Haydn and the Valve Trumpet

for Chip —
with the gratitude, admiration
and affection of the author

Craig

Haydn and the Valve Trumpet

CRAIG RAINE

ff

faber and faber

LONDON · BOSTON

First published in 1990
by Faber and Faber Limited
3 Queen Square London WC1N 3AU

Photoset by Wilmaset Birkenhead Wirral
Printed in Great Britain by
Richard Clay Ltd Bungay Suffolk

A CIP record for this book is
available from the British Library

ISBN 0–571–15084–5

to
KARL MILLER
without whom English letters
would be dramatically poorer,
in recognition of a lifetime's dedication
to literature.

Contents

Acknowledgements

Martin Amis first asked me to review for the *Times Literary Supplement*. For this – and many other generous actions, including his delighted permission to tell the story in 'Haydn and the Valve Trumpet' – I will always be grateful. Two editors deserve to be singled out from the many to whom I am obliged: Claire Tomalin at the *New Statesman* and the *Sunday Times* was noteworthy for discovering and supporting unknown talent, and Michael Church at the *Times Educational Supplement* was prodigal with his space. I owe a debt also to Tom Paulin, a friend with whom I have frequently disagreed, but who has been an invaluable goad time and again. Matthew Arnold, a critic I admire and Paulin dislikes, wrote: 'we like to be suffered to lie comfortably in the old straw of our habits.' Paulin is the needle in the haystack – and more often encountered than the proverb implies. Finally, to Mrs Valerie Eliot, I am grateful, as ever, for her generosity, example and encouragement.

Thanks are due to the editors of the following, where some of these pieces first appeared, often in a radically different form: the *Times Literary Supplement*, the *Times Educational Supplement*, the *Sunday Times*, the *Observer*, the *Guardian*, the *New Statesman*, *Quarto*, *Grand Street*, the *Poetry Review*, the *New Review*, the *Literary Review*, *London Magazine*, *The Times*, *Encounter*, the *London Review of Books*.

'Poetry Today' was first delivered at Central Hall, Westminster, on 18 October 1988 and was the annual lecture at the Froebel Institute College in 1989.

Introduction
Haydn and the Valve Trumpet

In the last act of *Don Giovanni*, the famished Leporello filches a titbit or two from the feast laid for his master and the *commendatore*. As he does so, a march can be heard in the distance, a tune which Leporello recognizes: 'Questa poi la conosco purtroppo.' Which is hardly surprising, because Mozart is making a musical pun on the stage action, by stealing his own 'Non più andrai, farfallone amoroso' from Act I of *Figaro*. In Liszt's orchestral Hungarian Rhapsody No. 5 in E minor, I hear the prefiguration of a theme in Dvořák's *Aus der neuen Welt* (1893). Liszt, of course, came first: his Hungarian rhapsodies of 1851–3 were based on his own *Magyar Dallok* pieces of 1840, which, in their turn, were based on gipsy music Liszt had heard. Is it possible that Dvořák, even though he began as an epigone of Liszt and Wagner, simply transcribed the same folk melody? And what ownership claims has Liszt on folk material? When the Stravinsky scholar, Lawrence Morton, examined the massive Anton Juszkiewicz anthology, *Litauische Volks-Weisen* (Kracow, 1900) – known to have been in Stravinsky's possession at the time *Le Sacre du Printemps* was composed – Morton found three melodies 'with obvious ties to subsequent material in the *Rite*', three melodies in addition to melody No. 157 which was previously acknowledged by Stravinsky (in André Schaeffner's 1931 biography) to be the source of the opening bassoon melody.

I know very little about music – so little that I have no way of establishing whether I have imagined the Liszt–Dvořák coincidence, and whether it is an instance of plagiarism or not; so little that I am unable to understand why Stravinsky appears to have concealed as a debt what is a perfectly honourable source; so little that, while I am perfectly sure of Mozart's humorous self-quotation, I do not know whether this is a commonplace among even half-educated Mozartians. It *must* be.

Yet, knowing so little about music, I therefore know something of Haydn's use of the valve trumpet. In this sense: on 3 August 1972, Michael Chanan wrote a longish piece in the *Listener*, seeking to answer the question, 'What did the trumpet mean to Haydn?' And he concluded: 'the valve instrument to some extent allows the separation of tone-quality from note-value, which means that all the effects which cannot be notated (and hence are called "inarticulate") can be smoothed out. *This* is what the trumpet meant to Haydn, the supreme Apollonian composer: smoothness and perfection combined with brilliance.'

Only a week later, a little week, a letter appeared in the correspondence columns, with this message: 'Please tell Michael Chanan that the valved trumpet was invented in 1818. Haydn died in Vienna on 31 May 1809. It is unwise to found a music(ologic)al theory on Haydn's use of the valved trumpet.'

Even those who are not musicians are familiar with Haydn's use of the valve trumpet. Though, inevitably, Michael Chanan's mistake is destined to indisputably classic status, the phenomenon features prominently in the unofficial history of criticism. Later in 1972, Martin Amis anonymously reviewed for the *Times Literary Supplement* a selection of Coleridge's verse, edited by William Empson and David Pirie. The anonymous mantle of 'Our Reviewer' somehow entailed a tone of amused condescension ambiguously tempered with compliment. After a fine show of patient openness to persuasion, our reviewer, with a further show of reluctant reproach, chid Professor Empson for the omission of Coleridge's prose gloss of 1817. Distracting, misleading it might be, yet beautiful at moments it certainly was; without the gloss, students and readers of the *Ancient Mariner* might be ill-served. Perhaps a place might have been found for it in an appendix?

A place had been found for it in an appendix. A fact Empson

pointed out in a peevish letter containing further complaints of misrepresentation. When 'Our Reviewer' replied, he began with an apology for a 'bad lapse', became argumentative and almost bold, and ended with the memorably desperate, 'Professor Empson always writes like an angel . . .' Smoothness and perfection combined with brilliance. Wriggle out of *that*, if you can, Empson.

Of course, some critics are undeterred by the single near-fatal collision with Haydn's use of the valve trumpet. A. Alvarez is an awesomely impaired yet fearless recidivist. My essay on Betjeman's poetry contains an example of Alvarez's propensity to pronounce from a position of wilful ignorance. Even earlier, in December 1973, the normally tolerant John Bayley noted the same tendency: 'the reader without some Russian cannot form much of an estimate of Mandelstam, though since he became a hot property that has not stopped the poetic PR men from trying: his widow's memoir *Hope against Hope* has not done any service to the poetry by enabling them to substitute for its reality the usual PR big words like "compassion". ("*Hope against Hope*, a book almost as fine in its sardonic compassionate way as Osip's own poetry" – A. Alvarez. Not knowing, as he says, any of the language, how can he know? What are his grounds of judgment? The take-over of the Christian name suggests some special and intimate hot line to the poet's *manes*.)' This is well said. Let us have no more non-Russian-speaking Russian experts and enthusiasts.

Let Blake Morrison, the former literary editor of the *Observer*, be an example to us all. On 21 December 1986, he wrote an appreciation of Irina Ratushinskaya's poetry to accompany the *Observer* Russian correspondent's exclusive interview with the newly exiled poet. 'Irina Ratushinskaya's place in the great twentieth-century tradition of Russian poetry already seems assured,' he wrote. 'She has been compared to Anna Akhmatova and Marina Tsvetayeva, passionate celebrators of individual life within the modern totalitarian state.' By 5 June 1988, reviewing her second collection of poems, *Pencil Letter*, Morrison could afford to be more critical. 'Without a knowledge of Russian it's difficult to be sure what she sounds like, let alone how major her talent is.' Morrison's retraction cannot have been easy but it does him credit, and it shows us that an admission of lack of competence can have its own authority.

Russian literature, foreign literature in general, what has now become known as world literature, have fostered their fair share of experts on Haydn's use of the valve trumpet. Restrained sceptics suddenly go on a mental binge. In October 1988, Anita Brookner was carried away and ravished by a tall dark strange idea while reviewing D. J. Enright's *Fields of Vision*: 'Enright's specialised knowledge of the central European tradition leads him to appreciate the work of writers usually found too extreme for English tastes: Canetti, Grass, Kraus, Singer, Milosz, Skvorecky. These writers are more dangerous than their English counterparts: bitterness, regret, wildness, fascination with God and the devil mark them out as heavyweights, not to be trifled with.' Is it an accident that Milan Kundera, an exceptionally intelligent and ironic writer, has no place on Anita Brookner's list? Equally, it is noticeable that laughter has no place on her list of dangerous qualities, of heavyweight qualities. I find her formulation suspect and sentimental. How can a 'fascination with God and the devil mark them out as heavyweights'? The *devil*. Surely a fascination with *him* is profoundly lightweight and reactionary? It is depressing to find all this dark ugly mental furniture, this hideous and uncomfortable lumber, acclaimed as austerely chic. It represents a nostalgia for pontification, for a time when issues seemed grander, harsher, more certain, more serious – when, to adapt *Cold Comfort Farm*, there was no butter in hell. I am irresistibly reminded of Burt Lancaster as an old gangster in Louis Malle's *Atlantic City*. As he idealizes bygone times, Lancaster is interrupted by his companion, who has just seen the sea. Lancaster dismisses it with a gesture and the verdict: 'You should have seen it in the old days.' Milan Kundera stands with Louis Malle: 'the art inspired by God's laughter does not by nature serve ideological certitudes, it contradicts them. Like Penelope, it undoes each night the tapestry that the theologians, philosophers, and learned men have woven the day before.'

4

Poetry – and particularly metre – is a noticeably hospitable micro-climate in which the valve trumpet can flourish. Edward de Vere, the Earl of Oxford, farted while bowing to Elizabeth I and, mortified, left England for seven years. On de Vere's return to court, Elizabeth, according to Aubrey, put the Earl at his ease with the words, 'My Lord, I had forgott the Fart.' In the same spirit, I have no wish to dwell on Tom Paulin's 'detection' of a Yeatsian 'echo' in Geoffrey Hill's sonnet 'Idylls of the King' – flawless example though it was of a critic blowing his own valve trumpet. I have also completely forgotten why his description of the sonnet as rhythmically monotonous was somehow less than just to Hill's workmanlike metrical variants. Rather let me turn – in the spirit of conservation – to Geoffrey Grigson's vatic assertion (supported by the citation of a line from the middle of a James Fenton poem) that first lines were an infallible test of poetic merit. Then there is Peter Porter's review of Fiona Pitt-Kethley's *Private Parts* in the *Observer* for 12 July 1987: 'there is one departure', he wrote, 'from her norm which would be welcome if it were applied more skilfully. She is determined to introduce a semblance of metre into many poems. But, to employ a metaphor of the kind she likes to use herself, she is really more at home in the world of five inches than of five feet. Witness such iambic regularities as "He walks his young Jack Russell by the sea".' But this line isn't the promised 'semblance' of metre, nor does it merit that ironical 'such iambic regularities'. The line is perfectly regular, if perfectly dull.

Almost exactly a year later, Jonathan Raban – always elegant, assured, unoriginal – was reviewing Bevis Hillier's biography of Betjeman. 'His main interest in Betjeman's verse is for what it can tell us about Betjeman himself, and this leads him to much injudicious quotation of snippets that it might have been wiser to have kept hidden. So, on West Hill, Highgate:

> . . . we were slightly richer than my friends
> The family next door: we owned a brougham
> And they would envy us our holidays . . .

. . . Ti-tumpty-tumpty-tum. Burbling along in this mood, garrulous and prosy, Betjeman is as sedative, and mildly addictive, as Valium.' What a remarkably inattentive ear Raban must possess, so remarkable it enables him to detect the valve trumpet's ti-tumpty-tumpty-tum in lines whose conversational emphases lie athwart the metric pattern. Betjeman's lines are the opposite of verse rising to the trot. They can be scanned as regular but not *heard* so – except by a critic mildly addicted to the lazy consensus.

Most of the pieces reprinted here have been rewritten, expanded, cut, touched up and improved. Where I have set the valve trumpet to my lips, daunted I have tried to silence it, though examples will undoubtedly remain. Let me end with my own confession. When I originally wrote my essay on Buddhism in Eliot's *The Waste Land*, I made no distinction between Buddhism and Hinduism. One sceptical correspondent to the *Times Literary Supplement* briefly wondered if I knew there *was* a difference. The distinction wasn't in the least crucial to my argument, but had I been less ignorant I would have acknowledged the distinction before disregarding it – as I now do. My blunder was, as it were, not even to realize a difference existed between a trumpet and a valve trumpet. When I told this story to Charles Monteith, my predecessor at Faber, and said I had rewritten the essay to accommodate a national reluctance to imagine Eliot in a dhoti rather than his famous four-piece suit, Charles smiled like an old India hand and said: 'Saffron robes. Dhotis are Hindu.' The dhoti remains, however, like a conscious act of contrition. I say among the trumpets, Ha, ha.

Mussolini's London Triumph

In *Transparent Things*, there is a bravura Nabokovian digression about a pencil which has spilled accidentally from the drawer of a desk. It is an unconsidered trifle on which Nabokov decides to focus his formidable attention. He considers it as no pencil has ever been considered before: 'it was not a hexagonal beauty of Virginia juniper or African cedar, with the maker's name imprinted in silver foil, but a very plain, round, technically faceless old pencil of cheap pine, dyed a dingy violet. It had been mislaid ten years ago by a carpenter who had not finished examining, let alone fixing, the old desk, having gone away for a tool that he never found. Now comes the act of attention.' And Nabokov pursues his pencil as far as the original pine tree. I think of historians, perhaps unjustly, as people with no time for pencils. Treaties, so to speak, are signed with fountain pens, gripped between important fingers, and overseen by famous faces.

I want you to consider one of history's lost pencils. I happened to open Malcolm Muggeridge's *The Thirties* – written and published in 1940, when history was still gossip – and out it fell. Discussing the literary pretensions of fascist dictators, Muggeridge lets slip that 'in the pre-Axis days, [Mussolini's] play, *The Hundred Days*, dealing with Napoleon's return from Elba, was produced at the Old Vic, and kindly received.' Under the heading 'Man of Culture', Denis Mack Smith, Mussolini's biographer, is brisk and dismissive: 'he claimed co-authorship in three plays though his own contribution, apart from the general themes, was nil. The three subjects he chose were Napoleon, Julius Caesar, and Cavour, and it is interesting that all dealt with much the same topic: a great man betrayed by his friends. All three plays were given a fantastic reception by the critics and compared to Shakespearean and Wagnerian drama at their best, though in private there was less enthusiasm. Two of them were turned into films about which a great fuss was made, without much box-office success.' Which two were turned into films, I find myself wanting to ask. And then again, what about that kindly reception at the Old Vic? Who was the person who actually wrote the plays for which Mussolini took the credit? What kind of pencils did he use?

Actually, in the service of humbler truths, Muggeridge is a little careless with dates and dull stuff of that kind. *Napoleon: The Hundred Days* by Benito Mussolini and Giovacchino Forzano ('adapted from the Italian for the English stage by John Drink-water', published by Sidgwick and Jackson at two shillings and sixpence net, and printed in 1932 by Billing and Sons Ltd, Guildford and Esher) was never performed at the Old Vic. It was performed at the New Theatre, St Martin's Lane (TEM 3878), with Robert Atkins as Napoleon and Arthur Wontner as Fouché. 8 Sharp Evgs. Mats. Thurs and Sat 2.15. The production was reviewed in *The Times* on 19 April 1932, and the same unsigned piece appeared again on 20 April, like a variation on the critic's theme: 'you feel again and again that the hands of the clock have been put back and that you are a spectator of scenes as they were in truth played.' Impressed, but not uncritical, he noted some overacting: 'the sniff of grease-paint is instantly in the air.' But these flaws are 'trifles' and 'the play's general effect is of a swift and necessary movement of destiny. It is, thank heaven, about something – something moving and important, and it is driven forward by a perceptive mind faithful to history and content to rely upon that faithfulness for dramatic effect.' Moving, import-ant, bent, apologizing, our critic tiptoes along Row K as the curtain closes, his final peroration already forming in his mind: 'it is a very uncommon experience in the theatre to feel the same quality of excitement that is there in the turning over of indisputable documents. Nothing here seemed falsified; no emphasis is forced, there being in the events themselves a natural and compelling emphasis. History lies quietly open; the comment of the Fates is implied; and the audience, without emotional beguilement, is continuously held.' Bravo, technically faceless old pencil, old stick.

Our critic isn't the only anonymous person in this connection. Though credited, Giovacchino Forzano is also anonymous, one can't help feeling. That 'perceptive mind faithful to history' should be plural given that the play was co-authored. Mussolini, it is somehow implied, is the perceptive mind in question. And at the celebratory lunch given at the Lyceum Club on 6 May, the absent Mussolini dominates proceedings by sending a personal telegram of praise which the Italian ambassador reads out. In the speeches that follow, John Drinkwater contrives to keep his distance from the piece: he will not say it is a great play 'because that is always a dangerous word to use'; instead, he confines himself to saying it has 'elements of greatness'. Robert Atkins is less cautious and expresses the honour he feels at being associated 'with so great a man as Signor Mussolini, with whose name are coupled in this play those of Signor Forzano and Mr John Drinkwater'. In spite of his conclusion – that the work would 'demand a bow even if these three men were nobodies' – one is left feeling that two of the three men *are* nobodies.

The play itself is really about the defeat of a somebody by a collection of nobodies. It doesn't quite answer to Mack Smith's summary, 'a great man betrayed by his friends'. Essentially, Napoleon is responsible for the defeat at Waterloo, though he attempts to blame it on his subordinates. But the interest lies not in the military defeat, rather in the psychological defeat Napoleon suffers at the hands of Fouché, the 'nobody' who is his Minister of Police. Napoleon represents passion, the military daemon, the double-edged gift of genius, whereas Fouché is a risk assessor, a creature of pure prose: 'I only became Minister in order that I might, in the public – you may say European – interest, control all eventualities.' Accordingly, he sees emissaries of every political shade and is finally rewarded when Gaillard negotiates the peace with Wellington. After St Helena has been arranged, they turn to the Bourbon restoration.

> WELLINGTON: The Bourbon restoration is inevitable.
> GAILLARD: The Bourbons. Yes. And the King's Ministers – ?
> WELLINGTON: The King's Minister will be Monsieur Fouché.
> GAILLARD: Exactly. As we had foreseen. Though there is a difficulty – ?
> WELLINGTON: That Monsieur Fouché sent his Bourbon Majesty's brother to the guillotine. Considerations of policy make that incident unimportant . . .

The computer has defeated the grand master. Against this cynical calculation is set a tragic ideal of sorts whose spokes-woman is Napoleon's mother, Letizia: 'Downfall is nothing, if one falls with greatness. It is everything if one falls basely. I had a son who was Emperor of France; a son who was King of Spain; a son who was King of Holland; and a son who was King of Westphalia. I always remembered that some day all those Kings might again be dependent on me for bread, as they were in Ajaccio. That was the reason for my thrift, my parsimony . . . about which my son, the Emperor, was so often amused.' Potentially, the idea is poignant, but the expression here, as elsewhere, has too much in common with the pencil. It is a little wooden and somewhat leaden, though perhaps less so than this stage direction for the defeat at Waterloo: *'There are cries of "Save himself who can!"'* The destruction of the Emperor's Guard and the French retreat are narrated by two injured French soldiers observing events from the window of a peasant's hovel. They miss very little, luckily enough. Napoleon appears at the end of the act, a fugitive horseman seeking directions and only recognized because one of his entourage calls him 'Sire'.

> FIRST SOLDIER: Do you know who that was?
> THE OLD MAN: It wasn't – ?

SECOND SOLDIER: Yes. (*Falling down*)

THE OLD MAN: Napoleon – fugitive. Well, you never know your luck.

FIRST SOLDIER: By the way, what's the name of this place?

THE WOMAN: We've got no name here. But the town, if you can call it a town, just over there, is Waterloo.

THE CURTAIN FALLS.

Yes, dramatic irony: nobody has become a somebody, Waterloo has made a name for itself. Somebody, Napoleon, has become a nobody. But I'm adding shape and symmetry to what is the merest dramatic opportunism. In reality, the point is horribly blunt.

Whatever Became of Brain Fever?

Of the thousand natural shocks that flesh is heir to, at least five or six have been struck off by the medical profession for reasons other than the march of scientific progress. Of course, some have been eliminated by medical advances. For example, the erysipelas which carries off William Morel in *Sons and Lovers*. This skin disease, commonly complicated with pneumonia, and caused by haemolytic streptococcus, was once highly contagious but is now easily curable by antibiotic therapy. Green sickness, the scourge of many an adolescent heroine, appears to have been rationalized out of existence. Other complaints may have been renamed: reviewing William Clarke's biography of Wilkie Collins, the critic John Sutherland was shrewdly baffled by the 'internal neuralgia' which Collins's mother endured and mused more constructively that the novelist's 'rheumatic gout' might be the (venereally transmitted) Reiter's Syndrome. Other diseases and diagnoses have simply gone missing. When, in Arnold Bennett's *The Old Wives' Tale*, Sophia Scales at last confronts the dead body of her scapegrace, absentee husband, Gerald, she contemplates his expression of 'final fatigue' – and, returning to Bursley, is herself rapidly overcome in the car. Only hours later, the doctor, on the landing outside the bedroom, is confiding: ' "U.P." ' Though the doctor's interlocutor nods his understanding, the modern reader is uncomprehending. These mysterious initials recur in Joyce's *Ulysses*, where the deranged Denis Breen is threatening legal action against those responsible for sending him a postcard on which the letters U.P. are written. Dublin wags are highly diverted, Breen's wife is angered and rueful – '–U.P.: up, she said. Someone taking a rise out of him. It's a great shame for them whoever he is' – but posterity is as baffled here as it was with *The Old Wives' Tale*.

H. G. Wells begins chapter 4 of *The History of Mr Polly* with this cynical, callous sentence: 'his father died suddenly – the local practitioner still clung to his theory that it was imagination he suffered from, but compromised in the certificate with the appendicitis that was then so fashionable.' Wells was writing in 1910, but in the previous century another complaint had been just as voguish. It was brain fever – a mysterious inflammation of the brain, which disposed of, or temporarily damaged, countless fictional creations, before it was itself deposed by the omnipotent appendicitis. The literary life of brain fever is now restricted to the occasional metaphorical reference, as when, in *Humboldt's Gift*, Citrine's gold-digging mistress, Renata, denounces Citrine's outlay on Thaxter and his journal of fresh ideas: 'What do you know about all these things, Charlie? You've got brain fever.' Renata is less *au courant* with medical lore, it would seem , than Asa Leventhal, the protagonist of Bellow's second novel, *The Victim*: there Leventhal's faintly robotic interior monologue avers that 'years ago everyone spoke of brain fever; now it was known there was no such sickness'. Leventhal is speaking, I'd imagine, for the consensus, but actually he is no better informed than busty Renata. There is such a sickness.

Whatever became of brain fever? The answer is that the term 'brain fever' is still used by the medical profession as a lay translation for encephalitis – that is, an inflammation of the brain caused by a virus. The trouble is that we laymen have mislaid it, largely because the affliction is now ignored by literature, whereas in the nineteenth century it was a dramatically active scourge. Nowadays, heroes and heroines are unaccountably immune. (Except in the USSR, where Pasternak's Lara from *Doctor Zhivago*, watched by a sceptical nurse, takes refuge in a bout of brain fever, after her failed attempt to shoot Komarovsky.) Perhaps we know too much. Perhaps we know too little. At any rate, the moment of change can be observed in the work of

D. H. Lawrence. In *The White Peacock*, Leslie suffers 'a slight brain fever' following his car crash. Two years later, in 1913, Mr Morel in *Sons and Lovers* complains of ' "nasty peens in his head" ' and Lawrence eschews 'brain fever' in favour of a longer, more self-consciously accurate statement: 'he was sickening for an attack of an inflammation of the brain.' In 1911, then, 'brain fever' could be used very loosely to describe any rise in body temperature. Since the term itself no longer described the particular illness, for precise cases its definition by 1913 replaced the by now promiscuously employed cognomen 'brain fever'. Thereafter, brain fever more or less disappears from literature. It is not replaced, however, by 'attacks of an inflammation of the brain'. The syndrome itself vanishes from the novel, though not from life, as medical testimony corroborates. Why is this?

Put it another way. Why did brain fever once feature so regularly in fiction and poetry? Perhaps literature was itself responsible for the deplorable laxness with which 'brain fever' came to be used. After all, Victorian novelists are not noted for their medical accuracy – their diagnoses can be highly imaginative and colourful. Consider the notorious Spontaneous Combustion of Krook in *Bleak House*. The event is merely a pretext for Dickens's powers of imagination and description: ' "I suppose it's chops at the Sol's Arms." "Chops, do you think? Oh! – Chops, eh?" Mr Snagsby sniffs and tastes again. "Well, sir, I suppose it is. But I should say their cook at the Sol wanted a little looking after. She has been burning 'em, sir! And I don't think;" Mr Snagsby sniffs and tastes again, and then spits and wipes his mouth; "I don't think – not to put too fine a point upon it – that they were quite fresh, when they were shown the gridiron." ' Brilliantly tasteless in its emphasis on taste, the passage is the perfect illustration of Valéry's dictum that the mind is a fly that will settle on anything. The thoroughness of Dickens's imagination has some of the grim relish one associates with Swift's 'A Modest Proposal'. Yet Dickens defends himself with cited case histories in his preface without discernible irony. Spontaneous Combustion for Dickens represented an imaginative opportunity – and one can't help feeling that brain fever represented not so much medical fact for the nineteenth-century novelist as a convenient short-cut to a dramatic climax. Illness, of course, was much more common, but even so brain fever, like alcohol and drugs, functioned as a great accelerator.

A brief anthology. According to the *OED*, brain fever first occurs in Marryat's *Peter Simple*, but it probably existed before its appellation. *Hysterica passio* has to serve as Lear, traumatized by his children and the elements, wanders mentally and physically. Jane Austen, too, has to settle, as it were, for a shabby circumlocution – 'sleepless pain and delirium' – when Marianne Dashwood succumbs in body and spirit after the same combination of inclement weather and disappointed love. The symptoms are aching for their proper sobriquet. If these two candidates seem unlikely, the *OED*'s citation looks equally improbable: 'I had a brain fever, which lasted six or seven days,' says Peter Simple. This, the first recorded use, appears as lax as many of the later usages when the term was in its decadence. He is probably suffering from simple sunstroke – the result of clinging to an upturned boat under a scorching Caribbean sun. Typically in the novel, brain fever has some emotional trigger which is absent in this case. The treatment is unconventional also: 'we were put into baths of brandy and water.'

If Peter Simple was cured by brandy, Lord Lowborough (another heterodox case in Anne Brontë's *The Tenant of Wildfell Hall*) could blame it for his troubles. After excessive losses at the gaming tables, followed by profound insobriety, followed by addiction to laudanum, he downs a bottle of brandy in one go. In the circumstances, the subsequent 'rather severe brain fever' seems rather a mild penalty, though one's faith in natural justice may be restored by the 'apoplectic fit' which precedes it. The circumstances are very different from those in chapter 8 of J. Meade Falkner's *The Lost Stradivarius* (1895), where Sir John Maltravers is found by his sister somewhat the worse for wear. Dr Empson diagnoses that he is 'suffering from a sharp access of brain-fever'. This has been brought on by sitting in an unlit picture gallery during a violent thunderstorm and seeing there the spectral figure of a long-dead, white-faced evil man. Not really surprising – was it? – that Dr Empson 'could not answer for any turn his sickness might take'.

Between these twin causes of booze and bogymen from the beginning of brain fever to its virtual end, there are other, more orthodox examples, in which brain fever is the physical manifestation of inner emotional turmoil. In Maupassant's *Une Vie*, Jeanne succumbs to brain fever in chapter 7 after she discovers that Rosalie has succumbed to her husband, Julien. Becky Sharp in *Vanity Fair* invents a plausible scenario to win the sympathy first of Jos and then of Amelia: 'my agonies were terrible when they took [my child] away from me; I thought I should die; but I fortunately had a brain fever, during which my doctor gave me up, and – and I recovered, and – and here I am, poor and friendless.' Behind that one unpredictable word 'fortunately' lies, I would hazard, the entire unwritten theory of brain fever as a necessary illness, as a safety valve for intolerable emotional stress. Thus when Jim tells Marlow, in *Lord Jim*, that he 'didn't get brain fever' in the open boat after the *Patna* had been abandoned, the case isn't parallel with that of Peter Simple – since Jim is under intense pressure of a psychological kind. He has taken the pulse of his own heroism and found it laggard. Amelia Sedley's own bout of 'fever' prostrates her 'after the death of George Osborne on the plateau of Mount St John'. Though it isn't specified as brain fever by Thackeray, the assumption isn't unreasonable since the young widow's hair is cut off in the usual way. The Victorians, however, were free with the scissors, as they are in this example from *The Pickwick Papers* which may, or may not, be brain fever: 'In proof of Bob Sawyer's being one of the funniest fellows alive, he proceeded to entertain Mr Pickwick with a long and circumstantial account how that gentleman once drank himself into a fever and got his head shaved.'

The theory of brain fever as a safety valve, useful for transposing emotional strains into physical expression, is somewhat modified by Henry James's 'The Madonna of the Future'. The painter's brilliant theory, 'the material for a hundred masterpieces', issues in the failure of a blank canvas: 'I need only the hand of Raphael. I have his brain.' Exposed, the decline follows, but the adverb 'fortunately' here does not apply: 'A violent fever had seized our patient, and the case was evidently grave. A couple of hours later I knew he had brain fever. From this moment I was with him constantly, but I am far from wishing to describe his illness. Excessively painful to witness, it was happily brief. Life burned out in delirium.' Brain fever could be fatal.

Not that it is in the case of Emma Bovary, when she receives Rodolphe's letter reneging on their projected elopement. First, she thinks of suicide but is deflected by the voice of her husband calling. Then she suffers a paroxysm and by midnight 'brain fever had set in'. Flaubert is painstakingly detailed about the treatment and the duration of the fever: 'for forty-three days Charles never left her side. He forsook his patients, sat up all night with her, and was continually feeling her pulse or applying mustard plasters or cold-water compresses.' Her symptoms are also recorded: 'what alarmed him most was Emma's condition of prostration. She didn't speak, and she didn't hear anything. She appeared even to be without pain, as though body and soul were resting together from all the shocks that they had suffered. By the middle of October she was able to sit up in bed with pillows at her back. Charles shed tears when he saw her eating her first slice of bread and jam.' A relapse follows, caused by the sight of the garden arbour with its painful amorous memories: this time the symptoms are more complex, ranging from dizziness to pains in the heart, head, chest and limbs.

In Goncharov's *Oblomov*, brain fever is the merest aside, but the emotional trigger remains identical as Oblomov confesses to Stolz: 'I had brain fever as it was, when I saw what an abyss lay between me and her, when I grasped that I wasn't worthy of her . . .' Dr Manette's account of his 'patient in a high fever of the brain' in *A Tale of Two Cities* lacks the detached narration of Flaubert. Dickens is in the grip of his plot and his broadest effects.

To find an equivalent of Flaubert in English, one had best turn to Mrs Gaskell's novella 'Cousin Phillis'. And, of course, there is no equivalent of Flaubert's 'first slice of bread and jam' – only the brain fever syndrome in its classic outline. Phillis falls in love with Edward Holdsworth whose surname proves to be ironical. Mrs

Gaskell drops a strong hint about his emotional unreliability when she notes that his whiskers and mustachios are somewhat in the foreign fashion. And, sure enough, he goes to Canada and Phillis embarks on a strict regimen of pining away. Just when her bloom has begun to return, Mrs Gaskell reveals that Holdsworth has married 'another'. Brain fever sets in as a symbolic moth flutters round a candleflame. Phillis collapses with 'a quivering of muscles round her mouth' and is carried 'slightly convulsed' to her bed. There, her hair is cut off (they order these things so much better in France) and wet cloths are applied. Eventually, the ice treatment succeeds.

Phillis's prototype is Mary Barton whose trials probably add up to brain fever, though Mrs Gaskell is never specific. First there is the shock of discovering that her father is a murderer as well as an opium addict. Mrs Gaskell conveys the trauma in plodding units, as if a conjuror were being photographed by Eadweard Muybridge, with a separate frame for every pass and sleight, concluding with the removal of a burly, red-eyed, squirming rabbit from a top hat: 'she sat down for an instant to think; and rising directly, went, with a step rendered firm by inward resolution of purpose, up the stairs; – passed her own door, two steps, into her father's room. What did she want there? I must tell you; I must put into words the dreadful secret which she believed that bit of paper had revealed to her. Her father was the murderer!' The exclamation mark quivers like a javelin on the page. Possibly, a girl might come to terms with this, but her mind is bound to boggle a bit when themansheloves is to be tried for the very same crime. And boggle it does. Sleepless nights follow as Mary sets about establishing an alibi for themansheloves. 'Armies of thoughts' meet and clash in her brain. Gradually, as she struggles to control her wandering mind, her brain refuses to recognize the sense when people speak to her: 'A veil seemed drawn over her mind, and she had no clear perception of what passed.' 'Her very words seemed not her own, and beyond her power of control, for she found herself speaking quite differently to what she meant.' By now it is plain that her hair is in some danger. Sure enough, on Jem's acquittal, Mrs Gaskell transports her heroine to 'the ghastly spectral world of delirium'. Her hair, however, is reprieved in parallel with her lover and wet cloths effect a cure.

Emily Brontë's Cathy, on the other hand, has her thick locks 'partly removed at the beginning of her illness'. Her brain fever follows a fit of temper on Linton's barring Heathcliff from Thrushcross Grange. As often in English, the fever isn't restricted to the character but also afflicts the prose style. After 'dashing her head against the arm of the sofa, and grinding her teeth, so that you might fancy she would crash them to splinters' – both medically inadvisable procedures – Cathy retaliates by barring herself in her room. There she has three sleepless nights (see Mary Barton above) and bemuses herself by tearing the pillow in her teeth. The resultant feathers are examined with a whimsical inconsequentiality borrowed from Ophelia. 'That's a turkey's . . . and this is a wild duck's' etc. Nelly Dean, unsurprisingly, is as unimpressed by this plagiarism as Pasternak's nurse: 'Give over with that baby-work,' she says, bringing the scene briefly to life. Cathy merely wanders to the mirror and refuses to recognize her own reflection. After five days of 'cold water and ill temper' (Nelly's epitome) Cathy blacks out, returns to childhood, raves, and, in short, gives way to 'what was denominated a brain fever'.

Her recovery is slow; her appearance is altered; her eyes no longer give 'the impression of looking at the objects around her'. She is unable to read a letter from Heathcliff and she struggles to arrange her ideas. It is a picture of general debility, but when Heathcliff reappears, other side-effects are evident. They embrace passionately. It transpires that Cathy's fingers have acquired preternatural strength. As the couple part, Cathy retains 'in her closed fingers a portion of the locks she had been grasping'. On the other hand, she is easily bruised: Heathcliff's fingers leave 'four distinct impressions . . . blue in the colourless skin'. As one wonders mildly about Heathcliff's thumb and its peculiar failure to make any impression at all, Cathy goes into labour and dies in childbirth.

In literary terms, Emily Brontë's account is stronger than either of Mrs Gaskell's but, without Nelly's sceptical presence and sour annotation, it would be wholly risible. Dickens, a far greater artist than both, but a writer constantly capable of the worst, plays down the distraught physical actions. Mere notation is replaced by the imaginative treatment of fever. Pip, in *Great Expectations*, undergoes the long, familiar apprenticeship of strain (discovering Magwitch is his benefactor, harbouring him, watching his trial and death) which issues in breakdown. Dickens writes (brilliantly): 'I confounded impossible existences with my own identity; that I was a brick in the house wall, and yet entreating to be released from the giddy place where the builders had set me; that I was a steel beam of a vast engine, clashing and whirling over a gulf, and yet I implored in my own person to have the engine stopped, and my part of it hammered off.' For a moment, Dickens is the Piranesi of prose. He risks more than Flaubert and yet brings it off.

Moreover, Pip's fever happens to be thematically significant. Its delusions are the climax of a life filled with delusions – the delusion that Miss Havisham is his benefactor, his deluded snobbery which makes him ashamed of Jo and repelled by Magwitch. On first seeing Miss Havisham, Pip sees an illusion of the young bride, and later imagines she is hanging by the neck in the old brewery. Add to this the way Pip harps on his 'poor dreams' and his remark 'Miss Havisham's intentions towards me, all a mere dream' – and one can see why Dickens, at the turning point of Pip's life, puts him to sleep, torments him with delusions, and allows him to wake up to the single reality in his life. Jo.

After Dickens, one wonders whether the other characters, including Liza and Stavrogin in *The Devils*, were suffering from anything worse than bad writing. And the temptation to laugh is strong. The psychology on offer seems so primitive, recent examples are so utterly rare. And yet: one thinks of a latent virus like *herpes simplex*, the common cold sore, which lives permanently in the brain and only travels to its other home on the lips when the host is physically depleted and psychologically depressed. That at least is no old wives' tale. Brain fever, unlike appendicitis at the turn of the century, isn't fashionable, but it may return, like padded shoulders or flared trousers or flowered shirts, to afflict us in the future as if it had never been away. Should this happen, most writers will fail in their descriptions, as they always have done.

The Waste Land

In March 1965, Stephen Spender, writing in *Encounter*, recorded that he had once overheard T. S. Eliot say 'to the Chilean poet Gabriele Mistral that at the time he was writing *The Waste Land*, he seriously considered becoming a Buddhist'. Were this snippet of literary gossip the sole instance of Eliot's interest in Indian thought, one might forbear to follow up the hint. On the face of it, a vermilion caste mark and a dhoti seem unlikely replacements for the famous Anglo-Catholic features 'of clerical cut' and the four-piece suit satirically invented for Eliot by Virginia Woolf. Eliot, of course, was a Boston Brahmin, but a Brahmin Brahmin is bound to strike us as unlikely.

Nevertheless, in Eliot's prose there are several references to the body of Buddhist and Hindu thinking. Possibly the earliest occurs in the *Athenaeum* for 28 November 1919, where the thirty-one-year-old Eliot, in the course of reviewing an edition of Donne's sermons compiled by Logan Pearsall Smith, suddenly demonstrates a daunting theological expertise which, for all its air of calm exposition, is challenging and pugnacious: 'the method – the analogy and the repetition – is the same as that once used by a greater master of the sermon than either Donne or Andrewes or Latimer: it is the method of the Fire-Sermon preached by the Buddha.' What a display of strength, what a deliberate invitation to the intellectually foolhardy to question the depth of his knowledge. Both the comparison and the judgement are knowingly unorthodox and thus aggressive in their assertions.

Eliot's confidence was rooted in his time as a student at Harvard, where, as he recorded in *After Strange Gods* (1933), 'two years spent in the study of Sanskrit under Charles Lanman, and a year in the mazes of Patanjali's metaphysics under the guidance of James Woods, left me in a state of enlightened mystification.' Later, in *Notes Towards the Definition of Culture*, Eliot was to be even more flamboyantly modest in disclaiming Indian scholarship. At the same time, though, he was direct and considered about the influence of Indian thought on his poetry. The authority of this aside, made in 1948, isn't that of the tyro reviewer with a reputation to make and sustain, but the authority of a great poet who is aware that his achievement does not rest on mystification. 'Long ago I studied the ancient Indian languages, and while I was chiefly interested at that time in Philosophy, I read a little poetry too; and I know that my poetry shows the influence of Indian thought and sensibility. But generally, poets are not oriental scholars – I was never a scholar myself.' The man speaking here is the same straightforward, candid, unassailable celebrity who, in 1956, described the notes to *The Waste Land* as 'the remarkable exposition of bogus scholarship that is still on view today' and who concluded, to the detriment of many a study, by expressing regret for 'having sent so many enquirers off on a wild goose chase after Tarot cards and the Holy Grail'.

One could, of course, express the drift of the argument so far as a football result: Indian Thought 2 (Spender, and Eliot), Fertility Myth 0. Or one could set the 'wild goose chase after Tarot cards' against the positive declaration 'I know that my poetry shows the influence of Indian thought and sensibility'. This is a little too simple, however. First, Eliot prefaces his repudiation of the Tarot cards with the statement, 'It was just, no doubt, that I should pay my tribute to the work of Miss Jessie Weston.' By this, I assume that Eliot intends to indicate that her work is in some way implicated, however generally, in the scheme of *The Waste Land*. That, to use Eliot's own phrase from the notorious notes, 'not only the title, but the plan and a good deal of the incidental symbolism . . . were suggested by Miss Jessie L. Weston's book on the Grail legend'. The apparent contradiction between 'wild goose chase' and the citation in the notes to *The Waste Land* cannot be resolved by an assumption of punctilious politesse on Eliot's part in 1956 – that he was simply paying tribute to her work as he might pay tribute, say, to Marie Curie. It is not a purely disinterested compliment. *From Ritual to Romance* is implicated in the structural plot of *The Waste Land*. As readers, we need to know the basic scenario – that the Fisher King is the impotent ruler of an infertile land; that the curse can only be lifted by the arrival of a stranger who can put or answer certain ritual questions. In parallel with this is the Grail legend, in which a knight searches for the cup used by Christ at the Last Supper; the knight journeys to the Chapel Perilous where he must put certain questions about the Grail; the plight of the land is then lifted. Thirdly, there are the vegetation ceremonies, in which the image or effigy of the fertility god is thrown into the sea to symbolize the death of summer, without which spring could not follow. The crucifixion and resurrection of Christ is assimilated to these traditions: one purpose of Frazer's *The Golden Bough*, itself acknowledged in the notes, is to present Christianity as a development of older pagan traditions.

To give a small instance of relevance, in the Grail legend, a choir of children sings at the ceremony of foot-washing which precedes the restoration of Antfortas by Parsifal and the lifting of the curse from the waste land. In Eliot's poem, we are treated to a farcical travesty:

> O the moon shone bright on Mrs. Porter
> And on her daughter
> They wash their feet in soda water
> *Et O ces voix d'enfants, chantant dans la coupole!*

And I would suggest that travesty – 'O O O O that Shakespeherian Rag' – is *The Waste Land*'s preferred *modus operandi*. The predicament of ancient Thebes – a sterile land caused by the incestuous marriage of Oedipus and his mother Jocasta – is consigned to a parenthesis, as Tiresias witnesses the indifferent sexual coupling of the typist and the young man carbuncular. Sterility itself isn't what it used to be.

The Fisher King isn't exactly a regal figure either as he fishes in the dull canal 'behind the gashouse'. The fourth section, 'Death by Water', travesties the vegetation ceremonies and, instead of the effigy of the fertility god, we have Phlebas the Phoenician, a trader interested in profit and loss. Finally, at the poem's end, we encounter 'the empty chapel', the Chapel Perilous, and the questions are asked and the answers are given – to what effect, it is difficult to tell. The Fisher King wonders 'Shall I at least set my lands in order?'

Indisputably, then, *The Waste Land* has a Fisher King of sorts, a vegetation ceremony of sorts, a ritual feet-washing of sorts, a Chapel Perilous of sorts, and a waste land of sorts where 'there is no water'. Why then did Eliot in 1956 repudiate the Tarot and the Grail legend as 'a wild goose chase'? The answer is very simple. He was, as he said, no scholar. He was a poet who had opportunistically seized on a useful metaphor to encapsulate a spiritual condition. In 'Shakespeare and the Stoicism of Seneca' (1927) Eliot comments on Donne's sources in a way that reflects on his own sources: 'Miss Ramsay, in her learned and exhaustive study of Donne's sources, came to the conclusion that he was a "mediaeval thinker"; I could not find either any "mediaevalism" or any thinking, but only a vast jumble of incoherent erudition on which he drew for purely poetic effects.' In fact, Eliot is quite honest about the superficial nature of his interest in anthropology. If those who have followed the wild goose chase of the Tarot pack had been willing to read, they could have read Eliot's candid admission of amateurism: 'I am not familiar with the exact constitution of the Tarot pack of cards.'

Eliot's repudiation is only the repudiation of special knowledge and his remarks should be seen in their context – a lecture on 'The Frontiers of Criticism' – where Eliot opposed the way in which scholarship frequently replaces the work of art, and the need to understand its internal economy and its formal dynamic, with the accumulation of data about the work of art. In a sense, then, Eliot in 1956 was reversing an earlier onslaught in 'The Function of

Criticism' (1923): 'interpretation is always producing parts of the body from its own pockets, and fixing them in place. And any book, any essay, any note in *Notes and Queries*, which produces a fact even of the lowest order about a work of art is a better piece of work than nine-tenths of the most pretentious critical journalism, in journals or in books.' By 1956, Eliot could see that 'facts', too, could be forced into place, that there was a need for interpretation – but interpretation which issued from a tactful sense of what poetry itself was likely to issue from. And, conversely, what poetry was itself unlikely to issue from. The last thing a poet is likely to attempt is a full-scale transposition of detailed anthropological theory into a poem of 433 lines – not only because Frazer's *The Golden Bough* is very, very long, but also because such a condensation would be a very unsatisfactory way of communicating the substance of Frazer and Jessie L. Weston. Not that literary scholarship believes that *was* Eliot's purpose; it merely behaves as if it believed that such a condensation was Eliot's purpose. Poetry has a saving stupidity, a saving ignorance, and scholarship stands in relation to poetry as the works of Henry Arthur Jones stand in relation to Shakespeare's: 'a play of Shakespeare's and a play of Henry Arthur Jones's are essentially the same type, the difference being that Shakespeare is very much greater and Mr Jones very much more skilful.' Poetry is unafraid of simplicity and *The Waste Land*, for all the particular demands it may make, exploits the various fertility myths in the simplest, most unsystematic way possible: 'it seemed as if, at that time, the world was filled with broken fragments of systems, and that a man like Donne merely picked up, like a magpie, various shining fragments of ideas as they struck his eye . . .' So Eliot in 1927, asking, one can't help feeling, for his own record of pilfering and felony to be taken into account.

It follows from the above that Eliot wasn't attempting either to freeze-dry Indian thought in its complex entirety when he remarked that his poetry showed 'the influence of Indian thought and sensibility'. All the same, in 1933 in *The Use of Poetry*, Eliot, as he examined the relationship between enjoyment of poetry and the system of beliefs embodied in the poetry, concluded: 'I am not a Buddhist, but some of the early Buddhist scriptures affect me as parts of the Old Testament do.' As the famous advertisement for Rakusen's matzos used to run: 'You don't have to be Jewish to enjoy Rakusen's crackers.' I doubt if we will ever know What Precisely Eliot's relationship to Buddhism was in the years preceding 1922. On the one hand, there is Spender's recollection. On the other hand, there is Eliot's statement in 1933, eleven years after the publication of *The Waste Land* and six years after his conversion to Christianity: 'I am not a Buddhist'. Yet, taken with its rider, it reads like an untroubled admission that he had once been at least drawn to the ambience of Buddhism. This hypothesis – which, I know, runs slightly counter to the critical point Eliot wishes to make in *The Use of Poetry* – receives some support in 1944 from the essay 'What is Minor Poetry?', where Eliot relates his boyish pleasure in Edwin Arnold's versified life of the Buddha, *The Light of Asia*: 'I must have had a latent sympathy for the subject-matter, for I read it through with gusto, and more than once.' In 1929, in his essay on Dante, Eliot described the *Bhagavadgita*, the great Hindu text which incorporates Buddhist elements, as 'the next greatest philosophical poem to the *Divine Comedy* within my experience'.

So what has been established? Only that Eliot had some knowledge of, and interest in, Indian thought, and that he believed his poetry showed the influence of Indian thought and sensibility. The question I should like to answer is this: given that the first section of *The Waste Land* to be composed was 'The Fire Sermon', an undisputed allusion to the Buddha's sermon at Uruvela, can we apply Eliot's statement to his greatest poem? How does *The Waste Land* relate, if at all, to Eliot's avowal that 'my poetry shows the influence of Indian thought and sensibility'?

The discovery of *The Waste Land Manuscript* in the Berg Collection of the New York Public Library and Valerie Eliot's subsequent meticulous edition enable one to garner the odd additional Indian fragment. To begin with, there are the lines:

> I am the Resurrection and the Life
> I am the things that stay, and those that flow.

27

> I am the husband and the wife
> And the victim and the sacrificial knife
> I am the fire, and the butter also.

After the opening quotation from St John XI:25, which begins The Order for the Burial of the Dead, what follows is closely modelled, as Mrs Eliot points out, on the *Bhagavadgita* IX, 16:

> I am the rite, the sacrifice,
> The offering for the dead, the healing herb:
> I am the sacred formula, the sacred butter am I,
> I am the fire, and I the oblation.

Perhaps the nearest Western equivalent of this evocation of the Infinite Substance is to be found in Spinoza's *Ethics*. But the passage isn't entirely straight in its rendition of Indian metaphysics. There is a rogue element, one item trailing whiffs of irony in this context: 'I am the husband and the wife' is a neutral statement whose neutrality is underlined by the subsequent 'victim and the sacrificial knife'. Again, there is an element of bathos, of travesty.

More crucial for the argument I wish to pursue are these lines about London:

> London, the swarming life you kill and breed,
> Huddled between the concrete and the sky;
> Responsive to the momentary need,
> Vibrates unconscious to its formal destiny.

Ezra Pound scrawled in the margin of the typescript this succinct verdict – Balls – and rightly, so far as the poetry is concerned. Eliot, in faint pencil, singled out one line and wrote 'Keep'. The line was:

> Vibrates unconscious to its formal destiny

but he did not keep it. Nor did he retain another line, two lines later, which explains what the 'formal destiny' was:

London, your people is bound upon the wheel.

This image occurs again in the manuscript:

The inhabitants of Hampstead are bound forever on the wheel.

Which wheel does Eliot have in mind? There are several candidates, including the medieval Wheel of Fate, King Lear's 'wheel of fire', the Buddhist Wheel of Law (*dhamma*) which incorporates the Noble Eightfold Path to Truth leading to the end of suffering, the medieval wheel of fire taken from the New Testament Apocrypha, Ixion's Wheel on which the father of the centaurs suffered for the attempted seduction of Hera. No doubt a tortuous case could be made for each of these spare wheels as well as many others. It is, however, not unreasonable to favour candidates with an Indian flavour in a poem whose author, as we know from Lyndall Gordon's biography, *Eliot's Early Years*, in August and October 1913, 'bought two books by Paul Deussen, *Upanishads des Veda* and *Die Sûtras des Vedânta*'. This must be a justifiable predisposition given that *The Waste Land* notes include this rebuke to spiritual provincialism: 'the complete text of the Buddha's Fire Sermon (which corresponds in importance to the Sermon on the Mount) from which these words are taken, will be found translated in the late Henry Clarke Warren's *Buddhism in Translation*.' Lastly, Eliot's poem reaches its emotional climax with the imperatives *Datta*, *Dayadhvam* and *Damyata* (elucidated in a note telling us that 'the fable of the meaning of the Thunder is found in the *Brihadaranyaka-Upanishad*') and concludes with the thrice-repeated 'shantih' (described in Eliot's note as 'a formal ending to an Upanishad').

Even so, I do not believe that Eliot intended the Wheel of Law, with its positive connotations, its promise of moral improvement, because the people who are bound upon the wheel are 'stunned', 'dazed', 'knowing neither what to think, nor how to feel' – a constellation of epithets scarcely appropriate to souls with spiritual amelioration in the forefront of their minds. The wheel I have in mind is *Samsara*, the Wheel of Becoming or Rebirth.

Granted the unignorable presence of Indian ingredients in Eliot's poem, it seems, prima facie, at least a plausible candidate. Ultimately, though, its acceptability will depend on how far I can show it to be central, crucial and simplifying. Is it a thread which, when pulled, produces a terrible tangle? Or, as it should, the resolution of a tangle into a continuous thread? I hope, in what follows, that the Wheel of Rebirth fits flush with the minimum of forcing.

Let me enter two caveats now. This wheel, whether it be *Samsara* or not, plays only a tiny role in *The Waste Land* as it finally emerged in 1922. We glimpse the wheel when Madame Sosostris examines her 'wicked pack of cards' and finds 'the man with three staves, and here the Wheel'. Each reader must decide for him- or herself how far an interpretation based on the entire *Waste Land* manuscript is still valid for *The Waste Land* after Ezra Pound and Eliot had dropped several hundred lines. Is the architectural master-plan crucially affected when whole wings are demolished by Pound on the grounds of poor workmanship ('inversions not warranted by any real exegience [*sic*] of metre', 'georgian', 'too tum-pum at a stretch')? With the dead wood did Pound also discard a vital structural beam?

The second caveat concerns Eliot's remark that he was never an oriental scholar. Patently, though he was no scholar compared to Henry Clarke Warren, he was a scholar compared to the majority of his readers. As often in the late prose, Eliot provides a hint, a nudge in the right direction, but accompanies it with a note of caution. Accordingly, I propose to apply only the simplest shared constituents of Buddhist and Hindu thought – rebirth, karma and nirvana – to Eliot's text. Since I am not an oriental scholar my information comes primarily from Sir Charles Eliot's classic, three-volume study, *Hinduism and Buddhism*. And, when I say 'simple', I do not discount the possibility of profundity. I merely mean 'central', or 'basic', rather than recherché.

In both of the major Buddhist schools of thought, the Theravada and the Mahayana, the Wheel plays a vital part in the idea of rebirth and the journey towards nirvana. Perhaps the most poetic description of rebirth occurs in the *Brihadaranyaka Upanishad* mentioned in Eliot's note to line 401: 'even as the caterpillar, when coming to the end of a blade of grass, reaches out to another blade of grass and draws itself over to it, in the same way the Soul, leaving the body and unwisdom behind, reaches out to another body and draws itself over to it.' Another image cited by Sir Charles Eliot is 'the chain, also known as the twelve Nidânas or causes'. But usually the Wheel is the preferred image of reincarnation. As it happens, F. L. Lucas, in an early and damning review, touched on the idea fleetingly, but left the supposition untested and speculative, since his main purpose was to recoil from Eliot's modernism: 'She [the Sybil at Cumae] typifies, I suppose, the timeworn soul's desire to escape from the "Wheel" of things.'

The original epigraph to *The Waste Land* was not taken from Petronius's *Satyricon*, but from Conrad's *Heart of Darkness*, shortly after the death of Kurtz. '*Did he live his life again in every detail* [my italics] of desire, temptation, and surrender during that supreme moment of complete knowledge? He cried in a whisper at some image, at some vision – he cried out twice, a cry that was no more than a breath – "The horror! The horror!" ' Pound, underrating Conrad's status as a writer, urged Eliot to drop the lines and find something weightier from an author who could stand the citation. Eliot replied, 'It is much the most appropriate I can find, and somewhat elucidative'. The passage was omitted. But how is it 'elucidative'? The title of *The Waste Land*, the general prefatory paragraph to the notes, point towards an infertile and arid world which needs to be rescued from this condition by rebirth – this condition being a metaphor for a spiritual state of dryness. In this scheme, rebirth is good, something to be sought after, and death is to be feared.

However, the quotation from Conrad activates a second, central oppositional strand, in which the 'horror' is living one's life over again, being trapped in continual suffering (*dukkha*) – of being, in other words, bound upon the Wheel of rebirth. In this scheme, rebirth is a necessary evil, while nirvana in which the self is extinguished is the most desirable state. Continuing consciousness is the evil to avoid. In fact, the epigraph from Petronius, in

31

which the Sybil wants to die, conveys the same information but rather less clearly. There, the 'horror' is the inability to die, which, though it amounts to the same thing, does not introduce the idea of rebirth.

Further evidence to support this reading comes in 'Death by Water':

> As he rose and fell
> He passed the stages of his age and youth
> Entering the whirlpool.

Phlebas, like many another drowning man, and like Kurtz, relives his life at the moment of death. Interestingly, the original version in French, 'Dans le Restaurant', makes the point more clearly:

> Le repassant aux étapes de sa vie antérieure.

Conceivably, Eliot is alluding to Baudelaire's 'La Vie Antérieure', of which Wallace Stevens, in 'Two or Three Ideas', wrote: 'the idea of an earlier life is like the idea of a later life, or like the idea of a different life, part of the classic repertory of poetic subjects.' Eliot's use of this 'classic repertory' is well in advance of the merely stock.

For instance, the puzzling 'The Death of Saint Narcissus', from which Eliot retained only the opening lines ('Come under the shadow of this gray rock . . .' etc.), belongs to the same collocation of ideas. It began as a poem about narcissism, about a man 'struck mad by the knowledge of his own beauty'. In the two surviving versions of the poem we can watch Eliot adapting this early material to his new Buddhist purpose.

> First he wished that he had been a tree
> To push its branches among each other.
> And tangle its roots among each other

These lines become, in the later version, less speculatively yearning and more downright:

First he was sure that he had been a tree . . . etc.

The emphasis shifts from a self-regarding, onanistic sensuality to the idea of reincarnation. Similarly, the lines

> Then he wished that he had been a fish
> With slippery belly held between his own fingers
> To have writhed in his own clutch . . .

become 'Then he knew that he had been a fish . . .' etc. And, finally, the lines:

> Then he wished he had been a young girl
> Caught in the woods by a drunken old man
> To have known at the last moment, the full
> Taste of her own whiteness . . .

likewise harden and become definite: 'Then he had been a young girl . . .' etc. The purpose of the adaptations is transparent enough. The later lines describe a series of incarnations or *vies antérieures*:

> First he was sure that he had been a tree . . .
> Then he knew that he had been a fish . . .
> Then he had been a young girl . . .

Saint Narcissus, however, did not figure in the final draft. Tiresias, though, did. Familiar, comfortably classical, Tiresias nevertheless fits into Eliot's Indian scheme without the slightest dislocation. He chose the hermaphroditical seer because he was, appropriately, 'throbbing between two lives'. There is no need to dwell on the significance of this, especially since Eliot explained, quite straightforwardly, in his notes to the poem what Tiresias's function was: 'although a mere spectator and not indeed a "character", [Tiresias] is yet the most important personage in the poem, *uniting all the rest* [my italics]. Just as the one-eyed merchant, seller of currants, melts into the Phoenician Sailor, and the latter is not wholly distinct from Ferdinand Prince of Naples, so all the women are one woman, and the two sexes meet in Tiresias. What Tiresias *sees*, in fact, is the substance of the poem.' To paraphrase, Tiresias is all the figures in the poem: they represent a series of incarnations, a series of lives which are all one life. Stephen Spender commented on this note: 'Now this all too easily might cause the student who reads the explanation first . . . to write in his notebook: "One-eyed merchant = Phoenician Sailor = Ferdinand Prince of Naples".' Precisely. That was Eliot's intention. If anything, the explicitness of the explanation is an example of Eliot's risking a flaw – by sacrificing the poem's *internal* integrity – for the sake of complete clarity. It is surely unsatisfactory that a note, a piece of apparatus, should be used to convey such crucial information.

Tiresias is not the only example of Eliot's ability to make over an apparently alien cultural fact to ideas of rebirth. There is also Philomela from Ovid's *Metamorphoses*:

> The change of Philomel, by the barbarous king
> So rudely forced; yet there the nightingale
> Filled all the desert with inviolable voice
> And still she *cried*, and still the world *pursues* . . .

The italics are mine. The change in tense, from preterite to continuous present, makes it clear that this is a continuous process – that defilements result in incarnations lower in the order of things. As a whole, 'A Game of Chess' illustrates this neatly and shows how *Samsara* can cope with falls from high to low estate. Firstly, there is Cleopatra who is alluded to in the magnificent blank-verse opening. Her modern reincarnation is placed in denatured magnificence. She does not hop thirty paces in the public street: she *threatens* something like it, an hysterical episode, but the closed car at four is more suited to her sapped vitality. She is Mrs Skewton young. Secondly, Eliot travesties and satirizes the married life of Albert Edward, Prince of Wales and later King Edward VII. His long-suffering wife, Alexandra, Princess of Denmark, gave birth to five children, Eddy, George,

Louise, Victoria and Maud. Though Louise's birth was the most troublesome, the Princess Alexandra's health was not strong and it was two full months after George's birth before she made a public appearance at Cowes:

> She's had five already, and nearly died of young George.

If Eliot treats the strict facts with poetic licence, it is surely because the joke has greater piquancy if it attaches to the reigning monarch. The echo of Ophelia's goodnight at the end of 'A Game of Chess' reminds us poignantly of another girl from the Danish court who was treated badly by a prince, and, incidentally, is an echo which preserves the Shakespearian harmony of the whole passage.

Before Eliot decided to use Ovid's Philomela, he evidently considered a more general treatment of lower incarnations. There is something eerily prophetic in these lines from 'The Death of the Duchess', describing the inhabitants of Hampstead:

> Dogs eyes reaching over the table
> Are in their heads when they stare
> Supposing that they have the heads of birds
> Beaks and no words

This is fantasy arising out of disgust, but it isn't difficult to see how the unfinished passage might have been adapted, possibly as the stanzas of 'The Death of Saint Narcissus' were altered, changed to show all things change. Kipling's account in *Kim* is populist rather than professional, yet useful for that reason: 'when the shadows shortened and the lama leaned more heavily upon Kim, there was always the Wheel of Life to draw forth . . . Here sat the Gods on high – and they were dreams of dreams. Here was our Heaven and the world of the demi-Gods – horsemen fighting among the hills. Here were the agonies done upon beasts, souls ascending or descending the ladder . . . Often the lama made the living pictures the matter of his text, bidding Kim . . . note how the flesh takes a thousand thousand shapes, desirable or detestable as men reckon, but in truth of no account either way; and how the stupid spirit is bound to follow the body through all the Heavens and all the Hells, and strictly round again.'

Although *The Waste Land* may appear to be a collection of brilliant dramatic monologues ('He do the police in different voices') they are unified in the person of Tiresias. He is not impersonating those people. He *is* those people. And the meaning of *The Waste Land* is that 'flesh takes a thousand thousand shapes':

> And I Tiresias have foresuffered all
> Enacted on this same divan or bed . . .

Reincarnation is also repetition, and repetition is also boredom. The last line of 'The Burial of the Dead' is a quotation from Baudelaire's 'Au Lecteur', which summons the airless void of ennui:

> C'est l'Ennui! – l'œil chargé d'un pleur involontaire,
> Il rêve d'échafauds en fumant son houka.
> Tu le connais, lecteur, ce monstre délicat,
> – Hypocrite lecteur, – mon semblable, – mon frère!

The Baudelaire is wonderful in the way it modulates from the accuracy of tears of boredom to the last hyperbolic refinement of *taedium vitae* which is an apathetic longing for death: 'Il rêve d'échafauds en fumant son houka.' And there is something thrillingly incriminating about tutoyer-ing the unknown reader – a real liberty is taken with the person. If the reader and all potential readers can be implicated in Eliot's scheme of reincarnations, the wide social spectrum of *The Waste Land* is only to be expected as 'flesh takes a thousand thousand shapes'. And this is why, theoretically, the flexible structure of the poem could have included many more poems, many more lives in addition to the Countess Marie Larisch, Elizabeth I, the working-class voice of Lil's friend, the young man carbuncular and so on. It could have included Fresca and Bleistein, two characters easily assimilated to the idea of rebirth. Just as Elizabeth I melts into a character from the lower middle class ('Highbury bore me'), so Fresca is fluid rather than fixed:

> . . . in another time or place had been
> A meek and lowly weeping Magdalene;
> More sinned against than sinning, bruised and marred,
> The lazy laughing Jenny of the bard.

The identity may vary, but the fallen predicament is the same:

> For varying forms, one definition's right:
> Unreal emotions and real appetite.

So much for Fresca's karma (volitional actions which determine the nature of the succeeding existence). Bleistein's karma is a desire for money. Consequently, his next life will be similar to the last. Eliot expresses this metaphorically in these lines:

> Though he suffers a sea change
> Still expensive rich and strange.

Neither is the long, deleted sea voyage an exception. As far as the theme of reincarnation is concerned, the voyage is a modern dress repetition of the Ulysses canto (XXVI) of the *Inferno*, and includes this anachronistic encounter with the Sirens:

> On watch, I thought I saw in the fore cross-trees
> Three women leaning forward, with white hair
> Streaming behind, who sang above the wind
> A song that charmed my senses . . .

The narrator thinks it is a dream, but it is, in fact, a memory of the former life on which the whole passage is modelled.

Similarly, the 'crowds of people, walking round in a ring' are literally going round in circles because they are bound upon the Wheel. And when Tiresias singles out one individual with the words 'You who were with me in the ships at Mylae!' there is no problem. Nothing requires exegesis. The statement is a statement of fact. Tiresias means exactly what he says. Stetson has also been reincarnated. A notorious local difficulty blends back into the text like vanishing cream. This is what I meant when I said that the concept of the Wheel of Rebirth should prove simplifying rather than complicating, and that this would be the strongest argument in its favour.

In the same way, Madame Sosostris, 'famous clairvoyante', is a macabre comic reminder that the soul survives physical death – she is a fake Tiresias who, by chance, happens to be right. And when she evokes 'Belladonna, the Lady of the Rocks', she also evokes Pater's sinister meditation on *La Gioconda* in *The Renaissance*, with its spectacular adherence to metempsychosis: 'She is older than the rocks among which she sits; like the vampire, she has been dead many times, and learned the secrets of the grave . . . The fancy of a perpetual life, sweeping together ten thousand experiences, is an old one . . .'

The soul, in this scheme, voyages wearily on, without rest, without finality. So it is appropriate that Eliot's evocation of Londoners 'under the brown fog of a winter dawn' should allude to Dante's *Inferno* Canto III:

> si lunga tratta
> di gente, ch'io non avrei mai creduto
> che morte tanta n'avesse disfatta.

'I had not thought death had undone so many' refers to those who 'spent Life without infamy and without praise'. Rejected by heaven and hell alike, 'they have no hope of death', 'Questi non hanno speranza di morte'. They exist in a kind of limbo, longing for death – longing for death like the Sibyl of Cumae.

Which brings us to the Dog 'that's friend to men'. I mentioned earlier that *The Waste Land* is driven by a central polarity – between the desire to be reborn (part of the vegetation myths) and the desire to avoid being reborn at all costs (the Buddhist prescription). Even the Buddhist–Hindu arm of the polarity includes the human desire to go on living: it is this thirst which binds human beings to the Wheel and causes them to be reborn. In Webster's *The White Devil*, to which Eliot's note refers us, the wolf is 'foe to men'. Here, the Dog is 'friend to men' because it digs up the buried corpse and stops it sprouting. Not death but rebirth is the thing to fear. On the other hand, the speaker is clearly anxious that the dog should not be allowed to interfere with the process of rebirth. At the end of the first section of *The Waste Land*, then, Eliot marshals his conflicting imperatives: the imperative to survive is as strong as the need to die. Eros and Thanatos are the Freudian version of this very human equation. Somehow, though, Eliot contrives to deprive them of all dignity in a way I find unsatisfactory. There is an atmosphere of sick farce for which we now have the adjective Ortonesque, alas. There is a determination to shock which is entirely febrile, as the punctuation demonstrates. Even the allusion to Baudelaire is very much weaker than the original.

'I will show you fear in a handful of dust': I don't think this is a reference to death either (however Donne used it) but a reference to the Sybil of the epigraph who was granted the long life she desired by Apollo – for as many years as she held grains in her hand. Eliot *begins* with an image of Time and Mortality:

> Your shadow at morning striding behind you
> Or your shadow at evening rising to meet you

but offers to show 'something different from either' the morning or evening shadows. It is the 'handful of dust' which, therefore, cannot be an image of mortality, but rather its opposite.

The hyacinth girl and the episode in the hyacinth garden are more problematic:

> 'You gave me hyacinths first a year ago;
> 'They called me the hyacinth girl.'
> – Yet when we came back, late, from the hyacinth garden,
> Your arms full, and your hair wet, I could not
> Speak, and my eyes failed, I was neither

> Living nor dead, and I knew nothing,
> Looking into the heart of light, the silence.

These very beautiful lines represent some great good, some intense spiritual afflatus. I take this as axiomatic, even while I experience certain difficulties of detail. I do this because, later in the poem, when things are going disastrously awry, the experience here is invoked ironically in the next section, 'A Game of Chess'. The ecstatic phrase 'I could not / Speak' returns shrewishly, as the woman chides her partner with his sullenness: 'Speak to me. Why do you never speak. Speak.' 'I knew nothing' is deformed by impatient anger: 'What are you thinking of? What thinking? What? / I never know what you are thinking. Think.' 'And my eyes failed' is twisted into a rhetorical question: 'Do you see nothing?' And the great climax, 'I was neither / Living nor dead', becomes a mere sarcasm: 'Are you alive, or not?' This negative version defines, I think, the initial experience after the hyacinth garden as positive. In fact, I should gloss it with a later quotation – probably planted by Eliot for just this purpose – in his Dante essay of 1929: 'The experience of a poem is the experience both of a moment and of a lifetime. It is very much like our intenser experiences of other human beings. There is a first, or an early moment which is unique, of shock and surprise, even of terror (*Ego dominus tuus*); a moment which can never be forgotten, but which is never repeated integrally; and yet which would become destitute of significance if it did not survive in a larger whole of experience, which survives inside a deeper and a calmer feeling.'

'Even of terror': that and the parenthetical reference to *La Vita Nuova* (Section III: I am your Master) explain the slight air of foreboding, of misgiving, which tinges the incident. (Eliot is always shrewd about the element of queasiness, the slight pang in all pleasure: consider, for instance, his account of first reading Edward FitzGerald's *Omar*: 'it was like a sudden conversion; the world appeared anew, painted with bright, delicious and painful colours.') The passage, too, is flanked by two quotations from *Tristan und Isolde*, one asking the whereabouts of '*Mein Irisch*

Kind', the other implying a negative response – '*Oed' und leer das Meer*.' It is uncomfortable also that the passage should begin with what feels like a qualification: ' – Yet . . .' Yet any awesome experience is bound to be awesome. Particularly here because Eliot is describing an experience of Enlightenment: 'Looking into the heart of light . . .' The name 'Buddha' means 'Enlightened'.

Can we be more precise? At the risk of trying to describe the indescribable, we can attempt a more formal definition, but Eliot's evocation is unsurpassable. Any more abstract account is liable to read as ploddingly as a police statement. Enlightenment, 'nirvana', is defined in *Buddhist Scriptures* (p. 247) as 'the ultimate goal of all Buddhist endeavour, the extinction of craving and separate selfhood, *a life which has gone beyond death*' (my italics):

> I was neither
> Living nor dead . . .

(Incidentally, Eliot's line-breaks on 'I could not / Speak' and 'I was neither / Living nor dead' are brilliant cliff-hangers both – full of suspense and angst.) This timeless moment of enlightenment is repeated in 'Burnt Norton', as the first in a series of four moments outside the tyranny of time and its cycle of rebirth and renewal:

> And the lotos rose, quietly, quietly,
> The surface glittered out of heart of light . . .

The lotus, of course, is often depicted as the seat of the Buddha.

However, the trouble with being 'neither / Living nor dead' is that this state can be difficult to distinguish from that of the crowd flowing over London Bridge – those who are 'odious to God and to his enemies'. On the one hand, there is nirvana. On the other hand, there is limbo. (Eliot may have dismissed his notes as 'bogus scholarship' but in 1950, in his essay 'What Dante Means to Me', he was strict about the necessity for at least this note: 'readers of my *Waste Land* will perhaps remember that the vision of my city clerks trooping over London Bridge from the railway station to their offices evoked the reflection that "I had not thought death had undone so many"; and that in another place I deliberately modified a line of Dante by altering it – "sighs, short and infrequent, were exhaled". And I gave the references in my notes, in order to make the reader who recognised the allusion, know that I meant him to recognise it, and know that he would have missed the point if he did not recognise it.') What is the precise moment when loss of self becomes hollowness, when the purged and pure is merely the empty? As the 1929 Dante essay explains so conveniently – since the moment can 'never be repeated integrally' but can only 'survive in a larger whole of experience', the larger context of aridity and emptiness is bound to taint the awesome moment. It is a reference point, but one that is under constant threat. How can one be sure the experience of enlightenment was not an illusion, given that so much else in *The Waste Land* is an illusion:

> Jerusalem Athens Alexandria
> Vienna London
> Unreal

The great civilizations of the Jews, the Greeks and the Egyptians have all decayed. Vienna and London, modern cities, will re-enact their fate. It is for this reason that Eliot, in his notes, refers to Baudelaire's

> Fourmillante cité, cité pleine de rêves,
> Où le spectre en plein jour raccroche le passant.

We are all of us ghosts, bound upon the Wheel, having had former lives in former cities: 'You who were with me in the ships at Mylae!' The disintegration of London is shadowed forth in the phantasmagoric scene-painting of 'What the Thunder Said'. There, despite 'the sandy road' and 'mudcracked houses', 'empty cisterns and exhausted wells', we are still in London.

> And upside down in air were towers
> Tolling reminiscent bells, that kept the hours

recall Saint Mary Woolnoth which 'kept the hours' in 'The Burial of the Dead'. In addition, the woman who 'drew her long black hair out tight / And fiddled *whisper* music on those strings' (my italics) is recognizably the neurasthenic from 'A Game of Chess' whose hair 'Spread out in fiery points / Glowed into words . . .' Equally, the 'bats with baby faces' are a nightmare version of her cupidons, who are, after all, babies with wings. What we have here is a nervous breakdown of reality itself. And my hunch is that, on the same principle, 'the empty chapel, only the wind's home' is at once the Chapel Perilous and St Magnus Martyr – just as the 'voices singing out of empty cisterns' are the Thames maidens. Not that either hunch can be positively proven.

'The Fire Sermon', predictably, is the easiest section of *The Waste Land* to interpret from the Buddhist point of view. Set ironically against the refrain from Spencer's 'Prothalamion' are a series of arid sexual encounters that bind their protagonists more firmly to the Wheel. Sir Charles Eliot broadens the concept of desire: 'This thirst (*Tanhâ*) is the craving for life in the widest sense: the craving for pleasure which propagates life.' Distasteful as some have found Eliot's asceticism, his intention is un-ambiguous: 'the collocation of these two representatives of eastern and western asceticism, as the culmination of this part of the poem, is not an accident.' Moreover, this asceticism conti-nued to interest him, as we can see from the epigraph to *Sweeney Agonistes*, taken from St John of the Cross – 'Hence the soul cannot be possessed of the divine union, until it has divested itself of the love of created things.' The Buddha at Uruvela advocated the same thing: 'All things are on fire . . . And with what are these things on fire? With fires of lust, anger and illusion, with these are they on fire, and so with the other senses and so with the mind. Wherefore the wise man conceives disgust for the things of the senses, and being divested of desire for the things of the senses, he removes from his heart the cause of suffering.'

Finally, a look at the very beginning of the poem and a glance at the last 33 lines. The first phrase of *The Waste Land* – 'April is the cruellest month' – has the force of an unquestionable fiat. There is, too, a surreal quality shared with 'The Naked Lunch', which is rooted in the oddness of the adjective. After all, the winter months, we might think, are more cruel. It is partly the weirdness of what the line says that gives it authority. Few readers ever ask why April should be stigmatized as the cruellest month. Yet the Wheel of Rebirth explains why with proper simplicity: April mixes 'memory' of former existences and 'desire' (*tanhâ*) for life which, necessarily, will prolong the period on the Wheel. As the *Bhagavadgita* warns so eloquently: 'their soul is warped with selfish desires, and their heaven is a selfish desire. They have prayers for pleasures and power, the reward of which is earthly rebirth.' Spring and renewal are, therefore, to be dreaded. In *The Family Reunion*, Eliot reverts to this idea so clearly that it is impossible to misinterpret him:

> Spring is an issue of blood
> A season of sacrifice
> And the wail of the new full tide
> Returning the ghosts of the dead
> Those whom the winter drowned
> Do not the ghosts of the drowned
> Return to land in the spring?

Mary replies to this speech of Harry's:

> And what of the terrified spirit
> Compelled to be reborn . . .

Spring, then, means only the renewal of old agonies, whereas 'dry bones can harm no one'.

The end of *The Waste Land* is difficult to interpret. Clearly, Eliot presents us with imperatives out of which arise the questions that, correctly answered, will lift the curse of sterility: '*Datta*: what have we given?' By analogy, the two further imperatives, *Dayadhvam, Damyata*, require a response too. Is the blight lifted?

It is not clear. First, the desired rain appears to fall: 'a damp gust /
Bringing rain.' Immediately, the poem rescinds this: 'the limp
leaves / Waited for rain.' The finale is likewise inconclusive,
though tipped towards pessimism despite the thrice-repeated
'Shantih', which (Eliot's note tells us) means 'The Peace which
passeth understanding'. Set against this 'formal ending to an
Upanishad' are 'the *arid* plain', the ruin of London Bridge and
the tower of the Prince d'Aquitaine, Arnaut Daniel in purgatory,
the loss of poetic inspiration evoked by the quotation from
'Pervigilium Veneris', and Hieronymo's madness. It is possible to
argue, as Eliot does in his essay on Dante (1929), that the
suffering of Arnaut Daniel is hopeful: 'the souls in purgatory
suffer because they *wish to suffer*, for purgation', Eliot maintains;
whereas Virgil, in limbo, has anaesthesia but no hope. Nevertheless, in context, Arnaut Daniel's 'hope' hardly strikes one as
robust.

Will metempsychosis help explain the curiously fragmented
conclusion of Eliot's poem? 'O swallow swallow' alludes to
Philomela, of course, and her transmigration may be paralleled
by the Prince d'Aquitaine who claims in Nerval's sonnet, 'j'ai
deux fois vainqueur traversé l'Achéron', Acheron across which
Charon ferries the dead. Conceivably, the Prince was Tiresias in a
former existence, but I believe the end to be not an invitation to
cryptography, but a gesture of cultural exhaustion – a scattering,
as it were, of the loose change left in the poet's pockets, a gesture
of poverty which tinges the word 'shantih' with irony.

As for the penultimate section in which the speaker responds to
the imperatives of the thunder, this, too, is ambiguous and
poised, if anything, towards pessimism. It is an account of an
emotional failure. 'Blood shaking my heart' and 'the awful daring
of a moment's surrender' are intended to summon the moment
after the hyacinth garden with its admixture of terror. But after
this moment of naked communion, not necessarily sexual, there
is subsequent withdrawal:

> We think of the key, each in his prison
> Thinking of the key, each confirms a prison

If one pursues the Dante passage cited in Eliot's notes, one is confronted with the story of Ugolino, who, despite his love, ate the flesh of his dead children. The general application might be summarized by Oscar Wilde's 'each man kills the thing he loves'. The 'aethereal rumours' at nightfall appear not to achieve anything more concrete than rumour and dream. Lastly, in the image of the boat, Eliot calls up his happiest memories of sailing, only to conclude with the wasted possibility: 'your heart would have responded'. Would have, but didn't. As the lady said:

> 'I have been wondering frequently of late
> (But our beginnings never know our ends!)
> Why we have not developed into friends.'

Waste, Eliot's enduring theme, is one reason why his greatest poem has the title he gave it.

The Awful Daring of T. S. Eliot:
A Centenary Essay

The task of the artist at any time is uncompromisingly simple – to discover what has not yet been done, and to do it. To do it, moreover, in a way which not only breaks with, but is also a logical extension of, the past. The late Hans Keller definitively observed that the greatest art is characterized by 'unpredictable inevitability' – a quality which T. S. Eliot possessed in abundance. Extravagantly inventive yet fastidiously word perfect, stylistically prodigious yet always recognizably himself, Eliot is the century's greatest poet. When *Poems – 1920* was reviewed by e. e. cummings in the *Dial*, even while he deplored the obstinately unconventional modernism of others, cummings noted Mr Eliot's 'skilful and immediate violins'. Of course, for a full description, one would now wish to add colours to Eliot's orchestra – a hint of crumhorn in the perfect pastiche of Prufrock's phrase 'to swell a progress', however out of character it may seem for one of Prufrock's cultural anxiety; serialism for 'Hysteria'; the thunder-sheet of *Dayadhvam*; the honky-tonk piano of *Sweeney Agonistes*; the organ fugue of *Ash-Wednesday*; the mixture of *sprechgesang* and *a cappella* of 'The Hollow Men'. None of these sounds was predictable, though all now strike us as inevitable.

Poetry lies at the centre of Eliot's achievement. But he was also a literary critic of originality and penetration, the influential editor of the *Criterion* from 1922 to 1939, a social critic, playwright, author of children's verse, the inspiration for a musical, a translator, a tireless lecturer, a quondam philosopher and a full-time publisher. To this one can add that he was a

47

purveyor of titles, as demonstrated by Waugh's *A Handful of Dust* and F. R. Leavis's *The Common Pursuit*, as well as (with increasing licence) two recent films, one Irish, one Canadian – *Eat the Peach* and *I've Heard the Mermaids Singing*. He was, too, a supplier of tags and coiner of phrases: 'I should be glad', he remarked, a little ruefully, in 1964, 'to hear no more of a bang and a whimper.'

There is, then, a great deal of Eliot, a great deal to Eliot and about Eliot – more, in fact, than it is possible to deal with in one short article. One might choose, therefore, to illustrate his unique temper by concentrating on a single essay, like that on Tennyson, replete as it is with Eliot's characteristic strengths – his grasp of detail and his gift for suggestive generalizations which frequently double as personal asides. Praising Tennyson's metrical virtuosity in 'Mariana', Eliot reveals the subtle discriminations of which his own ear was capable: '*the blue fly sung in the pane* (the line would be ruined if you substituted *sang* for *sung*) is enough to tell us that something important has happened.' The 'something important' is the disruption of the metre in the middle of the line. Whether this is, as Eliot claims, 'wholly new', is open to question: Wordsworth, describing a girl struggling to walk in a high wind, adds an extra syllable, a little stumble, as a way of representing her progress verbally: 'And seem'd with difficult steps to force her way.' The word 'difficult' is itself metrically difficult. In earlier poetry, there are many examples of radical disruption, including Wyatt's 'With naked fote stalking in my chambre'.

In his own poetry, Eliot's ear was both resourceful and almost completely reliable – the latter a much more rare quality than non-poets might suppose. Eliot's failures are not naked blunders, they are heavily camouflaged mistakes by a sophisticated ear. For example, '*This* is as I had reckoned' disguises, as best it can, that little pile-up of syllables at the beginning of the line. The italics Eliot so deplored in Arnold's poetry are here deployed to distract us from the initial stutter. The difference is enormous.

Eliot said that 'to be able to quote as Arnold could is the best evidence of taste'. By this standard, Eliot has near perfect taste. In 'What Dante Means to Me' (1950), he quotes an extended passage of *terza rima* from 'The Triumph of Life', with the encomium that Dante has inspired Shelley to 'some of the greatest and most Dantesque lines in English'. In fact, this is only half true – the syntax drifts as the lines move, with an air of suppressed panic, from one rhyme to the next – but Eliot's invocation of Dante also invents a flattering context for Shelley's verse. Its quality of relieved improvisation is masked because we read it as if it were Dante in translation and therefore make all kinds of unaudited allowances. For instance, the clumsy locution 'And that the grass, which methought hung so wide' is Shelleyan for *sparseness* presumably – but because we are familiar with Dante's direct clarity, we discount Shelley's blurred execution of his idea. Quoting 'Tears, Idle Tears' from *The Princess*, Eliot omits the last line with its variant refrain, and greatly improves the poetry by this stroke of editing. Praising Tennyson as having the finest ear for vowel sounds of any English poet, Eliot silently emends Tennyson's weakness for repetition – an area where Tennyson is notably gifted but sometimes oversusceptible, and where Eliot's skills are unmatched. Has anyone dared to use the simple connective *and*, as Eliot does in 'Prufrock' so insistently, both for its ability to summon ironically the epic world of, say, 'Sohrab and Rustum', and for its surprisingly powerful music? Consider, too, the hypnotic Bolero-like development of this passage:

> And would it have been worth it, after all,
> Would it have been worth while,
> After the sunsets and the dooryards and the sprinkled streets,
> After the novels, after the teacups, after the skirts that trail
>   along the floor –
> And this, and so much more? –
> It is impossible to say just what I mean!
> But as if a magic lantern threw the nerves in patterns on a
>   screen:
> Would it have been worth while
> If one, settling a pillow or throwing off a shawl,
> And turning toward the window, should say:

'That is not it at all,
That is not what I meant, at all.'

The Tennyson essay is also remarkable for the thoroughness of
Eliot's reading. Juvenilia which most of us would skip are cited
instead as evidence, and convincing evidence, of Tennyson's aural
inventiveness. Eliot's knowledge of the neglected, late dialect
poems, like 'Owd Roä', 'The Village Wife' and 'The Northern
Cobbler', permits him to cite Tennyson as an influence on
Kipling's *Barrack-Room Ballads*, thereby complicating our
notion of Kipling as the artistic son and heir of Browning. Unlike
many merely good writers, Eliot continued to read and to learn
from his reading rather than be confirmed by it. This is one reason
why he repeats himself less than any other modern writer – and
why, for other poets, he has become the model for variousness.
Because Eliot was such a powerful exemplar, Lowell could
change his style from the clotted theological intensities of 'The
Quaker Graveyard at Nantucket' – themselves closely modelled
on *Four Quartets* – to the relatively relaxed simplicity of *Life
Studies* and thereafter to the Marvellian formalism of *Near the
Ocean*. And if Seamus Heaney is currently purging his style in
search of something more austere, a poetry of 'the bare wire',
Eliot is a presence in that process, too. Even Larkin's resolute
refusal to develop as a poet was conditioned by Eliot's quick-
change artistry.

Writing of Arnold – an irksomely important and therefore
deeply resented intellectual father-figure, a Victorian sage familiar with the work of the de Guérins, Joubert, Heine, Goethe,
Tolstoy, Marcus Aurelius, Renan, Sainte-Beuve, Lamartine,
Pascal, La Bruyère, Voltaire, Spinoza and Rousseau, not to
mention the entire range of English literature – Eliot brings in the
eccentric verdict that 'Arnold was not a man of vast or exact
scholarship.' As for exactness, years ago F. W. Bateson compiled
a small anthology of Eliot's misquotations and trivial scholarly
blunders – without, so far as I am aware, displacing Eliot as a
critic. Yet even while he criticizes Arnold, Eliot mimics his tone of
lofty judiciousness: 'there is petulance in such a judgement,

arrogance and excess of heat.' Eliot is unjust, too, to Arnold's poetry. It is academic. Arnold, to have been a great poet, should have seen 'the boredom, and the horror, and the glory' – and, according to Eliot, knew only 'something of the boredom'. There is some justice here, given the poems Eliot chooses to discuss – but he completely ignores 'Dover Beach', a poem whose irregular rhymes, irregular line lengths, fluctuating stress-count provide the formal template for 'The Love Song of J. Alfred Prufrock', just as surely as Clough is godfather to its ironies and Browning to its way with the dramatic monologue. 'Dover Beach' is the poem *par excellence* which sees beneath the beauty to the horror and the glory:

> Ah, love, let us be true
> To one another! for the world, which seems
> To lie before us like a land of dreams,
> So various, so beautiful, so new,
> Hath really neither joy, nor love, nor light,
> Nor certitude, nor peace, nor help for pain . . .

When Eliot writes, early in his career, that 'the possessors of the inner voice ride ten in a compartment to a football match at Swansea, listening to the inner voice, which breathes the eternal message of vanity, fear and lust' – when Eliot writes so, he takes his cue from Arnold, the greatest ironist in the English language: 'this and that man, and this and that body of men, all over the country, are beginning to assert and put in practice an Englishman's right to do what he likes; his right to march where he likes, meet where he likes, enter where he likes, hoot as he likes, threaten as he likes, smash as he likes.'

This major and influential critical injustice aside, Eliot's criticism is notable for its absence of showily perverse flourishes, as the essay on Tennyson shows. The swift and exact discriminations are as thrilling in their way as watching a Chinese chef wielding a cleaver with power and precision, as if he could never make a mistake. Eliot made very few. Of Wordsworth, whose 'Tintern Abbey', 'Ode: Intimations of Immortality' and much of the

Prelude deal with the loss of vision, Eliot remarks somewhat mystifyingly: 'His inspiration never having been of that sudden, fitful and terrifying kind that visited Coleridge, he was never, apparently, troubled by the consciousness of having lost it.' His verdict on *Maud* is more typical: the meat, several distinguished lyrics, is set aside, while the bones, Tennyson's incoherent and melodramatic plot, is put to one side for a nourishing soup – the reflection that Tennyson fails here because he is undecided between lyric and dramatic expression.

Eliot finds in Tennyson's poetry, particularly *Maud*, evidence of emotion 'deeply suppressed': 'the real feelings of Tennyson, profound and tumultuous as they are, never arrive at expression.' This observation isn't limited to Tennyson. As early as 1919, Eliot wrote: '*Hamlet*, like the sonnets, is full of some stuff that the writer could not drag to light, contemplate, or manipulate into art.' And in the *Athenaeum* for the same year, he remarked of Donne that he possessed 'an Ego which nowhere in his works finds complete expression, and only furtively in his sermons'. So Tennyson is in distinguished company – company which, of course, includes Eliot himself. Eliot is attracted to the idea of a powerful, imperious, but apparently unprovoked emotion – whether it be in Tennyson's 'Tears, Idle Tears' ('I know not what they mean') or in *Hamlet* ('the intense feeling, ecstatic or terrible, without an object or exceeding its object, is something which every person of sensibility has known') – because he is mesmerized, throughout his poetic career, with the idea of powerful emotions which are, for whatever psychological reasons, suppressed and unable to achieve expression, except momentarily.

The great and persistent theme of Eliot's poetry, from first to last, can be summed up in the advice of Lambert Strether, the central protagonist of Henry James's *The Ambassadors*, to a young artist, little Bilham: 'Live all you can. It's a mistake not to.' For Eliot, the failure to live, the failure of emotion to find its proper expression, is an obsessive theme of his work. It begins with Prufrock's failure to ask the 'overwhelming question', to make his feelings known in a proposal of marriage. He cannot pop the question and, instead, acknowledges: 'I have measured out my life with coffee spoons.' This line is generally, even universally, perceived as conceding the triviality of Prufrock's existence, but it should be read completely otherwise – as a tragic statement of repression and stoical suffering, like John Davidson's clerk in 'Thirty Bob a Week' who sees his banal existence as 'walking on a string across a gulf' – the unglamorous heroism of the almost poor. Life's sweetness, even as Prufrock loads his spoon with sugar, is accelerating to its vanishing point. And he knows it, yet hasn't 'the strength to force the moment to its crisis'. The pretentious anti-heroine of 'Portrait of a Lady' finally claims our sympathy because her emotional desperation at last drives her to a directness that shames the narrator out of his cynically amused reserve. She can ask him 'why we have not developed into friends'. He can respond only with the authentically modern poetic note of queasy emotional uncertainty – 'not knowing what to feel . . .' Directly appealed to ('I am always sure that you understand / My feelings'), the young man remains aridly self-possessed and unable to give himself.

In 'Rhapsody on a Windy Night', the idea of preparing for 'life' is 'the last twist of the knife' because the poem has shown us only a simulacrum of life, the form without the substance, or the substance without the soul. A rusty, inelastic spring; a child with nothing behind its eye; a crab with instincts to pinch: life, in this poem, is portrayed as nothing more than a series of physical reflexes. And it is no accident that the 'automatic' hand of the child which pockets a toy should be echoed in The Waste Land by the typist who has stooped to folly with the 'young man carbuncular':

> She turns and looks a moment in the glass,
> Hardly aware of her departed lover;
> Her brain allows one half-formed thought to pass:
> 'Well now that's done: and I'm glad it's over.'
> When lovely woman stoops to folly and
> Paces about her room again, alone,
> She smoothes her hair with automatic hand,
> And puts a record on the gramophone.

53

Actions which once had consequence have now become weight-less. The people in *The Waste Land*, like Gerontion, have lost their passion. Ariel's song in *The Tempest*, which leads Ferdinand to Miranda and the prospect of innocent love, is demoted by Eliot: the lyrical 'Come unto these yellow sands / And then take hands' becomes instead 'On Margate Sands. / I can connect / Nothing with nothing.'

'The Hollow Men' are hollow because they, too, are without substance. They are not 'lost / Violent souls' – not real sinners who deserve hell and retribution, but people who have failed to live at all, failed even to sin, and have therefore been refused admission to hell. They fetch up rather in limbo, where they ruminate on 'death's other kingdom'. They are not unlike Kipling's 'Tomlinson', who is rejected by heaven and hell alike. But the significant reference here is to Canto III of the *Inferno* (already alluded to in *The Waste Land* notes): Virgil identifies the occupants of hell's ante-room as 'forlorn spirits', whose lives have been 'without infamy and without praise', beside whom 'the sinner would be proud'. Eliot's attitude is summed up in his essay on Baudelaire: 'so far as we do evil or good, we are human; and it is better, in a paradoxical way, to do evil than to do nothing; at least, we exist.' Again: 'the worst that can be said about most of our malefactors, from statesmen to thieves, is that they are not men enough to be damned.'

In *Sweeney Agonistes*, published in the *Criterion*, October 1926 and January 1927, the febrile socializing cannot hide the fundamental truth voiced by Sweeney. When asked by Doris what life is, he retorts that 'Life is death'. The (unfinished) piece closes with the lines, 'And perhaps you're alive / And perhaps you're dead'. As a result of Eliot's low-life cast, the theme is coarsely articulated but still related to the spiritual diffidence and crippled sensibility of 'Animula' – the 'simple soul', 'Fearing the warm reality, the offered good, / Denying the importunity of the blood'. And the doubtful nature of experience in *Sweeney Agonistes* – where the man who has kept the murdered girl in a bath of lysol is uncertain whether 'he was alive and the girl was dead' – anticipates 'Burnt Norton', whose speaker delineates an experience in all its vivid non-existence:

> Footfalls echo in the memory
> Down the passage which we did not take
> Towards the door we never opened
> Into the rose-garden.

Essentially, Eliot is conjuring an experience which has been tragically missed – something from the realm of might-have-been, a hypothesis of happiness. By the time of *Four Quartets*, Eliot certainly knew it was a mistake not to live all you can.

Which makes it odd that one criticism consistently levelled at Eliot is the charge of being 'anti-life'. Two of our cleverest critics, Ian Hamilton and John Carey, feel that Eliot presents a drained apprehension of life, marked with distaste. Yet it seems to me that, even where you would least expect it, Eliot's perceptions are exceptionally vivid. As a nature poet, for instance: the nightingales who 'let their liquid siftings fall'; the bees 'with hairy bellies'; 'sunless dry geraniums'; 'When the wind blows the water white and black'; 'scent of pine and the woodthrush singing through the fog'; 'the cry of the quail and the whirling plover'. As an erotic poet, Eliot's economy of means is equalled only by Wyatt. Wyatt's woman 'in thyn arraye' is matched by Eliot's 'Arms that are braceleted and white and bare / (But in the lamplight, downed with light brown hair!)' – everything in this couplet is charged and perfect, from the way Eliot spaces out his separate shocks with 'and' to that thoughtfully stationed comma after 'lamplight', which gives Prufrock and the reader pause. That comma represents a space to swallow – perhaps the first silent gulp in English poetry. The brackets aren't idling either: somehow Eliot makes them stand for shyness and sudden disclosure.

Even when Eliot appears aloof from his material, he notates it precisely, in a way superior to pages of worthy, well-meant, twittering inaccuracy: 'Sitting along the bed's edge, where / You curled the papers from your hair, / Or clasped the yellow soles of feet / In the palms of both soiled hands.' The internal rhyme, 'bed's edge', is suggestively claustrophobic. But Eliot is always good on feet – whether it be Doris 'padding on broad feet', or the 'unoffending feet' of Jesus, which share the adjectives 'pale and thin' with the water they are standing in. Eliot keeps an ironic distance, but both pairs of feet are registered rather than ridiculed or gagged at. Of course, Eliot answered for himself when he referred to Bertrand Russell and Aldous Huxley as 'two depressing life-forcers', with an 'enervate *gospel of happiness*'. He concluded: 'what chiefly remains of the new freedom is its meagre impoverished emotional life.' (It would be less meagre, you feel, if there wasn't a shortage of commas.) We may disagree with Eliot's chosen prescription – Christianity – but we cannot deny that he seeks a 'more varied, refined and intense enjoyment of life'. And in his Arnold lecture, Eliot obliquely rebuts the accusation that his own poetry is a 'poetry of indifference towards *life*'. Arnold argues that Wordsworth's poetry is great because of 'the joy offered to us in nature, the joy offered to us in the simple primary affections and duties'. To which Eliot rejoins 'by asking whether Wordsworth would be a less great poet, if he felt with extraordinary power the horror offered to us in nature, and the boredom and sense of restriction in the simple primary affections and duties?' As you might guess, the ironic repetition, without abatement, of the critical formulation, is a favourite ploy of Arnold's. And the point is good. That is to say, concede even the worst case against Eliot (which I do not) that his poetry is anti-life and the charge evaporates because the criteria applied are inappropriate. The criteria are extra-literary and subjective – as they are, it has to be said, when Eliot, in the course of deploring the loss of traditional moral orthodoxy and the subsequent replacement of it by the '*personal view of life*', lodges similar charges against Hardy in *After Strange Gods*: 'the self which he had to express does not strike me as a particularly wholesome or edifying matter of communication.' As readers, we cannot tell our writers what they must feel. Not unless we want to read hymns rather than poems: 'people who write devotional verse,' Eliot noted, 'are usually writing what they want to feel, rather than as they do feel.'

Neither in his prose nor in his poetry is Eliot the dry, indifferent, faintly chilly personage of popular myth – commemorated by Eliot in 'Lines for Cuscuscaraway and Mirza Murad Ali Beg' – 'How unpleasant to meet Mr Eliot! / With his features of clerical cut'. We know what he thought of human love. It can be 'the copulation of animals', he believed – which is clearly true and no one has captured the desolation of purely physical sex better than Eliot. 'To seize and clutch and penetrate.' On the other hand, in 'our intenser experiences of other human beings', he writes in the 1929 Dante essay, 'There is a first, or an early moment which is unique, of shock and surprise, even of terror (*Ego dominus tuus*); a moment which can never be forgotten, but which is never repeated integrally'. The poetic equivalent of this passionate submission to another human being (I am your Master) is:

> *Datta*: what have we given?
> My friend, blood shaking my heart
> The awful daring of a moment's surrender

We have come a considerable distance from those early critics who were able to see only cleverness in Eliot's poetry – from people like Richard Aldington who, in a letter praising Eliot's criticism, felt constrained to add, 'I dislike your poetry very much; it is over-intellectual and afraid of those essential emotions which make poetry.' Who now reads Aldington? And who, in the future, will read the foolish American critic Harold Bloom, who is certain that Eliot will be regarded as the Abraham Cowley of the twentieth century? To me this suggests two closing truths. First, more critics evoke Cowley than read him. Secondly, Eliot is a poet by whom critics are judged.

57

To Purify the Dialect of the Tribe

In 'Little Gidding', Eliot describes how, after an air-raid but before the all-clear, he 'met' what he calls 'a familiar compound ghost' – an encounter which is clearly based on Dante's meeting with Brunetto Latini in Canto XV of the *Inferno*. The ghost refers to their common literary endeavour:

> Since our concern was speech, and speech impelled us
>   To purify the dialect of the tribe . . .

At this juncture, the allusion is to Mallarmé's 'Tombeau d'Edgar Poe': 'Donner un sens plus pur aux mots de la tribu.' Yet Eliot intends by this phrase something different from Mallarmé, who appears to propose a kind of cultural toilette, the sprucing up of language. It is that for Eliot, too, but not in the way we might imagine when we read this passage from 'The Music of Poetry' (1942): 'no poetry, of course, is ever exactly the same speech that the poet talks and hears: but it has to be in such a relation to the speech of his time that the listener or reader can say, "that is how I should talk if I could talk poetry".' Though this, too, sounds like the gentrification of language, that is not quite what Eliot has in mind. If the gentrification of language were Eliot's programme, why should he invoke the vernacular of Mark Twain in 'American Literature and the American Language' (1953): 'I should place him, in this respect, even with Dryden and Swift, as one of those rare writers who have brought their language up to date, and in so doing, "purified the dialect of the tribe".' One has only to recall the opening of *The Adventures of Huckleberry Finn* to realize that the citation of Twain complicates our idea of what 'purification' might mean in this context: 'You don't know about me, without you have read a book by the name of *The Adventures of Tom Sawyer*, but that ain't no matter.'

Confronted by this paradox – that 'purification' might involve the introduction of colloquial 'impurities' – we can find help in *Constructions*, Michael Frayn's collection of agile and elegant philosophical aphorisms. In a discussion of metaphor, he also touches on cliché – the semi-comatose, generally benign twilight state that frequently overtakes the successful image. Linguistically undemanding, the cliché is therefore 'efficient'. The beaten track, so to speak, is 'better' than the track we make for ourselves, because it gains in speed of address what it loses in individuality. Frayn, however, restores the individuality of phrases which have lost their crispness by becoming common currency: 'the more one thinks about our common kit of metaphors for mental states and events,' Frayn writes, 'the less inclined one is to take it for granted, or dismiss it as banal. "At the back of one's mind", "to run over the alternatives", "to reach a decision", "something stirred in her memory", "he groped for words" – they're brilliant! A whole literature, really, trodden down into the soil like last year's leaves, fertilising whatever pushes above the ground now.'

One way of restoring the brilliance of a phrase is to work a variant of it, as Raymond Chandler does in *The Long Goodbye*: 'the girl gave him a look which ought to have stuck at least four inches out of his back.' What Chandler does here with *looking daggers*, Saul Bellow does in *Humboldt's Gift* with the expression, 'a turn-on': 'Why, Renata didn't need an ignition key to start a car. One of her kisses on the hood would turn it on.' These are relatively simple examples. A more complex instance occurs in V. S. Naipaul's *Finding the Centre*, where he describes how his father, Seepersad Naipaul, though a rationalist, found himself compelled by his own fear to make a sacrifice to the goddess Kali. It was a thoroughgoing humiliation and, shortly afterwards, Seepersad Naipaul went mad: 'he looked in the mirror one day and couldn't see himself. And he began to scream.' Behind these two sentences lies a whole literature of clinical hysteria, as well as the literary analogue of Bram Stoker's *Dracula*, where the vampiric count's reflection is characteristically invisible in the narrator's shaving mirror – but the primary source feeding Seepersad Naipaul's breakdown is the phrase, *to lose face*. It is the verbal trigger that determines the form which the madness takes. I assume that, while V. S. Naipaul is alert to the psychological mechanism at work, his father was not – but was rather the victim of language speaking through him. As W. S. Graham warily inquires: 'what is the language using us for?'

Eliot's endeavours in this area are both more sophisticated and more self-conscious. Even our notion of 'dialect' requires an adjustment and sometimes applies to a phrase which, if not exactly a cliché, is so commonly used as to demand transformation, or 'purification'. For instance, to stay with mirrors for a moment, in 'Portrait of a Lady' the young man is conspicuously unruffled: 'I keep my countenance, / I remain self-possessed'. Yet when the older woman taxes him with his coolness, his 'self-possession gutters'. He is suddenly self-conscious, but Eliot's way of expressing this adjective is to stage the phenomenon, instead of stating it: 'I feel like one who smiles, and turning shall remark / Suddenly, his expression in a glass.'

> The readers of the *Boston Evening Transcript*
> Sway in the wind like a field of ripe corn.

When Eliot begins a poem thus, we register the resolutely unpoetic cadence of the newspaper's name (to be repeated twice more, each time at the end of a line) – only to be seduced by the beauty of the second line. The beauty is, of course, ironical: the sense is that the readers of the *Boston Evening Transcript* go whichever way the wind blows. A sentiment Eliot expressed less enigmatically in, 'The Death of the Duchess', an unused section of *The Waste Land*: 'They know what they are to feel and what to think, /They know it with the morning printer's ink.'

'Cousin Nancy' is not a poem that normally attracts much critical attention. In it, Eliot conducts a whimsical examination of

the pitfalls awaiting the avant-garde and the outré. The freedom
of the opening verse reflects the actions of the nicotine-addicted
Miss Ellicott, whose iconoclasm extends to the physical world
itself:

> Miss Nancy Ellicott
> Strode across the hills and broke them,
> Rode across the hills and broke them –
> The barren New England hills –
> Riding to hounds
> Over the cow-pasture.

Against this latitude is set the deliberately cramped inversion at
the poem's end:

> Upon the glazen shelves kept watch
> Matthew and Waldo, guardians of the faith,
> The army of unalterable law.

The finale's almost prissy diction – 'upon', 'glazen' – contrasts
with the gossipy discursiveness of 'And her aunts were not quite
sure how they felt about it'. Formality overtakes and stiffens the
casual beginning.

How marvellously the metre of that last line lifted from
Meredith insists on the precise enunciation of 'unalterable', with
its little minuet of syllables. The changed rhythm and its classic
regularity make an implicit prediction for Nancy. Matthew and
Waldo have a message for her, and not just the obvious one of
disapproval. It is a message almost as rueful as that delivered by
Forster's knifed Florentine to Lucy Honeychurch – things change,
suddenly; life goes. Mr Arnold and Mr Emerson, anti-establish-
ment figures in their day, individualists, literary lions, have been
flea-ed and clipped. Domesticated and familiar (Matthew and
Waldo), they have become respectable upholders of the correct
view of things, 'the unalterable law'. Their prophecy for Miss
Ellicott is spinsterhood: she will end up *on the shelf* – unmarried,
as Arnold and Emerson are unread.

The bachelor Prufrock also has messages encoded in his monologue. It is a commonplace in literature to compare the sunset (or the sunrise) to blood. In *Dombey and Son*, Dickens produces his own variant: 'even the sky itself was changed, and had an execution in it plainly.' In *A Tale of Two Cities* the equation is more straightforward, as it is in Mallarmé's 'Les Fenêtres': 'et quand le soir saigne parmi les tuiles'. To this straightforward idea, Eliot imparts his modernist spin and delivers one of the great poetic googlies, which has proved unplayable for over fifty years:

> Let us go then, you and I,
> When the evening is spread out against the sky
> Like a patient etherised upon a table . . .

By turning the standard figure through 150 degrees, Eliot has remade the entire concept. The trope itself is changed and has an operation in it plainly.

Something similar happens when Prufrock, in a paroxysm of hesitation, tries to articulate his wish to be *transparent*: 'But as if a magic lantern threw the nerves in patterns on a screen'. He knows, however, he isn't really up to the part: 'No! I am not Prince Hamlet'. Nor is he John the Baptist: 'Though I have seen my head (grown slightly bald) brought in upon a platter, / I am no prophet – and here's no great matter . . .' In that case, the reader is intended to ask, why make the comparison at all? And what, since it cannot be literally true, does it mean that Prufrock has seen his head brought in on a platter? The explanation, should we be looking for one, is ready to hand in the subsequent lines: 'And I have seen the eternal Footman hold my coat, and snicker, / And in short, I was afraid.' Socially uneasy, Prufrock has, on occasion, *lost his head* – and this is Eliot's way of expressing the subjective magnitude of his panic.

'Mr. Apollinax', reputedly an account of Bertrand Russell's impact on America, exploits a similar cliché, in the course of a poem which more or less exhausts this technique in Eliot's *œuvre*. That the poet should refer so insistently at the end of his life, in poetry and prose, to this aspect of his work, long after he ceased to employ it, should be no surprise. He wanted to direct his readers to something we had consistently overlooked. The progress of Mr Apollinax through the United States is seldom free from laughter. He never stops. At one point, *he laughs his head off*: 'I looked for the head of Mr. Apollinax rolling under a chair'. He *curls up with laughter*, in a line which so dismayed Harriet Monroe at *Poetry Chicago* that it was cut without Eliot's consent: 'He laughed like an irresponsible foetus.' Pulling himself together, he is still subject to *waves of silent laughter*: 'His laughter was submarine and profound / Like the old man of the sea's'. His mirth is mainly because his audience is *out of its depth*: 'worried bodies of drowned men drift down in the green silence, / Dropping from fingers of surf.' The conversation of Mr Apollinax is too difficult, *over their heads*: Eliot looks for the head of Mr Apollinax 'grinning over a screen'.

> I heard the beat of centaur's hoofs over the hard turf
> As his dry and passionate talk devoured the afternoon.

How will his interlocutors, Mrs Phlaccus and Professor and Mrs Channing-Cheetah, ever manage to keep up with him? Although he is brilliant, he is actually wasting his time talking to them. Contrary to 'appearances' – that lively leg action imagined by the narrator – as far as his American audience is concerned, Mr Apollinax is *flogging a dead horse*. Hence the 'centaur': what horse could be more definitively dead than a centaur, were you intent on illustrating the common expression?

By his strategy of avoidance, by his brilliant circumlocutions, Eliot amuses us, certainly; and conveys to us at first hand exactly what it means to meet someone like Mr Apollinax. We are startled, appreciative, but, let it be admitted, scarcely less baffled than Mrs Channing-Cheetah. In fact, only now are we beginning to understand the poetic possibilities of our own dialect – which Eliot has taken and returned to us so purified that we barely comprehend it. It is, to adapt two lines from Eliot's 'Preludes', 'such a vision of the street / As the street hardly understands'. It is good to think that, in his centenary year, this great poet is no longer flogging a dead horse. We are beginning to understand what he meant, because at last we are once again asking of his poetry, as of other poetry, the overwhelming question so long suspended in Eliot criticism: how does this make sense? It is time to escape that deplorable state of affairs so accurately summarized by Valéry: 'most people have so vague an idea of poetry that the very vagueness of their idea is, for them, its definition.'

John Carey's Dickens

Prospective readers of *The Violent Effigy** should be warned that they are liable, like Major Bagstock, to laugh themselves black in the face. John Carey's study of Dickens is the wittiest ever, and likely to remain so. Few critics, except possibly the early acid Eliot, have his command of language or his eye for what is bad in an author.

Dr Carey takes one on a guided tour of Dickens's imagination – that part of his mind which, for psychological reasons, contains potent objects and ideas that occur repeatedly in his writing. It is like being shown round a cross between a junk shop and an emporium of surgical supplies. Dr Carey's Dickens is not the social reformer so often cheered to the podium (or the pulpit) – he is too much the crypto-fascist for that. The new Dickens, discovered in the secret recesses of his brain, cackles over bottled babies, tapeworms like 'unhealthy macaroni', wooden legs, red-hot pokers, umbrellas, combustible persons, guillotines, nooses, animated furniture, grindstones and amputated limbs.

This may seem a rather extreme view of Dickens. It is. But one is sympathetic to Dr Carey's discontent with the po-faced and pallid Dickenses normally presented in critical studies. Rightly, Dr Carey knows that, *finally*, we read Dickens for his brilliant detail – the good bits, like the stone-mason who points out the mistake in Mr Dombey's specifications with his pocket rule. Equally, Dr Carey knows that one cannot write a book which is

**The Violent Effigy: A Study of Dickens' Imagination* by John Carey, Faber.

simply an anthology of enjoyable moments – though, to his credit, *The Violent Effigy* sometimes reads like that. A thesis must be found to link the fragments. Alas. So Dr Carey gives us Dickens the unconscious artist, violent, anarchic and obsessed. Whenever there is supporting biographical material, like Warren's Blacking Factory, we feel tolerably convinced.

Otherwise, Dr Carey is forced to rely on lists of repeated images to prove an obsession. But, beckon a character from his context and he will, however minor, assume a spurious significance. In this way, certain items in the catalogue are actually make-weights – for instance, Dr Carey summons from obscurity the shadowy Mr Tungay (an amputee in *David Copperfield*) and offers him as evidence of a Dickensian obsession with wooden legs. He hardly merits the limelight. Again, Dr Carey sees Mr Vholes as a typically Dickensian effigy because he takes off his gloves 'as if he were skinning his hands'. But Dickens's starting point is not an unconscious obsession, but a piece of conscious wordplay, a literalization of a common expression – Vholes's clothes are 'skin-tight'. (I examine this phenomenon at length in my essay 'Dickens and Language'.) Lady Tippins, too, is on Dr Carey's list of effigies. But she is not, as he maintains, 'made up of lifeless bits'. Poultry, Dickens tells us, scratch in her neck as she talks. Occasionally, inconvenient items are omitted from Dr Carey's lists: his Dickens is sexually prudish and repressed, so the lesbianism of Miss Wade in *Little Dorrit* is quietly suppressed. Commenting on Dickens's philistine hatred of music, an obsession beginning with his jealousy of his musical sister, Dr Carey writes: 'Dickens' musicians are, in fact, a moth-eaten lot and they make a melancholy noise.' But where is Edith Dombey, who plays two instruments well and is neither moth-eaten nor (Dr Carey's other alternative) evil?

Dickens is so notoriously prodigal in his invention that Dr Carey assumes that repetition can only mean obsession. But there is another explanation – one which escapes Dr Carey because, in the interests of quantity, he makes no distinction between Dickens the journalist (on the look out for unusual copy) and Dickens the artist who re-used, sensibly enough, material collected on journalistic assignments. Here, Dr Carey double-counts what is really a single item, unaware that Dickens, like all great writers, was a literary conservationist who recycled his material. And this applies to images which, as all writers know, have two possibilities. A ploughed field is like a sea of clods, or, the sea is like a ploughed field. Thus, Dr Carey discusses Dickens's unlikely obsession with brollies and notes that Silas Wegg's furled umbrella is 'like an unwholesomely-forced lettuce'. And the next item is Betsey Prig's lettuce which has to be shut up like an umbrella! Similarly, he notices that nooses in *Barnaby Rudge* are compared to garlands. But he fails to list the garlands in Jaggers's house which remind Pip of nooses – or to draw the proper conclusion.

These are small examples, but throughout his creative life Dickens re-used material – like that other notoriously prodigal 'genius', Shakespeare, of whom Pasternak wrote: 'What cunning, what ulterior purpose can be imagined in the mind of this highly reckless man . . . who was not ashamed of slips of the pen and who, yawning with fatigue in the face of history, remembered less of his own work than any high school pupil knows of it today?' If economy has not presented itself as an explanation to Dr Carey, neither has amnesia.

His obsession with Dickens's obsession produces some curious results. He draws a sexual inference from the two fights in *Great Expectations*. Pip defeats the pale young gentleman, spied on by Estella who then, in her role as fair maiden, gives the victor the traditional kiss. She is, says Dr Carey, 'sexually stirred' – an excessive description of a peremptory peck. Accordingly, when Jo floors Orlick as easily as Pip dispatched the pale young Pocket, it must follow that Mrs Jo is sexually stirred. Does Dr Carey seriously believe that Mrs Jo's thighs fall apart at the sight of a clenched fist? If so, her apron-bib, with its load of ironmongery, must be taken as evidence of an aptitude for bondage and an interest in constriction suits. A more accurate guess would be that the marriage is unconsummated.

This exuberant pursuit of the improbable points to a larger flaw in *The Violent Effigy*. It is not simply a local distortion like

Dr Carey's disingenuous description of Jo and Orlick as locksmiths in the section on locks. Rather, it demonstrates that a concentration on the unconscious, imaginative Dickens (following a purge of the inferior prose) reduces the novels first to brilliant details, then to incoherent fragments.

Dr Carey has no sense of the novels as wholes. If he had, it might have struck him that there are four fights in *Great Expectations*: Magwitch v. Compeyson, Pip v. Herbert Pocket, Jo v. Orlick, and Orlick v. Pip. In only one case does the gentleman defeat the underdog, because only once is the gentleman a true gentleman – Jo. While one sympathizes with Dr Carey's scorn for 'the critics who labour to unearth their "meanings", as if great works of art were to be cherished, in the last resort, for whatever moral droppings can be coaxed from them', one insists, all the same, not on the moral value of 'meaning', but on its structural value.

Dr Carey is blind to structure in Dickens, for his Dickens is a Pavlovian artist – 'several aspects of the execution scene show that Dickens's imaginative powers have been aroused'. And, when Dickens carefully adds a simile to the *Chuzzlewit* manuscript, likening the flies on a corpse to 'dried currants', Dr Carey sees, not art, but Dickens's 'imagination entrapped by the scene'. This dovetails with his other assumption about the way artists work – they express themselves. 'Dickens' need to express his violent and murderous instincts' and so on. It is an oddly unsophisticated view of the artist from someone as sophisticated as Dr Carey. But it sorts well with his fragmented attitude to the novels, once their structural integrity is waved aside.

Take Captain Cuttle who is, for Dr Carey, just another amputee to itemize. His special role in *Dombey* attracts no comment other than that his salty presence undermines Dickens's windy sea-symbolism. As for his hardness, Silas Wegg, we feel, would have done just as well.

Dombey, however, is a novel about feeling. Its central symbol is the wooden midshipman who stands outside an interior which is overflowing with warm emotion. Apart from the drips (Walter, Florence, the Carker brother and sister), the characters divide into two camps. There are those like the wooden midshipman whose hard exteriors are needed to contain thumping hearts – Captain Cuttle, Susan Nipper, the superficially crusty Mr Toodle, Mrs MacStinger, Mrs Pipchin, Good Mother Brown, Edith Dombey, Mr Dombey, Mr Feeder and even Diogenes the dog. On the other hand, there are those characters who make a show of feeling to hide their heartlessness. Bagstock's behaviour is a parody of friendship, heartiness and hospitality – yet he is Mephistophelean. Mrs Skewton who constantly implores Florence to implant kisses on the wizened cartilage of her ear is, nevertheless, without feeling. Carker – Dr Carey's witness to testify to Dickens's obsession with dentures – smiles continually in a show of friendship. Outsides are the opposite of insides – which is why the metallic oaken Cuttle is irreplaceable.

In ignoring this structure, Dr Carey overlooks a vital imaginative stimulus – the stimulus of strict form which, paradoxically, liberates the artist. If the artist were free to 'express' his obsessions, the result would be silence, not therapeutic utterance.

Finally, for all its extremism, *The Violent Effigy* is a valuable, stimulating book, worth reading especially for its evaluative judgements. But it has to be read with scepticism, otherwise one is totally seduced by its panache.

Dickens and Language

In *The Slavonic Review* for May 1949, George Katkov argued that *David Copperfield* was one of the sources of Dostoevsky's *The Possessed*. In particular, he saw Stavrogin as a Steerforth divested of Dickensian sentimentality. In other words, Dostoevsky used his source critically. My purpose is to argue that Dickens used his linguistic sources in a similarly creative way, and, further, that his method is essentially poetic.

In his notebooks, Valéry has written: 'Poetry is the use of certain singular properties of language, a use that consists *in regenerating the meaning by the sign, and the sign by the meaning.*' The opening of *Little Dorrit* at once clarifies and illustrates this utterance. It is a description of Marseilles sweltering under a hot sun: 'Everything in Marseilles, and about Marseilles, had stared at the fervid sky, and had been stared at in return, until a staring habit had become universal there. Strangers were stared out of countenance by staring white houses, staring white walls, staring white streets, staring tracts of arid road, staring hills from which verdure was burnt away.' Dickens means us to be disconcerted, and we are. It is a surrealistic landscape full of eyes.

And yet, the source of this extraordinary perception is the perfectly ordinary phrase, 'the glare of the heat'. Dickens, by producing a logical synonym for 'glare', has restored the metaphoric force, the original meaning, to a phrase which had lost it through over-use. The sign and its meaning have been regenerated. The result is rather like the Magritte painting of a birdcage which contains, not the expected bird, but an egg. In both cases, the authentic queasy surrealistic frisson is caused by the expected presented in an unexpected way. Though not normally a reliable guide in poetic matters, in this case Cocteau has remarked soundly enough: 'take a commonplace, clean and polish it, light it so that it produces the same effect of youth and freshness and spontaneity as it did originally, and you have done a poet's job.'

This sensitivity to language is often the basis of typically Dickensian fantasy. The description of Chancery in *Bleak House*, for instance, includes this jewel: 'Eighteen of Mr Tangle's learned friends, each armed with a little summary of eighteen hundred sheets, bob up like eighteen hammers in a pianoforte, make eighteen bows, and drop into their eighteen places of obscurity.' It is a wonderfully precise image. There is an exact correlation between the padded heads of the hammers and the bewigged barristers, and yet the starting point of the fantasy is in a piece of implicit wordplay: '"Several members of *the bar are still to be heard* [my italics] I believe?" says the Chancellor, with a slight smile.' Dickens simply acknowledges the pun and literalizes it.

It is clear that Dickens was a man constantly on the look out for whatever language itself might offer. *Dombey and Son* begins: 'Dombey sat in the corner of the darkened room in the great armchair by the bedside, and Son lay tucked up warm in a little basket bedstead, carefully disposed on a low settee immediately in front of the fire and close to it, as if his constitution were analogous to that of a muffin, and it was essential to toast him brown while he was very new.' The paragraph is an exquisitely periphrastic reworking of the commonplace phrase to 'keep someone warm as toast'.

Examples in which language itself prompts the imagination are not difficult to multiply in Dickens. We might start with Montague Tigg in *Martin Chuzzlewit*. The 'shabby-genteel' Tigg has a wardrobe which demonstrates the extremities of poverty. Tigg's dress, Dickens informs us with facetious irony, 'can hardly be said to have been in any extremities, as his fingers were a long way out of his gloves, and the soles of his feet were at an inconvenient distance from the upper leather of his boots.' And so forth. The oxymoron is rather forced. Dickens is more successful with Miss Tox in *Dombey and Son* for whom Tigg is a crude prototype. She is a genteel lady in reduced circumstances, someone of 'limited independence'. But before Dickens discloses her financial circumstances, we are *shown* Miss Tox's inability to make ends meet: 'it was observed by the curious, of all her collars, frills, tuckers, wristbands, and other gossamer articles – indeed of anything she wore which had two ends to it intended to unite – that the two ends were never on good terms, and wouldn't quite meet without a struggle.' The indirectness of Dickens's method seems itself an example of tactful decorum totally suited to Miss Tox.

Again, instead of telling us that Mr Vholes in *Bleak House* has skin-tight clothes – which would be banal – Dickens tells us that he takes off his gloves as if he were skinning himself. And then his fantasy rises some distance above its linguistic moorings as Dickens adds that Mr Vholes takes off his hat as if he were scalping himself. Speaking of tightness, one thinks, too, of *Pickwick Papers* and the reception for Count Smorltork, at which Mr Jingle elaborates (in his own characteristically elliptical telegraphic idiolect) an extended authorial fantasy arising out of the social squeeze: ' "Ah," cried the voice, as its owner pushed his way among the last five and twenty Turks, officers, cavaliers, and Charles the Seconds, that remained between him and the table, "regular mangle – Baker's patent – not a crease in my coat, after all this squeezing – might have 'got up my linen' as I came along – ha! ha! not a bad idea, that – queer thing to have it mangled when it's upon one, though – trying process – very." ' Sometimes, as here, the verbal starting point is not difficult to locate: to feel like a fish out of water becomes, in *Pickwick Papers*, subject to a comic displacement, 'as much out of his element as a dolphin in a sentry box'; rather than the standard 'withering look', Dickens opts for this variant, 'Mr Pott darted a look of contempt, which might have withered an anchor'. Again from *Pickwick* (the early work, as one might expect, displays its new invention more frequently than the later): 'the old lady, quite unconscious that she had spoken above a whisper, drew herself up and looked carving knives at the hard-headed delinquent.' Just as 'carving knives' replace the more usual *daggers*, so Hardy in *The Wood-landers* tiptoes rather archly around the idea of a sharp east wind: 'a north wind was blowing – that not unacceptable compromise between the atmospheric cutlery of the eastern blast and the spongy gales of the west quarter.'

These examples all flirt openly with the cliché and are clearly related, therefore, to the kind of paradoxical wit practised by Kingsley Amis when he remembers his father's 'catholic distaste', or the somewhat mechanically inverted maxims of Oscar Wilde, like his 'work is the curse of the drinking classes'. On the whole, however, Dickens's invention and gusto prevent one returning the verdict of 'automatic' or 'habitual' – as one is often tempted to with Wilde. Time may be running out for Mrs Dombey in the usual deathbed way, but Dickens produces a fertile and grotesque variant – a race between the doctors' watches. 'The race in the ensuing pause was fierce and furious. The watches seemed to jostle and to trip each other up.' To be fair to Wilde, he, too, can transform his linguistic sources as radically as Dickens on occasion. In *The Importance of Being Earnest*, Jack Worthing's name and peculiar ancestry are Wilde's ironic comment on the importance Victorians attached to *having a handle to your name*. Jack was found in a cloakroom at Victoria Station on the Brighton line. His only handle is the two literal handles of the handbag in which he was found.

In the more direct variants, Dickens differs from Wilde because, even there, his economy of means is less stringent, less elegant, if you like, but also less glib. Wilde inverts: 'if one tells the truth one is sure sooner or later to be found out.' Dickens perverts: Paul Dombey doesn't go down with measles like other children; 'this dangerous ground in his steeple chase towards manhood passed, but he still found it very rough riding, and was grievously beset by all the obstacles in his course. Every tooth was a break-neck fence, and every pimple in the measles a stone wall to him. He was down in every fit of the hooping cough . . .' This kind of elaboration is increasingly favoured by Dickens, though he never forsakes the simpler instance either, as in Mrs Pipchin's unflinching gaze: Dickens transfers her ability to look hard at things to the eye itself. Her 'hard grey eye' looks 'as if it might have been hammered at on an anvil without sustaining any damage'.

Now, however, I would like to consider less obvious examples in which Dickens's technique is to expand as well as literalize.

Take Mrs Sparsit's staircase: 'Now, Mrs Sparsit was not a poetical woman; but she took an idea *in the nature of an allegorical fancy* [my italics], into her head. Much watching of Louisa, and much consequent observation of her impenetrable demeanour, which keenly whetted and sharpened Mrs Sparsit's edge, must have given her a lift, as it were, in the way of inspiration. She erected in her mind a mighty Staircase, with a dark pit of shame and ruin at the bottom; and down those stairs, from day to day and hour to hour, she saw Louisa coming. It became the business of Mrs Sparsit's life, to look up at her staircase, and watch Louisa coming down. Sometimes slowly, sometimes quickly, sometimes several steps at one bout, sometimes stopping, never turning back. If she had once turned back, it might have been the death of Mrs Sparsit in spleen and grief.'

It is, arguably, the most eery and sustained fantasy in Dickens. But what does it allegorize? Clearly, it is an emblem of ruin, part of whose effectiveness lies in its apparent solidity and its associations of grandeur. But one can say more. The fantasy originates in an acute verbal awareness, in a linguistic scrutiny of an apparently lifeless cliché – in this case, 'coming down in the world'. Dickens has made an extraordinarily imaginative leap from his initial stimulus, the everyday phrase. Mrs Sparsit herself has come down in the world; she has been compelled to accept what she calls her 'annual compliment', her wages as a servant, from Mr Bounderby. It is, therefore, appropriate that she should be at the bottom of the staircase waiting for Louisa to reach her level. And, here too, Dickens is examining another commonplace expression – this time one applied exclusively to servants – 'below stairs', which is where Mrs Sparsit is.

Admirers of *Ulysses* will recall with pleasure this passage from the 'Sirens' section: 'under the sandwichbell lay on a bier of bread one last, one lonely, last sardine of summer.' It's exquisite, but it isn't original. The source is chapter 14 of *Pickwick Papers*: there, one of the items in the 'commercial room' is 'the mortal remains of a trout in a glass coffin'. The two phrases are sufficiently dissimilar in detail for one to write the coincidence off as the harmony of genius, rather than unconscious plagiarism, were it not for another, odder coincidence. In the Dickens, a serving maid responds to the flirting of a customer: ' "Let me alone, imperence" '. How strange that Joyce should also add a mispronunciation of 'impertinence' to his description of the fish. The boots of the Ormond Hotel, when threatened by the barmaid, Miss Douce, with a complaint to the management about his impertinent insolence, answers: 'imperthnthn thnthnthn.' But if Dickens is Joyce's source, what is Dickens's source? The language, of course, but the precise trigger for this fantasy isn't clear until *Dombey and Son*, when Dickens repeats the figure rather more elaborately, though still without revealing his complete thought process. After the christening of Paul Dombey, the principals return for a 'cold collation', 'set forth in a cold pomp of glass and silver, and looking more like a dead dinner lying in state than a social refreshment'. Behind this effective but enigmatic fantasy is an instance of wordplay – a phrase common to serving maid and undertaker alike. Like tables, corpses are *laid out*.

Nowadays, of course, we speak of laying the table and of laying out bodies, but as recently as 1922, Eliot's typist in *The Waste Land* was laying out her food in tins. The *OED* cites Conan Doyle: 'the deal table was laid out . . .' And also H. T. Ellis: 'refreshments were laid out in an adjoining room.' A dead dinner 'lying in state' suppresses its key phrase, *laid out*, yet concealment is not remoteness. One might compare a similar example in Auden's poetry, a description of telephone wires seen from a train: 'the wires I watched from train, / Slackening of wire and posts' sharp reprimand.' The image, from the poem '1929', tells without telling us why. We assent before we understand why 'reprimand' feels so appropriate. Behind the lines is the common schoolboy notion of 'the slacker'.

Periphrasis is another technique Dickens brings to bear on the cliché or the commonplace. Mrs Gradgrind is, we learn, 'a little, thin, white, pink-eyed bundle of shawls, of surpassing feebleness, mental and bodily.' To this hostile witness, Dickens adds the phrase that she is 'like an indifferently executed transparency of a small female figure, without enough light behind it.' She is, in other words, a bit dim, not very bright.

To continue with *Hard Times* a moment, a sustained and central fantasy in the novel also avoids mentioning the key word. I am thinking of the symbolic opposition of the circus to the industrial complex of Coketown, which is expressed largely through Dickens's transformation of industry into 'the melancholy mad elephants' of steam pistons and the 'monstrous serpents of smoke'. Why 'melancholy'? Why 'mad'? On the one hand, all the circus animals proper are shown to be immensely gifted and virtually human: one thinks of Merrylegs asking for directions to Sleary after his master has died. On the other hand, debased human beings, like Tom Gradgrind, dwindle into animals: when Tom is blacked up and disguised, Dickens shows us 'his hands, with the black partly worn away inside, looking like the hands of a monkey'. This paradoxical nub – that the animals are human, while the human beings are animal – is perfectly illustrated by Bitzer's definition of a horse. 'Quadruped. Graminivorous. Forty teeth, namely twenty-four grinders, four eye-teeth, and twelve incisive. Sheds coat in the spring; in marshy countries, sheds hoofs, too. Hoofs hard, but requiring to be shod with iron. Age known by marks in mouth.' The definition scarcely encompasses what a horse is actually capable of, as Bitzer is to discover when, with calculated irony, he is thwarted by 'a horthe that'll do anything but thpeak' – including 'danthing, till the morning'. The core of energy behind this sophisticated schema is one phrase – 'animal spirits' – a superabundance which can either find an outlet in *horseplay* and the high spirits of the circus, or become depressed, low and 'melancholy' like the aforementioned elephant pistons.

The examples of this almost abnormal sensitivity to language are manifold in Dickens. From *Great Expectations* alone one might choose, say, the lawyer Jaggers and his disconcerting habit of constantly washing his hands. Jaggers delegates responsibility whenever possible and dislikes hearing of illegal court procedures which he has himself, as a matter of fact, set in train. He is, in other words, 'washing his hands of the whole affair', but Dickens shows us this rather than tells us. Again, he does not say that Miss Havisham is 'living in the past', he literalizes the phrase. Likewise, he does not say that Wemmick's house at Walworth has as its rationale the phrase 'An Englishman's home is his castle', he simply makes the house a mock-up of a castle, with cannon, flagstaff, crenellations, and drawbridge.

In *Bleak House*, there is Phil Squod whose experience of life's vicissitudes has literally made him 'go to the wall', as the expression is: 'He has a curious way of limping round the gallery with his shoulder against the wall, and tacking off at objects he wants to lay hold of, instead of going straight to them, which has left a smear all round the four walls, conventionally called Phil's mark.' In *David Copperfield*, there is Mr Mell's flute playing: 'When he had put up his things for the night, he took out his flute, and blew at it, until I almost thought he would gradually blow his whole being into the large hole at the top, and ooze away at the keys.' Again, an ordinary phrase has been expanded and literalized: this time it is 'to put the whole of oneself into something'. And, when the young Wilkins Micawber sings, 'he had a certain expression of face, as if his voice were behind his eye-brows; where it presently appeared to be'. Once more, by literalizing the commonplace (in this case the observation that his voice was extremely high), Dickens brings off an unusual effect.

But perhaps the two finest examples occur in Copperfield's first dissipation. The drunken David attempts to smoke with disastrous results: 'Somebody was leaning out of my bedroom window, refreshing his forehead against the cool stone of the parapet, and feeling the air upon his face. It was myself. I was addressing myself as "Copperfield", and saying, "Why did you try to smoke? You might have known you couldn't do it." Now, somebody was unsteadily contemplating his features in the looking-glass. That was I too.' Behind this brilliant writing is the everyday idiom, 'I wasn't feeling quite myself today', but overhauled and reconditioned. In the same chapter, Dickens rewrites and expands the banal phrase, 'the room swam before my eyes'. Again, he offers a periphrasis of genius: 'The whole building looked to me as if it were learning to swim; it conducted itself in such an unaccountable manner, when I tried to steady it.'

However, if the examples of this technique are manifold in Dickens's novels, the sceptic wants to know, and rightly, whether those many folds are pleats or crumples, organized or accidental. Then, he wants to know if Dickens is unique in this respect. The answer to the first question is that Dickens was certainly conscious that he scrutinized and reworked common speech. In chapter 41 of *David Copperfield*, he writes: 'I had (and have all my life) observed that conventional phrases are a sort of fire-works, easily let off, and liable to take a great variety of shapes and colours not at all suggested by their original form.' One could not have clearer proof of a conscious artistic intention.

The answer to the second question is that Dickens is not unique, though criticism has ignored this technique in others as much as it has ignored it in Dickens. The concern to renew language is common to almost every good poet. One thinks of 'East Coker':

> And so each venture
> Is a new beginning, a raid on the inarticulate
> With shabby equipment always deteriorating . . .

Or one thinks of Eliot saying in 'The Social Function of Poetry': 'But most people do not realize . . . that unless they go on producing great authors, and especially great poets, their language will deteriorate, their culture will deteriorate and perhaps be absorbed into a stronger one.' Dickens shares with Eliot this view of the central importance of language to a culture. In *Copperfield* he writes, apropos of Mr Micawber: 'We talk about the tyranny of words, but we like to tyrannize over them too; we are fond of having a large superfluous establishment of words to wait upon us on great occasions . . . As we are not particular about the meaning of our liveries on state occasions, if they be but fine and numerous enough, so the meaning or necessity of our words is a secondary consideration.' Dickens goes on to prophesy national disaster unless we use words more carefully, more consciously.

Let me end by citing examples of the technique from Shakespeare and Lewis Carroll. 'My heart is turned to stone,' exclaims Othello, and then Shakespeare redeems the cliché by literalizing it: 'I strike it and it hurts my hand.' *Alice's Adventures in Wonderland* and *Through the Looking-Glass* are, with the exception of *Finnegans Wake*, the most sustained inquisitions of conventional idioms in English literature. Three examples chosen from many: firstly, when he appears as a witness, the Hatter, under cross-examination by the Queen of Hearts, is so thrown by her crossness that 'he trembled so, that he shook off both his shoes' – which is decidedly more graphic than merely *shaking in his shoes*. When the guinea-pig is suppressed for noisiness in court, 'they had a large canvas bag, which tied up at the mouth with strings: into this they slipped the guinea-pig, head first, and then sat upon it.' Because it is a *guinea*-pig, it is contained in a purse. Lastly, there is the Hatter's watch, which is 'two days wrong': ' "I told you butter wouldn't suit the works!" he added, looking angrily at the March Hare.' Butter – with, or without, crumbs – is, of course, a bad idea. And yet it is only a comically short distance away from a very good idea – that of *oiling* the works.

The most telling, the most macabre example, however, of a resuscitated figure of speech was at Bikini in 1946 when an atom bomb exploded with another bombshell painted on its side – Rita Hayworth.

Invented Languages

'Experimental prose is death', Kingsley Amis once hedged. Actually, it is life. Take two words from Lewis Carroll and Hopkins – *gimble* and *twindle*. Both are a concentrate of language: dilute the Carroll word, and the slithy toves are gambolling nimbly. *Twindle* is a combination of twirl and dwindle. This lively inventiveness is, as it were, ordinary language plus cosmetics: the expressive features are heightened. In any case, ordinary English has been improving and inventing itself from the beginning. Like skin, it renews itself with unobtrusive efficiency. In this long-term experimentation, grammar has changed, letters like thorn, eth, yogh and wynn have gone missing; words have been borrowed from other countries and meanings have shifted. *Nice*, for example, now means *pleasant*; formerly, it meant *discriminating*. In *Northanger Abbey*, Henry Tilney scolds Catherine Morland for using it in the modern sense. In vain. Language is for the people and by the people: experimental writers are merely a self-conscious reflection, a more talented version of linguistic process.

Consider Nadsat in *A Clockwork Orange*, Anthony Burgess's forceful mélange of Russian words, cockney rhyming slang, and a rather formal English. Its vitality is unquestionable: *smeck*, the Russian for laugh, conveys exactly the right hard sound of thuggish laughter; *sponge-meat* is better than spam. More importantly, the hero avoids the stale by creative circumlocution: like Dickens's beadle, who substitutes 'I'm on broken bottles' for 'I'm on tenterhooks', Alex prefers 'brought out the red like an old

friend' to the neutral 'she bled'. The macabre politesse under-
scores the violence of the act. Nadsat, however, is not simply
literary: minority groups have always invented private languages.
Dialect, for instance, is a function of class as well as geography.

The Goncourt Journal describes Javanese – the argot used by
Paris prostitutes and borrowed from schoolgirls. Basically, it
involved the repetition, after every syllable, of two syllables
taking the same vowel, so that 'How are you?' became 'How dow
gow are dar gar you doo goo?' Hearing it, the Goncourts report,
created 'the effect of a stiff brush scouring one's ears'. In Joyce's
A Portrait of the Artist, there are two invented languages, apart
from the brilliant baby-talk which opens the book. A youngster
volunteers the information that his parents have 'goneboro
toboro lookboro atboro aboro houseboro', and Cranly speaks
fluent dog-Latin: 'Ego credo ut vita pauperum est simpliciter
atrox, simpliciter sanguinarius atrox, in Liverpoolio.' In other
words, the lives of the Liverpool paupers are simply bloody
atrocious. Again, in *Oliver Twist*, the thieves employ a vivid slang
– *barkers* for pistols, *persuaders* for skeleton keys, crow-bars and
the arcana of house-breaking. Once more, one's ears are scoured,
for the language is not the Artful's 'high cockalorum' but
thoughtful and witty euphemism.

Experimentalism is, therefore, not restricted to the avant-garde
– you can find it in Mayhew. It is not even confined to this century
or to glum intellectuals. Jane Austen and Dickens provide
passages of stream of consciousness long before Joyce and
Virginia Woolf. Miss Bates, in *Emma*, is an undiscriminating
torrent, jumbling together letters received, her mother's spectacle
rivets, a leg of pork, the size of a salting-pan, her bonnet and
spencer, Jane standing in the passage and Hello, Mr Knightley.
The stream of consciousness is not a literary technique, patented
in 1922, it is a fact of life. Dickens's Flora Finching and Joyce's
Molly Bloom are not uniquely unable to punctuate speech and
thought: 'Oh good gracious me I hope you never kept yourself a
bachelor so long on my account but of course you never did why
should you, pray don't answer, I don't know where I'm running
to,' burbles Flora, washed away by a rising tide of words. Who

doesn't recognize the type from their own circle of acquaintance – friendly, torrential, time-consuming?

Seen correctly, experimentalism is *anything* that alters standard English – it is only prejudice that excludes comedy. Its inclusion brings some surprises. Which painter guyed his own landscapes by writing on the canvas, against the appropriate features, *ski, rox, korn*? Marcel Duchamp? Claes Oldenberg? In fact, it was Edward Lear. Beerbohm emerges as a radical experimentalist, too. This is his version of the *Dictionary of National Biography* in 1997: 'Fr egzarmpl, a riter ov th time, naimed Max Beerbohm, hoo woz stil alive in the twentieth senchri, rote a stauri . . . It iz a summwot labud sattire' and so on. There is no reason why experimentalism should not be funny. More often than not, it is. What, for example, could be more amusing or more experimental than the elimination of nouns from a character's speech, forcing him into panicky circum-locutions like 'er, prickly stuff' for 'holly'? The experimenter in question is Kingsley Amis, whose *Ending Up* includes a character who suffers from selective aphasia.

In fact, every *good* writer invents the language for himself. We call it *style*. No one could mistake Milton's elaborate periods or his Latinate diction. *Finnegans Wake* is an extreme example of invented language, but in *Ulysses* the placement of the adverb in perfectly orthodox sentences will tell one Joyce is the author. Conrad was acutely aware of his own stylistic signature. Badly off and short of copy, he wrote to Ford Madox Ford: 'if you have something written that you do *not* care for *in the least* send it on. I'll put in a few of my jargon phrases and send it off.' Every reader is familiar with Conrad's brand of heavily adjectival desperanto ('an implacable force brooding over an inscrutable intention') – that stilted pessimism parodied by Beerbohm. Parody is, of course, the vindication of the argument, since it depends absolu-tely on individualistic authorial adaptation of the language.

Style may seem a long way from invented language but, in reality, it is not possible to invent a language *ex nihilo*. Modifi-cation, more or less radical, is all that is feasible. William Barnes, the Dorset poet and philologist who influenced Hopkins, reconstructed English by eliminating Latin loan-words and inventing pure Anglo-Saxon equivalents. Panacea became *allheal*, photograph a *sunprint*, alienate became *unfriend*, depilatory became *hairbane*, diaphanous became *thorough-shining*, forceps became *nipperlings*. The scope of Barnes's reforming zeal and the wonderful freshness of a word like *loosensome* for laxative, however, should not conceal his reliance on common raw materials. On the other hand, *Orghast*, Ted Hughes's invented language, concentrated on the purely auditory and drew sounds from the diaphragm inspirationally – without reference to other languages. These sounds for universal objects (the sun, light, dark, etc.) were supposed, in theory, to transcend national barriers. Finally, Hughes and his producer, Peter Brook, realized that they were creating something more analogous to music than to language. 'If it doesn't work musically', said Hughes, 'it doesn't work at all.' Semantic considerations were unimportant: 'The deeper into language one goes, the less visual/conceptual its imagery, and the more audial/visceral/muscular its system of tensions. This accords with the biological fact that the visual nerves connect with the modern human brain, while the audial nerves connect with the cerebellum, the primal animal brain and nervous system direct.'

This may read like a perversely framed prescription to get back to the grunt, but actually it produced a kind of choral music – not experimental prose. Orwell would have been appalled by its premises. Newspeak, the linguistic nightmare of *Nineteen Eighty-Four*, aims ultimately to 'make articulate speech issue from the larynx without involving the higher brain centres at all' – precisely Hughes's recipe. Newspeak *is* experimental prose, though, and a test case. Orwell hates it, but if my argument holds good, it should be vital and expressive.

Orwell's invented language is lagged with extraneous prejudices. But strip off the bias, the reiterated statements that Newspeak was designed to prevent self-expression, and one is left with a rather striking language. 'Oldthinkers unbellyfeel Ingsoc' is translated by Orwell as 'Those whose ideas were formed before the Revolution cannot have a full emotional understanding of the principles of English socialism.' What a ponderous and null paraphrase it is, beside the graphic economy of the original. 'Unbellyfeel' is obviously better than the automatic formula, 'cannot have a full emotional understanding of', which has all the verve of a lexicographer's definition. *Prolefeed* is another excellent coinage – sprinting ahead of Orwell's windy and winded equivalent, 'the rubbishy entertainment and spurious news which the Party handed out to the masses'. *Duckspeak* for mindless oratory is good, too, as are the grim euphemisms, like *joycamp* for penal settlement.

Inside Orwell, there is a magisterial grammarian, appealing to our linguistic Toryism. Newspeak is intended to affront our sense of tidiness – Orwell expects our mental hygiene to find verbal promiscuity distasteful but 'an almost complete interchangeability between different parts of speech' is a common feature of Shakespeare, Milton and Newspeak. 'The dark backward and abysm of time', says naughty Prospero, misusing an adverb as a noun. And even when Newspeak is shorn of irregular inflexions (*stealed*, *thinked*), Orwell is still appealing to our grammatical conservatism. Regularity may be tidy, we are supposed to think, but it's still wrong.

Really, ungrammatical usage can be highly effective, particularly if its intrinsic comic potential is linked to serious subject matter – as it is in John Berryman's poetry. His *Dream Songs* are about suicide, guilt, lust and remorse, yet their diction is slangy, clownish and ungrammatical. Form and content (the tired pantomime horse) really do come together to make the perfect tragifarce. We laugh till we cry – *laughtears*, Joyce calls it. Henry, the narrator, meditates on his irrational guilt:

> But never did Henry, as he thought he did,
> end anyone and hacks her body up
> and hide the pieces, where they may be found.

The use of the preterite locates the situation in the past, as something completed. But all the time, that *hacks* insists on its continuous immediacy. The guilt will not go away.

84

Another 'offensive' feature of Newspeak is the formation of negatives by the prefix un, as in *ungood*. Curiously, the poetry and prose of e. e. cummings (a man more anti-Soviet and anti-totalitarian than Orwell) exploits this idea on the side of democracy. The true individual, he writes, is not 'an undream of anaesthetized impersons, or a cosmic comfortstation, or a transcendentally sterilized lookiesoundiefeelietastiesmellie'. Cummings is a mixed writer: his achievement is marred by sentimentality and didacticism. But these failings are unconnected with his experimental language. A line like 'love is thicker than forget' is feeble. Deprive it, however, of its linguistic quirkiness and its worsens appreciably. The breakdown (admittedly unfair) reveals two phrases: blood is thicker than water; lovers never forget. Each is not so much a cliché as a *thought-crime*. Cummings's satires are less prone to sudden, diabetic collapse. Take this aggressively modernist extract from a drunk's belligerence towards the Chinese:

> dem
> gud
> am
> liddl yelluh bas
> tuds weer goin
> duhSIVILEYEzum

Enter Beerbohm and Lear and the epistolary Pound – to share the bow.

Joyce, the master of linguistic invention, illustrates the prime function of the experimentalist – to revitalize the outworn. In *Finnegans Wake*, one reads endless variations on the banal and ordinary. Seduced becomes *sinduced*, Finnegan lives in 'the broadest immarginable way', take up your partner becomes (in a sexual context) 'tuck up your part inher', truce in the trenches at Christmas becomes a 'muddy kissmans', salesmen are *palesmen*, denies becomes *denays*, photograph becomes *fadograph*, tears are *bouncing brimmers*, vocal chords are *talktapes*, envelopes are *gummibacks*, the stars are *dimtwinklers*, Ireland becomes

85

aleland, a single man's apartments become 'a bachelure's flat', at the funeral 'all chimed in with the eatmost boviality', far-off times are 'pharaoph times', people cannot 'say aye to aye', a kaleidoscope is a *collideorscope*, orphans cast on the parish are 'waif-strays on the perish', and the streets are 'paved with cold'. There is nothing dead about this experimental prose. Under Joyce's obstetric hand, language is safely delivered into the future – a future which includes, perhaps, a vernacular invigorated by the weird poetry of the City, or of aeronautics and space travel. I am thinking of, for instance, Caryl Churchill's *Serious Money*, in which the poetry was generated not by the crude use of rhyme but rather by the play's willingness to exploit a flourishing argot: 'if the market moves in a big way we'll get cremated.' From the City, too, comes the recent phrase, 'a dead cat bounce' – which describes a slight, entirely illusory value recovery in shares that have fallen catastrophically. When, in January of 1989, two American planes shot down a Libyan MiG-23, the *Independent* enterprisingly published a transcript of the cockpit conversation released by the US state department. Not for anything a layman might learn, but for the hypnotically evocative and impenetrable language: 'OK. Bogeys appear to be coming jinking to the right now, heading north. Speed 430. Angels 5,000, now in descent.' *Bogeys* are MiGs; *Angels* is altitude. Language has to be invented again for this experience to carry its uniqueness unblunted: 'Pilot: I've got a second one on the nose right now. Pilot: OK. I'm high cover on you. Pilot: Lock him up. Lock him up.'

Babylonish Dialects

1. How do we think? In words? Exclusively in words? Consider Nabokov on the stream of consciousness in *Ulysses*: 'it exaggerates the verbal side of thought. Man thinks not always in words but also in images, whereas the stream of consciousness presupposes a flow of words that can be notated: it is difficult, however, to believe that Bloom was continually talking to himself.'

2. How does one refute Nabokov? By saying this is true, but only because we are not always thinking while we are conscious? By offering up Wordsworth on his couch, in *vacant* or in *pensive* mood?

3. What about the other mental phenomena which inhabit Wordsworth's vacancy – the dreams, the emotions, those daffodils? They cannot be verbalized, though they undoubtedly exist.

4. I see the current Oxford Professor of Poetry in the street and E. P. Thompson on the train. Both are talking to themselves. They are thinking aloud. If I was closer, I could bathe in their stream of consciousness, hear their words. For a second, I see myself with my trousers rolled up: is this a thought or a picture?

5. 'How can I tell what I think till I see what I say?' asks E. M. Forster. This implies that all thinking is verbal, that without language we cannot think. This is what happens to Ralph in *Lord of the Flies*: 'he lost himself in a maze of thoughts that were rendered vague by his lack of words to express them.'

6. On the other hand, Forster is also saying that we cannot articulate thought without using language. True. But that still leaves inarticulate thought, Ralph's 'maze of thoughts' in which he is lost.

7. Wittgenstein is masturbating. His mind is continuously occupied for five minutes, shall we say, by a series of obscene pictures – not by the words 'cock' and 'bum'. This is a thought process even though it is unrelated to language.

8. Music is a language to which we listen in order to experience a distinct penumbra we could not describe. Much poetry initially works in this way, too. 'Genuine poetry', said Eliot, 'can communicate before it is understood.' A philosopher might retort: for people who cannot think, this passes for thought.

9. But most of the time, we are at the mercy of language. If we introspect, we see in our minds the words, 'if we introspect'. And surely we can be misled by language, as Wittgenstein explains metaphorically: 'philosophers often behave like little children who scribble marks on a piece of paper at random and then ask the grown-up "What's that?" It happened like this: the grown-up had drawn pictures for the child several times and said: "this is a man", "this is a house", etc. And then the child makes some marks too and asks: what's *this* then?'

10. Often language tells us what to think. Poetry, though, can use language to help us escape this tyranny of language. T. S. Eliot said of Edward Lear's poetry that it was not non-sense but a parody of sense. As readers, we are like Wittgenstein's child, but from deliberate choice. We hear the language and, while we know there is no sense to it, we experience the *sensation* of thought. The mind is Pavlovian: it salivates at the sound of a word, as if there was here real food for thought. The nebulous effect corresponds to something within our minds before we have said what we think. Lewis Carroll understood this perfectly, as we know from *Through the Looking-Glass*. Confronted with 'Jabberwocky', Alice accurately describes her mental responses: 'Somehow it

seems to fill my head with ideas – only I don't know exactly what they are!'

11. Poetry written in dialect belongs to the world of non-sense and the world of sense – depending on how familiar you are with the dialect.

12. All great poetry is written in dialect. This is Johnson on Milton: 'through all his greater works there prevails an uniform peculiarity of *Diction*, a mode and cast of expression which bears little resemblance to that of any other former writer, and which is so far removed from common use, that an unlearned reader, when he first opens his book, finds himself surprised by a new language . . . Of him, at last, may be said what Jonson says of Spenser, that *he wrote no language*, but has formed what Butler calls a *Babylonish dialect* . . .'

13. It follows that if all great poetry is written in dialect, then it is all poised between sense and non-sense – which seems unlikely until you consider, say, Southey's reaction to the *Ancient Mariner* ('many of the stanzas are laboriously beautiful, but in connection they are absurd or unintelligible') and Wordsworth's insistence that new art must create the taste by which it is to be enjoyed.

14. Most bad poetry is written in the dialect of the previous age. Some bad poetry is written in the dialect of no particular age – only the dialect of poetry. But if language dates, no language dates quicker than the self-consciously timeless, which is already dated.

15. Wordsworth's dialect, Hopkins's complicated dialect, Frost's simple American dialect – we have mastered them all. The task is to invent a new dialect or even dialects.

16. Why? There are two reasons. We become so familiar with a dialect that we no longer hear its individuality. Or the dialect becomes in time more and more difficult: presumably some such thought is behind A. L. Rowse's scheme to render *Romeo and Juliet* into modern English.

17. And there is a further reason. The advantage of dialect is this: if nonsense poetry can create in us the sensation of thought, then dialect can create in us different thoughts. Alter the language and you alter thought. Our ways of thinking are renewed.

18. Why should we want to do this? Let me quote Wittgenstein again: 'the idea is worn out by now and no longer usable . . . Like silver paper, which can never be quite smoothed out again once it has been crumpled. Nearly all my ideas are a bit crumpled.' Good: let us have some uncrumpled ideas, if not some new ones; let us change the language.

19. The bonus of dialect is easy to see. 'Wee, sleekit, cow'rin, tim'rous beastie' alters our thought, our perception, gives us a clearer idea of the mouse than standard English. Everything vivid here would cloud at the mere approach of A. L. Rowse.

20. Hopkins wrote to Robert Bridges that he had been reading *Two Years Before the Mast*: 'all true, but bristling with technicality – seamanship – which I most carefully go over and even enjoy but cannot understand . . .' This is true of any dialect; we enjoy without at first fully understanding. But what is the nature of the enjoyment? Compare the opening of *The Tempest*: 'Down with the topmast! yare! lower, lower! Bring her to try with maincourse.'

Quite. Shakespeare is bluffing. He is adding spices to his recipe. Neither he nor we may know exactly what they are, but we can taste the tiny, authentic explosions. They give us the sensation of thought by their confident, but ultimately opaque, particularity.

21. In *Riddley Walker*, Russell Hoban uses language like Molesworth in *Down with Skool*: 'She said, "Its some kynd of thing it aint us but yet its in us. Its looking out thru our eye hoals. May be you dont take no noatis of it only some times. Say you get woak up suddn in the middl of the nite. 1 minim youre a sleap and the nex youre on your feet with a spear in your han. Wel it wernt you put that spear in your han it wer that other thing whats looking out thru your eye hoals. It aint you nor it dont even know your name. Its in us lorn and loan and sheltering how it can."'

One is immediately struck by the way Hoban completely escapes the comedy implicit in the Molesworth idiom, then by how little has been changed – the odd spelling, haphazard punctuation. Yet the effect is enormous: the change in the language has actually changed the thought. The woman is discussing the soul, but much more vividly than if Hoban had confined her to that word. The concept is renewed.

22. In the same way, MacDiarmid's poem, 'The Bonnie Broukit Bairn', renews our acquaintance with the stars after centuries of stale classical mythologizing:

> Mars is braw in crammasy,
> Venus in a green silk goun . . .

They are no longer simply stars, but aristocrats in a laird's hall. The metaphor on its own would take us this far, but the dialect brings with it an implicit sense of class awareness: we are underlings of no importance and what is true of the earth is also true of man's place in the universe. Both are fixed systems.

23. In *The Inheritors*, Golding invents a dialect for his Neanderthal people. Again, the language employed alters our perception of even the simplest things, like a canoe: 'they were digging the water and the log was sidling across the river.' Or an echo: 'their words had flown away from them like a flock of birds that circled and multiplied mysteriously.' In both these examples, Golding refuses the easy noun ('he writes no language') and with it the easy thought. The initial obscurity, the moment of non-sense, puts us in touch with our non-verbal thoughts, or their simulacrum. And even after the necessary translation is effected, the strangeness lingers.

24. Nothing is more difficult than being open-minded. The mind is a vast country whose borders are closed. We know less than we think about its economy. It is teeming with peasants, productive souls, who are hard-working but mute. There are elections, about which we hear. Language is the prime minister

who tells us the results, like a spokesman reading quite confidently from a brief he was handed in the dark, or simply found in his inside pocket.

Hopkins's Poetry

'Tuncks is a good name. Gerard Manley Tuncks. Poor Tuncks,' wrote Hopkins in one of the earliest Journal entries. With time, this whimsical sally has come to seem visionary as well as merely curious. It is as if Hopkins foresaw the patronizing critical judgements to come and decided to transfer them, well in advance, to a more appropriate recipient – Tuncks, poor Tuncks. In 'Fosterage', for example, Seamus Heaney retails some literary advice he was given in 1962, presumably by Michael McLaverty, the poem's dedicatee:

> But to hell with overstating it:
> 'Don't have the veins bulging in your biro.'
> And then, 'Poor Hopkins!' . . .

Others have seen Hopkins in a less varicose predicament. Claude Colleer Abbott, editor of the correspondence with Bridges, offers an overweight glutton to balance his praise: 'he was too greedy as poet and prosodist, and too anxious to "load every rift . . . with ore".' Even 'Dearest Bridges', as Hopkins habitually addressed him, found the poetry violent and artificial if we are to judge from Hopkins's extant replies. In his introduction, though, Bridges was more temperate, mildly disparaging the metaphors as often affected. Poor Hopkins.

Or should it be poor Tuncks? For, against those critics like Austin Warren who conclude their praise with head-shaking over the way copious detail destroys poetic organicism, there are many admirers – admirers who see the biro bulging with muscle, the affectation as originality, the overloading as prodigal richness. Yet even Hopkins had his doubts: of 'The Sea and the Skylark' he writes to Bridges that 'the saying of it smells, I fear, of the lamp, of salad oil'. And again, 'I find myself that when I am tired things of mine sound strange, forced, and without idiom, which had pleased me well enough in the fresh heat of composition.' Of the slightly bungled 'Loss of the *Eurydice*', he volunteers: 'Everybody cannot be expected to like my pieces. Moreover, the oddness may make them repulsive at first . . . Indeed when, on somebody returning me the *Eurydice*, I opened and read some lines, reading, as one commonly reads, whether prose or verse, with the eyes, so to say, only, it struck me aghast with a kind of raw nakedness and unmitigated violence I was unprepared for.'

One notes, however, that these concessions to Bridges's conventional taste concede little that is absolute: they simply admit that Hopkins, too, is capable sometimes of reading with fatigued attention or without using his ear. As a rule, he defended his output resourcefully and more stoutly, perhaps, than many of his admirers who might, for instance, have grave doubts about the moribund final line of 'Duns Scotus's Oxford' or even the balance of 'Inversnaid', where a powerful reference to Despair as a type of vertigo is abandoned in the celebratory rondo of the last stanza.

There is no question either that Hopkins could be impossibly obscure, as the explanation of 'sakes' in 'Henry Purcell' bears out: 'it is the *sake* of "for the sake of", *foresake*, *namesake*, *keepsake*. I mean by it the being a thing has outside itself . . .' Equally, 'Andromeda' continues to baffle us with its allegory, even though Hopkins offered it to Bridges as an endeavour at 'a more Miltonic plainness and severity'. This jibbing at particularities doesn't, however, confront the general problem of Hopkins's poetry which, though it can be simple, strikes many readers as massively overdone, whether bulging with veins or muscles.

The case against Hopkins is put most forcibly, if anachronistically, by Dryden, whom Hopkins revered. As it happens, however, it is also the case against Shakespeare: 'yet I cannot deny that he has his failings; but they are not so much in the passions themselves as in his manner of expression: he often obscures his meaning by his words, and sometimes makes it unintelligible. I will not say of so great a poet that he distinguished not the blown puffy style from true sublimity; but I may venture to maintain that the fury of his fancy often transported him beyond the bounds of judgement, either in coining of new words and phrases, or racking words which were in use into the violence of a catachresis. 'Tis not that I would explode the use of metaphors from passions, for Longinus thinks 'em necessary to raise it: but to use 'em at every word, to say nothing without a metaphor, a simile, an image, or description, is I doubt to smell a little too strongly of the buskin.'

Or of the lamp. Or salad oil. Poor Shakespeare. Poor Hopkins. Poor, poor Tuncks. One might almost leave the argument there, with Dryden wriggling on his own point, evidently embarrassed to convict his favourite writer of vulgarity. But why did Dryden find himself in this uncomfortable position? Anxiety of influence appears to be the main cause: he was seeking a theoretical route out of the creative cul-de-sac presented by the achievement of Shakespeare and the metaphysicals. The pressure of the past shows itself in the rejection of the conceited style after the early 'Annus Mirabilis' and in every rewrite of Shakespeare, however bold we may find them. Hopkins, on the contrary, was more deeply assured of his own originality and wrote to Bridges: 'the effect of studying masterpieces is to make me admire and do otherwise.' This was more radical than any of Dryden's recurring attempts to polish up Shakespeare or his effort merely to refine the numbers.

Refinement, in fact, is one key to Dryden's limitations as a critic. It led him, for instance, to reject Jonson as a 'perfect pattern of imitation' – on the curious grounds that Jonson's forte, low-life conversation, could hardly be expected to amuse gentlemen in the theatre when they avoided it in the streets. Dryden's literary taste, it is clear, was a function of his social taste. Literature should be polite, easy and polished, not vulgarly straining for effect. Hopkins saw things differently. For a start, as James

Milroy points out in his excellent study,* he was a fascinated student of low-life and rustic language – a word-hoard he plundered to make his utterly distinctive style. Secondly, his idea of poetry involved continuous effort. This much is obvious from his comments on Hardy and Blackmore, where his praise is tempered by a crucial reservation: 'these writers only rise to their great strokes; they do not write continuously well.' Hopkins did, or tried to, repeatedly insisting to Bridges that his work was free from padding. He wrote with unbroken and candid artifice – an artifice which, with the exception of the terrible sonnets, has led inevitably to the charge of artificiality.

This charge is best refuted, paradoxically enough, by the critic who did most to establish it on the critical statute-book – Dr Johnson. Johnson may have condemned 'Lycidas' and the metaphysicals for insincerity and artificiality, but he inadvertently answers himself in his defence of Shakespeare's failure to observe the unities. They are not binding, he briskly avers, because 'it is false that any representation is mistaken for reality'. Similarly, in the case of Hopkins, only a naive reader would confuse artistic utterance with real utterance. Art, even the art that hides art, is, after all, artificial.

James Milroy avoids these large issues. His purpose is to explain and describe Hopkins's use of language rather than defend or evaluate the canon. Yet, underlying his scrupulous objectivity is the idea of *tout comprendre, c'est tout pardonner* and his scattered reservations only serve, by their rarity, to endorse Hopkins's poetic practice.

Dr Milroy's Hopkins is a philologist whose aesthetic arises out of a conviction that 'the poetical language of an age should be the current language heightened'. By current language, Milroy conclusively proves, Hopkins meant *speech*, not prose, influenced as he was by the new science of philology, led by Max Müller and Jacob Grimm. The conclusions that follow from this simple distinction are manifold: sprung rhythm is shown, as Hopkins always maintained, to be based on natural speech rhythm; the

*The Language of Gerard Manley Hopkins by James Milroy, André Deutsch.

many inconsistent 'archaisms' in Hopkins's diction turn out to be current in conservative dialect usage; the disjointed syntax that disturbs so many readers is seen as true to the grammar of *speech*, with all its parentheses, verbless exclamations, explanatory repetitions and reprises of the main verb.

If this is the case, though, why does much of Hopkins seem utterly different from speech? Milroy's answer takes up the second half of his book which is an account of the different ways Hopkins *heightened* current language – phonetically, through consonant and vowel rhyme so complex that Dr Milroy resorts to tables and diagrams; in his diction, where Hopkins freely coined from root-words, a practice he felt was legitimized by the work of Müller and Barnes; and, finally, in his syntax.

There are so many sensible insights in Dr Milroy's book (like his observation that Hopkins's inversions could not have been forced on him by the supreme freedom of sprung rhythm, but must be deliberate) that reservations seem carping. Even so, some of his pages are distinctly hard going. The grammarian's bent scarcely allows for a simple Hopkins at all. Sometimes, things are 'explained' in the manner of Johnson's notorious definition: NET – 'anything made of interstitial vacuities'. Finally, at some points, Dr Milroy overstates the case for the philologist Hopkins, partly because he stretches the meaning of 'inscape' a long way beyond its primary meaning of 'pattern' and 'design', a meaning which is clearly assigned in a letter to Bridges (15 February 1879): 'No doubt my poetry errs on the side of oddness. I hope in time to have a more balanced and Miltonic style. But as air, melody, is what strikes me most of all in music and design in painting, *so design, pattern or what I am in the habit of calling "inscape" is what I above all aim at in poetry*. Now it is the virtue of design, pattern, or inscape to be distinctive and it is the vice of distinctiveness to become queer. This vice I cannot have escaped' (my italics).

'Harry Ploughman', for instance, is a complex poem but not so linguistically enriched as Dr Milroy maintains. In the description of the blown hair on Harry's arms ('a broth of goldish flue / Breathed round'), Dr Milroy argues for *broth* as a kind of semantic carrier, infested with associations from 'the semantic fields in which it is normally used in ordinary language'. The trouble is that these associations are entirely unhelpful in their irrelevance: 'the *broth* of the whirlpool is also applicable to Harry Ploughman's arms.' Hopkins's image is thus effectively smothered. Equally, we learn that *ropes* are not simply ropes, but also clouds and waterfalls; that *curded* means not only 'hardened' but is also associated with clouds. Which is all very well in its way, except that Hopkins is describing hard muscles, not insubstantial, misty ones.

'Harry Ploughman'

Eliot, in *After Strange Gods*, complained that Hopkins's poems sometimes struck him 'as lacking inevitability – that is to say, they sometimes come near to being purely *verbal*, in that a whole poem will give us *more* of the same thing, an accumulation, rather than a real development of thought or feeling'. The criticism that Hopkins is merely a sound-poet can be discounted at once. There is nothing *abstract*, as music is abstract, in Hopkins's extremely concrete poetry. It has its music, of course, but it never aspires to the condition of music, in Pater's yearning formula. Rather, Eliot's displeasure is focused on those poems whose form resembles a capacious travelling trunk – delightfully and apparently infinitely accommodating until the lid, a sturdy moral precept, is forced down over the contents. It is the arbitrary curtailment as much as the sweet disarray which exaggerates the sense of mere accumulation. Thus, in 'Epithalamion', the brilliant observation of the swimmers ('bellbright bodies *huddling* out' against the cold) breaks off for the anti-climactic explication, the theological justification (which Eliot affects to envy) – 'what the water? Spousal love.' Literary convention, as much as Hopkins's religious bent, dictates this fatally disjunctive form.

Augustan sensibility, with its strong didactic quality, reached its apogee in *Rasselas* where, for Imlac, the natural world is only important as it is 'useful for the inforcement or decoration of moral or religious truth'. The poet, according to Johnson, remarks 'general properties and large appearances: he does not number the streaks of the tulip'. Hopkins stands at the mid-point

99

between the moral Johnson and Joyce who repudiated moral interference in *A Portrait of the Artist as a Young Man*. 'The artist, like the God of creation, remains within or behind or above his handiwork, invisible, refined out of existence, indifferent, paring his fingernails.' Such a thoroughgoing rejection was impossible for Hopkins, and Conrad's definition of art as 'a single-minded attempt to render the highest kind of justice to the visible universe' might have struck him as not quite respectable.

The single exception to the moral idea has always been the love poem, which can simply celebrate or lament – and, even then, often with some moral generalization about, say, female fickleness. 'Harry Ploughman' is a homosexual love poem which describes the beauty of the labourer with all the obsessive detail of an Elizabethan sonneteer cataloguing his mistress's eyebrows, eyes, cheeks, breasts and limbs. The unconsciously felt weight of this tradition permits Hopkins to exclude overt moralizing. The problem of form is, however, intensified: deprived of a moral argument, the poem is deprived of development, of a beginning, middle and end – particularly if there is no obvious narrative for, unlike the novel, there are no established stopping points like births, marriages and deaths. Indeed, Whitman did not stop. The poem must generate its own form, as 'Harry Ploughman' does. It moves from close-up to panorama, from the hair on Harry's arms to the figure moving in the landscape.

The single, paradoxical portmanteau word, 'churlsgrace', epitomizes everything that makes Hopkins an original poet. For him, poetry is not limited to the conventionally beautiful. Yokel-beauty, a rough paraphrase of 'churlsgrace', is not, prima facie, a promising subject, but, as Wallace Stevens realized, 'everything is beautiful if you say it is'. Herbert, Hopkins's literary ancestor, also exploited the possibilities of the unpoetic and mundane. And all three, Hopkins, Herbert and Stevens, tacitly subscribe to Constable's diktat: 'I have never seen anything ugly. Dog turds cathedralling to the sky.'

Hopkins, like Herbert, can be sentimental ('his wind-lilylocks-laced') or literary, as in this line from 'Spelt from Sibyl's Leaves': 'Only the beakleaved boughs dragonish damask the tool-smooth bleak light'. The melodrama of 'dragonish' dilutes the strong 'beakleaved', but the characteristic touch is the authentic 'tool-smooth' with all its connotations of the everyday, the *domestic*. Similarly, Hopkins's image of the hair on Harry's arms blown *gently* by the wind is 'a broth of goldish flue [fluff] / Breathed round'. In other, less economical words, the wind blows the hair as we blow on soup to cool it. In the same way, Harry's ribs are compared to a plate-rack, his bulging calves to barrels, his thigh muscles to rope (a subtle variant on the more usual *knotted* muscles), and the tensing muscles to the coagulation of a hard curd. Only the comparison of the bent knee-joint to a nave clashes slightly with the uniformly appropriate domestic opening. After this troop of images marching in step, comes Hopkins's *tour de force*, the extended conceit in which the muscles are compared to a well-drilled regiment. It is a kind of animated anatomical drawing by Calcar for Vesalius.

From exterior and interior detail, Hopkins then steps back, consummately contrasting the grace of Harry's 'liquid waist' with 'the wallowing o' the plough'. His eye is absorbed by the object, like the eye of a painter. (Incidentally, Hopkins's drawings are highly accomplished.) The cheek reddens with effort and the curls are first lifted, *then* tangled by the wind. The two final comparisons (of the creases in Harry's boots to frown-marks, of the furl of the iron-hard furrow to a fountain) may seem more poetic than painterly – until we remember that Picasso said, 'Reality lies in how you see things. A green parrot is also a green salad *and* a green parrot. He who makes it only a parrot diminishes its reality.' Painting simply had to catch up.

A Toad Run Over

Swinburne, naked and drunk, sliding down the banisters; Morris with a black eye from an apple-fight; Hunt trapping sparrows and painting their heads green before releasing them; Rossetti's scheme to train an elephant as a window-cleaner to attract custom, and his purchase of a Brahmin bull because it had eyes like Janey Morris – few artistic movements can supply so much slapstick and whimsy. It is easy to see the Pre-Raphaelites and their associates as the Marx Brothers of Victorian art. They specialized in sophisticated naivety: 'Why?' asked Rossetti, when the sergeant barked the order 'right about face' to the Artists' rifles. Millais visited the 'High Priest of Craniology', Donovan, and asked, pointing to a head of Dante, 'Who may that old lady be?' Rossetti followed him and elicited the phrenological information that Keats and Dante owed their poetic genius to scrofula 'provoking an irritability in the brain'. Their wordplay was as quick as Groucho's 'Why a duck?' – Rossetti wrote limericks ('There is a dull Painter named Wells / Who is duller than anyone else'); Edward Lear thought Millais might introduce a 'Millais-neum' of art; Hunt's friend, Thackeray, cut by Lord Wensleydale, yelled in a nursery voice, 'Dear, dear me! I'm afraid I've greatly offended Lord Tuesdaydale!'

In this cast of zanies, William Michael Rossetti naturally assumes the role of Zeppo Marx – described by James Agee as 'a peerlessly cheesy improvement on the traditional straightman'. The younger Rossetti was a civil servant like Trollope and Peacock (whose phrase, 'an athlete in pedestrianism', covers

William Michael neatly). Later, he became log-rolling art critic for the *Spectator* in addition to his part-time duties as factotum to Dante Gabriel – 'Tin is no more; spout that pin of mine' being a typical fraternal directive. Though not incapable of asperity ('dinner and dreariness' with his editor), William Michael's experiments with mesmerism somehow give the temper of the man. On the first occasion, the hypnotist pleaded lack of practice; on the second, as it appeared to be working, the hypnotist stopped, afraid of possible catalepsy; subsequently the magic twice failed. A series of non-events, in fact.

His diary antedates the sensational years of Pre-Raphaelitism. Thrill-seekers will have to go elsewhere for Lizzie Siddal's death by an overdose of laudanum, Rossetti's exhumation of her body to retrieve his notebook, his chloral addiction and attempted suicide, as well as minor events like the murder of Howell, Ruskin's quondam secretary – found in a Chelsea gutter with his throat cut, a ten-shilling piece jammed between his clenched teeth. William Michael's journal is a sober affair – 'My journey to Cowes was unmarked by any particular incident', he notes racily. Keats's 'Isabella', he computes, has twenty-four faults, 'with a reservation on my part of eleven in addition'.

Thanks to Professor Fredeman's labour of love, or love of labour, we now have the unexpurgated PRB Journal.* It is chockablock with stunning disclosures: 'In a walk we took after dinner, we found in the middle of the road a toad run over.' Even so, the diary remains incomplete – in a sensible moment (oddly explained by Professor Fredeman as possible derangement), Dante Gabriel ripped out an estimated 30 per cent. Moreover, moments of high excitement, like Dickens's hilarious and philistine attack on Millais, find William Michael unable to locate his fountain pen. The result is a flat, retrospective summary. Worse, the day-to-day journal is silent about the inception of the PRB, so that no inconvenient details emerge to contradict William

---

The PRB Journal – William Michael Rossetti's Diary of the Pre-Raphaelite Brotherhood, 1849–53 (& other Pre-Raphaelite Documents) edited by William E. Fredeman, Oxford.

Michael's later account – in which Dante Gabriel (his brother) and Ford Madox Brown (his father-in-law) are given primacy.

The rival, and only coherent version is that of Holman Hunt, whose *Pre-Raphaelitism and the Pre-Raphaelite Brotherhood* is dismissed by Professor Fredeman as a turgid amalgam of prejudices. (Only a boondoggling bibliographer could fail to appreciate Hunt's marvellous ear for dialogue, Jewish, Cockney, Irish or Carlylean.) While it is true that Dante Gabriel had a forceful personality, the fact remains that, in the first instance, his entrepreneurial flair failed him. It was he who recruited the duds to the Brotherhood – Woolner, Collinson, and William Michael. In addition, he simply could not paint. Brown and Hunt alike record his rages over drapery or a fidgety angel. Rossetti was incapable of fulfilling Ruskin's seminal dictum – 'Go to nature in all singleness of heart, selecting nothing, rejecting nothing' – as the uncompleted *Found* bears witness. His early paintings are striking but inept struggles towards the pure Hunt doctrine, and he was soon to abandon them for the Higher Boots portraits of Janey Morris and Fanny Cornforth.

In the second, *aesthetic* phase of Pre-Raphaelitism, Rossetti was undoubtedly the leader. Not even Hunt disputes that. But nothing could be further from pure Pre-Raphaelitism. One has only to compare the second title of *The Germ* ('Art and Poetry: Being Thoughts Towards Nature') with Burne-Jones's pronouncement that a picture should be 'a beautiful romantic dream of something that never was, never will be . . . in a land that no one can ever define or remember, only desire'.

Brown, being a great painter, is less easy to place than Rossetti. His *Take Your Son, Sir!* is unquestionably a Pre-Raphaelite masterpiece, unfinished as it is. It shows a woman, shrewishly buck-toothed, offering a naked baby to a whiskered loon, who can be seen in the mirror behind her head. Her expression, in its way, is more tellingly ambiguous than that of the Mona Lisa – at once blank and hard. The mirror makes a sharply ironic halo, startling in an illegitimacy picture. It belongs with Hunt's *The Awakening Conscience*, that triumph of neo-Hogarthian iconography, as a brilliantly ugly painting. Prettiness was never part of genuine Pre-Raphaelitism, but its absence has led to the devaluation of Hunt and Brown. The reluctance to accept Hunt's cogent and detailed version of events (in which Brown is essentially a loner, gifted enough to pick up what he needed from Hunt and Millais) must surely stem from a distaste for his pictures. The taboo against ugliness dies hard.

Hopkins, who reservedly admired Ruskin, was strangely critical of Hunt's detailed garishness. In his Journal (12 June 1874), he writes of Hunt's *Shadow of Death*: 'the feet not inscaped but with a scapeless look they sometimes no doubt have . . . and veined too, which further breaks their scaping. On the whole colour somewhat overglaring . . . Shavings and all the texture too tufty and woolly . . . The saws and other tools seemed over-blue. No inscape of composition whatever – not known and if it had been known it could scarcely bear up against such realism.'

It is odd, this protest against Pre-Raphaelite extremism, because Hopkins is the sole successful Pre-Raphaelite poet. Though all the founder members of the brotherhood wrote poetry, only Dante Gabriel and Morris offer real claims. 'The Haystack in the Floods', 'Sir Peter Harpdon's End', 'Riding Together' leave a strong, ineffaceable taste in the mouth but their casual, drab, unhurried brutalities derive from Morris's private pessimism rather than any Pre-Raphaelite picturesque stereoscopic medievalism. As for Rossetti, once discount the mixed 'Jenny' and the pleasing 'My Sister's Sleep' and only ponderous rhetoric remains: 'Dumb tears from the blind sky' is the kind of line one is deaf to. It was left to Hopkins to manage the cramped, intense detail of the pure Pre-Raphaelite prescription. 'Tom's fallowbootfellow piles pick / By him and rips out rockfire homeforth' could be an animated detail from Ford Madox Brown's *Work*. The Pre-Raphaelites looked to the purity of Raphael's predecessors: Hopkins evoked an English free of Latin. In Millais's *Winter Fuel*, Hopkins remarked 'a rawness . . . unvelvety papery colouring, especially in raw silver and purple birchstems, crude rusty cartwheels, aimless mess or mingle-mangle of cut underwood in under-your-nose foreground'. Fourteen years later, he caught the same effect in 'That Nature is a Heraclitean

Fire': 'in pool and rutpeel parches / Squandering ooze to squeezed dough, crust, dust; stanches, starches / Squadroned masks and manmarks treadmire toil there / Footfretted in it'.

By comparison, William Michael's *Mrs Holmes Grey* (printed in an appendix to Professor Fredeman's book), while avowedly exemplifying Pre-Raphaelite principles, is glumly literal and bereft of intensity. It reads like the *News of the World* done into the blankest of blank verse, and its effect is best conveyed by William Michael's jottings on hypnosis: 'The sensation is not one of drowsiness, nor in the least . . . of unconsciousness, but simply of inability to resist closing the eyes and dropping backwards.'

Stanley Spencer

'Diana called for me and we went to the Tate', Evelyn Waugh's
1955 diary records, 'to see the Stanley Spencer exhibition where I
should have liked to linger but she rushed, missing the point and
thinking him quaint and whimsical, where I see him realistic and
proletarian.' *C'est tout.* An earlier entry notes a visit to Burgh-
clere and pronounces Spencer's paintings there 'splendid'.
Waugh's characteristic categorical brevity is as different from
Spencer's prodigal prose as the novelist's spare drawings are from
Spencer's teeming compositions. Where Waugh snubbed experience daily with a phrase ('It was my birthday yesterday'), Spencer
left behind him three million prolix, sparsely punctuated,
ungrammatical words that are the record of his infatuation with
experience and himself* – a dense and driven passion that was the
absolute antithesis of Waugh's *taedium vitae.*

In John Rothenstein's rather meagre selection from this mass of
material and in the affectionate memoirs of Spencer's friends,
there is much to support Waugh's brief notice of the Tate
retrospective. Spencer was indeed 'realistic and proletarian'. For
him, the ordinary was more numinous than the conventionally
visionary. This world constantly imposes itself on the other-
worldly so that, for example, Christ and the twelve apostles are
metamorphosed by Spencer's imagination: 'I want to paint
J. C. & Co. like a football team, don'tcha know, sitting there

Stanley Spencer – The Man: Correspondence and Reminiscences edited by John
Rothenstein, Elek.

in two rows with their arms folded like this, and looking tough.'

He never experienced that conflict between the divine and the mundane dramatized so compassionately by Eliot in his Ariel poems, where the Magus and Simeon discover a sadly human inelasticity of spirit in the face of apocalyptic events. In Spencer, one can't help feeling, the religious is almost a pretext for the human. His two crucifixions of 1947 and 1958 centre not on Christ but on human activity – the carpenters banging in the nails with fierce concentration; the exhausted workman resting both hands on a wall after the labour of tamping down the earth at the foot of the cross. The simple craft of here and now meant more to him than the metaphysical possibilities offered by theology and it is entirely typical that his last words should have been a compliment to his nurse. 'Beautifully done,' he said of her injection, though the hereafter was only minutes away.

Nothing is disenfranchised in Spencer's art. A skein of wool, a patch of floor receive his concentrated regard, just as the chamber-pot under the bed is brought to our attention in Rembrandt's etching of Joseph and Potiphar's wife. His letters and conversation simply extend this polite interest to a whole variety of shy details and topics. Shown a slide of a stained-glass window that depicted the laying-out of Lazarus, Spencer concentrated on the women: 'I bet they've done that kind of job many times before, you can see by their expressions as they work that one is saying to the other "say, Jane, did you have a good time last night when you were with your boy friend?"' Again, when he was asked why the disciples in his *Last Supper* had their feet crossed, he replied that it was because they'd heard it all before.

It is a typically shrewd, ironical observation, realistic and proletarian in the sense that it undermines the establishment view. Yet one rapidly wants to expand Waugh's encapsulation. Spencer *could* be quaint and whimsical – delightfully so. Moreover, he was a hectic autodidact who read, we learn, the *Odyssey*, *Don Juan*, *Gulliver's Travels*, *The Idiot*, most of Chekhov's plays and some of the stories, Sophocles and 'Europides', Ibsen and *Alice in Wonderland*. Too poor and too preoccupied with his beloved Cookham to venture abroad much, Spencer nevertheless had an astonishingly retentive memory for and a deep appreciation of the Italian art he had absorbed from books. He was quite capable of sketching the designs at the foot of the Florence campanile, explaining them with vivid enthusiasm.

In fact, there were many Stanley Spencers and just as Waugh was wrong to be so categorical, so John Rothenstein is mistaken, though well-meaning, in selecting those letters that best reflect the public Spencer he and other friends knew. His aim is to prove that Spencer was not sexually depraved, that Dudley Tooth was the best of all possible dealers for the financially feckless artist, and that Spencer's second, gold-digging wife, Patricia Preece, had been white-washed in the Maurice Collis biography and in Louise Collis's sequel, *Stanley Spencer: A Private View*. On the last two counts, he succeeds absolutely.

As for Spencer's alleged sexual abnormalities, Rothenstein largely ignores them. Even so, we learn that Spencer delighted in 'low stories' and that the local builder remarked that 'his trouble is he's secky'. In any case, the Astor collection includes a drawing of Stanley on a double lavatory with his first wife, Hilda, a delicate erection balanced like a long-stemmed wine glass on his lap. On the subject of Spencer's mild fetishism, his interest in the sexual behaviour of animals, Rothenstein has reacted against Louise Collis's lurid presentation and maintained a stiff decorum. The truth is that Spencer was only averagely interested in sex — that is, like the rest of us, he thought about it variously and a great deal. It is time to lay aside the prudishness which condemns and that which protects. The entire correspondence and writings should be printed, or at least a sizeable chunk. The last word should go to the artist: 'I can go round the grounds with Lord Astor and in a superficial vicarious way say, yes, yes, lovely and so on, and both of us are getting quietly nowhere; until at last I am crying and pining to get home and back to that happy homely realm of thinking about myself and all my special brew of thoughts, when all the Stanleys, this me and that me, can come out like children coming out of school.' It's long overdue for sexy Stanley to come out and play.

Henri Le Douanier Rousseau

Nowadays, Henri Rousseau is a lazily accepted member of the modernist pantheon, just as he was once automatically reviled.* In fact, he is a very uneven painter, though that may seem a paradoxical charge to lay against a primitive, the *donnée* of whose work is a necessary technical incompetence. All the same, it remains true that his greatest pictures (*A Carnival Evening, The Promenade, Football Players, Surprised!, One Centennial of Independence, The Snake Charmer, The Sleeping Gipsy* and *The Dream*) are few, however remarkable. Other paintings are less successful and there are a great many straightforward bummers. Unless we recognize this scale of achievement, we are in danger of patronizing Rousseau just as much as his early detractors did. While we congratulate ourselves on a broad-minded generosity, we are merely indulging our sentimentality.

Henri Rousseau painted in pidgin, so to speak. His simplicity is quite different from that of, say, Matisse. Matisse solves his artistic problems elegantly in two lines, with brilliant intuitive formulae which then find their way into the hands of lesser artists. Rousseau, by contrast, is invariably long-winded and garrulous. His problems are all solved in longhand on the backs of huge manila envelopes: the pictures are a long sum, a painstaking accumulation, complete with the odd mistake in the working. And it is here, of course, that his particular charm resides. Because the sophisticated vocabulary of the academic painters he

The World of Henri Rousseau by Yann Le Pichon, Phaidon.

admired was beyond him – a closed lexicon – he invented a new periphrastic language with its own charm. Just as the pidgin speaker has no word for helicopter or piano, and therefore invents 'mixmaster b'long Jesus Christ' and 'man im bockis you fight him he cry', so the best of Rousseau capitalizes on his limitations. His paintings thus manage to avoid the deadness of academic technique and provide instead a periphrastic freshness.

There are two reasons for his popularity. The modernists adopted him because, in his unschooled way, he blundered unconsciously towards an approximation of their own position. In all the arts, there comes a point when what were originally artistic discoveries dwindle by dissemination into mere technical tricks. As Matisse said, 'It is perilous to fall under the influence of the masters of one's own epoch, because the language is too close to ours, and one risks taking the letter for the spirit.' Thus Picasso makes Juan Gris his postman, bequeathing him the cubist style to popularize, while he himself moves on to new discoveries. On the face of it, Rousseau appears similarly innovative, if by default.

The second reason for Rousseau's acclaim is more complex. There are painters like Holbein, Memling and Carpaccio who raise technique to such a pitch that it becomes invisible. Take, for instance, Holbein's portrait of Sir Richard Southwell in the Uffizi: we register the spoilt mouth, the incipient double-chin, the jaw-line dark with closely shaven bristles, the scar on the neck. We do not register the medium. It does not exist. We see only *das Ding an sich* – a scar. Or in a Giorgione, the technical problem of rendering fur is so achieved that we see only fur. Modern painting is a self-referring, self-conscious language: 'An artist should observe nature but never confuse it with painting', Picasso told Brassaï. 'It is only translatable into painting by signs.' And to Pignon he observed: 'I don't want to do a nude as a nude. I want only to say breast, *say* foot, *say* hand or belly.' This kind of sign language solicits the viewer to admire the ingenious economy of its signs – a toy car for a gorilla's face, handlebars and a saddle for a bull. The medium is no longer invisible, so that Degas's *Woman Sponging Her Leg in the Bath* invites our admiration: the water isn't only water; it's also flakes of lime-green pastel, a breathtaking illusion, which elicits our praise by drawing attention to the sign.

Rousseau, of course, was inarticulate by comparison. But we are never allowed to forget technique in his work. It is always visible and often clumsy. In this curious way, he joins the moderns. However, compare one of his jungle masterpieces, *Surprised!*, with one of his jungle failures (*Fight Between a Jaguar and a Horse* or *The Lion Hunter*) and you rapidly discover the limitations of a limited technique. Everyone is familiar with *Surprised!* Substitute a Stubbs tiger for Rousseau's domestic cat, which looks as if it has just been propelled outdoors by a pair of rubber-soled tartan slippers, and the whole effect would vanish. The 'failure' of technique is finely balanced. Similarly, the repeated unifying motif of stripes in the painting is ostentatious to just the right degree. We are buttonholed without being bored. The lightning and the weather effects are bold but unclichéd. In *The Lion Hunter*, on the other hand, the endearing becomes merely ludicrous, the lion's snarl the grin of teeth fresh from a tumbler of Steradent. And in *Fight Between a Jaguar and a Horse*, the disarray of the horse's mane is mechanically mirrored in the vegetation. The discovery of *Surprised!* has become a cliché, a monotonous repetition. In his jungle paintings, there is, despite a copious surface, a paucity of signs, so that in *The Lion's Meal* we encounter bunches of bananas which dutifully echo the lion's mane and protuberant ears.

Rousseau enthusiasts usually appeal to poetry. But they are using the word in a very limited sense — one related to poetic licence, which in the end says no more than that the paintings are inaccurate because they are inaccurate. Rousseau has two great strengths: he is a brilliant colourist, whose canvases are rendered null by black and white reproduction, and he is, at his best, a master of atmosphere. *The Sleeping Gipsy*, for example, has a satisfyingly simple organization — the lute and the vase taking up the rigid posture and the striped caftan of the sleeping negress — but nothing can really explain the painting's haunted emptiness. Is it because the palomino lion is at once dreamlike and realistic? Or is it to do with Rousseau's uncharacteristically bare canvas?

Why does *Football Players* succeed? On the one hand, there is a ludicrous Spot-the-Ball quality of unrealism. No one is looking at the ball. On the other hand, there is something strangely and accidentally compelling in the figures: they aren't simply paralleled; they are eery twins. Randall Jarrell said that 'a good poet is someone who manages, in a lifetime of standing out in thunderstorms, to be struck by lightning five or six times; a dozen or two dozen times and he is great.' Rousseau isn't a great painter; he is a good painter – and the evidence is here in this beautifully produced book of reproductions, which are accompanied by sources and analogues. There is a useful biographical table at the back of the book. Otherwise, forget the text: it is tawdry, incoherent, bogusly psychoanalytical and pretentious as only the French can be. And badly translated to boot.

Fairground Art

Apart from its authors, Geoff Weedon and Richard Ward, it is difficult to envisage a properly qualified yet objective reviewer for *Fairground Art** – a charming, extensively illustrated and scholarly study. One excludes, naturally, all the enthusiasts credited in the bibliography. As for me, I spent a proportion of my adolescence hanging around the rides, but, preoccupied by my appearance and the proper management of the crêpe-soled dodgems on my feet, I failed to appreciate my garish surroundings were popular art. However, I once worked at St Giles's Fair in Oxford on George Pickard's Boadicea Spinner (illustrated, gratifyingly enough, on page 221) and my father once fought a light heavyweight called George Dicko in a fairground boxing booth just before the war. Dicko was a thing of family legend – hairy as a coconut, fanged, frightening, disfigured, with both ears tight as the heart of a lettuce. My father smashed his nose like a walnut. Hence my pedantic expertise which allows me to correct a tiny slip on page 291, where the authors identify a bespectacled moustached face on a boxing booth as 'the BBC commentator, Kenneth Wolstenhome'. In fact, it is a portrait of Raymond Glendenning. Wolstenhome was clean-shaven and a football commentator.

Fairground Art is a paean to the pleasures of naming. Deliciously technical throughout, crammed with spartan facts and

Fairground Art: The Art Forms of Travelling Fairs, Carousels and Carnival Midways by Geoff Weedon and Richard Ward, White Mouse Editions.

esoteric vocabulary, it is guaranteed to appeal to the Gradgrind in all of us. The Joyce who wrote 'Ithaca', the Kipling of 'McAndrew's Hymn' and *Many Inventions*, would have loved it: 'the rounding boards were built up from half-inch thick yellow pine board twelve inches wide, tongue and grooved together, the top made a little wider to create a dome effect. Top and bottom sweeps were cut to bend and the nosing was made on a spindle moulder. Twelve battens were screwed at intervals through the boards and sweeps, to secure the shape . . .' Quite. Put like that, you could practically knock together a merry-go-round yourself. Now that you know the nosing should be made on the spindle moulder. No sweat.

As against this real world with its workshop Esperanto, its 'inlines, outlines, drop shadows and shaded brushwork', its Manders Flamboyant Enamels, there is the world of the fair itself. Like Sleary's circus in *Hard Times*, the fair is a potent symbol of the mass imagination. On waste ground, overlooking allotments or railway sidings, roundabouts gather like the crowned heads of Europe. Under a perspiration of electric light bulbs lies the gaudy plunder of the popular imagination – an imagination vulgar, rapacious, economically straitened. The fair, unlike the circus, has no real animals so that, although Weedon and Ward gamely discuss horses, say, in terms of realism, the illustrations show us an idealized, heraldic bestiary. The horses have no depth of chest. They are sexless and on page 21 there is a wooden pattern for producing metal castings of horse genitalia: 'apparently the intention was to alternate stallions with mares on Savage roundabouts. However, the gyration of the ride suggested a hot pursuit, so to placate Victorian propriety the stallions were gelded and the pattern put into storage.' After this early veer towards realism, fantastification took over and, for instance, horses became centaurs – half beast, half Baden-Powell. Bejewelled like an outbreak of boils, transfixed by gilded skewers, they cease to be animals and become declarations of greed.

The imprecision of conception contrasts with the precision of making. The real poetry in this book lies in the painstaking exactitude with which the creative process is described and not in

116

the products of that process. In his *Degas*, Ian Dunlop reports the following aphorism made by Degas to George Moore: 'Among people who understand, words are not necessary. You say humph, ha, ha, and everything has been said.' The craftsmen who are quoted in *Fairground Art* share the same unpretentious professionalism: 'he'd use just a bit of chalk on these great big rounding boards – up on the scaffolding – next thing you'd see a great big fig leaf and a lion.' Yet, if this makes it seem easy, Weedon and Ward also pursue the richly technical: 'the Scenic cars were carved from yellow pine, built up in blocks, shot, glued and later touch nailed both sides with two-inch oval nails.' One responds here to the chaste precision, whereas the popular imagination is both inexact and derivative. It's interesting to note, for example, how little the authors are bothered by plagiarism. But if imagery borrows from itself, instead of de-lineating life, the result is always artistic disaster. You can see this in even a great writer like Nabokov when he wants to write beautifully instead of precisely: he opens a casket from Hatton Garden and scatters a fistful of rubies in the general direction of beauty. But they're paste, with highlights by Manders Flamboy-ant Enamels. In the end, then, one is disappointed by fairground art for the same reason. The objects reach for a facile poetry and one only has to compare these animals with the creatures realized by Picasso to sound their glibness. Picasso's owl, for instance, is economical, witty, accurate and made from humblest ingredients – the blade of a mattock and a few screws. Looking at the illustrations in *Fairground Art* made me think of the vision of heaven in *Pearl* with its unremittingly lavish monotony. All the same, this is a fascinating, if finally uncritical book, because reality always returns to the text: 'a number of Louis Quinze fronts seem to have crossed the English channel via Gavioli's London agent Chiappa, including those destined for Twigdon's Coliseum, Murphy's Bioscope and Alf Ball's New Lyceum.' *Alf Ball* . . . I like it, but you can keep the Louis Quinze fronts.

The Language of John Donne*

In 1936, a gleeful Dylan Thomas informed Vernon Watkins that he had lunched with 'Pope Eliot'. Despite a faint edge of malice, the sobriquet is an index of Eliot's enormous and, on the whole, well-deserved critical prestige. As a poet, he spoke *ex cathedra* and his booming, authoritative pronouncements have produced a multitude of echoes in subsequent criticism. His essay, 'The Metaphysical Poets' (1921), for instance, has been profoundly influential, even though it is an example of papal fallibility. Take this typical antithesis: 'It is to be observed that the language of these poets is as a rule simple and pure . . . The *structure* of the sentences, on the other hand, is sometimes far from simple.' The reader has scarcely murmured 'Amen' before he encounters, four pages later, a rogue echo of undiminished volume – the same proposition in exactly inverted form. Eliot is drawing an analogy between the difficulty of modern poetry and that of the metaphysicals: 'we get, in fact, a method curiously similar to that of the "metaphysical poets", similar also in its use of obscure words and simple phrasing.'

When Eliot expounds his famous theory of the dissociation of sensibility in the same essay, the argument is no more coherent. Primarily, he is making a distinction between two types of poetic sensibility. Concurrently, however, he distinguishes between the poet and the less fortunate ordinary man, for whom the disparate experiences of falling in love and reading Spinoza 'have nothing

John Donne: Language and Style by A. C. Partridge, André Deutsch.

to do with each other'. In pursuing the second distinction, Eliot undermines the first. On the one hand, he argues for a general unification of sensibility in all poets, as opposed to the man in the street: 'a degree of heterogeneity of material compelled into unity by the operation of the poet's mind *is omnipresent in poetry*' (my italics). On the other hand, he maintains that Donne, his contemporaries and his predecessors are to be differentiated from later poets like Tennyson and Browning, because they wrote before 'a dissociation of sensibility set in', before a mysterious 'something' happened to 'the mind of England' – whatever that mythical entity might be.

In fact, as a poet of argument, Donne is intimately related to Dryden and Browning in particular – two of the poets Eliot chose to sever him from. It is no accident that the author of 'Bishop Blougram's Apology' was notorious in nineteenth-century drawing rooms for his proselytizing on Donne's behalf. Both poets are metrically rough. Pound's description of Browning in his pastiche, 'Mesmerism', could apply equally to Donne: 'Here's to you, Old Hippety-Hop o' the accents.' Both are dramatic poets, though even Donne's most robust openings ('For Godsake hold your tongue, and let me love') look etiolated beside Browning's matchless bravura in, say, 'Mr Sludge', with its volatile mixture of mollification, snarled aggression and physical violence:

> Aie-aie-aie!
> Please, sir! your thumbs are through my windpipe, sir!
> Ch-ch!

The effects are obvious and impeccable – the way Sludge persistently observes, *in extremis*, the disparity of rank; the brilliant printed equivalent for wordless choking. Here, Browning is on his own.

As an argumentative poet, too, Browning is superior to Donne and matched only by Dryden – Dryden whose expository gift so excluded the dramatic that, in *All for Love*, Antony and Cleopatra debate decorously where Shakespeare makes them quarrel. 'Bishop Blougram's Apology' and Dryden's 'Religio Laici' effortlessly and lucidly sustain complex, consecutive argument. Donne, by and large, argues no better than Eliot. His breathless logic is often presented with some of the jerky rapidity that one associates with the Keystone Cops falling over themselves:

> I heard mee say, Tell her anon,
>   That my selfe, (that is you, not I,)
>   Did kill me, and when I felt mee dye,
> I bid mee send my heart, when I was gone,
> But I alas could there finde none,
>   When I had ripp'd me, and search'd where hearts did lye;
> It kill'd mee againe, that I who was still true,
> In life, in my last Will should cozen you.

Of course, no one would claim that 'The Legacie' represents Donne at his very best, but the poem is not untypical of the *Songs and Sonets* – either in the preponderance of argument or its inept conduct. It is curious also to note how little these lines conform to the received idea of Donne and the metaphysicals, as we find it expressed in, for example, Pope's *Essay on Criticism*:

> Some to *Conceit* alone their Taste confine,
> And glitt'ring Thoughts struck out at ev'ry Line.

Struggling with 'The Legacie', one recalls rather Dryden's moan about the limited resources of the language: 'Poetry requires ornament; and that is not to be had from our old Teuton monosyllables.' Latinisms, however, are not the only means of ornament, though Donne did use them, always sparingly and sometimes with fine appropriateness:

> When love, with one another so
> Interinanimates two soules . . .

The other obvious ornament available to Donne was metaphor, a device he employs with great unevenness and far less frequently than one might suppose. At his worst, we hardly need

Rosemond Tuve's painstaking study of Elizabethan and meta-physical imagery to tell us that he is drawing monotonously on a common stock. The hyperbolic images become stale within the canon. On the other hand, Donne can be brilliant:

> So kisse good Turtles, so devoutly nice
> Are Priests in handling reverent Sacrifice.
> And such in searching wounds the Surgeon is
> As wee, when we embrace, or touch, or kisse.

The doves are quite standard, but the comparison with the surgeon blazes with originality. The secret is that, in this elegy, Donne is free from the responsibility of sustained argument: the organizing principle is a straight comparison between Donne's beautiful mistress and another's ugly mistress, conducted through a series of discrete statements like epigrams.

Where there is no intricate argument to pursue, Donne is at his best. Sex, the pain of parting, the fear of physical decline are never untouched by intellectual play, but they elicit the effectively simple in Donne:

> As liberally, as to a Midwife, shew
> Thy self: cast all, yea, this white lynnen hence

and, 'Sweetest love, I do not goe':

> But thinke that wee
> Are but turn'd aside to sleepe

and, 'His Picture':

> My body'a sack of bones, broken within,
> And powders blew staines scatter'd on my skinne;
> If rivall fooles taxe thee to'have loved a man,
> So foule, and course, as, Oh, I may seeme than,
> This shall say what I was . . .

Here, the unexpected force of that plain 'Oh' catches exactly the metrical stress and is made to tell in an utterly uncomplicated way.

In his greatest work, the *Anniversaries*, the overall argument is again simple – a *contemptus mundi* that allows Donne to concentrate on the lavish illustration of his theme. Similarly, the famous 'stiffe twin compasses' image may be intricate in itself, but it is intricate with the clarity of a Hilliard miniature because it depicts absolutely straightforward emotions. The compasses are 'stiffe' since the lovers are reluctant to part; this is the sole element that is left by Donne for the reader to puzzle out. The comparison has a deeply imagined metaphoric justness lucidly undertaken. Its mystery is 'like the Sunne, dazling, yet plaine to all eyes'. Metaphorically, Donne outstrips Dryden and Browning, as they are more than a match for his argumentative verse. The latter brings to mind Mr Woodhouse's comment on Mrs Elton: 'She speaks a little too quick. A little quickness there is which rather hurts the ear.' And if Pope Eliot defended Donne's difficulty, we ought to realize that he was also defending himself against the charge of obscurity. Further, Eliot's obscurity is radically different in kind from that of Donne whose only real follower in recent times has been William Empson. Predictably, Empson's zealous emulation produced a poetry in which elaborate argumentation buried his human starting points so thoroughly that they now only survive in his later explanatory notes.

A. C. Partridge also has a weakness for notes and *John Donne: Language and Style* is disappointing largely because it never transcends annotation. Indeed, by treating Donne's work in groups (the *Elegies*, the *Satyres*, *Songs and Sonets* etc.) he effectively precludes the possibility of any general argument about his alleged subject. He takes instead one or two gobbets from each group for comment when one might have expected him to write chapters on diction, syntax, metaphor and scansion, ending with a final chapter on style. Of course, these topics are touched upon, but in a shoddy, piecemeal way. Partridge's study has no real overview.

But how informative is the commentary he does offer? On elementary matters like Elizabethan orthography (*I* for *ay*; *then* for *than*) he is clear enough. An 'O' level candidate would find this useful. The same candidate, however, would be baffled by, for instance, this comment on 'To Sir Edward Herbert, at Julyers': 'He [Herbert] was eleven years Donne's junior, and had written a satirical exercise on *The State Progress of Ill* (1608), which was indebted to Donne's satires; *hence* [my italics] the references in the following passage to the Ark of Noah.' The enigmatic connective is explained only if one consults (as Professor Partridge has done) W. Milgate's edition of the *Satires, Epigrams and Verse Letters*: Milgate bothers to quote the end of Herbert's poem:

> The World, as in the Ark of *Noah* rests,
> Compos'd as then, few Men, and many Beasts.

Here and elsewhere, one is better off with the original commentary, rather than Professor Partridge's truncated transcription of it.

In literary matters, Professor Partridge's book is sadly adrift. From Donne's 'The Anagram', he extracts the following message: 'Content yourself with a homely woman, if she has no physical handicaps.' Actually, Donne's poem is a steady crescendo of insult ('though seaven yeares, she in the Stews had laid / A Nunnery durst receive, and thinke a maid') but Professor Partridge is impervious to its irony. Likewise, his misinterpretation of the *Nocturnall upon S. Lucies Day* is a collector's item of perversity. Not for the Professor a lament for a dead woman, rather an allegorical account of Donne's spiritual autobiography, his turn from flesh to the spirit. Equally entertaining is the criticalese: 'many phrases, such as *much deare treasure* (33), acquire a metonymic significance that engrosses the mind through aptness and intellectual fecundity.' Again, Milgate's notes solve the problem of Professor Partridge's exposition. He means that 'much deare treasure' alludes to Matthew 6:20.

Finally, two gems: 'rhythmical thinking' and 'thought-generated tropes'. As opposed to oil-fired tropes, presumably?

Ben Jonson: Dramatist

'It is such a comfort to meet a man and not have to tell him to wash his face, wipe his feet, and remember the date (1914) on the calendar', Ezra Pound wrote of Eliot. Jonson was another poet whose special gifts were called forth by the contemporary. On the flyleaf of the British Museum's Quarto version of *Volpone*, the handwriting of Jonson's dedication to Florio is, typically, not in the Secretary, but in the more up-to-date Italian hand. Coleridge claimed that 'there is not one whim or affectation in common life noted in any memoir of that age which may not be found drawn and framed in Jonson's dramas.'

But Jonson's kinship is not simply to the tradition of artistic, documentary journalism – Hogarth and Rowlandson, Daumier's London and Meryon's Paris. He is also the pioneer of the bizarre, racy, and often grotesque urban poetry of modern life. He begins a line which continues through Pope's *Dunciad* to Baudelaire's *Fleurs du Mal* and the Eliot of 'Gerontion' and *Sweeney Agonistes*. Compare Jonson's

> With all your Broathes, your *Menstrues*, and *Materialls*
> Of Pisse and Egge-shells, Womens termes, Mans blood,
> Hayre o' the head, burnt Cloutes, Chalke, Merds, and Clay

with the sick beauty of 'Gerontion' – 'Rocks, moss, stonecrop, iron, merds'. Both are great poets of decadence, poets of the city, the antithesis of pastoral. And between them is Baudelaire who wrote, 'The pageant of fashionable life and the thousands of floating existences – criminals and kept women – which drift about in the underworld of a great city; the *Gazette des Tribunaux* and *Le Moniteur* all prove to us that we have only to open our eyes to recognize our heroism . . . a new and special beauty, which is neither that of Achilles nor yet that of Agamemnon.'

This paradox of the brutally beautiful (though we find it everywhere in 'The Windhover') will always be slighted by the well-bred. Dryden, for example, chose *Epicoene* as Jonson's best play for its skilful plot, clever dénouement and, most importantly, for 'the conversation of gentlemen'. In other words, because it was most readily assimilable to the dominant upper-class *ton* of Restoration drama, where bawdy acquits itself with decorous language. In fact, *Epicoene* – essentially a dramatic *imitation* of Juvenal's Sixth Satire upon women – lacks the genuinely contemporary low-life material which, elsewhere, stimulates Jonson's singular poetic gifts. We are conscious, therefore, that *Epicoene* is merely elegant prose, whereas the prose of *Bartholomew Fair* often deceives us with its quasi-poetic richness of imagery – asked how the pigs are cooking, Mooncalf replies, 'Very passionate, mistress, one on 'em has wept out an eye.' This, and the differentiated argots of Knockem, Whit, Ursula and even Zeal remind us of the poetic prodigality of Synge's Irish.

The Alchemist and *Volpone*, on the other hand, are almost wholly written in a flexible blank verse which has all the fluency of prose. Few readers are aware that the opening exchange between Face and Subtle in *The Alchemist* is a decasyllabic line:

FACE: Believe't, I will.
SUBTLE: Thy worst. I fart at thee.

When Shakespeare creates contemporary scenes, he usually confines himself to (brilliant) prose, but Jonson's elastic line was the triumphant technical instrument which enabled him to bring the contemporary into poetry and to express his vision of modern decadence.

It is this vision which led Jonson, in the Folio version of *Every Man in his Humour*, to change the locale from Florence to London. It accounts for the attenuation of the overt moral strain in his later work; Jonson's perspective becomes too comprehensive, horrified and *historical* to be satisfied by trite individual penances. He has seen, in Eliot's phrase, 'the boredom, and the horror, and the glory'. The horror finds emblematic expression in the puppet show of *Bartholomew Fair*, where the present is shown in ironic relation to the past. The great love story of Hero and Leander, in a modernized degenerate form, mirrors the action of the play. Hero is a whore, Leander is a 'dyer's son' who shares her favours with two whoremasters, Damon and Pythias. Cupid is a publican, so that alcohol, not sentiment, provokes not love, but lust. 'Modern for the times, sir, that's all', its author remarks. 'I'll be allied to them presently', Cokes replies – and he is. His fiancée, Grace, is Hero to his Leander, while Quarlous and Winwife enact the quarrelsome roles of Damon and Pythias (in ancient times the by-word for friendship). And, in the sub-plot, Leander–Littlewit's wife, Hero–Win, is made drunk by Cupid–Ursula, and procured for prostitution by the bawds, Whit and Knockem, vying like Damon and Pythias.

In *Volpone* a similar device exposes the poverty of modern wisdom, where the song of Androgyno describes the progress of Pythagoras's soul from Apollo, through whores and animals, to its present lodgement in an hermaphrodite, 'When wit shall wait upon the Fool'. Again, the emblem reflects the action: in the seduction scene, for example, Volpone's voluptuous fantasies chart the progress of 'our wandering souls' in terms of metempsychosis. It is hardly progress. When he and Celia have 'weary'd all the fables of the Gods', they reach 'more modern formes', namely 'our most artefull Curtezans'. Equally, Jonson's use of Aesop and the animal names fit well with the idea of transmigration. In *The Alchemist*, it is the ideal of the Golden Age which stands in ironic contrast to the scramble for gold to finance depravity.

Jonson's moral 'horror' is, however, tempered by his feeling for the 'glory'. It is, of course, a queer glory, but less strange if we compare it to *Ulysses*. Jonson glories in bodily functions as much as Joyce. In the same way Jonson identifies with his con-men: Mosca, Volpone, Subtle, Face and Brainworm are all pseudo-dramatists, playing roles and directing the action. Co-existing with a Juvenalian misanthropy is a humane Chaucerian acceptance, and it is from this polarity that Jonson's greatest poetry springs. Finally, the aloof poet is matched by the (necessarily) embroiled dramatist.

In a less abstract sense, the controlled invention of Jonson's stagecraft equals that of his language. One thinks of Corbaccio's deafness, of anticipatory character delineation, of the resourceful way Jonson reserves fresh characters (like Kastril and Dame Pliant) until the third act, of the integrated sub-plots. (Even *Every Man In* balances the abuse of Kitely's house by Wellbred with the abuse of Cob's by Bobadill.) Then there are the brilliant openings – the masked narrative exposition of *The Alchemist*, and the Induction of *Bartholomew Fair* which disarms, by anticipation, the potential criticisms of the groundlings *and* the wits. Consider, too, how well Face and Subtle are balanced: Face bamboozles Dapper and Drugger, while Subtle is passive, secondary. Yet Face abdicates when Subtle is snarling at the Puritans or cringing piously with Sir Epicure.

The clumsy exception is *Every Man in his Humour* where soliloquy dominates and the dialogue often reads like concurrent soliloquies (reminding one of Jonson's tedious man in *Timber* – 'I spake to him of *Garlicke*, hee answered Asparagus'). In this apprentice work there is no *liaison des scènes*; two characters, or one, enter the empty stage, talk and exit. Stephen and Bobadill are insufficiently distinguished and together they foreshadow the silly vapours scene of *Bartholomew Fair*. Knowell's moralizing soliloquies (taken from Juvenal) are irrelevant to the action and recall, as Dryden said, 'the tedious visits of bad company'.

But after this play, the theory of humours ceases to confine Jonson. The characters of Jonson's maturity are real people, not humours, and they live in a real world. Jonson suggests the teeming life behind the flats: in *The Alchemist*, there are characters we never see – the 'good wives', the fish-wife, the 'Baud of

Lambeth'. And the gulls, Dapper and Drugger, have off-stage biographies. Just as Wasp remembers Overdo when he was 'Adam Scrivener, and writ for twopence a sheet', so Dapper's world is one where, to keep up appearances, a watch is lent to one who dines with the sheriff. He consorts with the small poets, reads Ovid, is bored by his job, while the poor hypochondriac, Drugger, tells his ailments to a yawning audience with a poignantly simple-minded egotism. Drugger's 'peece of fat Ram-Mutton' is as vividly particular as anything in Dickens. In *Volpone*, Corvino's 'and no pleasure, / That thou shalt know, but backwards' suggests familiarity with physical degradation which is quite absent from Kitely's stagey presence. Corvino is more real to us than Webster's Duke Ferdinand or Browning's Franceschini because Jonson *domesticates* the glittering world of Italian revenge tragedy. Corvino's rococo rantipole is the more terrible for the sweetly wheedling jocularity which varies his attack – but it convinces us primarily because the mountebank speech has provided a context – the squalid reality of sixteenth-century Venice.

Andrew Marvell

Marvell is perhaps the most elusive of English poets – the one who comes nearest to Keats's definition of 'the poetical character itself', as distinguished from 'the Wordsworthian or egotistical sublime'. 'It is not itself – it has no self – it is everything and nothing – It has no character; it enjoys light and shade.' Marvell's poetry accommodates the gracefully imaginative ('Musick, the Mosaique of the Air') and the extrovert, the breezily crude ('See but their *Mairmaids* with their *Tails of Fish* / Reeking at *Church* over the Chafing-Dish' – the description of Dutch women from 'The Character of Holland'). 'Fleckno' is as robust as Browning; 'Tom May's Death' anticipates the gusto of Byron's 'Vision of Judgement'; 'Upon Appleton House' is noteworthy for the panache of its extraordinary inventiveness, while 'The Nymph Complaining' has the enigmatic simplicity of the Petrus Cristus portrait of *einer jungen Frau* in the Dahlem at Berlin. 'The First Anniversary of the Government under O.C.', on the other hand, is ultimately in the Miltonic epic mode. Marvell's politics are equally difficult to pin down: 'Tom May's Death' is royalist; the 'Horation Ode' is a monarchist's tribute to Cromwell; 'The First Anniversary' is a sincere panegyric to Cromwell's vigour and belligerence, whereas 'The Garden' and 'Appleton House' sing peace and retirement.

These things are puzzling only if seen as inconsistencies. Actually, they are the hallmark of flexibility and Marvell's poetry is characterized by the free play of intelligence, a clear-eyed detachment which mediates between conflicting points of view, an unwillingness to dogmatize, an intellectual largesse. In the 1681 Folio there is no 'irritable reaching after fact and reason', as Keats put it. And yet, despite the numerous genres used by Marvell, despite the contrast between, say, the jingoism at the end of the 'Horation Ode' or 'Holland' and the 'easie Philosopher' of 'Appleton House' – despite this, there is something which is recognizably Marvellian throughout. It is a distinctive classic grace, an impersonality which is not lofty, something we may express in a final paradox – it is the conjunction of an intimate tone and impersonal subject matter. Marvell looks forward to Pope and the Augustans. There is no personality, no soul-searching in his verse – and yet we recognize his talking voice.

'The Garden' illustrates Marvell's characteristic balance between playful wit and sober seriousness. It is primarily a poem extolling the virtues of a natural, retired, contemplative life against the active life – as we can see from 'Hortus', the Latin version (essentially an expansive version of the first four stanzas and the last), and from Marvell's translation from Seneca, 'Climb at *Court* for me that will'. Its arguments *qua* arguments are inadequate: the witty surface caricatures and travesties the opposing point of view rather than refutes it. Thus, it concentrates on the self-evident absurdity of choosing 'uncessant labours' rather than repose; natural beauty is, we are informed, superior to female charms; the gods themselves, in reality, were not interested in seducing their mortal loves, but were engineering their metamorphosis; the body (5), the mind (6) and the soul (7) are catered for in the garden which is (8) like Eden before the Fall, indeed, before the possibility of the Fall; finally, there is praise for the gardener's dial which permits us, appropriately because florally, to be conscious of the duration of our enjoyment. Evening has come with its 'milder sun'.

At the same time, there is, beneath this lightness, an *under*statement of the fleeting quality of human existence which stiffens the playful surface. The poem reads as a celebration of the natural world until we are turned back by a single ambiguous line in the final stanza: the bee '*Computes its time* as well as we'. The bee, in other words, calculates its end, its death. Vistas open. The garden loses its particularity and becomes an emblem of the natural world, created by the Gardener, God – compare 'Appleton House's' descriptions of England as 'The Garden of the World'. The 'dial *new*' is the natural world itself after the Fall, a place of cycles, time, growth and decay. Significantly, the dial does not tell the hours, but the months of the zodiac: nature, however justly celebrated, reminds us of our end. Marvell is uniquely the English poet whose temperament could accommodate, *simultaneously*, joy in the 'sweet and wholesome hours' of life and a sober recognition of imminent extinction.

Accordingly, on a second reading the emphases shift. We still respond, of course, to the superficial *élan* which puns on 'upbraid' (plait and chide), and offers a witty pseudo-argument against ambition – namely, if the reward of success is leaves, they are more easily obtained in a garden. But now the *real* argument shows itself in two delicate euphemisms: the 'short and narrow vergèd shade' implies the grave, while the 'garlands of repose' suggest floral tributes. As Marvell says in 'Appleton House', man 'superfluously spread / Demands more room alive then dead'. What price ambition *now*, the poem whispers.

Similarly, Stanza 2 no longer simply establishes a parallel between the garden and Eden because of the common presence of Innocence. It sets a limit to that parallel: 'Your sacred plants, *if* [my italics] here below'. The garden, nature, is only *like* Eden.

Again, Stanza 3 sets the evergreen against the blooming (and fading) white and red. And Marvell's 'How far these beauties hers *exceed!*' implies not only that nature is more beautiful, but also that it will *last longer*.

Stanza 4, too, becomes more than a witty theorem with a whimsical view of Greek mythology offered as 'proof'. Once more, Marvell offers a deft euphemism for death – 'When we have run our passion's heat' – and follows it with the inevitable corollary that we will return to the earth, the organic world. The gods become, not lovers, but bleakly emblematic hunters – 'The gods, that *mortal* beauty *chase*' (my italics). Marvell's use of the present tense makes the universal application clear: Daphne and

Syrinx thus become a type of man's progress from beauty to the grave – 'Rolled round in earth's diurnal course / With rocks and stones and trees'.

Stanza 5, ostensibly a straightforward and superb celebration of the natural world, ends with a reminder of the Fall and its consequence – that all flesh is grass. Likewise 6 celebrates the satisfactions of contemplation, the pleasures of imagination. In the official poem, the last two lines – 'Annihilating all that's made / To a green thought in a green shade' – are an epigrammatic summation and repetition of the first six, namely, the power of the mind to contain within itself all matter. The under-argument insists, however, that these lines *advance* the argument. Thus, the mind (like Pliny's ocean) reflects, and therefore contains, the natural world. Moreover, it can imaginatively create transcendent, extra-mundane worlds which relegate the world of nature ('all that's made') to the status of 'a green thought in a green shade'. In other words, the soul is bound elsewhere, and the material aspect will be *annihilated* – the word assumes its full power. Stanza 7 continues this line of thought: the body is cast aside, and the soul prepares for its longer 'flight' to heaven.

In Stanza 8, there is, on the one hand, the flippant witty misogyny which states that Paradise without a wife is equivalent to two Paradises. But, on the other hand, there is the under-argument which draws together the debate about post-lapsarian nature – viz. if Adam and man had not been betrayed by Eve, man would indeed have had the choice of two Paradises, the heavenly and the earthly. And this is the view advanced by Milton in *Paradise Lost* V (Raphael *loq*.):

> Your bodies may at last turn all to spirit,
> Improv'd by tract of time, and wing'd ascend
> Ethereal, as wee, or may at choice
> Here or in Heav'nly Paradises dwell'.

As it is, Marvell argues, man is fallen, must die and leave the earthly Paradise: ''twas beyond a *mortal's* share' (my italics). Ultimately, it is this underlying theme of mortality which brings an argued coherence to what might otherwise degenerate into a witty riff of impromptus.

The Garden

1
How vainly men themselves amaze
To win the palm, the oak, or bays,
And their uncessant labours see
Crowned from some single herb or tree,
Whose short and narrow vergèd shade
Does prudently their toils upbraid,
While all flow'rs and all trees do close
To weave the garlands of repose.

2
Fair Quiet, have I found thee here,
And Innocence, thy sister dear!
Mistaken long, I sought you then
In busy companies of men.
Your sacred plants, if here below,
Only among the plants will grow.
Society is all but rude,
To this delicious solitude.

3
No white nor red was ever seen
So am'rous as this lovely green.
Fond lovers, cruel as their flame,
Cut in these trees their mistress' name.
Little, alas, they know, or heed,
How far these beauties hers exceed!
Fair trees! wheres'e'er your barks I wound,
No name shall but your own be found.

4

When we have run our passion's heat,
Love hither makes his best retreat.
The gods, that mortal beauty chase,
Still in a tree did end their race.
Apollo hunted Daphne so,
Only that she might laurel grow.
And Pan did after Syrinx speed,
Not as a nymph, but for a reed.

5

What wondrous life is this I lead!
Ripe apples drop about my head;
The luscious clusters of the vine
Upon my mouth do crush their wine;
The nectarene, and curious peach,
Into my hands themselves do reach;
Stumbling on melons, as I pass,
Ensnared with flowers, I fall on grass.

6

Meanwhile the mind, from pleasures less,
Withdraws into its happiness:
The mind, that ocean where each kind
Does straight its own resemblance find,
Yet it creates, transcending these,
Far other worlds, and other seas,
Annihilating all that's made
To a green thought in a green shade.

7

Here at the fountain's sliding foot,
Or at some fruit-tree's mossy root,
Casting the body's vest aside,
My soul into the boughs does glide:
There like a bird it sits, and sings,
Then whets, and combs its silver wings;

And, till prepared for longer flight,
Waves in its plumes the various light.

8

Such was that happy garden-state,
While man there walked without a mate:
After a place so pure, and sweet,
What other help could yet be meet!
But 'twas beyond a mortal's share
To wander solitary there:
Two paradises 'twere in one
To live in paradise alone.

9

How well the skilful gardener drew
Of flowers and herbs this dial new,
Where from above the milder sun
Does through a fragrant zodiac run;
And, as it works, the industrious bee
Computes its time as well as we.
How could such sweet and wholesome hours
Be reckoned but with herbs and flowers!

Dr Johnson

The trouble with new books about Johnson's life is that they are never new. Inevitably, much information is retailed secondhand from Boswell and Mrs Thrale, and though Margaret Lane* enterprisingly supplements these sources with the biography of John Hawkins (a less famous friend of Johnson), the anecdotes are wearing a little thin by now. There is, one concludes, a limit to how often it is possible to turn Johnson's choler. Miss Lane's window display – her well-chosen and beautifully reproduced illustrations, her clean style – is professional but unpersuasive. We have seen the goods before. Johnson stands, like Stephen Dedalus, in 'new secondhand clothes', selling at a new price of £6.95.

This is scarcely a matter for blame, but it does mean that originality is only possible in two areas. One is the period background which Boswell took for granted; the other might be a reassessment of Johnson's literary reputation. Margaret Lane chooses the former and, on the whole, her deployment of historical records is more novel than the familiar sound of His Master's Voice. The exact procedure for being touched for the King's Evil, the disposal of night soil, a Grub Street poet naked in bed with his writing hand poking through a hole in his blanket, foxes raiding the coops in the environs of Cavendish Square, right of way in London streets – these are some of the interesting facts she includes. There is only one grumble. Her book is aimed at a

*Samuel Johnson and his World by Margaret Lane, Hamish Hamilton.

non-specialist market and, reasonably enough, avoids a fussy spattering of dates – except that it betrays her into a chronological ambiguity. In her brief, sociological commentary on Johnson's 'London' (1738), she refers to the Mohocks as a threat to law-abiding citizens after dark. In fact, the Mohocks (a club of upper-class thugs) flourished in 1711–12, as we know from Swift's *Journal to Stella*: 'Did I tell you of a race of Rakes calld the Mohacks that play the devil about this Town every night, slitt peoples noses, & beat them &c.' The arrests which Swift reports two days later suggest that they were unlikely to be on the rampage in 1738.

Apart from this solitary slip, Miss Lane is excellent on the background. Her comments on Johnson's literary output, on the other hand, are sound but cursory. One could hardly call her an enthusiast, and yet her sensible brevity is perhaps preferable to Christopher Ricks's desperate attempt to transplant an Empsonian heart into Johnson's poetry (*New Statesman*, 6 August 1965). Margaret Lane, as it were, confines herself to taking its temperature, whereas Professor Ricks puts it in traction after claiming extraordinary acrobatic feats for it. Poetry Johnson? Among the many epithets retailed by Boswell – 'DICTIONARY JOHNSON', 'that great CHAM of literature', 'Pomposo', 'Rambler Johnson', '*Jean Bull Philosophe*', 'the Caliban of literature', 'the Demonax of the present Age', 'Oddity Johnson' – *Poetry* is the notable absentee. One might stop there, exclaiming with Johnson, 'Nay, Sir, if you will not take the universal opinion of mankind, I have nothing to say' – were it not that posterity has singled out five poems of commendation: 'The Vanity of Human Wishes', 'London', 'On the Death of Dr Robert Levet', 'A Short Song of Congratulation' and the Drury Lane 'Prologue'. It is a short list by any standards.

Accordingly, Professor Ricks set out to add to it, promoting inferior poems like 'An Epitaph on Claudy Phillips, A Musician', and divining a series of 'tacit metaphors'. His starting point with the Phillips epitaph was a Dr Wilkes's attempt which the competitive Johnson capped when Garrick quoted it approvingly. Wilkes's version began:

> Exalted soul! whose harmony could please
> The love-sick virgin, and the gouty ease.

Johnson, to any normal eye, *eliminated* this 'clumsy mention of the gout':

> Phillips! whose touch harmonious could remove
> The pangs of guilty pow'r, and hapless love,
> Rest here distress'd by poverty no more,
> Find here that calm, thou gav'st so oft before.
> Sleep, undisturb'd, within this peaceful shrine,
> Till angels wake thee, with a note like thine.

Professor Ricks, however, thinks that 'Johnson subdued the metaphor gracefully . . . "Touch" widens out from the musician's fingers to suggest those of a doctor who can remove "pangs" and (in the next lines) can give calm and an undisturbed sleep.' It is a curiously instructive piece of criticism, a dazzling mantle cast over humble verses for an itinerant violinist. Let us unpick the Professor's natty stitching, the texture of nimbly worked association.

The naked lesson is that Johnson's poetry will not respond to Empsonian techniques. There is no proof that Johnson was subduing his predecessor's obtrusive professionalism. But grant the point, then Professor Ricks, in the process of unsubduing Johnson's metaphor, plunges the reader into just that indecorum which Johnson (according to this reading) was seeking to avoid in an epitaph. That is, Professor Ricks seems unaware of the implications of deciding that Phillips is a doctor as well as a violinist. The train of association set up cannot be halted until it reaches the terminus: grant a *doctor*, what then are the pangs of hapless love? Obviously, they correspond to Wilkes's 'love-sick virgin', but according to the logic of Professor Ricks's medical metaphor, they must now be read as a euphemistic periphrasis for the clap. Unlucky, even hapless. The epitaph takes on burlesque features unintended by Johnson.

It is just this kind of inadvertent association that Johnsonian theory was designed to eliminate: 'words being arbitrary must owe their power to association, and have their influence, and that only, which custom has given them ... the most heroick sentiments will lose their efficacy, and the most splendid ideas drop their magnificence, if they are conveyed by words used commonly upon low and trivial occasions, debased by vulgar mouths, and contaminated by inelegant applications' ('Abraham Cowley'). Johnson, then, was sensitive to association as a danger, not as a virtue, and accordingly chose a diction which ruled out words with a spin-off into the indecorous: 'limpid streams', 'verdant meads', 'flow'ry vales', 'the balmy Blessings of Repose', 'crystal rill', 'verdant hill' and 'the Steeps of Fate' are represent-atively adventurous samples from a vocabulary whose asso-ciations are strictly limited to polite literature.

Professor Ricks is equally quick to exploit the chance verbal echo of being *touched* for the King's Evil: 'The associations of "touch" even reach to the healing power of the sovereign (Johnson had been touched as a child for the King's Evil), which impinges beautifully on the dour fact of Phillips' lowly poverty.' The word *sovereign*, of course, is never used in the epitaph, and (as Margaret Lane points out) Queen Anne lost her touch in Johnson's case – his neck had to be lanced while he played with a custard, leaving him with scars visible on his death mask. If biographical facts are to be employed in exegesis, they should be used *in full*. Moreover, this method of biographical association should be 'good' for other apparently innocuous poems.

Let us apply the same method to 'Miss Hickman playing on the Spinet':

> Bright Stella, form'd for universal *Reign*,
> Too well You know to keep the *Slaves* You gain.
> When in Your Eyes resistless Lightnings play,
> *Aw'd into Love, our conquer'd hearts obey,*
> And *yield*, reluctant, to *despotick* Sway.
> But when your Musick sooths the raging pain,
> We bid propitious Heav'n prolong your reign,
> *We bless the Tyrant, and we hug the Chain.* (my italics)

Music again, and another anthology of clichés, it seems. We remember Johnson on Ogilvie's poems: 'And his diction too is not his own. We have long ago seen *white-robed innocence*, and *flower-bespangled meads*.' On the other hand, consider Johnson's padlock, sold at Manchester in 1823; the entry in his diary for 24 March 1771, 'De pedicis et manicis insana cogitatio' (insane thoughts of fetters and manacles); his letter in French to Mrs Thrale, 'Je souhaite, ma patronne, que votre autorité me soit toujours sensible, et que vous me tenez dans l'esclavage que vous savez si bien rendre heureuse'; Mrs Thrale's diary for May 1799, 'I have been more to him for Intimacy, than ever was any Man's Valet de Chambre'; and her marginalia, 'but the Fetters and Padlocks will tell Posterity the Truth'. Add to these her further remark (not quoted by Margaret Lane who soft peddles the question of masochism) apropos Johnson's conviction that a young woman had such power she might 'tye a Man to a post and whip him if she will' – 'This he knew of him self was *literally* and *strictly* true I am sure.' All these pointers towards a sad erotic masochism in Johnson could be used to give body to the half-starved diction of 'We hug the Chain' and the other italicized phrases.

Johnson's comment on such Ricksian innovation remains applicable: 'Truth will not afford sufficient food to their vanity; so they have betaken themselves to error. Truth, Sir, is a cow which will yield such people no more milk, and so they are gone to milk the bull.'

What of Johnson's major poetry? The consensus is that Johnson must be judged according to Augustan theory. As he himself said, and Eliot echoed, 'To judge rightly of an author, we must transport ourselves to his time, and examine what were the wants of his contemporaries, and what were his means of supplying them' ('John Dryden'). Nevertheless, Johnson would not have agreed with Virginia Woolf that progress in the arts is circular rather than forwards. He believed, for example, that Dryden had refined our numbers. In other words, Johnson's own theory allowed for the idea of improvement – logically, this should apply to his own narrow ideas. Even when we have allowed for Augustan theory, the *tout comprendre* does not entail *tout pardonner*. As Johnson remarked of Warton's poetry, when Boswell protested that its idiosyncrasies were rooted in his knowledge of Old English, 'What is that to the purpose, Sir? If I say a man is drunk, and you tell me it is owing to his taking much drink, the matter is not mended.'

The fact is that Johnson's theory of poetry was inadequate. Unlike Eliot, who employs the Johnsonian manner so effectively in 'The Function of Criticism' ('and the name I suggest is Whiggery'), and whose notorious self-portrait ('a classicist in literature, a royalist in politics, and an Anglo-Catholic in religion') describes Johnson so well as to suggest conscious emulation, Johnson's criticism was not the by-product of his poetry workshop. Rather the reverse. Propriety, poetic diction, no oddities of thought or diction, generalities and moral purpose are some of the deadening rules laid down by the magisterial Johnson. On the whole, his poetry is best when he plays truant from them.

Take the poem on Levet, who emerges from Margaret Lane's book (like many other minor characters usually elbowed to one side by Johnson) as an interestingly unfortunate man. Most of it is blandly conventional – 'Condemn'd to hope's delusive mine', 'In misery's darkest caverns known', 'where hopeless anguish pour'd his groan', 'Death broke at once the vital Chain'. The good moments violate his own criterion of rigorous generality ('This business of a poet is to examine, not the individual, but the species; to remark general properties and large appearances. He does not number the streaks of the tulip . . .'):

> Yet still he fills affection's eye,
> Obscurely wise, and coarsely kind . . .

With the two last words, the truth, idiosyncratic and exact, pops out. There are aphids on Levet's tulip. And we are encouraged to place more trust in the play on welling tears and the inward eye of memory in the preceding line. Equally, the play on 'talent' (with a biblical allusion) later in the elegy, has an implicit quality not often seen in Johnson.

The rest is humdrum, like his notes for a number of the *Rambler*, which remind one of the tired Bloomonologue of *Eumaeus*: 'Hope predom. in youth. Mind not unwillingly indulges unpleasing thoughts. The world lies all enamelled before him, as a distant prospect sun-gilt.' ('To vary the time-honoured adage', as Joyce ironically puts it.) How much less interesting are these cracker-barrel aphorisms than even Johnson's microscopic notations from his Paris diary: 'Rhinoceros, the horn broken and pared away, which, I suppose, will grow; the basis, I think, four inches 'cross; the skin folds like loose cloth doubled over his body, & cross his hips . . . Among the birds was a pelican, who being let out, went to a fountain, & swam about to catch fish. His feet well-webbed: he dipped his head, & turned his long bill sideways.' In themselves, these quirky entries refute Johnson's notion in the *Lives* that 'we are perpetually moralists' and his complaint that innovators 'seem to think, that we are placed here to watch the growth of plants, or the motions of the stars. Socrates was rather of the opinion, that what we had to learn was, how to do good, and avoid evil' ('John Milton'). Poetry needs pelicans as much as it needs moral texts. In the same way, Boswell's dutiful encomiums bore us, whereas his picture of Johnson swinging absent-mindedly on a gate, absorbed in the *Mémoires de Fontenelle*, is queer and touching in its particularity.

Too much of Johnson's poetry is moral aphorism in a vacuum, where the images and metaphors are ornaments to the truth rather than the embodiments of its living substance. This emphasis on moral guidance is inherited by Arnold: 'it is important, therefore, to hold fast to this: that poetry is at bottom a criticism of life; that the greatness of a poet lies in his powerful and beautiful application of ideas to life – to the question: How to live.' Arnold is more sophisticated than Johnson, but his touchstones reveal a similar belief, at bottom, that moral nuggets can be prised out of their context. In fact, they can not, and a touchstone like 'Ripeness is all' depends heavily upon its context – Edgar's immediately consecutive imperative, 'Come on', and Gloucester's reply, 'And that's true too', ground the aphorism in ordinary reality. Neither Johnson nor Arnold would have appreciated this sufficiently, abstracters both.

It is not that one would wish, whimsically, to prefer Johnson's poetic 'frisks' (like the poem on Mrs Thrale's thirty-fifth birthday) to the major work. But the merits and demerits of the latter must be precisely delineated. Unlike Johnson's conversation, with its homely illustrations, his poetry is fatally abstract. We cannot accept Dr Leavis's testimony that, for example, in lines 143–56 of 'The Vanity of Human Wishes', 'the style is remarkable for body', and that 'abstractness here doesn't exclude concreteness':

> Yet should thy Soul indulge the gen'rous Heat,
> Till captive Science yields her last Retreat;
> Should Reason guide thee with her brightest Ray,
> And pour on misty Doubt resistless Day;
> Should no false Kindness lure to loose Delight,
> Nor Praise relax, nor Difficulty fright;
> Should tempting Novelty thy Cell refrain,
> And Sloth effuse her opiate Fumes in vain;
> Should Beauty blunt on Fops her fatal Dart,
> Nor claim the Triumph of a letter'd Heart;
> Should no Disease thy torpid Veins invade,
> Nor Melancholy's Phantoms haunt thy Shade;
> Yet hope not Life from Grief or Danger free,
> Nor think the Doom of Man revers'd for thee!

It is difficult to see how Dr Leavis has persuaded himself that these abstractions ('Science', 'Reason', 'Doubt', 'Kindness', 'Novelty', 'Sloth' etc.) are also concrete. What gives them 'body' except his say-so? Each example in the catalogue – from 'resistless Day' to 'Melancholy's Phantoms' – is characterized by the nullest diction and metaphor. Concrete? Johnson, too, once complained that 'he was sometimes so languid and inefficient, that he could not distinguish the hour upon the town-clock'.

The passage's power, such as it is, works (capturing some of the calm thoroughness of Johnson's pessimism in *Rasselas*) through the sustained cadenza of the syntax – which moves with perfect clarity from couplet to couplet, until the resolution of the subjunctive mood comes to release our response. The 'should's pile up, then comes

> Yet hope not Life from Grief or Danger free,
> Nor think the Doom of Man revers'd for thee!

The mastery here is that of a great prose writer – as Dr Leavis rightly insists, while producing the oddest reason for his belief.

For a poet (*pace* Professor Ricks), Johnson's ear was too crude. The evidence need not confine itself to his dimness when he tackles Cowley's metrical innovations, or his disturbing failure to distinguish between Donne and Cleveland. The proof is there in his own verse: 'Nor whilst she Simons acts persues', 'Yet still one gen'ral Cry the Skies assails'. One recalls Tennyson's mordant phonetic rendering of the opening lines of *The Rape of the Lock*: ' "Amrus causiz springs", horrible! I would sooner die than write such a line!!'

Eighteenth-century Poetry

In 'Burnt Norton', T. S. Eliot tells us that 'human kind / Cannot bear very much reality'. You could say the same thing about eighteenth-century verse with more justice. The Augustans could bear much more propriety than now seems tolerable. They were easily shocked by breaches of decorum: Dr Johnson commenting on Shakespeare's *King John* picked out the line, 'The earth that serves as paste and cover to our bones', and noted, 'an image not of the most sublime kind – taken from a *pie*'. The nose-wrinkling italics are, it seems, typical of the period. It was the same great arbiter of taste who, in his life of Cowley, argued the need for a poetic diction.

Poetic diction, of course, is always with us. At any period, there is always the temptation to back-slide, to take off the bicycle clips only in order to put on a pair of spats. We all like the patina of easy association that comes with the slightly antique. A single word like 'upon', which long ago vanished from ordinary conversation, will provide a bogus afflatus: take, for instance, Geoffrey Hill's 'Ovid in the Third Reich'. Whereas most of us look down on people, Hill's speaker has learned 'one thing: not to look down / So much upon the damned'. The word may be historically appropriate and authenticated by props as the perfect choice for Ovid (43 BC–AD 18) in the Third Reich (1933–45). It is certainly dated – as is Hill's line 'The body is but husk and excrement' which deploys the Yeatsian 'but' for 'only' like the sob in a pub tenor's top note. Geoffrey Grigson is another poet with a weakness for easy saloon bar effects:

> And I say 'Oh, if you had elected to stay, had
> Elected to stay' – liking that form of my words –

Perhaps the woman in question decided to go because Grigson's golden treasury couldn't keep her in the style to which she was accustomed. 'You ought to be ashamed, I said, to look so antique.' There is, too, another kind of poetic diction, which is less archaic but just as unsatisfactory – a kind of legospeak in which sunsets are invariably 'raw' and blackbirds inevitably 'scold'. Both kinds of poetry gratify the reader instantly since they do not require us to think. They appeal to a conditioned reflex.

The eighteenth century, though, is different because it had a theory which was responsible for producing what Arnold called a 'provincial and second-rate' literature. The great strength of Roger Lonsdale's massive anthology* is that it complicates Arnold's flat verdict. Lonsdale has read far more poetry of the period than anyone ever – including Arnold – and about a quarter of his contents have never been reprinted since their first publication. Like the historians Christopher Hill and E. P. Thompson, he has rediscovered the anonymous mass, both the literally 'anon' and the effectively anon. And the results are equally surprising to those of us who can imagine Dr Johnson turning away with disgust from Philip Larkin's 'awful pie' – his literary taste offended, rather than his taste buds.

In this anthology there are poems about bricklaying, hypnotism, cricket, billiards, tennis, golf, shrimps, workhouses, iron foundries, constipation, urban pollution, landladies, air balloons, a louse, laudanum, elopement, compost, kites, gin, homosexuality, boxing, rope-dancing, bowls, eels, tortoises, giving up smoking, lavatories at sea. In summary, thus, it looks as if we were mistaken about the eighteenth century. The list appears surprisingly modern and it would be possible, like James Fenton, to quote a genuinely maverick poem like Swift's 'The Humble Petition of Frances Harris', with its easy colloquial brogue, and claim that modern poetry began in 1701. A line like 'However,

---

*The New Oxford Book of Eighteenth Century Verse edited by Roger Lonsdale, Oxford University Press.

she stole away my garters, that I might do myself no harm', you could argue, anticipates the second half of Eliot's 'A Game of Chess' and the brilliantly recorded demotic of 'It's them pills I took, to bring it off, she said.' However, it would be wrong. Roger Lonsdale, to his credit, makes no such claim. Considering the appeal of those poets who emerged in the 1780s, he acknowledges that their new qualities of realism implicitly downgrade their forerunners: 'we may have to concede, in fact, that emotional and stylistic inhibitions are what continue to strike many readers most forcibly about the verse of the earlier period.'

Actually, the emotional inhibition is created by the stylistic prohibition: diction drives out experience. Consider Hetty Wright, a newcomer previously excluded by David Nichol Smith, Dr Lonsdale's predecessor. She was, we learn, unhappily married. For this, we must thank the notes. Her poem on the subject, 'Wedlock. A Satire', is about as personal as a policeman's courtroom testimony. It proceeds in an orderly manner from couplet to couplet, from cliché to cliché: marriage is 'Eternal foe to soft desires, / Inflamer of forbidden fires . . .' Her other poem, 'To an Infant Expiring the Second Day of its Birth', is also, I assume, based on personal experience and potentially affecting. In the event, though, the tiny corpse and any reality it might have had are buried by the diction:

> Tender softness, infant mild,
> Perfect, purest, brightest child;
> Transient lustre, beauteous clay,
> Smiling wonder of a day.

These melodious door chimes echo pleasantly in the brain but are answered by the paediatrician in us – who points out that babies do not smile for four weeks.

Mrs Wright is followed by John Dyer, whose 'Grongar Hill' graphically illustrates the difficulty of early eighteenth-century verse, particularly with real names. The poets themselves were clearly bothered: given the body of Augustan verse, as lifeless and bloodless as a marble effigy, a real name is as embarrassing as a kidney transplant. Hence the profusion of Clios, Chloes, Celias and Sapphos. Dyer prepares the ground, 'painting fair the form of things' with assiduous cultivation. We see 'the purple ev'ning', hear the 'yellow linnet' and 'the tuneful nightingale', see 'Phoebus riding high' – only to encounter the name 'Grongar' with the painful surprise of a parent standing on a bit of sticklebrick in the middle of the night. Thomas Tickell has much the same problem in his elegy for Addison, when he also attempts to encompass the death of Craggs:

> These works divine, which, on his deathbed laid,
> To thee, O Craggs, th' expiring sage conveyed . . .

It is one thing to purify the dialect of the tribe and quite another to pasteurize, homogenize and process it to the point where the language is so dead that sheep, say, cannot be mentioned without bringing a blush to the reader's cheek, and become in James Thomson 'the bleating kind'. Thomson is so mannered ('ruddy fire', 'beaming tapers', 'cheerless gloom', 'bellying clouds') that one responds with real shock when he isn't on automatic pilot: 'The foodless wilds / Pour forth their brown inhabitants . . .' You wouldn't normally notice an adjective like 'brown', but you do in this context.

Clearly, the writers themselves were uneasy with these restrictions. At the same time, they could never quite escape the prevailing neo-classical mode. Dialect poems alone escape the gen'ral doom – including an excellent and well-found transcription of Geordie, as well as Burns, of course. That list of 'modern' subjects proves to be less contemporary when you consider the poems. 'The Bricklayer's Labours', for instance, may look promising in prospect, but it turns out to differ from the prevailing norm as one test-card differs from another:

> At length the soft nocturnal minutes fly,
> And crimson blushes paint the orient sky;
> When, by a kind of drowsy stretch and yawn,
> I ope my eyes, and view the scarlet dawn . . .

Obviously, this bricklayer is about as typical as the Monty Python lumberjack. Mary Collier's washerwoman, too, is absurdly genteel for the job: 'At length bright Sol illuminates the skies, / And summons drowsy mortals to arise.' Perhaps she 'did' for Mr Pope.

When these writers take on the ordinary and the unpoetic, they hardly ever do it straightforwardly. It's either Sunday best or laboured mock-heroic, itself an admission of uneasiness, as in the poem on golf:

> A mighty blow Pygmalion then lets fall;
> Straight from th' impulsive engine starts the ball . . .

Thomas Mathison, the author, knew about golf clubs. He mentions them a couple of lines later, but he can only do so by appealing to the alternative decorum of the mock-heroic. If golf is beneath the Miltonic heroic mode, then the writer turns instead to the example of Pope. The same thing is true of the verses on bowls, billiards and those other promising subjects. The quotidian is assimilated to the given style, rather like a television set encased in a rosewood pseudo-Corinthian cabinet.

Eliot blamed the badness of so much eighteenth-century verse on Milton: 'he certainly did more harm than Dryden or Pope.' Remembering that washerwoman, I'm not so sure. The problem for the average writer then was not just the theory of poetic diction, but what produced it – the presence of major writers who had invented their own styles. Things are not so very different now. A genuinely representative anthology of twentieth-century poetry would probably demonstrate the deleterious effect of Eliot and Auden and Hughes. Nothing is harder than to invent a style. Nothing is easier, or more popular among readers, than to copy it. Eventually, of course, the great figures stand out alone, as they do in this anthology, but for a time at least (to adapt Auden) they 'become their admirers'. One of the heartening aspects of this anthology is that, over a century, one can see this process in action and then the inevitable reaction – a reaction Roger Lonsdale admirably illustrates by his inclusion of parodies. One

in particular is worth singling out, 'Sarah Hazard's Love Letter'.
First we are given the prose 'source': the girl is unmarried and
pregnant, 'therefore Der Charls, cum ashor, and let us be mared
to safe mi vartu, and if yow have no munni, i wil pawn mi new
staies.' A cod note explains that 'the girl's sentiments were much
the same with those of Ovid's heroines, were theirs to be stripped
of poetical decorations'. A poem follows in which the experience
is gift-wrapped:

> Dear object of my love, whose pow'rful charms
> With bliss ecstatic filled my clinging arms!
> That bliss is past; and nought for me remains,
> But foul reproach, and never-pitied pains!

The date of this poem is 1747, three years after the death of
Pope. For a time, thanks to Dr Lonsdale's painstaking and
exemplary editing, we can see parody come into its own. There
are ten parodies in the next hundred pages – not all of them
directed at Pope, but indicative of restlessness. Though there are
few great poets in the mid-century, the general level is higher, or
at any rate, less uniform. Gray and Collins are particularly
interesting to watch as their talent battles against Pope's genius.
Inevitably, they are forced into the margin, especially Collins,
with his regional gothic. Gray's 'Elegy' remains his only successful poem. Elsewhere, his experimentation amounts to little.

Dr Lonsdale has done his work well. We have a slightly
different eighteenth century to come to terms with after his
massive research. None the less, perhaps Arnold was right. There
are a great many dull poems in this anthology and very few
genuine finds among the previously unreprinted work. One might
single out Jonathan Richardson, who is represented here by four
poems about his dead wife. The second poem carries the author's
note, 'Really dreamed, July 14–15, 1726' – and certainly this is
true. The poet dreams of his wife, sees her, but knows it is a
dream. He embraces her just the same and is about to say that her
shade gives him more pleasure than he can get from living
women, when he realizes she will be offended if he admits the

possibility of other women had even crossed his mind. His scruple, in fact, is unnecessary, since he still loves her, but the calculation is convincingly tender towards her feelings, and captures the quirkiness of dreams. In another dream she passes him without acknowledgement. In yet another, they talk to each other in their private pet language. These experiences are sadly arbitrary, but important enough to the writer to tell them straight, without flourishes. They are not great poetry, but they manage to include a little of that reality the eighteenth century found so hard to bear.

John Davidson

Perhaps the best-known fact about John Davidson is T. S. Eliot's testimonial for 'Thirty Bob a Week': 'I am sure that I found inspiration in the content of the poem, and in the complete fitness of content and idiom: for I also had a good many urban images to reveal.' As a result, the nineties poet survives, but survives in sepia, a flash in the pan, the photographer's name, T. S. Eliot, prominently embossed on the print. In Yeats's *Autobiographies*, Davidson appears as a squat, pugnacious Scot on the fringes of the Rhymers' Club. Posterity remembers him – if at all – as the author of one poem, wearing his toupee with smouldering belligerence.

The facts of Davidson's life are as meagre as a life of poverty and literary hack work could make them. Born in 1857, the son of a minister, he abandoned Christianity, dropped out of Edinburgh University, married, fathered, and school-mastered, before pursuing an unsuccessful literary career in London. In 1909, in Penzance, he ordered a large whisky and a cigar at a local hotel – and disappeared. His body was found at sea six months later, with a possible bullet hole through the skull. The coroner's verdict was the non-committal 'Found Dead', but suicide seems the obvious inference. Certainly, no one murdered Davidson for his money. He left an estate of £319.

He left, too, a large body of poetry, now ably edited by Andrew Turnbull, on which, alas, the verdict must also be 'Found Dead'. Davidson is not a great forgotten poet. But the autopsy has a profound interest for the literary historian: Davidson is a linkman, a figure who bridges periods and demonstrates that literary revolutions are not inaugurated overnight – either by Wordsworth or Ezra Pound.

The early poetry is derivative. 'The Rev. Habakkuk McGruther' is Burns's 'Holy Willie' in dilute form. His 'Cheops' is the thinnest alias for Shelley's 'Ozymandias'. He apes Keatsian synaesthesia:

> Subdued almost, our sense can hardly tell
> The music for the odour; it perceives
> A sweetly-scented tune, a sweet-toned smell.

Tennyson's *Idylls* overshadow 'A Ballad of Launcelot'. Morris's more vividly particular medievalism – his minute painterly detail, the anomie of his protagonists, the sarcastic dialogue of 'Sir Peter Harpdon's End' – dominates 'John Baliol at Strathcathro'. Blake stands behind the torturing angels of 'Insomnia'. Even Davidson's *Fleet Street Eclogues* are Arnold's 'The Scholar Gipsy' writ small: the 'strange disease of modern life' finds an antidote in pastoral escapism. The result is strained and utterly improbable, Wordsworth with a lisp:

> BASIL: Oh, little flower so sweet and dear!
> SANDY: Oh, humanest of flowers that grow!
> BRIAN: Oh, little brave adventurer!
>   We human beings love you so!

The subject is a daisy.

If Davidson's stylistic sources are wide and contradictory, his content is no less enigmatically eclectic. On the one hand, there is his counter-decadent Imperialism, his cries of Merrie England and *Lebensraum* – a curried chauvinism which leaves one gasping for the relative coolness of Kipling. On the other hand, Davidson's ballads defend the innocence of man's sexuality and defy heaven and hell, the bogies of organized religion. His scientific, quasi-evolutionary ideas are imaginative, too, even if

the poetic results falter. Consider, for example, his quirky
reflections in 'Snow':

> Once I saw upon an object-glass,
> Martyred underneath a microscope,
> One elaborate snow-flake slowly pass,
> Dying hard, beyond the reach of hope.
> Still from shape to shape the crystal changed,
> Writhing in its agony . . .

Unfortunately, Davidson does not stop there – he never does –
and his real originality comes across best in truncated quotation.
The materialist, metaphysical rationale of 'Snow' (most clearly
expressed in 'The Vivisector') is not *poetically* original, merely
bizarre, as if Arthur C. Clarke were rewritten by Milton: 'the
myriad fibrilled intellect', 'eternity installed in ganglioned tissue'.
In fact, the *echt* in Davidson lies in his ability to locate pathos and
improbable tragedy in the everyday. Its appearances are rare,
momentary and unmistakable. It is in this narrow area that
Davidson anticipates and enables Eliot and modernism.

Stylistically, 'Thirty Bob a Week' is less unusual and accomplished in its grasp of common speech than the bravura Kipling: 'I
cut mine on a leek, which I eat it every week.' Nor is it remarkable
because Davidson gives the anonymous their say – the Leonard
Basts, the Jude Fawleys, the Pooters of modern England. The
poem's extraordinary quality lies in its vision of the unnoticed
heroic tragedy beneath the banal. The *hero* is as commonplace
and as strangely brave as the snowflake:

> It's walking on a string across a gulf
> With millstones fore-and-aft about your neck;
> But the thing is daily done by many and many a one;
> And we fall, face forward, fighting on the deck.

'The thing . . .' marvellously adumbrates the bereft, inarticulate
actuality which is given its eloquent due in the remainder of the

verse. In these lines, the close of 'The Love Song of J. Alfred
Prufrock' is intimated – the romanticism of the unromantic, the
warm bath of words after the assault course of ironies.

The dilemma *par excellence* of the modernist is to unify the prose
and the passion, the squalor of industrial modernity with the lyric
impulse, to reconcile 'Truth and Calliope / Slanging each other
sous les lauriers', as Pound puts it in his exemplary *Cantos*.
Davidson was an early pioneer, and one might add to these
antitheses another from 'Thirty Bob a Week': 'she's made of flint
and roses, very odd.' The vorticists rejected the roses and embraced
the flint: in *Blast*, Wyndham Lewis said of the English, 'they are the
inventors of this bareness and hardness, and should be the great
enemies of Romance'. In a poem like 'Pastoral', William Carlos
Williams is less truculent than Lewis, but just as self-consciously
programmatic in his assertion that 'fences and outhouses'
'smeared a bluish green' are 'of vast import to the nation'.

Eliot and Pound, on the other hand, saw the challenge was to
integrate the flint and the roses. Davidson, among others, showed
the way:

> An unseen roadman breaking flint,
> If echo and the winds conspire
> To dedicate his morning's stint,
> May beat a tune out, dew and fire
> So wrought that heaven might lend an ear,
> And Ariel hush his harp to hear.

One responds to the intention here and ekes out the achievement
with goodwill – ignoring the disastrous closing rhyme of 'ear' and
'hear'. In 'The Isle of Dogs', 'The Thames Embankment',
'London', 'November' and a few other poems, Davidson effects a
makeshift marriage between the ugly and the beautiful:

> Across the viaduct trailing plumes of steam,
> The trains clanked in and out.
> > Slowly the sun
> Undid the homespun swathing of the clouds,

> And splashed his image on the northern shore —
> A thing extravagantly beautiful:
> The glistening, close-grained canvas of the mud
> Like hammered copper shone . . .

'The glistening, close-grained canvas' is genuinely seen; the rest is Gully Jimpson; the unquoted remainder continues more like E. M. Forster's worst exalted passages. Nevertheless, it is an outlook, an attitude — if not ever a vision — which leads to the tender susceptibility of Eliot, the 'inexplicable splendour of Ionian white and gold', the piercing incongruity of 'some infinitely gentle / Infinitely suffering thing' in the midst of modern ugliness. It is also genetically related to the end of 'Mauberley':

> The sleek head emerges
> From the gold-yellow frock
> As Anadyomene in the opening
> Pages of Reinach . . .

> The face-oval beneath the glaze,
> Bright in its suave bounding-line, as
> Beneath half-watt rays,
> The eyes turn topaz.

If Anadyomene and Edison join hands here, it is because Davidson brought them together — clumsily, wordily, prophetically.

Wilfred Owen

Wilfred Owen's tiny corpus is perhaps the most overrated poetry in the twentieth century. There are two reasons for this anomaly: first, the other poetry of the First World War is undistinguished and, therefore, an excellent foil; second, criticism finds itself embarrassed by the historical facts – the horror of trench-warfare. As Yeats wrote of W. E. Henley, 'I thought his prose violent and laboured, but I was ready, as were all those others, to test myself and all I did by the man's sincere vision.' One might say the same of Owen – that his life and death as a soldier make literary criticism seem pedantic and invalid. 'Above all', Owen wrote, 'I am not concerned with Poetry. My subject is War, and the pity of War. The Poetry is in the pity.' But is it? Is Owen another Hardy, that genius who wrote frequently appalling prose and yet produced great novels?

Owen's main defect is ultimately educational: he has read, quite uncritically, too much bad Keats and worse Shelley, and so associates poetry with the merely poetic. One can see this in the unashamedly archaic diction: 'Later they found the English ball', he writes in 'S.I.W.', when he means *bullet*. It becomes imposs-ible, as Owen stipulates, to apply the criterion of sincerity to a poetry whose language is so frequently artificial and literary: 'Against more days of inescapable thrall', 'whom no compassion fleers'. Few poets have written more clumsily than Owen: 'But who these hellish?', 'Drooping tongues from jaws that slob their relish', 'It seemed they pushed themselves to be as plugs', and 'Their old wounds, save with cold, can not more ache'.

And he is prepared to write nonsense if the rhyme demands it; as when he describes a bayonet 'Blue with malice, like a madman's flash'. What *is* a madman's flash, except a vague *poetical* property? Nor is it pedantic to ask, when Owen writes 'the crowing sirens blare', if they indulged in these mutually exclusive activities of crowing and blaring at the same time. And when he writes 'And with old winds pondered / Over the curse of this chaotic world', we recognize Shelley's presence, but it hardly explains why the winds are 'old' or why they are cogitating — except that they often do in bad Romantic poetry.

Too much of Owen's poetry wishes to evoke rather than describe, and too much of that evocation takes the form of emotional blackmail, largely because Owen is insensitive to the possibilities of understatement. With the rare (and not wholly perfect) exceptions of 'Spring Offensive', 'Send-Off', 'Anthem for Doomed Youth' and 'Futility', Owen's poetry is written with the volume turned full up. He lacks the essential quality of the poet — a good ear — as we can see from 'Love's wine's thin' (!) or 'Stuck in the bottom of his throat of phlegm' (where any competent poet would have eliminated the repeated 'of'). Instead he relies on mechanical alliteration ('where shell-storms spouted reddest spate', 'But wound with war's hard wire whose stakes are strong') and overstatement ('like limbs knife-skewed', 'And saw a sad land, weak with sweats of dearth').

And how much less telling is the overstatement of a poem like 'Mental Cases' than Owen's prose description of a battalion broken up by artillery fire: 'we carried on like a crowd moving off a cricket field.' Here, Owen's reaction is spontaneous and authentic, and we may be surprised that, in his poetry, he did not make more of the *contrast* between war and ordinary life. When he does, as in the beginning of 'Spring Offensive', he touches on a source of real power, but even there, verbosity and archaism flaw the poem. It is a technique used brilliantly by Sassoon in the only masterpiece to emerge from the First World War, *Memoirs of an Infantry Officer*: 'At six-forty-five the final bombardment began . . . Barton and I sat speechless, deafened and stupified by the seismic state of affairs, and when he lit a cigarette the match flame staggered crazily. Afterwards I asked him what he had been thinking about. His reply was "Carpet slippers and kettle-holders". My own mind had been working in much the same style, for during that cannonading cataclysm the following refrain was running in my head:

> *They come as a boon and a blessing to men,*
> *The something, the Owl, and the Waverley Pen.*

For the life of me I couldn't remember what the first one was called.'

We see a glimpse of this quirky, unpredictable honesty in the best line of 'Dulce Et Decorum Est' – 'Gas! GAS! Quick boys! – An ecstasy of fumbling' – where eager love-making is introduced into a horrifyingly inappropriate context. 'Drunk with fatigue' (the men staggering along) has something of the same quality, of civvy street and trench-mud in close juxtaposition. But the beggars and hags, the comparison of the gassed man's face to that of 'a devil's sick of sin' *and* that of a man about to be hanged, are irretrievably literary. On the other hand, 'the *haunting* flares' is a precise description of the after-image left by bright light. The 'gargling' in the 'froth-corrupted lungs' is equally accurate. Yet, 'obscene as cancer' and 'bitter as the cud / Of vile, incurable sores on innocent tongues' is the rhetoric of Speakers' Corner.

It is significant that Philip Larkin should temper his admiration of Owen with unease. While he believed Owen's poetry to be 'an eternally resonant monument to one of the most dreadful corners of history', while he thought Owen 'the only twentieth-century poet who can be read after Hardy without a sense of bathos', the admiring Larkin also registered unease – unease that our response isn't pure, that we are moved not simply by the poetry but also by the appalling historical events out of which it came. 'We should now be able to separate his work from the temporal accidents of his lifetime,' Larkin avers, only to continue, 'yet it is just these accidents that condition the nature of his achievement, and make independent critical assessment so difficult.' Inadvertently, Larkin supplies us with the perfect illustration of this imperfect state of affairs: 'Lines such as "The Poetry is in the pity" and "The eternal reciprocity of tears" will never lose their enormous impact that is utterly free from affectation.' The first quotation isn't a line of poetry at all. It is from Owen's preface and – a slip, nothing more – taken for poetry by Larkin. And why not, if the poetry is in the pity, rather than in Owen's lines?

Siegfried Sassoon

In August 1957, Siegfried Sassoon was received into the Catholic Church. It was the culmination of, and consolation for, a lifelong search for belief. *Poet's Pilgrimage** is a selection designed to show 'the spiritual aspect of his poetry from youth to age'. Sassoon's editor, Felicitas Corrigan, has interleaved the poems with relevant extracts from his prose works, his diaries and letters. Apart from a lengthy introduction, editorial interference is sparing – fortunately so, because her comments scarcely persuade one of her critical competence. Her vocabulary, one of bold largesse, precludes fine discrimination: 'every phrase of his best poetry is a mystery of significance and music'; 'a sonnet of exquisite perfection'; 'lyrics of white-hot intensity'. Such generosity is vitiated by its generality.

Consider, too, her inaccurate account of Sassoon's famous pacifist gesture. Dame Felicitas makes it ridiculous by, paradoxically, omitting the absurd. Sassoon was heroically *prepared* 'unflinchingly' to face 'the scorn of fellow-officers' but, instead, had to face his colonel's 'kindly tolerance' in a moving scene at the end of *Memoirs of an Infantry Officer*. Nor is it strictly accurate to say that Sassoon was 'incarcerated' at Craiglockhart – incarcerated men do not play golf every day. Similarly, Dame Felicitas's description of him as 'the Angry Young Man who hurled his Military Cross into the Mersey' is a distortion as well as a cliché. Sassoon's self-mockery becomes uncomplicated

---

Siegfried Sassoon: Poet's Pilgrimage by Felicitas Corrigan, Gollancz.

heroism: 'I ripped the MC *ribbon* [my italics] off my tunic and threw it into the mouth of the Mersey. Weighted with significance though this action was, it would have felt more conclusive had the ribbon been heavier. As it was, the poor little thing fell weakly on the water and floated away as though aware of its own futility.'

Dame Felicitas is hardly more reliable when she writes about the poetry. For instance, her brief remarks about 'Devotion to Duty' misplace and blunt its emphasis. In this poem, Sassoon, like Wilfred Owen in 'The Parable of the Old Men and the Young', uses a biblical parallel (in this case, David, Bathsheba and Uriah) to indict the self-interested motives of those responsible for war. Dame Felicitas, looking for the religious perspective, misleadingly brackets it with 'Ancient History', a poem in which Adam laments the death of Cain. The two poems are not comparable except on the most superficial level: 'Devotion to Duty' exploits an ironic parallel between past and present, while 'Ancient History' simply reinterprets received myth.

None the less, it is clear that Dame Felicitas has followed Sassoon's own lead. In his later years, he was bored and irritated by those who praised his war poetry and otherwise dismissed his entire *œuvre* as Edwardian. *Poet's Pilgrimage* is a memorable portrait of a man awaiting the Georgian counter-revolution, some literary coup which would result in the restoration of Walter de la Mare and Ralph Hodgson, Henry Tomlinson and John Drinkwater. In disgruntled obscurity, Sassoon is baffled by the clever young chaps who continue to praise Ezra Pound when he has exposed him in a talk delivered to the Bank of England Literary Society in 1935. Bartók's work is 'poltergeist music'. An elephant by Henry Moore would certainly suffer from elephantiasis. He has never 'perused' Robert Lowell. His consolations include letters from equally puzzled Edwardian friends and the unexpected visit of a Sherston fan who turns out to be a CID man from Scotland Yard. These personal details, the crustiness, the nervousness, the egotism and the odd courage of a forgotten man with what Dame Felicitas charmingly calls an 'Ivor Novello profile' – these make this book worth reading.

But does *Poet's Pilgrimage* force the reader to admit that the later poetry has been unjustly ignored – like the Kipling that nobody read? Sassoon himself was in two minds. Courageously and correctly, he writes: 'It would seem that the "content" of my poems amounts to nothing except an exhibition of echoings from other minds'; and 'They are, as usual with me, deficient in imagery and full of abstractions.' And in 1952 he wrote an 'Apologia' which begins:

> My words – that non-surprising choice –
> My thoughts – not found evocative –
> My untransparent tone of voice –
> Forgive.

Later, reading the poems of Dylan Thomas, he notes bleakly: 'They make my own poverty of language painfully apparent.' On the other hand, he argues that he scores 'through absence of literary artifice', the 'essential simplicity and naturalness' of his language. Unfortunately, his diction contradicts this at every turn: 'slavedom', 'envisioned', 'worldhood' 'trophydoms', 'enharmonized', 'holpen', 'influent essence', 'unscienced thirst', 'unfulfillment', 'gloom-girt winds of time', 'Aeonian-rapt remoteness', 'unmeaningness', 'heart-envisioned', 'believement' 'abidant', 'frustrate brain', 'indubitant and absolved' and, worst of all, 'meditationment'. In addition to Milton's disease (transmitted by Hardy), Sassoon is afflicted by syntactical rickets:

> Hastes he once more to harmonize and heal?
> I know not.

Inversion on the scale of these last poems the reader admires not. 'Rogation' in its entirety will convince any reader that these criticisms are not a chance result of random selection. The last two lines of this moribund poem are typical:

> Hope of our humility, resistless Rood,
> Beyond our bodements bring beatitude.

Looked at carefully, 'Rogation' explains why the Georgians, like the poor, are always with us. Considered unhistorically, the Georgians are those who can never escape their models. In the case of 'Rogation' the model is Milton's organ music – as if God spoke only Latin. Familiarity and usage, not originality, are important. One is never surprised by Georgian poetry. A 'thou', a 'thee' or a 'thy', the merest mention of a word like 'nescient' is enough to reassure the reader that this is religious poetry. It is significant that Sassoon was proud of his gift for parody.

The same thing applies to much of Sassoon's inferior prose. For example, in *The Old Century*, he writes that when he visited his dying father at Eastbourne 'there must have been moments when I half-unconsciously connected the sound of the incoming waves with the idea of death'. The idea probably came from Paul Dombey whose spirit was still lurking down the coast at Brighton. In *Sherston's Progress* (1936) he writes (having been shot in the head): 'I had been young and exuberant, and now I was just a dying animal, on the verge of oblivion.' There is no acknowledgement to Yeats's 'Sailing to Byzantium' (1928) because the Georgian never borrows intentionally. It is not a question of plagiarism, rather of vague reminiscence – as in this passage's debt to *Great Expectations*: 'The solicitor used to come down from London for the day. I can remember him carving a duck with evident relish, and saying in somewhat unctuous tones, "Have you considered, my dear Miss Evelyn, the well-worn subject of a school for our young friend on my left?" ' This is a mélange of Jaggers and of Pumblechook who addresses Pip as his 'young friend' and who passes from the pork to Pip's moral education. In the same way, Sassoon's best war poetry derives from the *Barrack-Room Ballads*. But, though Sassoon's views may be more acceptable, he has written nothing as good as 'The "Mary Gloster" ' and, from a purely technical point of view, Kipling is plainly superior.

How then did Sassoon produce his one real masterpiece, *Memoirs of an Infantry Officer*? In his other prose works there is a struggle between his originality and his models, in which the stereotypes win. They can be clearly divided. On the one hand,

taking *Memoirs of a Fox-hunting Man* and *The Old Century*
together, there is the vivid and the accurate. Sassoon notices
voices – his mother's 'calling voice' of 'politeness tinged with
reserve', his nanny's ingratiating, legacy-seeking voice 'which
wasn't the same as her everyday one', the voice which is 'more
like being read aloud to than talking'. He observes the flies
buzzing round a horse's ears, the click of a parasol, cook flapping
a wasp away from a tin of golden syrup, a man who strolls up and
down his lawn like a wicket-keeper changing ends. He reminds us
of Signorelli's 'Crucifixion' at Sansepolcro when he describes a
cloud as 'a hooded giant with clumsy expostulating arms'. He
shows a real world of beeswaxed parquet floors, gate-legged
tables, filled with the 'soft clatter' of pigeon wings. Its inhabitants
wear leather gauntlets to cut the lilac and hang calendars which
bring 'The Relief of Ladysmith' to their larders.

On the other hand, there are the stale prose rhythms of 'time's
wavering shadows are falling across the glade'. Woodland
branches 'whisper' through the 'sleepy summer afternoon' until
the reader takes the soporific hint. Variants of 'Elysium' occur
eight times. Sassoon stares into the 'blue distance' five times. And
superficially gruff masters have a twinkle in their eyes three times.
This is hardly surprising since they eke out an existence in a world
where boys 'bag' things, 'rag' each other, get into fearful waxes
and generally have a ripping time. Perhaps, after all, Sassoon was
mistaken and those twinkles were tears? In this world of
stereotyped response, all characterization is necessarily at the
level of the school magazine's *Valete* column: 'Good old Gould!
Successive generations of Marlburians . . .' For the same reason,
the village cricket team is choc-a-block with wooden-legged
umpires and one-eyed Dickensian wicket-keepers – a ghastly
array of 'evergreen country characters' that leaves one longing for
Hardy's rustics.

It is precisely this uncritical acceptance and conformist prose
which prevents *The Old Century* from being compared to the
classic account of childhood, *A Portrait of the Artist* – despite
their respective heroes' shared fascination with words. And if at
moments during *Memoirs of a Fox-hunting Man* one is reminded

of the Tolstoy who described Vronsky's race in such daring detail, the impression is quickly undermined by sentimentality. Sometimes Sassoon is so busy conforming that he actually contradicts himself, as when he revisits Edingthorpe in order to reclaim 'a transient experience' which he has forgotten. Once there, succumbing to its charms, he writes of its 'unforgettable flavour'.

With *Memoirs of an Infantry Officer*, though, the uniqueness of the events deprived Sassoon of possible models. As a result, his writing is consistently fresh. His self-scrutiny is candid, critical and humorous. He admits to being irritated by even those he is fond of, like Aunt Evelyn and Barton. He is malicious about an officer who lards his conversation with archaisms like 'anent' and 'for the nonce'. He wonders if shells ever collide in mid-air. The thud of distant shells reminds him of 'someone kicking footballs' and, setting out to avenge the dead Kendle, he forgets him entirely as he notices the grating of a grenade-pin on his teeth. But not all the writing is in this serio-comic vein: the 'unknown territory in front was dark, and I stared at it like a man looking from the side of a ship'. If Sassoon had written as well as this consistently, he would have been a figure of real stature. As it is, English literature has one great work from him – almost by accident.

The Thirties Poet

'I found his poetry extremely congenial', writes Roy Fuller in his introduction to Kenneth Allott's poems.* 'For example, my poem "The Barber" is a crib for tone and attack of his "Lament for a Cricket Eleven".' There was a lot of cribbing in the thirties, though not many own up as gracefully as Roy Fuller. This is Auden furtively lifting the lid of his desk to sneak a glance at his Faber and Gwyer (in 'Journey to Iceland'):

> Here let the citizen, then, find natural marvels,
> a horse-shoe ravine, an issue of steam from a cleft
> in a rock, and rocks, and waterfalls brushing
> the rocks, and among the rocks birds.

The basic ingredient comes from 'What the Thunder Said'. Auden has just added water:

> Here is no water but only rock
> Rocks and no water . . .

Consider, too, the progress of Yeats's 'rook-delighting heaven' as a right answer to be whispered round the remove, changed by every surreptitious ear. In Auden's 'May', it becomes the banal 'swan-delighting river'; in Allott's 'City Nocturne', much later in the chain, it becomes the Bunterishly overweight 'bird-alighting

---

*Collected Poems by Kenneth Allott, Secker and Warburg.

estuaries'. This example is an adequate, if miniature representation of the thirties poetry ladder.

More interesting than Auden's debts to his great predecessors are the mutual borrowings among the younger poets, a general craning over shoulders. Here, Auden was the major creditor for, despite his occasional loans from his elders and betters (Yeatsian beggars, for instance), he quickly cultivated a distinctive style of his own – poetic eccentricities of dress which his contemporaries assiduously adopted as the uniform of a thirties school. For a poet like Allott, this was disastrous: he stands, somewhat blurred, on the back row of the school photograph, a man remembered for his marvellously slavish imitations of an Auden who sits in the centre of the front row, with the ball at his feet.

It does not follow, however, that *Collected Poems* is without interest. On the contrary, it exercises an eery fascination as a reference document in the literary history of the period. Because there is so little that is individual, let alone idiosyncratic, the shared tendencies of the time are registered the more sharply in Allott's poetry. He is that impossible phenomenon, the average thirties poet – signing his work with invisible ink, ineffably anonymous, drunk on the spirit of the age. If, for example, Auden left off the definite article, he was aped by a similarly denuded Allott:

> Never an hour
> But city of communicable prose
> Expels from fundament
> Its viscid traffic north . . .

or:

> On flags in farmyard kitchen
> Under flitch of bacon.

Then there are the quirky inversions of the thirties, invented by Auden to lift a poetry which was, by and large, more rigidly colloquial than the occasional excursus into the vernacular by

Yeats and Eliot. Yeats, nodding to his secretary Pound, might slip into his diction the odd 'bum' but, on the whole, his rhetoric remained unchanged except for a purge of Shelleyan adjectives. One could never call him a chatty poet. The new school was more doctrinaire in its casualness (it had to be to stake a claim to modernity) and boldly used contemporary slang like 'piece of skirt', 'lingo', 'booze', and 'fagged'. Auden's counter-balance was poems that employed a deliberately poeticized syntax:

> I, crouching behind a sheep-pen, heard
> Travel across a sudden bird . . .
> Nor speech is close nor fingers numb,
> If love not seldom has received
> An unjust answer, was deceived.

In Allott's 'Calenture' this mannerism, Jamesian in its willed ugliness, degenerates into a syntactic tic: 'What was mislaid not St Anthony shall find.' MacNeice was another culprit in 'Trilogy for X':

> When clerks and navvies fondle
> Beside canals their wenches . . .

This last quotation also adumbrates the social self-consciousness of the thirties, a tendency to classify which was as prevalent as polio, and just as crippling. Auden, of course, brings it off because his social types are also individuals. With natural authority, he manages to impose on us vignettes which are at once the definite and indefinite article:

> the tall
> Professor in the mountains with his large
> Tweed pockets full of plants . . .

His sharper eye distinguishes what James would have called 'The Real Thing', where MacNeice achieves only the dull 'clerks and navvies' and the inept 'wenches'. Allott is equally embarrassing. 'The hinds and the wives are jogging to the fair', or worse –

> drummers who gulp whisky
> Easing their crippled burning feet from shoes
> Of suede or patent leather . . .

It is the maladroit offer of an alternative which prompts one to ask if drummers were shod exclusively in suede or patent leather, and to continue with a supplementary question – did they *never* sip their drink?

The other alternative frequently offered by thirties poets is the bifurcated simile. Here, it is difficult to say with any certainty who was the least certain: Auden with his 'heart like a clever / Conjuror or dancer', or his 'unremarkable actions / Like ploughing or a tipsy song', or Allott with his *echoing* 'actions are like mirrors or railway arches', or MacNeice in the *Autumn Journal* where

> the windscreen wiper
> Kept at its job like a tiger in a cage or a cricket that sings
> All night through for nothing.

Perhaps the resurgence of interest in the Metaphysicals was responsible for this staccato version of Donne's swift and fluent movement from image to image. Be that as it may, the alternatives create a feeling of uncertainty and fumbling where exactitude is intended. Two wrongs, as always, do not make a right – and in the case of MacNeice, two rights undoubtedly make a wrong.

Other shared features in this stylistic twinning are a tough attitude to the traditionally sentimental (one thinks of Auden's lovers in an 'ordinary swoon' and Allott's lovers with their 'outlandish lingo') and a modish way with scientific imagery: in Auden, violence is 'pandemic like a new disease'; in Allott, summer is a 'ballet of Fahrenheit and Réaumur'. And when Allott compares loving to 'the illusory movement of a wave', one feels the pressure, not of good poetry, but of the need to be intelligently modern. Behind these images lies not so much the upsurge of science as Eliot's initial avant-garde trump – 'the evening is spread out against the sky / Like a patient etherised upon a table'.

Moulded by the pressure of this immediate modernist tradition, Auden eventually becomes a literary conservative, excluding, for example, from his *Collected Shorter Poems* lines that expressed a desire for more new architecture. 'I have never liked modern architecture', he confessed, symbolically giving the game away. Allott, at an earlier date, had already retired hurt, unable to keep up the pace set by Eliot and Yeats. At first, however, Auden schooled himself in Eliot's lofty cosmopolitanism, and Allott followed. Europe was the great guarantee against provincialism in Auden: Macao is 'a weed from Catholic Europe'; in his 'Bride in the 30's' there are 'the sixteen skies of Europe' and the moon 'climbs the European sky' whereas, in 'Dover', he notices 'High over France, a full moon' and aeroplanes that 'drone through the new European air'. His contemporaries took these lines and copied them like schoolboys in detention: thus Auden's 'All the dogs of Europe bark' turns up in MacNeice as

> But all of them must now align against the beast
> That prowls at every door and barks in every headline.

Allott gamely keeps up with his 'Exodus':

> From this wet island of birds and chimneys
> Who can watch suffering Europe and not be angry?

In this fetishistic preference for 'Europe', there is a touch of what A. O. Lovejoy, in his 1933 William James Lectures at Harvard, called 'metaphysical pathos'. It more aptly still describes 'Time' as it appears in the poetry of the period. Again, Auden is the inventor and, accordingly, deploys it with confidence, if a little monotonously. In Allott, though (*pace* Roy Fuller who admires its use), Time is little more than a monolithic prop, purloined from Auden, a guarantee of bogus sublimity to be trundled on at every opportunity.

Is there, then, nothing good in Allott? Roy Fuller praised him as a phrase-maker, but he could not make poems – because he never knew when to stop, and the same thing applies to his phrases. For example, the excellent line 'Slip with the lyric purpose of the eel' is followed by the bungled

> Out of the histrionic hug of evil
> Without that accoucheur, the miracle.

In three lines, Allott staggers from the pet-shop to the church, via the theatre and the maternity hospital, without an *A–Z* to lead us through the maze of streets.

With John Fuller this problem of the well-made phrase and the well-made poem recurs.* He has always been a resourceful and even arty poet. A new admixture of simplicity makes *The Mountain in the Sea* his best volume to date, though the stunning phrases are still in evidence – 'bushes / Sprung with the weight of bees', raspberries' 'plump facets padded like dusty cushions', sleeping bags like 'quilted chrysalises', the moon as an 'understudy, practising with silent lips', mushrooms 'White and soft as conjurors' gloves', the segments of a halved grapefruit like a 'dartboard'. Sometimes, it is true, this search for the unusual phrase creates some absurd circumlocutions, a rum poetic diction. Looking through binoculars, for instance, becomes 'The eyes sweep out through tubes' – a periphrasis to set against 'the rolling circle's speed' chased by Gray's Etonians. Overall, though, John Fuller (to borrow Arnold's distinction) trades in *simplicité*, not its semblance, *simplesse*. 'In the Room', like the other poems, touches on the theme of eventual death and at the same time exhibits a calm reverence for the dumb, inarticulate acts which make up life from minute to minute. Fuller sees his children as fragments – knees to be attended to, a hand bunched over an eggcup, a foot, an empty sandal – the future, in fact, seen out of

---

*The Mountain in the Sea by John Fuller, Secker and Warburg.

the corner of one's eye. Meanwhile, there are parental responsibilities:

> The long nail
> Curled slowly away from the scissors.

This may have less brio than Fuller's Audenesque *Epistles to
Several Persons*, but it has more weight, and the voice is his own
indubitably. One thinks of Vuillard's colourful domesticity or of
Stanley Spencer's daily documentary drawings at Cookham – of
Hilda helping him to put on his collar, of Hilda cutting his nails,
of other acts which, simple in themselves, strike one with the
force of meditation.

The Mountain in the Sea is a thoughtful, pleasing collection,
flawed only by a tendency to create whole poems around single
observations, or to foist moral conclusions where they are not
needed.

Writers in the Second World War

As Ivan Denisovich pockets a precious bit of hacksaw blade, Tsezar discusses the merits of Eisenstein with prisoner X 123. There's something oddly persistent about intellectuals. In a rather bizarre way, they validate Descartes's *Cogito*. I am therefore I think. Robert Hewison's absorbing account of cultural life during the Second World War* corroborates this clear and distinct perception. If not an England, there'll always be a Brains Trust: internees on the Isle of Man, we learn, started up an unofficial university, a kind of concentrating camp. After the initial scare, the gloomy prognostications of H. G. Wells, and the disappearance of Auden and Isherwood to America, the show went on. Some of it on the road — war-work in the provinces was encouraged by touring troupes of theatricals.

Jolly good show. Or was it? The real subject of *Under Siege* is not the democratic dissemination of culture to the sticks, but the reactions of the London literary mandarins to the war. At first, there was a certain amount of panic — I am therefore I funk. Some tried to circumvent the threat of conscription by joining Victor Cazalet's anti-aircraft battery at Rochester, where James Pope-Hennessy was librarian and chaps could potter round the barracks in their silk pyjamas. Cazalet's greenhouses ensured a supply of fresh flowers. Dylan Thomas, who candidly admitted that he wanted to put little into the war ('certainly not my one and

*Under Siege by Robert Hewison, Weidenfeld and Nicolson.

only body'), volunteered for the battery, but his one and only was rejected on medical grounds.

Another scheme involved Lord Esher, who proposed that an informal committee, including Desmond MacCarthy and John Lehmann, should choose fifty writers and artists to be exempted from conscription. Since they would almost certainly have chosen duds, one learns with pleasure that the War Office vetoed the proposal. After this febrile activity, things settled down. Writers wishing to be part of the war effort were snubbed by the bureaucrats who (rightly, in my view) regarded them as peripheral to the struggle with Hitler. The alienated intellectuals then entered their third Cartesian stage – I am therefore I brood. However, this brooding, widespread though it was, hatched very little in the way of good art. Many intellectuals felt they were prevented from being great writers by circumstances beyond their control. To Cyril Connolly's pre-war list of the enemies of promise (booze, sex, domesticity, talk, journalism, worldly success) could now be added the war. War meant a shortage of paper and typewriters, conscripted printers, the sense of being dehumanized by the machine of state, lack of security, the absence of an individual or collective myth. Above all, it now seems, war meant excuses, excuses. The strength of Mr Hewison's book is that it recreates this ethos in depth; the weakness is that it never rumbles the bogusness. The obvious distinction between writers and intellectuals is not made – the distinction between *I am therefore I write* and *I am therefore I want to write*. Keith Douglas and Alun Lewis, the only war poets of stature, simply wrote, using the materials to hand. The intellectuals wrote about writing, ignoring Connolly's salient question in *The Unquiet Grave*: 'How many books did Renoir write on how to paint?'

Connolly is the spokesman of failure, shrewd enough, one guesses, to realize that his novel, *The Rock Pool*, was merely plausible – knowingly nasty, short on characterization and convincing dialogue, long but uncertain on style. Naylor, the central character, is a heavily ironic self-portrait and a prediction of failure. Unfortunately, he is the *only* character. Connolly desperately wanted to be a great writer, but the prose style on which he relied almost exclusively was fickle. He could write with unnerving panache: Naylor is preparing a biography of Samuel Rogers – 'unconsciously he had chosen a man who, besides being easy to do, and rather coming into fashion, was also, by his snobbery, his great wealth, and a certain niggling smallness of soul, by no means unsympathetic.' Elsewhere, describing a girl dancing, he parenthetically swats 'the morbid redundancies of Ravel's *Bolero*'. Art, good or bad, stimulates him. On the other hand, nature and women (each of them alien to Connolly's mannered consciousness) defeat him entirely. A mouth 'like a crushed blackberry' is conferred on his dyke anti-heroine, Toni van Kandersteg. Connolly's *métier* was the epigram: 'we all like obscurity when it is on our own plane: great artists like Epstein and Orpen know how to provide for the public the bewilderment it deserves.' Novels, though, are not made out of epigrams. 'The warm night, on which summer's hold could yet be imagined as faintly relaxing' is always there, alas.

The weakness of *Under Siege* appears most clearly in its treatment of Julian Maclaren-Ross – a tragic figure according to Robert Hewison. Dan Davin's *Closing Times* also remembers him, affectionately if ruefully, as a man who squandered his early brilliance. What brilliance? As a short-story writer, Maclaren-Ross tried to domesticate the vernacular style of Hemingway. Here is a sample: 'It was in a café and she was a WAAF. What was he writing was it poetry . . . You can tell yourself that the uniform does not matter that you are the same underneath but it does matter and you are not the same because the attitude of others makes you what you are and of course to a private soldier the attitude of others is entirely different and you yourself are different too.' After a page of this, the ventriloquist's dummy is ready to gabble – the legs go limp, the mouth drops like a draw-bridge, and a burly arm reaches across the Atlantic and plunges violently up the shirt tails. The effect is less pronounced in his other stories, but essentially Maclaren-Ross wasn't more than a mimic. He picked up the inflexions not of individuals but of classes. The title 'A Bit of A Smash in Madras', with its crude tang of colonialism, is itself a giveaway. His ear was glib rather than accurate. In his *Memoirs*, he recounts the difficulties of adapting *A Gun for Sale* for radio. How could sound convey Raven's crucial deformity? Graham Greene suggested a waitress saying, 'Ugh, he ain't arf an ugly bastard. That 'air [*sic*] lip of his makes me want to retch.' Maclaren-Ross, coarsening the coarse, amended this to 'fair turns me stomach up'. Jolly good show.

Light Verse

Light verse bears close affinities to self-abuse: it may not be the real thing, but it has its own peculiar satisfactions. To begin with, poet and reader enjoy the surmounted difficulties of form. John Fuller's testing form is the 'standard habbie', taken from Burns and so called by Allan Ramsay after Robert Sempill's 'Life and Death of the Piper of Kilbrachan or, the Epitaph of Habbie Simpson'. From it Mr Fuller extracts some dazzling rhyme sequences (incognito–SEATO–*Quito*–pardons–*Emperor Hirohito–Kew Gardens*) as witty as, say, Auden's 'Akureyri–very dreary' or MacNeice's 'gaffelbitar–Rye-vita'. The Master, however, remains the master.

The danger of light verse (as of self-abuse) is that it can seem private. One recalls Auden's in-joke in *A Letter to Lord Byron* – 'documentaries by the GPO' – which refers to 'Night Mail', written for Grierson's documentary. Or, worse, the arcana of the MacNeice–Auden joint composition, 'Last Will and Testament', which rivals in obscurity the Villon it parodies. To take an example from *Epistles to Several Persons,** one wonders what an American would make of this:

> Managerial boobs
> And answers that you won't take no for
> From *Fine Tubes*.

**Epistles to Several Persons* by John Fuller, Secker and Warburg.

Presumably, the innuendo will be lost as *Fine Tubes* fails to ring the door chimes. Baffled Harvard professors should consult the *New Statesman* for 27 August 1971, 10 March 1972, and 28 July 1972. There they will find James Fenton's articles on the longest strike in Britain's history and will inevitably ask themselves whether the reference is legitimate without a note.

The answer is yes, because Mr Fuller has turned to advantage the danger of privacy. The compiler of *Nemo's Almanac* (a literary quiz of impossible difficulty, designed to keep the most learned academic busy for a full year) has mined his new volume with references. But the references are calculated to baffle the merely academic: thus, granted the knowledge that Luigi Nono is an Italian composer and Charles Ives an early American experimentalist, will the same person know that Olga Korbut is a Russian gymnast or that Paul Newman played Eddie Fingers in Robert Rossen's film, *The Hustler*? How many people know that 'Rolling Down to Rio' is a Kipling shanty set by Edward German *and* that Frank Bough is a BBC sports commentator *and* that Dave Wottle is the be-capped United States and Olympic 800 metres champion?

In addition to this competitive quiz element, there is the pleasure to be derived from Mr Fuller's play with decorum — something he perhaps learnt from Burns. Burns begins with an uneasy mixture of Lallans and the educated neo-classic style reserved for moments of high seriousness. It is a mélange which ruins 'The Cotter's Saturday Night' and 'The Vision', but eventually Burns used high-style reference for comic purpose. Take his list of the forty-five Scottish MPs in the English Parliament under the terms of the Act of Union:

> *Erskine*, a spunkie norland billie;
> True Campels, *Frederic* an' *Ilay*;
> An' Livistone, the bauld *Sir Willie*;
>   An' mony ithers,
> Whom Auld Demosthenes or Tully
>   Might own for brithers.

In the same way, Mr Fuller's elevated references (Pablo Sarasate, Stockhausen, Deuteronomy) are deliberate breaches of light verse decorum, particularly when they occur in the splendid isolation of the short last line, with all the arhythmical force of a clerihew.

But nothing will convince the person who instinctively loathes the 'crambo-jingle', the 'spavet *Pegasus*', as Burns put it. Despite its long history, the verse letter has never really been accepted: Burns's Muse, 'the tapetless, ramfeezl'd hizzie', has never been welcome in literature's polite drawing room. And perhaps there is a case for insisting on the puerility of the exchange between 'wan-fukkit funling' Dunbar and 'cuntbittin crawdoun' Kennedy – a slugfest of unparalleled tedium. Equally, one might easily forget Keats's verse letters to George Felton Matthew, George Keats, Charles Cowden Clark and J. H. Reynolds; the case for verse is not improved when the poet's inspiration is an admitted lack of inspiration, all too clearly illustrated:

> There must be too a ruin dark and gloomy,
> To say 'joy not too much in all that's bloomy'.

And even when the obvious failures have been eliminated, the fact remains that, since the Romantics, wit and poetry have raised some forbidding eyebrows. Arnold, for example, condemned Burns by the absurd standard of Dante's 'In la sua volontade é nostra pace' – a touchstone guaranteed to brain any light verse unlucky enough to come into contact with it. Moreover, it is foolish to defend verse on ground chosen by its enemies: a cry of *vive la différence* is more effective than Byron's totalizing of Pope's images (23) in the attack on Lord Hervey: 'Whether I made out a case for Pope, I know not; but I am very sure that I have been zealous in the attempt. If it comes to proof, we shall beat the Blackguards. I will show more *imagery* in twenty lines of Pope than in any equal length of quotation in English poesy, and that in places where they least expect it: for instance, in his lines on *Sporus* . . . Look at the *variety*, at the *poetry*, of the passage – at the *imagination*: there is hardly a line from which a *painting* might not be made, and *is*.' Alas, given these grounds, Arnold, brushing aside Byron's pocket calculator, comes back with:

> To Hounslow Heath I point, and Banstead Down;
> Thence comes your mutton, and these chicks my own

— and condemns Dryden and Pope as 'classics of our prose'. On the whole, it seems better to insist, with Auden, on the incomparability of poetry and verse:

> By all means let us touch our humble caps to
> *La poésie pure*, the epic narrative;
> But comedy shall get its round of claps, too.
> According to his powers, each may give;
> Only on varied diet can we live.
> The pious fable and the dirty story
> Share in the total literary glory.

As a defence, this refusal to fight is better than Eliot's insistence that, for some people, thought (wit thinly disguised) *is* emotion. But the trouble with literary pacifism, the frank admission of inferior status, is that verse never knows its place. When Auden writes 'I'm writing this in pencil on my knee, / Using my other hand to stop me yawning', the rise into serious poetry is only stanzas away. Burns, too, is constantly lapsing into the real thing:

> When lintwhites chant among the buds,
> And jinkin hares, in amorous whids,
>   Their loves enjoy,
> While thro' the braes the cushat croods
>   With wailfu' cry!

And one remembers Pope's description of Villiers's death, which rivals Hogarth:

> In the worst inn's worst room, with mat half-hung,
> The floors of plaister, and the walls of dung,

On once a flock-bed, but repaired with straw,
With tape-ty'd curtains, never meant to draw,
The George and Garter dangling from that bed
Where tawdry yellow strove with dirty red,
Great Villiers Lies . . .

It is a beautifully constructed sentence, guiding the eye from object to object, until we reach the marvellously deferred subject. Mr Fuller, too, is not guiltless of writing well. And if Pope reminds us here of Milton and Arnold's comment on the opening of *Paradise Lost* – 'So chary of a sentence is he, so resolute not to let it escape him till he has crowded into it all he can, that it is not until the thirty-ninth word in the sentence that he will give us the key to it, the word of action, the verb' – Mr Fuller often reminds one of Pope. In the letter to Angus Macintyre, for example, there is a surreal fantasy about bringing Oxford's academic procedure to the countryside: it is as good as Pope's fantasy in the *Epistle to Bathurst* about the abolition of all currency. And there are genuinely evocative moments:

> an interrogator's cigarette
> Quietly glowing.

The problem of the 'form that's large enough to swim in' is insoluble and will remain so. Chaff and grain lie side by side, demanding a catholic response from the reader. Mr Fuller's mixture is not, finally, as potent as Pope's. There are too many empty stanzas (created by the impetus of his ornate form) for the comparison to be sustained. But *Epistles to Several Persons* will be welcomed for its skill by all who like light verse, while those who do not may retort, like Thom Gunn, that

> It's better
> To go and see your friend than write a letter.

Subject Matter in Poetry

My subject matter is subject matter. Is it true, as it sometimes seems, that certain subjects are inevitably more interesting than others, however much we may protest that they are merely different? For instance, does Robert Lowell's *Life Studies* intrigue us more than, say, Tony Harrison's family reminiscences in *Continuous*? If so, is it because Lowell's technique is more sophisticated and fluid than Harrison's vigorously clanking sonnet sequence in which the rhymes come like a boisterous game of snap? Or is it because the Lowell family tree is richer in eccentricity and event than that of Harrison? Where Lowell can boast a Great Aunt Sarah thundering 'on the keyboard of her dummy piano' and 'risen like the phoenix / from her bed of troublesome snacks and Tauchnitz classics', Harrison's relations are more familiar figures, bickering on Blackpool's Golden Mile or locked into their ordinarily absurd theatre of non-communication:

> Your life's all shattered into smithereens.

> Back in our silences and sullen looks,
> for all the Scotch we drink, what's still between 's
> not the thirty or so years, but books, books, books.

As this last line makes amply clear, Harrison is the only eccentric in his family. Even so, the predicament of the deracinated scholarship boy is a familiar enough subject. That is its appeal.

Any upwardly mobile reader will identify with it. I suppose, too, that it is just possible there are upper-class readers so articulate and cocooned that they find Harrison's background exotic in a way comparable to Lowell's. I doubt it, though. In any case, shouldn't both hypothetical readers reject that padding 'all', even while they reluctantly accept the decorum of the cliché: 'Your life's all shattered into smithereens'? Not to mention the awkward rhyme, 'between 's', which boldly attempts vernacular, though the actual phrase remains maladroitly formal: 'what's still between'.

As far as subject matter goes, Lowell unquestionably appeals to the snob in us, the desire to know the secrets of the grand. Harrison appeals to the inverted snob in us and, for some, that will be a greater appeal. Most readers, though, will react like Elizabeth Bishop: 'And here I must confess (and I imagine most of your contemporaries would confess the same thing) that I am green with envy of your kind of assurance. I feel I could write in as much detail about my Uncle Artie, say, – but what would be the significance? Nothing at all. He became a drunkard, fought with his wife, and spent most of the time fishing . . . and was ignorant as sin. It is sad; slightly more interesting than having an uncle practising law in Schenectady maybe, but that's about all. Whereas all you have to do is put down the names!' Elizabeth Bishop is, of course, overstating the case. One of the reasons why one withholds one's agreement is precisely the wish that she *had* written about her Uncle Artie. Few poets have written better about the apparently insignificant – from her 'Filling Station' to the anonymous, timid commuter-soul of 'The Man-Moth', from 'Jeronimo's House' to 'Manuelzinho':

> I see you all up there
> along with Formoso, the donkey,
> who brays like a pump gone dry,
> then suddenly stops.
> – All just standing, staring
> off into fog and space.

Clearly, there is a place for interestingly uninteresting subject matter. We know this from Miss Bates and the spectacle rivet. We know from Chekhov that the provincial and the defeated have their proper significance. Even Tolstoy, dealing with grand themes in *War and Peace*, succeeds best, not when he ruminates about History, but when he adds brilliantly mundane footnotes to the illuminated scroll of recorded events: Rostov's fractional pause and subsequent guilt because his French opponent has a dimple in his chin; 'one bandy-legged old French officer, wearing Hessian boots, who was getting up the hill with difficulty, taking hold of bushes'. These details are more memorable than the names of the battles in which they occur.

All the same, it is difficult to resist the appeal of striking subject matter. In 'The Music of Poetry', Eliot remarked: 'the best contemporary poetry can give us a feeling of excitement and a sense of fulfilment different from any sentiment aroused even by very much greater poetry of a past age.' Eliot assumed the reason for this to be that contemporary poetry was nearer to the reader's own everyday speech. I think it more likely that immediacy of subject matter is the proper explanation for this excitement.

For example, Carolyn Forché's recent book, *The Country Between Us* (Jonathan Cape, 1983), received great acclaim in America – largely, one suspects, because a number of her poems were about El Salvador. Her impact in England, a year or so later, was considerably less as the frisson of *actualité* diminished. (This has since reappeared – too late to affect her reception.) Yet if it was possible to see the unevenness of her work more clearly, it remained true that, technical deficiencies aside, some poems retained a crude momentum. In particular, a prose-poem, 'The Colonel', in which gruesome events were baldly narrated, with only a couple of disastrous poetic flourishes. War and atrocities are powerful subjects. Nevertheless they are subject to the law of diminishing returns, however strong their initial impact. Hardly any good poems came out of the conflict in Vietnam and most of those were written by James Fenton, a poet alert to the eerie surrealism of war. What happens when the war is banished from the front page and into the history books? Pound said, in the *ABC of Reading*, that 'literature is news that STAYS news.' Eliot, on the other hand, was less sanguine and noted ruefully that even good literature dates: 'the majority of poems one outgrows and outlives, as one outgrows and outlives the majority of human passions: Dante's is one of those which one can only just hope to grow up to at the end of life.' Moreover, Eliot was sceptical about the capacity of style to preserve dead subject matter. Discussing journalism in his essay 'Charles Whibley', he writes: 'literary style is sometimes assigned almost magical properties, or is credited with being a mysterious preservative for subject matter which no longer interests. This is far from being absolutely true. Style alone cannot preserve; only good style in conjunction with permanently interesting content can preserve.' 'Even poetry', he tells us, 'is not immune,' and he asks rhetorically: who 'can now read through the whole of *The Faerie Queene* with delight'?

Yet there are good poems with ostensibly dead subject matter. For instance, Herbert's 'A Wreath', which explores the Christian idea that humility contains a greater glory. For most non-Christian readers (and for a few Christians) this proposition can hardly seem the red-hot tip it once was. It is no longer news. No one is going to reel away from the notion seared with surprise. However, a Christian might easily re-formulate Pound's dictum to read: literature is truth that STAYS true. For the moment, I address myself to agnostic readers.

> A wreathèd garland of deservèd praise,
> Of praise deservèd, unto Thee I give.
> I give to Thee, Who knowest all my wayes,
> My crooked winding wayes, wherein I live –
> Wherein I die, not live; for life is straight,
> Straight as a line, and ever tends to Thee –
> To Thee, Who art more farre above deceit
> Then deceit seems above simplicitie.
> Give me simplicitie, that I may live;
> So live and like, that I may know Thy wayes;

> Know them, and practise them; then shall I give,
> For this poore wreath, give Thee a crown of praise.

What remains news here is not the ostenible, paraphrasable subject matter, but its stylistic demonstration. Herbert's lines are themselves braided with repetitions like a wreath: the end of each line turns to become the beginning of the next. The plaint is also a plait, in which the repetition is at first inverted ('deservèd praise', 'praise deservèd') and finally straightforward as simplicity wins over crookedness. Even as he prays for true simplicity, then, Herbert demonstrates his own human reluctance to forsake intricacy, 'the crooked winding wayes', though he does so up to a point. The subject matter of the poem is also its form. In this case, the style does preserve the subject matter because it is the subject matter. Equally, Napoleon's Russian campaign is not news any longer, but Tolstoy's treatment of it is. Later in his career, Eliot came to see this: 'Real poetry survives not only a change of popular opinion but the complete extinction of interest in the issues with which the poet was passionately concerned.'

If the treatment of subject matter is everything, we should not be too worried when Peter Porter tells us, referring to his family, that they are 'quite without distinction'.* In this, he is at one with Elizabeth Bishop and Tony Harrison, the former a great poet. However, like Elizabeth Bishop, Porter feels the immediate force of Lowell's claim on our interest: '[my family] may be reasonably called "Old Colonial", but hardly in the patrician sense of Robert Lowell's or, to stick to Australia, Patrick White's. None of the Porters has ever made *Who's Who in Australia*, though family legend has it that my great grandfather was Lord Mayor of Brisbane for a time in the 1880s . . . I have to dress up my material: it is very ordinary stuff.'

This is modest and charming. It will also serve as an introduction to Peter Porter's primary subject matter. He is richly intrigued and preoccupied by status throughout the collected

---

Collected Poems by Peter Porter, Oxford University Press.

poems – social status, sexual status ('trying to keep it up with the Joneses!') and literary status. He is baffled and resentful about his own ontological status, the given and apparently unalterable climate of unhappiness in which he lives and moves and has his being:

> It is the little stone of unhappiness
> which I keep with me. I had it as a child . . .

He is fascinated by the ability of others to commandeer status, the effortless arrogance of, say, Joyce:

> I never knew when to stop
>
> If I'd been christened Stanislaus
> I'd have claimed the throne of Poland.

The early and middle satirical poems bring a connoisseur's eye to the world of consumer durables and status symbols. It is hardly an accident that two poems, one early, one late, are entitled 'The Picture of Nobody', or that the phrase turns up in yet a third poem.

'I have to dress up my material'. One turns forewarned to Porter's poems about his ancestry – looking forward, indeed, to the poet's promised 'cavalier indifference to fact'. But a poem like 'A Christmas Recalled' leaves one baffled by its dullness. If this is the dressed-up version, what can the plain truth have been like? Only a moral addiction to the truth, however flat, could explain this stanza:

> In this time I heard my uncle calling my mother:
> 'Marion, I've made a new one, give it a try.'
> I saw my face stretched in his cocktail shaker
> When I wiped the condensation off. We were
> A drinking family and I would quietly lie
> Eight years old drinking Schweppes in bed, their
> Noise a secure lullaby, drinking up my fear.

189

This is, of course, an early poem and Peter Porter's preface states clearly that he does not want 'to act the prig to the man who wrote these poems' and has therefore changed as little as possible. But was it, one asks, really a 'cavalier indifference to fact' that produced the line: 'Marion, I've made a new one, give it a try'? Was his uncle Ron Glum? The undemanding rhyme scheme creates its own problems, too: the penultimate line of the stanza, for instance, with its protrusive 'their' jutting out like a leg in traction. And there is a fidelity to the echoic hangover in the three times repeated 'drinking' that may not be intentional. Only the cocktail shaker begins to approach the vivid and even that is ponderously imagined beside Lowell's particularity in a similar vein of childhood reminiscence:

> his illegal home-made claret
> was as sugary as grape jelly
> in a tumbler capped with paraffin.

Despite Porter's sense of Lowell's patrician grandeur, I doubt if one can account for the qualitative difference by the superiority of the Winslow cocktail cabinet. For one thing, the hooch is illegal. For another, in all probability Lowell invented the drink with a 'cavalier indifference to fact'.

The aural shortcomings here are not an isolated instance in his work and bother even his admirers. For John Lucas, who admires Porter's savage attacks on metropolitan manners, verbal clumsiness is simply the price to be paid for Porter's fecundity and invention — the cost of weariness after years at the typewriter bashing the smoothies. For others perhaps less taken by the satirist, less nostalgic for consumer bric-à-brac and brand-names, the difficulty is in deciding whether the ear is tin, zinc or, on occasion, polythene:

> What is locked in a book
> Of a Civil War, of a king . . .

Might this be King Ofa, by any chance? Double genitives, rush hours of present participles, clumsy repetition, syntactic chaos, whimsical punctuation, ugly assonances and a widespread aural ineptitude never leave Porter's poetry. In the end, one becomes an indulgent screw greeting familiar old recidivists. A brief selection from the early volumes: 'The Unicorn's Horn', 'In the shrinking morning shadows', 'Dangling in his hessian wrap. / In his own house an old mother', 'Time eats savoury lechery,' 'Old Terrestrial in hospital', 'O the cancer atolls, growing by writing light', 'After the pictures of the sweetness of fonts', 'Have nothing to lose but your brains but you cry', 'To wearing old stockings', 'Picture, or when I joined in when they', 'I came to this spot full of the smell / Of wild honeysuckle', 'And fish choking in unbreathable blue', 'He came to hear / the silver pornographer lecture', 'Within an ant's tremor'. The later work supplies: 'grilling all writing but his own', '*God make gardeners better nomenclators*', 'stripping for the shining theatre instruments', 'looking at me to turn me to stone', 'Vulcan's and Venus's trespasses', 'Offering shining emphasis', 'Mornings weaving through the mud', 'You asked in an uncharacteristic note', 'I see her hand on an envelope', 'She in an urn'. What have you done this time, In An Un? Though Porter swears by the English language ('This is language / I would go into the jungle with'), in practice his deployment of it is back-slappingly enthusiastic rather than subtle:

> so useful for asking for fasteners in
> As well as for caning professors

Forsooth.

The strange thing is that, in the later poetry, these inveterate faults begin to co-exist with a genuine eloquence, a gift for phrase-making which Porter sums up shrewdly in the title 'A Philosopher of Captions'. The other thing that remains the same is his obscurity. It is often said that as his poetry has developed it has become more obscure, but two early poems, 'Jack and Jill' and 'The Unicorn's Horn', will disabuse anyone of that notion. Porter's own account (in a recent interview) is accurate and endearingly funny: 'it's interesting that what I regard as my best book, the one published in 1972, called *Preaching to the Converted*, marks the point at which my poetry got farthest away from Group practices, and returned to what I'd been doing before I entered the Group; a rather dense, oracular, even obscurantist, rhetorical kind of writing. I think I've always had that side to myself, which many of my friends deprecate. When I told Vernon Scannell that I'd had some poems translated into German, his reply was "I thought they were in German already."'

The relationship of eloquence to obscurity in Porter's later work is revealingly glossed in a *New Statesman* piece he wrote about William Empson. Porter's own poetic strategy is expounded along with Empson's: 'people were not used to poems which began so laconically: "and now she cleans her teeth into the lake." But the originality of the poem lies in its enormous power of modulation, within a few lines, so that it ends as magnificently as anything in Milton or Pope.' Again, and even more revealingly: 'it departs from the plain and known into the empyrean (so many of his final lines are resonantly in the stars), and does not need to cross continents or fill up Broch-like spaces with lexical soup.' In fact, this is what Larkin does so well – the shift from the blunt and sometimes foul-mouthed to the final singing resonance. The difference between Larkin and Empson and Porter is the undistributed middle in the work of the latter two – the reader doesn't get it. What lexical soup there is contains enigmatic lumps that are difficult to swallow.

Consider Porter's 'A Philosopher of Captions'. It begins laconically enough ('The knowledge anyway is worth something') and ends in the stars ('That pain is the one immortal gift of our stewardship'). The problem is that, while the last line bursts brilliantly in the dark empyrean, it leaves behind a milk bottle thick with smoke – the rest of the poem. As far as I understand 'A Philosopher of Captions', it seems to be about a perennial Porter concern – namely, his poetic status: a subject which exercises most poets but which most prefer not to write about since it is a vulnerable area, though Seamus Heaney's 'Exposure' is a brilliant account of poetic uncertainty. And a lucid account, unlike Porter's:

> The knowledge anyway is worth something,
> That no person from this liner-browed brain
> Will reach the height of those grave captains
> Whose Dantesque walk and Homeric facing
> Still flare on our desolate concrete plain
> So late; that I am a philosopher of captions.

In this opening stanza, the metaphor is fudged but just intelligible. Lines on the cogitating brow suggest, via a pun, an ocean-going liner with captains on the bridge. At the same time, the ringing plains of windy Troy are brought up to date with 'our desolate concrete plain'. The gist seems to be that the poet will never be Dante or Homer, only a philosopher of captions. This is clear despite the bodged dovetailing of ship and concrete plain. The final line of the poem ('That pain is the one immortal gift of our stewardship') relates to this presumably by the menial role of steward in which Porter casts himself in contrast to the captains.

However, the centre will not hold. Stanza two describes (I think) poetic apprenticeship prior to the gradual sense of individual poetic identity:

> This special authenticity must grow on one
> After baffled if dutiful years putting down
> Some orders of words towards definition –
> Here space a fear and there placate a pun,
> Or adjudicate through childhood, one noun
> Up and another down, with everything a fiction.

The last three lines are a confused evocation of confusion – the poetic process as placating now words themselves, now auto-biography, according to their needs and demands. But I am unsure what exactly is being described by 'one noun / Up and another down'. It is a poetic process I am unfamiliar with, though I recognize the influential presence of Eliot's 'intolerable wrestle /

With words and meanings'. Nor do I like the sound of 'words towards'.

The third stanza attends to those who have achieved a measure of success. But they are no longer naval types bent over the binnacle. They are 'the shouters, the ones met at stations by crowds':

> One can only admire them, join the acclamation
> And worry at their simplifying stance. The text,
> After all, belongs to its explainers; those clouds
> Are felt only as rain; an acceleration
> In the speed of madness, harder saving from the wreck.

Eh? Halfway through, the light is switched off. It never really comes on again either. Do the lines mean that Porter is puzzled at the way poetic heroes accept their success – because finally everything lies with the critics, not in their own hands? The clouds are presumably an illustration of this thesis: they make their effect only as they touch others down below. The last line and a half return the reader abruptly to P & O and may mean that failure after success is worse than no success in the first place. The bigger you are, the harder you fall: 'In the speed of madness, harder saving from the wreck.'

The final stanza refuses nevertheless to relinquish all hubristic poetic ambition:

> But the power is still somewhere in us, hovering
> In the forehead auditorium of sounds . . .

Why? The answer seems to be that one has a responsibility to one's lived experience, one's past, one's memories, that will not go away. But the image for this is hermetic and bizarre.

> Those who were with us and have changed their shape
> Come back, like old ladies with parcels moving
> To the chair beside us; embarrassment abounds
> That pain is the one immortal gift of our stewardship.

The psychological wrinkle about old ladies and parcels is too idiosyncratic for me to understand fully, altogether too personal.

Though it is possible, then, to salvage meaning from this poem, it remains a disaster. The nature of the disaster is interesting and typical: the metaphors are mixed and mismanaged. Metaphor is never an agent of clarification in Porter's work. It is a device for disguising the banal: 'Perhaps you should say something / A bit more interesting than what you mean,' words tell him in 'English Subtitles'. In fact, he usually says less, not more, than he means. Porter's strength is for quasi-choral last lines, like this evocation of marital difficulty in 'Old-Fashioned Wedding', which is indebted to 'The Whitsun Weddings':

> After this huge
> Joke, a terrible deluge
> The speeding innocents know nothing of,
> Mad hours, silence, subterfuge
> And all the dark expedients of love.

In the same poem, sexual misadventure is treated metaphorically and ponderously, first impotence, then defloration:

> In the flurry of guy ropes let down,
> And crushed flowers in delicate cups.

'Cups', which is needed for the rhyme scheme, is inappropriately rigid and unyielding for what it describes and 'delicate' does not save it.

'Old-Fashioned Wedding' is typically pessimistic, part of Porter's poetic personality and of a piece with the early poetry: 'honest, loveless, childhood Peter', the poet dogged by bad-luck and self-disgust. In this area, there is little of Larkin's saving humour. The dominant note is anger and envy:

> To be above the tearing fingers of the ruck
> You need good teeth, a good income, good luck.

There is something so persistent in the rage that it becomes depressing and unattractive. You want the poet to change the subject.

In 1974, tragically, it was changed for him by the sudden death of his wife:

> Rather, I think of a woman lying on her bed
> Staring for hours up to the ceiling where
> Nothing is projected – death the only angel
> To shield her from despair.

The preoccupation with the literary ladder survives since it was evidently a topic much discussed:

> it is not a small thing to die,
> But looking back I see only the disappointed man
> Casting words *upon* the page. Was it for this
> I stepped out *upon* the stairs of death obediently?

(My tetchy italics.) In the poems about his wife, Porter's new eloquence, already evident in *Living in a Calm Country*, sadly finds an adequate subject. The poems are freighted with remorse, regret, tenderness, guilt and memory. Obviously harrowing to write, they are also difficult to criticize. The best moments are the most simple:

> The curtain of your life was drawn
> Some time between despair and dawn.

These are not fine lines. They are great poetry. So is this passage from the same poem, 'An Exequy':

> I owe a death to you – one day
> The time will come for me to pay
> When your slim shape from photographs
> Stands at my door and gently asks

> If I have any work to do
> Or will I come to bed with you.

There are other great moments, too, never sustained for long enough. But they serve to make the reader feel the anguished force of Porter's outcry:

> Her clothes are syntax, so that I read
> someone else's poem and I am there
> on the banks of salvation
> or crying in a furnace. Why has thou
> held talent above my head
> and let me see it, O my God!

In the face of this, who has the temerity to notice the slight ungainliness of 'Why has thou / held talent above my head' – and to wonder why the poet resisted the full biblical 'hast', creating instead an awkward hybrid? 'An Exequy' has its moments but always it stands in the shadow of its great predecessor and the eloquence isn't always pure:

> This introduction serves to sing
> Your mortal death as Bishop King
> Once hymned in tetrametric rhyme
> His young wife, lost before her time . . .

Isn't 'mortal' an otiose adjective? What other kind of death can there be? 'The hand is stopped upon the clock', 'Upon a sculpted angel group': isn't 'upon' archaic padding? 'With what halt steps' is similarly antiquated. Yet criticism seems an impertinence. Certain poems in this group stand out: 'The Delegate', 'An Angel in Blythburgh Church', 'The Easiest Room in Hell', 'Non Piangere, Liù', 'Talking to You Afterwards', 'Alcestis and the Poet'. None of them, though, are perfect, however much the subject matter tells us that they must be.

Poetry and Philosophy

With his thesis on F. H. Bradley behind him and *Four Quartets* some way ahead, T. S. Eliot was sceptical about the place of philosophy in poetry. 'We have the same respect for Blake's philosophy', he wrote in 1920, 'that we have for an ingenious piece of home-made furniture.' And even Dante's shop-bought Thomist philosophy strikes him as an irrelevant bonus – a kind of magnificent desk, a miniature Arc de Triomphe on which Dante could rest with confidence while he got on with the business of writing poetry. Nor is Eliot alone. Arnold, for instance, deplored the tendency of Wordsworth's early admirers to recommend the metaphysical lumber in the poet's attic. Earlier still, Coleridge regretted, rightly or wrongly, filling his pleasure dome with Kantian sideboards and secondhand dressers from Herr Schelling.

Of the modernists, only Wallace Stevens has come out in favour of the poetic possibilities of philosophy, and even he has many reservations. In his essay 'A Collect of Philosophy', he argues that 'it is often the case that concepts of philosophy are poetic', yet rejects Leibniz's theory of monads, Lucretius and the relevant bits of Milton, Pope and Wordsworth. He is, in fact, only interested in those lofty philosophical ideas which ignite the imagination – that is, when philosophers are more like poets than philosophers, however much their aims might ultimately diverge. Stevens isn't interested in a set of six dining-room chairs or a three-piece suite – only in the odd sublime sofa richly brocaded with metaphor. His selectivity, though, didn't pre-empt criticism.

Randall Jarrell, echoing Valéry's complaint that 'poetry is a bad medium for philosophy', once described the later work of Stevens, overboldly in my view, as 'G. E. Moore at the spinet'.

Clearly, there are problems. In Charles Tomlinson's poetry,* nature has always been a mental event, not so much evoked as philosophically annotated. It is Wittgenstein at the triangle or thirteen ways of looking at a blackboard. Admirers find it uncompromisingly austere. Detractors find it pedantic. Peering scrupulously at phenomena over a pair of depressed clericals, as it were, Tomlinson describes the dialectic between their flux and the orderly cast of the perceiving intelligence: 'One sees. But not merely the passive mirrorings of the retinal mosaic – nor, like Ruskin's blind man suddenly struck by vision, without memory or conception. The senses, reminded by other seeings, bring to bear on the act of vision their pattern of images; they give point and place to an otherwise naked and homeless impression. It is the mind sees.' Against the mind's categorizing imperative, though, phenomena assert their own irreducible reality: bird skulls, for instance, 'resist the eyes' imaginings with the blade of a beak which no lyrical admiration can attenuate to frailty'.

In other words, thesis and antithesis are locked in an endless Hegelian embrace, where nature and the mind take turns for who's on top in the missionary position. It's a dry, joyless business even when, as often, Tomlinson's subject is the appropriately protean one of water:

> There is a geometry of water, for this
>   Squares off the clouds' redundancies
> And sets them floating in a nether atmosphere
>   All angles and elongations . . .

Other favourite subjects for Tomlinson are wind, light and clouds – all of them suitably unstable phenomena. But, like Monet at

*Selected Poems 1951–1974 by Charles Tomlinson, Oxford University Press. *The Shaft* by Charles Tomlinson, Oxford University Press.

Étretat, Tomlinson (himself a painter) constantly returns to water. With this difference: it is water, water everywhere, and every drop to think:

> Its strength is here: it must
> Account for its opposite and yet remain
> Itself, of its own power get there.
> Water is like logic . . .

You might expect a painter to be more interested in rendering visual effects and less in analysing them like the worst kind of art critic: 'A whitish smoke / in drifting diagonals / accents, divides / the predominance of street / and chimney lines, / where all is either / mathematically supine / or vertical, except / the pyramids of slag.' Such a painstaking passage reminds one of George Moore's comment that Kipling tracked down the details of a sunset like a detective in a divorce case – except that here you wouldn't convict. First he sees it, then you don't.

The Shaft, Tomlinson's new volume, pursues nature as before through various *trompe-l'œil* effects and temporary perfections. In addition, however, it opens with a number of poems on historical subjects, including Charlotte Corday's assassination of Marat, an event which, in consecutive poems, he presents from both points of view – the stabber and the stabbed, thesis and antithesis. In an earlier volume, he wrote around the murder of Trotsky where, improbably, the assassin was more perturbed by the 'whispered roar' of falling papers and his heightened perception of ordinary objects than by the task in hand. Here, too, at the crucial moment, there is a failure of language and imagination:

> She struck him from above. One thrust. Her whole
> Intent and innocence directing it
> To breach through flesh and enter where it must,
> It seemed a blow that rose up from within:
> Tinville reduced it all to expertise . . .

In fact, Tomlinson is more interested in the ironies of history than in the actual murder, more touched that she should have gone to the guillotine believing she had stopped the Terror. But it's difficult to respond to this pathos when the murder itself is disposed of so feebly. There is nothing concrete in the poem and certainly nothing to rival Browning's brilliantly prurient imagination in *The Ring and the Book* where the bystanders deduce the type of weapon from the shape of the wounds:

> Triangular i' the blade, a Genoese,
> Armed with those little hook-teeth . . .

Curiously, another historical murder produces the best moment in Michael Schmidt's otherwise disappointing fourth collection.* Sisera recollects his fatal encounter with Jael, including the moment before the hammer blow when, he remembers, the spike 'pricked' his brow. It is a superbly imagined moment of accuracy and understatement. If *A Change of Affairs* had more comparable insights, one might think that Schmidt's newly adopted stance of austerity was justified. As it is, one remembers his earlier work, *Bedlam and the Oakwood* and *Desert of the Lions*, with regret – even if those books were themselves nostalgic for, respectively, the Lowell of *Notebook* and Elizabeth Bishop.

A Change of Affairs opens with an allegorical poem, ostensibly about Noah. The diction is deliberately undistinguished, as if it had been written to be translated easily, and the lines drift uncomfortably in and out of iambic metre. Noah gets his instructions from God in a dream but he is reluctant to start work on the ark because he's fond of the earth and doesn't want to see it inundated. He knows that, although God is the final cause, he is the necessary efficient cause of the flood. Shem can only see the situation in terms of family aggrandizement: 'The earth will all be ours, though,' he clumsily ruminates. Japheth wants to build the ark so he can have forty days of idleness and a lazy life thereafter. Ham is a craftsman, uninterested in the moral issues. Straight

A Change of Affairs by Michael Schmidt, Anvil.

away, he starts pricing wood. Noah's final word in the poem is 'I don't believe the dream was meant for me.'

The trouble with this kind of poem is that it offers so few stylistic rewards that one must judge it by the quality of its moral perceptions and the neatness of its allegory. The moral is surely rather obvious not to say banal: the ark was built, therefore evil took place, as it always does, not by a conscious choice of one wicked person, but because it is easier to give way to the desires of others than maintain a position of isolated virtue. As for allegorical neatness, isn't God a bit of a loose end? Since He is, by definition, good, isn't it odd to cast Him as the villain upstairs?

Originality in Poetry

On 22 May 1920, a confident e. e. cummings wrote to his father: 'after all, sans blague and Howells, it is a supreme pleasure to have done something FIRST.' No one, probably, would deny cummings his originality or dissent from this aggressive, if unspecific, denunciation:

> certain ideas gestures
> rhymes, like Gillette Razor Blades
> having been used and re-used
> to the mystical moment of dullness emphatically are
> Not To Be Resharpened.

If modernism means anything, it means originality. Picasso exclaimed to his dealer, Kahnweiler: 'It's magnificent to invent new subjects. Take Van Gogh: Potatoes, those shapeless things! To have painted that, or a pair of old shoes! That's really something!'

And yet, while we accept this apotheosis of originality, how many of us have the intellectual chutzpah to assent to the inevitable corollaries as they affect, for instance, Renaissance art in general? Picasso again: 'People are always talking about the Renaissance – but it's really pathetic. I've been seeing some Tintorettos recently. It's nothing but cinema, cheap cinema. It makes an impression because there's plenty of people, plenty of movement and grandiloquent gestures. And then it's all about Jesus and the Apostles.' Surely, one thinks, this is the *reductio ad absurdum*? Is originality so important that it can banish the output of an entire era to the lumber room?

Just the same, originality *is* important and, ironically enough, it's by this, his chosen standard, that one eventually dismisses cummings as a major poet. There is little point in being FIRST if there isn't a second or third. And the total absence of followers is easily explained in the case of cummings. His originality, even as he describes it to his father, is a relatively trivial thing: 'such minutiae as commas and small i's, in which minutiae my Firstness thrives . . .' Strip off the modernist make-up, the distracting false eyelashes, and there is cummings the old-fashioned troubadour, fearlessly sentimental about flowers and spring and death and love and beauty. His father, keenly unsentimental, called it 'slobber', with particular reference to 'spring omnipotent goddess'. The poet could only appeal to his allegedly transfiguring manner. There is originality and there is top-dressing. No one copies the latter.

A great many poets, though, have followed Auden, including James Fenton. In a recent *New Review*, he argued that the *Collected Poems* represent 'a great pattern-book for subsequent poets to use as they wish'. The theoretical justification for this stance, in Fenton's view, is the example of Auden himself whose originality is grounded in the extraordinary range of his borrowing: 'Auden's real decline began when he had worked through the whole gamut of possible forms and influences.' A paradoxical account of originality, you might think, but sound enough – except that it is too narrowly technical an account of Auden's genius. True, there is a vast wardrobe of borrowed clothes, but the Anglo-Saxon byrnie, hose and doublet, toga and Jamesian top-hat are effortlessly transformed into the familiar crumpled suit and carpet-slippers because Auden's subject matter was deeply idiosyncratic. He invented new subjects as much as he re-invented old styles.

In cummings, for instance, children are traditionally innocent; in Auden, they're often guilty and the effect of this innovation is easily traced in subsequent poetry. 'Huge tears are in the pond', Peter Porter's reminiscence of childhood, for example, is also a reminiscence of Auden's 'The boiling tears amid the hot-house plants'. The danger of emulating Auden's technical range, then, is that it is inextricably bound up with his characteristic gifts. You try to borrow a fiver and find yourself in debt to the tune of a fortune. Thus, Fenton's 'The Pitt-Rivers Museum, Oxford' (in his earlier book, *Terminal Moraine*) ends:

> he calmly pushed open the gate
> And entered the wood near the placard: 'TAKE NOTICE MEN-
> TRAPS AND SPRING-GUNS ARE SET ON THESE PREMISES.'
> For his father had protected his good estate.

But this menacing, unfamiliar ground is, in fact, oddly familiar. We've been here before in Auden's 'No Change of Place':

> Will neither go nor send his son
> Further through foothills than the rotting stack
> Where gaitered gamekeeper with gun and dog
> Will shout 'Turn back'.

The echoes in *A Vacant Possession** are more generalized but just as pervasive, yet there is something identifiably Fentonian. His starting point is Auden's statement: 'Present in every human being are two desires, a desire to know the truth about the primary world, the given world in which we are born, live, love, hate and die, and the desire to make new secondary worlds of our own or, if we cannot make them ourselves, to share in the secondary worlds of those who can.' Those who can, do; those who can't, leech. Fenton can. His fictional worlds impose themselves on us (and on him) as they might on the mind of a madman – which is why the poems are prefaced by an extract from *Rasselas* where the astronomer complains that he has suffered 'chimeras to prey upon me in secret'.

'Song', for instance, continues the nonsense mode of 'Lollipops of the Pomeranian Baroque' and 'The Kingfisher's Boxing

---

A Vacant Possession by James Fenton, TNR Publications.

Gloves' in his previous collection. It is a short humoresque that examines the night-life of slugs and spiders – an underworld, in fact: 'the slugs / Wind up another night of sluggish trade.' 'Song' is, however, distinguished from other nonsense poetry by the way in which it constantly flirts with meaning: we almost take it seriously because it almost takes itself seriously. The other poems, though very different in tone, are also partly about the relationship of the purely imagined to the real. The last, 'In a Notebook', repeats the same description of a Vietnamese village during the war but offers two alternative endings, the first imagined, the second real. Here, the imagination is seen to be irresponsible. Elsewhere, it is compelling, inventive, a brilliant liar.

'Prison Island' is obviously a fiction, full of poignantly urgent political advice that has been superseded by time, yet delighting in its own dubious status. How can we be moved by the merely invented, it seems to ask. The text of the poem is a letter from a political prisoner on one of the Lipari islands off north Sicily to a friend on the mainland. The time is uncertain, but before Garibaldi drove out the Bourbons from Sicily and Naples in 1860–1. It begins:

> That's the Naples packet slipping out of harbour
> With a fat Bourbon guard and a hold full of capers
> So perhaps my letter will have escaped the censors.

But if the poem is the letter, how can it include information about its fate after it was sent? This deliberately gives the fictional game away and allows Fenton his implicit question: how can we be troubled by a chimera?

'Nest of Vampires' imposes on us the scenario of an adolescent about to leave the posh family seat for good, as a result, we infer, of his father's bankruptcy. 'The house is all packed up' and it is real enough, except that, for the boy, it has always been mixed up with fiction – the world of Wilkie Collins's *The Moonstone*, mystery stories and nursery rhymes. The title is, I take it, a lurid illustration of how the boy usurps reality: the large house is viewed through blood-tinted spectacles and leased out to Count Dracula. Though their conversation survives in fragments, real people scarcely impinge on the boy's rapt imaginings of secret rooms and covert signals. The primary world is deposed.

'A Vacant Possession' begins once more with an empty house, but this time the poet is moving in, with bewildering imaginative speed. The furniture is, of course, purely mental, as the sudden time changes make clear. After only an afternoon and night, Fenton writes 'What shall we do the next day?' instead of 'What shall we do tomorrow?' Once again, though, we're convinced by the detail (a mixture of the ordinary and the bizarre) until our disbelief is quite suspended by Fenton's final trump: the narrator goes into his bedroom for something he's forgotten, then can't remember what it is. Given the poet's *carte blanche* to invent, what could be more convincing than this 'failure' to do so?

Reading Ted Walker's well-made collection, *Burning the Ivy*,* I was reminded of the joke about the man who invented television – in 1975. It worked but it wasn't sufficiently original. In order to praise Walker's animal poems, you'd have to forget that Ted Hughes invented animals in 1956. Naturally, there are good lines (Walker's ram has a 'black / scrotum tight with tottery lambs') but even the best have a remaindered feel about them. Moreover, Hughes isn't the only poltergeist throwing his weight around in these poems. Heaney's Grauballe man 'seems to weep / the black river of himself' and we find this trick of self-reference in Walker's 'Logs': 'Dumped from the truck, they / clobber onto themselves.' Frost, however, is the main ghost in this cadence:

> Powdery mortar has begun to fall
> As fall it did our first winter here.

Throughout *Burning the Ivy*, one is aware of a white-haired figure guiding Ted Walker's elbow as he sagely moralizes over his various agricultural tasks. But there are also touches of Betjeman

**Burning the Ivy by Ted Walker, Jonathan Cape.

('Between the Acts'), Eliot's 'Burnt Norton' ('*Tendrils* of summer warmth / Clasp October; the leaves *cling*'), the awkwardly reverent Larkin ('I stood apart against an awkward headstone') and Auden's 'Their Lonely Betters' (fish 'do / not know they cannot be mad'). In the end, you feel that literature itself is the really fatal influence.

Berryman and Inclusiveness

In his famous essay, 'Beyond the Gentility Principle' (1962), A. Alvarez announced that 'the great moderns experimented not just to make it new formally, but to open poetry up to new areas of experience'. The implicit image, that of the poet as explorer, is typically rugged, but the proposition itself is uncontroversial. Poets have been making things new for a long time. To take a trivial example, Cowper's *The Task* begins with the deliberate comic shock of 'I sing the SOFA' – signalling a greater poetic inclusiveness. More seriously, Wordsworth's *Prelude* is a great innovatory poem of psychology, while his 'Preface' to *Lyrical Ballads* foresaw a time when the poet would 'be ready to follow the steps of the Man of Science' – a prediction realized (alas) in Tennyson's *The Princess*, with its 'shale and hornblende, rag and trap and tuff'. Poetry, then, is a suitcase that constantly aspires to the condition of a trunk. In proclaiming this, Alvarez was in good company.

But what, in 1962, were the 'new areas' to be? Genocide, death camps, the psychology of evil? Alvarez gestured in these directions yet, sensibly, flinched away from any final prescriptiveness, even at the cost of some polemical bathos: 'what poetry needs, in brief, is a new seriousness.' All pretence of theoretical rigour thus abandoned, Alvarez argued from examples. Berryman was a leading exponent of what he had in mind – a poet of increasing variety, inclusiveness and interest. Suicide, alcoholism, fame, fatherhood, bereavement, facial blemishes ('a blackhead at the base / of her smooth nose looks sullenly at me') and incontinence in childbirth are some of his subjects:

> I press with horrible joy down
> my back cracks like a wrist
> shame I am voiding oh behind it is too late

Just the same, it's mildly ironical that Alvarez's nominee for the 'new seriousness' should be a poet whose favoured mode proved so often to be humorous and clowning – so much so, in fact, that Lowell singled it out in this last book, *Day by Day*:

> Just the other day,
> I discovered how we differ – humour . . .

It's an overgenerous judgement that wasn't always true. However mechanically rhetorical Lowell could be on occasion, he was delicately humorous in his greatest, pioneering book, *Life Studies*. There, describing his father's 'sensationally sober' Chevrolet, he dispenses some accurate banter:

> The local dealer, a 'buccaneer',
> had been bribed 'a king's ransom'
> to deliver quickly a car without chrome.

Commander Lowell's harmless hyperbole reaches us sprigged with tenderly teasing inverted commas.

Berryman's humour was of a different kind, self-absorbed and more rumbustiously ironical: 'Legman assman bustman, abominable Henry.' The urgent sexual preferences dispense with the polite pauses of punctuation. In effect, Berryman had only one subject – himself – and even during the forties when he was dutifully writing public-Audenesque, his diaries were crammed with pages of self-analysis. Some readers find Berryman's egotism claustrophobic and it's true he can be repetitive on the subject of fatherhood (Little Twiss muttering Latin on the steps of Smith and Vassar) and ignorance (the unread *Ubu Roi*, for example).

Nevertheless, as Tennyson noted of *Maud*'s mad narrator, 'different phases of passion in one person take the place of different characters'. Berryman was various and knew it, sometimes as an affliction:

> Cross am I sometimes with my little daughter:
> fill her eyes with tears. Forgive me, Lord.
> Unite my various soul,
> sole watchman of the wide & single stars.

These beautiful, eloquent, unsentimental, self-reproachful lines are from a perfectly made prayer in *Love and Fame*, one of a series generally reckoned to be unsuccessful. The objections are that the humour is misplaced and brash, the reverence tritely formulaic, the vision of God negligible beside Berryman's own omnipresence. But although the religious poetry is uneven, every poem has its vivid moments and there are some totally achieved prayers where the humour and the reverence complement each other perfectly:

> Holy, as I suppose I dare to call you
> without pretending to know anything about you . . .

Prayer, a distinct sub-category of religious poetry, suits Berryman because its traditional blend of praise and request accommodates his egotism. In prayer, God never has our undivided attention and Berryman's praise is always refreshingly opinionated: 'endower of Earth so gorgeous & different from the boring Moon . . .' Here, within a single line, the cheek qualifies the reverence and vice versa, but elsewhere the qualification can work across the whole poem, redeeming lines that, taken out of context, might seem either trite or brash.

This latest, posthumous volume of unpublished work is, on the whole, inferior.* Yet it has moments of wild comedy and terror that stay in the mind:

*Henry's Fate by John Berryman, Faber and Faber.

He slept longer than usual:
one cliff he had to descend, clinging to mosses,
woke him though.

Berryman has always been an expert on the pains of sleep. There are, too, moments of eloquence like this terminal sunset: 'the sun burned down . . .' *Henry's Fate* is a timely reminder of Berryman's skills – the convoluted demotic that derives from Hopkins, the daring promiscuity of tragedy and farce, the ability to open up 'new areas of experience'.

After Berryman's formidable directness and prodigal gifts, reading the poetry of A. Alvarez* and Harold Pinter† is like being whisked away from a banquet and plunged into a world of austerity – poetry aspiring to the condition of a ration book. Alvarez tries to fulfil his own inclusive prescription but succeeds only superficially. His poems, written between 1953 and 1976, attempt intimate, difficult subjects – suicide, sexual jealousy, abortion, the onset of age, failed love. Mostly, though, Alvarez can include this experience only by treating it obliquely and euphemistically. Even the abortion is sentimentalized: 'You vanished. Later came violence.' 'Violence' tells us more about Alvarez's guilt than the fact of surgery, and the quaint scraps of dialogue are equally literary: 'I bleed still', the girl is supposed to have said, rather than 'I'm still bleeding.'

Alvarez recently disclosed that, while reading *Bleak House* in 1964, he realized for the first time that literature was about *pleasure* – not technique or the search for identity or any other critical formula. 'It was like Saul on the road to Tarsus.' I find this disarming admission at once courageous and damaging. It certainly illuminates his poetry, most of which was written before the revelation. We are a long way from pleasure of any kind in *Autumn to Autumn* because the critical police are out in strength. Accordingly, little is risked and nothing achieved beyond the habitual resort to a timid, moody pastoral which excludes the ostensible subject. As Mrs Gradgrind says, 'I think there's a pain

Autumn to Autumn by A. Alvarez, Macmillan.
†*Poems and Prose 1949–1977* by Harold Pinter, Eyre Methuen.

somewhere in the room' – but finding it in these poems is like looking for a hypodermic in a haystack. They are thin not trim, dull not austere.

Not so the early poems of Harold Pinta, as he was known when he published fraudulent imitations of Dylan Thomas in *Poetry London*:

> Now in the quaver of a roisty bar, the wansome lady
> I blust and stir,
> Who pouts the bristle of a sprouting fag.

You can't get more inclusive than that. It's like being offered a sweet and carrying off a brawling cluster of liquorice allsorts. Pinter, though, quickly realized that this chaotic, barely intelligible prodigality was not his *métier*. The later poems, more characteristically, offer very little beyond the rustling of an empty paper bag. I confess I understood very few of these poems, but those which aren't written by the Pinter encoding-machine hardly persuade one to persevere.

Poetry Today

The problems of the poet today are almost identical to the problems of the poet a century ago today. This is what Eliot was driving at when he said, in 'The Music of Poetry', that 'every revolution in poetry is apt to be, and sometimes to announce itself as, a return to common speech'. Poetry is always tempted by diction whose sell-by date has long since been passed. Even though poetry is always capable of dealing with the unpoetical, for every generation of poets this requires a special effort. Poetry's business is to replace old plant equipment and constantly retool. Philip Larkin, for instance, admired the development of Betjeman's style in *Summoned by Bells* for its flexibility: it was, wrote Larkin, a blank verse 'resigned to swallowing anything, even "Don't throw old blades into the w.c." ' And this is Ted Hughes on Shakespeare's language: it has 'the air of being invented in a state of crisis, for a terribly urgent job, a homely spur-of-the-moment improvisation out of whatever verbal scrap happens to be lying around, and this is exactly what real speech is.' Not very different, it turns out, from what Hughes has to say about *Crow*: 'songs with no music whatsoever, in a super-simple and a super-ugly language which would in a way shed everything except just what he [Crow] wanted to say without any other consideration and that's the basis of the style of the whole thing.' In other words, both Hughes and Shakespeare have invented a functional style, a verbal waste-disposal unit into which anything goes. Even old razor blades.

If there isn't this sustained effort to accommodate the unpoeti-

214

cal, poetry is likely to revert to the poetical – to be high-minded, high-sounding, a kind of warehouse for the storage of antique ideas and genteel soft furnishings, where nothing is ugly because nothing is particular; where everything is under an Antarctica of dust-sheets. This idea of 'poetry' makes it synonymous with 'beauty'. In *Three Sisters* Masha breaks down. Stuck with her boring husband, the Latin master Kulygin, with Vershinin drifting inexorably out of her life, she breaks down and begins to recite poetry: 'A green oak by a curving shore, / And on that oak a chain of gold . . .' At which point, Masha gets stuck, muddles the words, sobs. The possibility of poetry has left her life and she knows it will never return. What she means by poetry – beauty, Moscow, emotional excitement, a less drab existence, spiritual afflatus – isn't quite what poets mean by poetry. (Significantly, Masha is quoting from a Pushkin fairy tale.) Poets hate this sanitized, sentimental, overly spiritual version of what they do. They always want the unpoetical.

But, in order to make poetry do what prose can do unblinkingly – swallow those used razor blades – it is a mistake to reduce poetry to prose. Just as poets should resist the poetical, so they should also resist any self-imposed attempts to reduce their options.

In one of his essays, George Orwell says that Englishmen regard the proper pronunciation of a foreign language – particularly French – as an infallible sign of effeminacy. There is a similar prejudice against poetry – a prejudice which is indigenous and easy enough to illustrate – a prejudice which regards poetry as a sort of fancy sauce copiously masking our old Teuton monosyllables. In *Pickwick Papers*, Sam Weller's father sees his son writing a valentine, and says: ' "Poetry's unnatural; no man ever talked poetry 'cept a beadle on boxin' day, or Warren's blackin', or Rowland's oil." ' Nigel Molesworth in *Down with Skool* shares Mr Weller's suspicion of poetry: 'you have to sa the weedy words and speke them beaitfully as if you knew what they meant. Fotherington-tomas thinks this is absolutely super and when he sa he wander lonely as a cloud you think he will flote out of the window.' Fotherington-Thomas, you'll recall, is the school wet. If we personified poetry according to these attitudes, we'd arrive at something with a centre-parting, a name like Cuthbert, carrying a narcissus in its limp hand.

And things aren't very different in the States, where Saul Bellow reports, in *Humboldt's Gift*: 'the country is proud of its dead poets. It takes terrific satisfaction in the poets' testimony that the USA is too tough, too big, too much, too rugged, that American reality is overpowering. And to be a poet is a school thing, a skirt thing, a church thing. The weakness of the spiritual powers is proved in the childishness, madness, drunkenness, and despair of these martyrs. Orpheus moved stones and trees. But a poet can't perform a hysterectomy or send a vehicle out of the solar system. Miracle and power no longer belong to him. So poets are loved, but loved because they can't make it here.' Behind this statement, of course, are a group of dead American poets – John Berryman, Hart Crane, Randall Jarrell, Delmore Schwartz, Sylvia Plath – who were victims of the Savage God, as A. Alvarez called his study of writers who committed suicide.

This prejudice against poetry – as a school thing, a skirt thing, a church thing – isn't entirely accurate. That doesn't stop it being shared, in a strange way, by writers themselves.

John Berryman, who killed himself by jumping off the Washington Avenue bridge in Minneapolis after years of alcoholism and mania and depression, is one of the poets implicitly referred to in Saul Bellow's analysis of poetry – so he is a good place to start mounting a counter-thesis, that poetry is a tough thing, a trouser thing, a truth thing. In *His Toy, His Dream, His Rest*, Song 134 recites some of the trials attendant on poets in academe. Berryman, or, rather, Berryman's alter ego, Henry, is feeling sick, yet responsible to his pupils, 'his little children'. The poem is calculated, since it touches on diarrhoea, to send Fotherington-Thomas not floating out of the window, but making a dash for the nearest lavatory.

> Sick at 6 & sick again at 9
> was Henry's gloomy Monday morning oh.
> Still he had to lecture.

They waited, his little children, for stricken Henry
to rise up yet once more again and come oh.
They figured he was a fixture,

nuts to their bolts, keys to their bloody locks.
One day the whole affair will fall apart
with a rustle of fire,
a wrestle of undoing, as of tossed clocks,
and somewhere not far off a broken heart
for hire.

He had smoked a pack of cigarettes by 10
& was ready to go. Peace to his ashes then,
poor Henry,
with all this gas & shit blowing through it
four times in 2 hours, his tail ached.
He arose, benign, & performed.

There are a great many things one could say about this poem, but
first I want to select one word, 'ached', for its exactness. Anyone
who has ever patted himself or herself gently dry will empathize
with Berryman. Song 134 isn't an example of artless candour,
though. It demonstrates a wide medley of tones, and ghosts
Henry's predicament with Christ's resurrection. Berryman uses
both – these tones, and the after-image of Christ – for the same
end, to strand the reader between the ludicrous and the tragic, the
jokey and the clinically depressed, between upbeat and downfall.
Take the second line: 'was Henry's gloomy Monday morning oh.'
How is this line to be read? Is that 'oh' there to recall the briskness
of the traditional ballad, with a rising cadence-oh? Or does the
'oh' have only the exhaustion and depression of barely voiced
pain? And when his students wait for stricken Henry 'to rise up
yet once more again and come oh', the problem is compounded
for the reader. How do we read the tautology of 'yet once more
again'? As comic impatience with repeated demands? Or as a
Beckett-like re-enactment, grimmer for its inelegant repetition?
The central stanza alludes to Yeats's 'Second Coming', particularly the bleak prognosis that 'things fall apart, the centre cannot

hold'. But Berryman substitutes for the austere dignity of 'things', the more colloquial 'the whole affair', so that the most heightened rhetoric of the poem begins, as it were, with a misquotation. 'He had smoked a pack of cigarettes by 10 / & was ready to go. Peace to his ashes then . . .' How do we read the phrase '& was ready to go'? First, he was ready to leave the house and lecture; he was ready to start. Second, he was ready to go; he was ready to die. 'Peace to his ashes' covers both. It is a joke about cigarette ash, and it is a comment on someone to all purposes dead. And the last line: 'He arose, benign, & performed.' Behind this 'arose' and the earlier 'rise up' is the Christian idea of the Ascension. But where Christ performs miracles, Henry simply performs. This performance – of the lecture, Berryman's jaunty endurance – is comparably miraculous from Berryman's point of view.

I could go on. But the earthy Berryman has something to say in his poetry about this, too, in Song 170:

> – I can't read any more of this Rich Critical Prose,
> he growled, broke wind, and scratched himself & left
> the fragrant area.
> When the mind dies it exudes rich critical prose,
> especially about Henry, particularly in Spanish, and sends it
>   to him
> from Madrid, London, New York.

Let us leave Berryman. At least we have learned that poetry isn't necessarily limited to the strictly polite. Not that it ever has been entirely restricted: the indecent generally found a place in the comic genre. 'This Nicholas was risen for to pisse' we read in Chaucer's 'The Miller's Tale' – which also includes a proleptic, if inevitably accidental, reference to Berryman's Rich Critical Prose: 'This Nicholas anon leet fle a fart, / As greet as it had been a thonder-dent.' Since these are natural functions, since people still have to get up in the middle of the night, it's no surprise to find the same thing in Larkin's 'Sad Steps': 'Groping back to bed after a piss', the poem begins. However, what makes Chaucer different from poetry today, is that in his day there was critical separation between the comic-and-earthy and the serious, whereas in Larkin the two are part of a single vision. The typical Larkin poem opens with, as it were, the scrunch and squeal of the tin-opener and ends with the music of the spheres: 'When I see a couple of kids / And guess he's fucking her' modulates into 'The sun-comprehending glass, / And beyond it, the deep blue air, that shows / Nothing, and is nowhere, and is endless.'

Despite Larkin's advertised hatred of modernism, he learnt a great deal from Eliot as well as Yeats. In *The Waste Land*, there is suffering – 'Burning burning burning burning' in 'The Fire Sermon'. On the other hand, there is the comic relief (beautifully integrated) of Lil and Albert, where, as in Berryman's poem, the comically low is ghosted by something clearly higher in the scale. In this case, the pub goodnights ('Good night, ladies, good night, sweet ladies, good night, good night') echo the 'good night, sweet ladies' wished by mad Ophelia. In his poetry, Eliot often donned motley – as and when it was appropriate – since he realized that poetry today, poetry yesterday and poetry tomorrow all face the same simple problem. Which is to effect, by whatever means come to hand, the introduction of poetry to life and to see if a permanent match can't be arranged. Eliot's classic statement of this credo occurs in his essay 'What Dante Means to Me', written in 1950: from Baudelaire, Eliot learned this important lesson, 'that the sort of material that I had, the sort of experience that an adolescent had had, in an industrial city in America, could be the material for poetry; and that the source of new poetry might be found in what had been regarded hitherto as the impossible, the sterile, the intractably unpoetic. That, in fact, the business of the poet was to make poetry out of the unexplored resources of the unpoetical; that the poet, in fact, was committed by his profession to turn the unpoetical into poetry.'

Baudelaire, the poet of the day before yesterday, says much the same thing. While Arnold in his essay on 'The Study of Poetry' insists on 'the advantage to a poet to deal with a beautiful world' and complains to Clough that the age itself is unpoetic, Baude-

laire has taken on the problem: in an art review, Baudelaire says
that 'the painter, the true painter for whom we are looking, will
be he who can snatch its epic quality from the life of today and
make us see and understand, with brush or with pencil, how great
and poetic we are in our cravats and our patent-leather boots.'
The problem is unchanged today – except that, of course, cravats
and patent-leather boots now strike us as extraordinarily trac-
table poetically. The past is always a poetic place – which is why
we have in English poetry a sepia school, whose poems are guided
tours of the trenches in the First World War. Here the moral
terrain is smooth and one returns pleasantly sad from the nips one
has been taking from a hipflask abrim with compassion. Even
Eliot's past is a poetic place now – in fact, became so very rapidly.
Rex Warner, a friend of W. H. Auden's, recalls taking walks past
the gasworks because they had been hallowed poetically after
appearing in *The Waste Land*. Even the patent-leather boots, so
to speak, became poetic properties for post-Eliot generations.
Eliot was notorious in his lifetime for dressing, not like a poet, but
like a bank clerk. In the early sixties, though, I remember that
George MacBeth set out on his poetic career in a morning coat
and striped trousers – they had become the sign of the poet, rather
than the sign of a banker. What, of course, *doesn't* become poetic
from the past is the poetic. The poetic becomes the poetical, the
ridiculous – as one can see from 'Sad Steps', the Larkin poem
cited earlier for its poetic earthiness:

> Groping back to bed after a piss
> I part thick curtains, and am startled by
> The rapid clouds, the moon's cleanliness.
>
> Four o'clock: wedge-shadowed gardens lie
> Under a cavernous, a wind-picked sky.
> There's something laughable about this,
>
> The way the moon dashes through clouds, that blow
> Loosely as cannon-smoke, to stand apart
> (Stone-coloured light sharpening the roofs below)

High and preposterous and separate –
Lozenge of love! Medallion of art!
O wolves of memory! Immensements! No,

One shivers slightly, looking up there.
The hardness and the brightness and the plain
Far-reaching singleness of that wide stare

Is a reminder of the strength and pain
Of being young; that it can't come again,
But is for others undiminished somewhere.

'Sad Steps' is a poem in triplicate: the rhymes are in triplicate (piss, cleanliness, this; plain, pain, again); the adjectives are in triplicate ('high and preposterous and separate'); and Larkin's argument is threefold, a dialectic. His thesis is the given fact of the moon, with its one neutral attribute – 'cleanliness'. The antithesis is the moon's poetic past, not so much recalled as sent up rotten: 'Lozenge of love! Medallion of art! / O wolves of memory!' and, best of all, 'Immensements!' The synthesis, the *tertium aliquid*, is the moon's present, genuine poetry, which Larkin can only approach after he has chortled and hooted at the idea of poetry, fashioned to the traditional recipe:

The hardness and the brightness and the plain
Far-reaching singleness of that wide stare

Is a reminder of the strength and pain
Of being young; that it can't come again,
But is for others undiminished somewhere.

In other words, Larkin has more than a touch of Molesworth in his ridicule. 'Lozenge of love': tell me, isn't that the work of that sensitive artist, Fotherington-Thomas? Nor is Larkin alone in letting Molesworth have his say. Marianne Moore began her poem entitled 'Poetry' with the declaration: 'I, too, dislike it.' The entire poem, in its shortened final version, continues: 'Reading it, however, with a perfect contempt for it, one discovers in / it, after

all, a place for the genuine.' Marianne Moore is wary and
sceptical where Larkin is gleefully philistine – but both acknowledge, finally, its proper power.

Another even more reluctant, but paradoxically prolific practitioner is Tony Harrison. Harrison is the classic deracinated
intellectual – a writer who has complicated relations with his
working-class background. Initially, Harrison's education – getting 'unbearably excited / poring over Kafka and *King Lear*' –
inclined him to despise his antecedents. Now, though, Harrison
mistrusts the arts because they appear to exclude a great swathe
of uncultured experience which he has come to value. In 'A Good
Read', Harrison is addressing his dead father:

> I've come round to your position on 'the Arts'
> but put it down in poems, that's the bind.

> These poems about you, Dad, should make good reads
> for the bus you took from Beeston into town
> for people with no time like you in Leeds –

> once I'm writing I can't put you down!

Harrison now cares so little for the educated discourse he has
been taught to master that he actively chooses to adopt the brisk
and simple judgements of his father – 'a good read'; 'couldn't put
it down'. They are also blank judgements – unarguable and
uninformative because they do not attempt to describe what is
being discussed, only offer an opinion arising out of it. And you
could argue that Tony Harrison wants to provide a kind of poetry
which is so simple it can be described adequately in this way. The
surface of the poem, its beauties or its uglinesses, what Marianne
Moore calls 'all this fiddle', is of no concern to Harrison because
it would be of no concern to his father. There is something
studiously primitive about Harrison's poetic means – the iambic
pentameter and full rhymes – the meat and two veg of poetry.
Nor is Harrison especially concerned to arrange it appetizingly
on the plate: 'I've come round to your position on "the Arts" '

sacrifices without a qualm the not particularly stringent requirements of his metre to preservation of a colloquial turn of phrase,
'I've come round to'. 'But put it down in poems': a poet who
cared about sound wouldn't slap down 'but' and 'put' next to
each other. There is, too, a great deal of gristle and inelegance as
well as a kind of queasy authenticity in the closing lines. They are
not 'the best words in the best possible order' – Coleridge's
definition of poetry – they are any old words arranged artlessly
and awkwardly:

> These poems about you, Dad, should make good reads
> for the bus you took from Beeston into town
> for people with no time like you in Leeds . . .

This is ordinary speech – shapeless, without periodicity, without
punctuation, as long as a lungful of breath, repetitive. The
sentence has no dynamic. It merely accumulates: 'for the bus you
took from Beeston into town / for people with no time like you in
Leeds.' I don't think Tony Harrison would dispute this description or mind it. He isn't interested in art. He has *chosen* to write in
this way: for all its apparent artlessness, this is a deliberate artistic
decision. The risk for Harrison is that the surface clumsiness may
alienate us. The reward for Harrison is that, given this rhetoric of
roughness, no one is going to doubt his sincerity. Once his
sincerity has been established, Harrison can chance his arty
finale, the trickiness of his last line:

> once I'm writing I can't put you down!

This is at once a boast about how readable Harrison finds his own
work – put in the modest form of saying how fascinating he finds
his father – and at the same time a confession of failure. The
delineation of his father will never be definitive. 'I can't put you
down' has a double meaning and the second meaning is artistically self-conscious. For all his disclaimers, then, Tony Harrison
is a strategist like any other poet. In the end, whatever appearances may suggest, all writing is writing. It is never life, however

much the writer would like it to be, however much the writer strives to close the gap.

But to say this does not mean that Tony Harrison will therefore give up trying to get his father down on paper. Walter Pater and Oscar Wilde both said that all art aspires to the condition of music. They were both wrong. All bad literature aspires to the condition of literature. All good literature aspires to the condition of life. We know that words are only words, but this doesn't mean we shouldn't spend our lives arranging words and choosing words and coining words so that we are deceived by our own illusion of life. Joseph Conrad's preface to *The Nigger of the 'Narcissus'* states the task of the writer simply and movingly. It is 'to make you hear, to make you feel – it is, before all, to make you see. That – and no more, and it is everything.' Every serious artist believes this. And it is why a great many mistrust poetry. They do not want to aspire to the condition of literature – and poetry appears to offer more opportunities for the artificial than most other art forms. Tony Harrison may forgo a great deal in the way of metaphor, cadence, allusion, preferring his rhetoric of clumsiness, but compared to many poets of Eastern Europe, who forgo rhyme and metre also, he isn't as lean and spartan as he might like to think.

Miroslav Holub, the Czech poet, has written: 'I like writing for people untouched by poetry; for instance, for those who do not even know that it should at all be for them. I would like them to read poems as naturally as they read the papers, or go to a football game.' In Poland, after Nazi occupation and the Holocaust, many poets felt that art was an insult to the great European trauma which had been endured – and that the only acceptable poetry was anti-poetry. Without in any way minimizing the collective experience of Eastern Europe, I want to take this idea of anti-poetry and put it in context. All good poetry is anti-poetry. Consider, for instance, the blurb to the 1948 Penguin *Selected Poems* of T. S. Eliot: 'There are no poetic "subjects" in this book, no conventional nightingales and daffodils, and there is no acceptance, either, of the traditional rules of metre and rhyme.' As you know, there *are* nightingales and daffodils in Eliot's poetry, just as there is rhyme and metre. Nevertheless, the blurb-writer is right. Eliot's nightingales are not conventionally poetic:

> The nightingales are singing near
> The Convent of the Sacred Heart,
>
> And sang within the bloody wood
> When Agamemnon cried aloud
> And let their liquid siftings fall
> To stain the stiff dishonoured shroud.

If there is a better description of falling bird-shit in English literature I would be pleased to encounter it. Two exact words – 'liquid siftings' – persuade us for a second that writing and life have come together like the images in a stereoscope. That is to say, truth to life is possible without depriving poetry of its repertoire of aesthetic resources.

The trouble is this: the word 'poetic' has been used in the past to suggest something untrue to life. When we talk about 'poetic truth' we mean, in fact, something which isn't actually true – but which conceivably we might like to be true. Whenever E. M. Forster uses the word 'poetry', his cheeks are flushed in pursuit of some transcendent experience. Two people kiss in *Howards End* and Forster rattles on about it, unrattled by the arguments of sceptics: 'But the poetry of that kiss, the wonder of it, the magic that there was in life for hours after it – who can describe that? It is so easy for an Englishman to sneer at these chance collisions of human beings. To the insular cynic and the insular moralist they offer an equal opportunity. It is so easy to talk of "passing emotion", and to forget how vivid the emotion was ere it passed.' *Ere it passed*. You can see what Forster means: he wants to be true to the temporary hyperbole of romantic emotion, but actually he overstates his position and substitutes afflatus for inflation.

In *Raise High the Roof-Beam, Carpenters*, J. D. Salinger conducts a similar guarded seminar on the themes of sentimentality and poetry. Just as Forster fends off the 'insular cynic', so

Salinger, through his protagonist Seymour Glass, tips off the reader that he has considered the nature of sentimentality. Seymour Glass's journal records seeing a film with his fiancée. 'I looked at her several times in the dark when Greer Garson's son's plane was missing in action. Her mouth was open. Absorbed, worried. The identification with Metro-Goldwyn-Mayer tragedy complete. I felt awe and happiness. How I love and need her undiscriminating heart. She looked over at me when the children in the picture brought in the kitten to show it to their mother. M. loved the kitten and wanted me to love it. Even in the dark, I could sense that she felt the usual estrangement from me when I don't automatically love what she loves. Later, when we were having a drink at the station, she asked me if I didn't think that kitten was "rather nice". She doesn't use the word "cute" any more. When did I ever frighten her out of her normal vocabulary? Bore that I am, I mentioned R. H. Blyth's definition of sentimentality: that we are being sentimental when we give to a thing more tenderness than God gives to it. I said (sententiously?) that God undoubtedly loves kittens, but not, in all probability, with Technicolor bootees on their paws.' Intellectual credentials thus rigorously in place – here is a writer who can resist a kitten – Seymour proceeds to sentimentalize his future mother-in-law, in a very sophisticated way. Mrs Fedder is 'irritating, opinionated', 'a person deprived for life, of any understanding or taste for the main current of poetry that flows through things, all things.' So far, so good: 'she might as well be dead, and yet she goes on living, stopping off at delicatessens, seeing her analyst, consuming a novel every night, putting on her girdle, plotting for Muriel's health and prosperity.' What is sentimental about this analysis?, you may be wondering. What is sentimental is the conclusion: 'I love her. I find her unimaginably brave.' Mrs Fedder could only be brave if she considered her life as meaningless as Seymour does. There is something disgusting and self-advertising about Seymour's love – as if love were a brand of kitchen detergent able to absorb even the most unpleasantly stained characters.

What Seymour has done is to apply 'poetry' to life – to ennoble it, to sweeten it, to tinker with the truth. Poetry, in this sense, is opposed to truth. Conveniently, Salinger provides an example for us. Seymour hears his kid brother Zooey on the radio: 'Zooey was in dreamy top form. The announcer had them off on the subject of housing developments, and the little Burke girl said she hated houses that all look alike – meaning a long row of identical "development" houses. Zooey said they were "nice". He said it would be very nice to come home and be in the wrong house. To eat dinner with the wrong people by mistake, sleep in the wrong bed by mistake, and kiss everybody goodbye in the morning thinking they were your own family. He said he even wished everybody in the world looked exactly alike. He said you'd keep thinking everybody you met was your wife or your mother or father, and people would always be throwing their arms around each other wherever they went . . .' It's an odd passage, isn't it? It has its own appeal which shouldn't be underestimated: it is undoubtedly cute. But which families, you wonder, has the writer actually encountered? In some families, a confusion of identities, thinking everyone you met was your wife or your husband or your brother, might lead to people throwing fists at each other. It is cute, undeniably, but it is also an edited version of reality – which, for some people, is a definition of poetry. Whereas I would argue that poetry is the fullest version of reality – *without* maintaining that the fullest version of reality is necessarily the nastiest version of reality.

In *The Use of Poetry*, T. S. Eliot quotes the poet and philosopher T. E. Hulme: 'the great aim is accurate, precise and definite description. The first thing is to realise how extraordinarily difficult this is . . . Language has its own special nature, its own conventions and communal ideas. It is only by a concentrated effort of the mind that you can hold it fixed to your own purpose.' While it is true that language is constantly presenting us with, as it were, emotional kits that do our feeling for us, powerful writers are as much to blame – at any rate, are much more *responsible*. Our great writers explode clichés of feeling, the old habitual and automatic responses – but in due course become their own clichés.

For instance T. S. Eliot, it need hardly be said, has been a hugely influential figure – not only through his poetry, but also through his criticism, even when the criticism is slightly at odds with the poetry. The poetic personality found in the poetry is much more agile and varied than the idea of the poet which we find in the criticism. Eliot wished to see himself as a poet of intense concentration, of unity of sentiment. He was anxious, as a shy New Englander, not to be like Matthew Arnold, whom he stigmatized as a poet of 'impeccable demeanour'. Rather, Eliot wished to be a poet able to see 'the boredom, and the horror, and the glory'. This, I submit, is fundamentally Romantic, despite his frequent declarations for classicism. Even while Eliot argues for impersonality, the figure he projects is recognizably tormented, marked-off, marked-out, one whose gifts are inseparable from personal suffering: 'poetry is not a turning loose of emotion, but an escape from emotion; it is not the expression of personality, but an escape from personality. But, of course, only those who have personality and emotions know what it means to want to escape from these things.' These sentences from 'Tradition and the Individual Talent' advocate one thing – impersonality – but implicitly boast about a superabundance of its opposite – personality. In *The Use of Poetry*, Eliot outlines a personal theory of inspiration, which, though it is studied in its distance from the Yeatsian brand, is nevertheless a Romantic theory. Eliot expresses it negatively, as 'the sudden lifting of the burden of anxiety and fear which presses upon our daily life so steadily that we are unaware of it . . . that is to say, not "inspiration" as we commonly think of it . . .' This may not be 'inspiration' as we usually think of it, but it is an unpredictable mental event for all that, and related to the group of hardy, half-conscious assumptions which belong to the *poète maudit*.

Deep down, for instance, Eliot believed that poetry and suffering were inextricably bound up with each other. In 1933, he surveyed his career in a way that inadvertently reveals this naive and involuntary equation of poetry with suffering. 'No honest poet can ever feel quite sure of the permanent value of what he has written: he may have wasted his time *and messed up his life for nothing*.' A wonderfully unguarded psychological moment this: there, under all Eliot's sophistication, is the idea that a poetic career involves the poet in messing up his life – for nothing, or for something – but certainly being unhappy. Eliot deserves his exemplary status, but the time has come to question what he has so hypnotically imposed – the belief that great poetry is unhappy poetry. The rule is not a rule but an accident of Eliot's temperament given a singular authority by his literary achievement. We have mistaken a contingent feature for an essential feature, misled perhaps by the force of Eliot's argument when he opposes a different assumption in Arnold – that poetry is fundamentally uplifting. Eliot was quick to laugh at this last idea and right to laugh at it: 'Can we say that Shakespeare's poetry is great', Eliot asked, 'because of the extraordinary power with which Shakespeare feels estimable feelings?' The question answers itself. We don't go to Shakespeare for uplift. Yet while Eliot's sense – that great poetry is gloomy, unsmiling, faintly tortured, and that anything else is suspect – partly arises in reaction to Arnold, it also derives in some measure from precepts first formulated by Arnold.

In theory, we resist hierarchy. Genres are discrete and each must be judged only by the appropriate criteria. We insist with Auden that light verse should have its 'round of claps'. And yet. For all these protestations, a visceral preference remains, atavistically heedless of the inviolable integrity of each genre. You can see it, half-disguised, in Randall Jarrell's sturdily negative review of e. e. cummings in 1954. Jarrell conscientiously lists the merits (humour, intelligence, charm, innocence) and the demerits (sentimentality, monotony, complacency) but he has already dropped the atom bomb before pitting conventional views against each other. 'If cummings is a great poet, what are you going to call Eliot and Frost? Rilke?' Jarrell is right. cummings is not a great poet. But it isn't fair to mobilize our prejudice by comparing the gravitas of Eliot, Frost and Rilke with the grin of cummings.

Behind Jarrell stands Eliot, and behind Eliot stands Arnold, and behind Arnold stands Aristotle's notion of 'high seriousness' as 'one of the grand virtues of poetry'. It is high seriousness that

Chaucer lacks, so that, although his poetry has 'a large, free, simple, clear yet kindly view of human life', Arnold can debar him from the pantheon: 'Chaucer is not one of the great classics.' What hope, then, is there for Pope and Dryden, convicted as 'classics of our prose'? Not even the *saevo indignatio* of the *Dunciad* qualifying as unhappiness, there could be little chance of cummings being accepted into the small band of the elect. Clough's poor showing relative to Arnold can be partially attributed, I believe, to his preference for irony and humour. Arnold's irony and humour are confined to his prose. Arnold, of course, is no longer an influential figure. His criticism is read, though less than Eliot's, and Eliot's poetic example is much more potently influential than Arnold's.

Eliot's poetic example is the force which leads Philip Larkin, in a review of Stevie Smith, to select a passage from her novel, *The Holiday*, which has the authentic grimness of a Larkin line: 'There is little landscape where you are going and no warmth.' Immediately, then, Larkin has managed to discount the Stevie Smith whimsy by establishing a dark inner core. His piece ends with another quote, in which she explains:

Why does my Muse only speak when she is unhappy?
She does not, I only listen when I am unhappy
When I am happy I live and despise writing
For my Muse this cannot be but dispiriting.

Larkin comments: 'Perhaps this explains it. For all the freaks and sports of her fancy, for all her short pieces that are like rejected *Pansies* and her long pieces that are like William Blake rewritten by Ogden Nash, Miss Smith's poems *speak with the authority of sadness*.' My italics. For all the qualifications Larkin enters – and there are too many too accurately expressed to leave Stevie Smith enthusiasts complacent – we assent to the idea of 'the authority of sadness'. But why should sadness have special access to authority? In itself, misery guarantees nothing. What Larkin really means is that her poems sometimes speak with, not the authority of sadness, but the allure of sadness. For sadness is alluring. A side of human nature is susceptible to the darker view of things. There is comfort, cold comfort, in the comfortless, as witness the enduring popularity of Housman and the pull of Graham Greene's pseudo-Conradian pessimism. 'Housman is the poet of unhappiness,' writes Larkin, accurately enough. 'No one else has reiterated his single message so plangently.' And there, more or less, Larkin rests his case, as if it were self-evident. A proper account of Housman might easily find in the reiteration a formula, saved only by the metre and Housman's beautiful variants. The trouble with 'the eternal note of sadness' is that it is so reliable, so automatic, regular and eternal. It is the emotional equivalent, often, of fast food. And, in fact, Arnold was, on occasion, properly suspicious of it.

In 1853, in his famous preface to his poems, Arnold identified modernism as 'the dialogue of the mind with itself', and you don't have to look far to find examples: Eliot's 'Sometimes these cogitations still amaze / The troubled midnight and the noon's repose,' or Larkin's 'Talking in Bed':

> And dark towns heap up on the horizon.
> None of this cares for us. Nothing shows why
> At this unique distance from isolation
>
> It becomes difficult to find
> Words at once true and kind,
> Or not untrue and not unkind.

For Arnold, 'the dialogue of the mind with itself' was a matter of regret. The qualities he associates with 'only the great monuments of early Greek genius' have disappeared. And these qualities are 'the calm, the cheerfulness, the disinterested objectivity'. By now it must be obvious where I would like to stand – on the ground of 'disinterested objectivity' without presuming in advance to say whether that will be calm or cheerful or rueful or melancholy. Without, in fact, wishing to append any qualifying adjective at all, the idea of acceptance is what I should like to propose.

Oddly enough, the best illustration I can find of what I mean by *acceptance* is provided by T. S. Eliot in his consideration of I. A. Richards's five spiritual exercises for poets. Richards suggested topics for meditation. The second topic was 'The facts of birth and of death, in their inexplicable oddity'. Eliot was brisk: 'I cannot see why the facts of birth and of death should appear odd in themselves, unless we have a conception of some other way of coming into the world and of leaving it, which strikes us as more natural.'

Acceptance, too, should cover acceptance of the resources of poetry. For instance, who said 'for my part I like a florid style: if your motto is "Cut out the adjectives", why not go a bit further and revert to a system of grunts and squeals, like the animals'? The writer was defending Conrad. It was Orwell, who was to be famous for the plainness of his own style, yet knew that the English language, any language for that matter, is a resource like any other resource. If it were food, not words, we would listen less to those who always counsel restraint – plain style or simplicity (as it prefers to be known) amounts to a row of beans, sometimes appropriate, sometimes not. Eliot said memorably of Dante that his was 'a *visual* imagination' and that his similes are there 'solely to make us *see more definitely* the scene which Dante has put before us', whereas Shakespeare's metaphors '*add* to what we see'. Dante's similes are intensive and Shakespeare's metaphors are expansive. Yet Eliot does not declare a preference: 'Between men who could make such inventions as these there can be no question of greater or less.' This is not a generally held view: the vulgar consensus is that simile is a threadbare device while metaphor is lavish and sumptuous. In fact, it depends how each is used. There are those who actually prefer neither and defend this position by quoting Dr Johnson on the metaphysicals, with special reference to Abraham Cowley. Art is never mistaken for life. No one believes the constructed elegy and the involuntary sob are interchangeable. Those allegedly artificial devices, simile and metaphor, are not restricted to art, however. 'Accurate, precise and definite description', T. E. Hulme's goal, will employ simile and metaphor because they are effective, natural modes, even if they are not universal modes. This is illustrated in Richard Hoggart's fine autobiography, *A Local Habitation*, when he examines figures of speech used by his Aunt Annie: 'She loved language and especially metaphor; I doubt if she forgot any colourful image she heard. Grandma and I enjoyed them, the others seemed not much to respond to them. I drew on her more than anyone else in recording working-class metaphors in *The Uses of Literacy* . . . I do not imagine Aunt Annie invented any of those images; she knew how to use them, though.'

It's strange, then, to watch even intelligent critics trapped on the narrow ledge of their *a priori* theories. Consider, for instance, Blake Morrison and Andrew Motion on Heaney's 'Grauballe Man' in their introduction to the *Penguin Book of British Contemporary Poetry*. You might expect these two critics to seize on the vividness of Heaney's imagery: 'The grain of his wrists / is like bog oak, / the ball of his heel / like a basalt egg. / His instep has shrunk / cold as a swan's foot / or a wet swamp root. / His hips are the ridge / and purse of a mussel, / his spine an eel arrested / under a glisten of mud.' Of this virtuoso focus of imagery, its needles of light sharp on detail after detail, the two editors offer this analysis: the imagery 'seems only likely to distance and disperse the body. As Heaney's eye ranges over the anatomy it transforms skin and bone to a clutter of inanimate things.' Heaney, so we are told, isn't describing; he is 'asserting the deadness of the corpse by exploring its resemblance to things'. I should have thought that the similes are there, as Dante's are, 'to make us *see more definitely*'.

I hope it won't be thought that I wish to reject plain language as a resource. On the contrary, I embraced it quite consciously when I wrote an opera libretto – knowing that Auden had remarked in *Secondary Worlds* that only one word in seven is audible in opera. Given that, and given that I had to write songs for characters who might be without great metaphorical resources, I naturally chose what in my preface to *The Electrification of the Soviet Union* I called the rhetoric of plainness. What I object to about plainness in language is the way its advocates appear to believe it is a guarantee of sincerity. It is only the guarantee of the *appearance* of sincerity – as honest Iago, himself a great plain-speaker, would be quick to explain.

> IAGO: O monstrous world! Take note, take note, O world.
> To be direct and honest is not safe.

Rhyme is another resource, like metre, that should be available. In 1919, Eliot, in his 'Reflections on *Vers Libre*', commented: 'There is no campaign against rhyme. But it is possible that excessive devotion to rhyme has thickened the modern ear. The rejection of rhyme is not a leap at facility; on the contrary, it imposes a much severer strain upon the language. When the comforting echo of rhyme is removed, success or failure in the choice of words, in the sentence structure, in the order, is at once more apparent. Rhyme removed, the poet is at once held up to the standards of prose.' Everything Eliot says in this passage strikes me as still true – except the statement that 'there is no campaign against rhyme'; in poetry today, there is a campaign for rhyme. I was recently offered by Houghton Mifflin, an American publisher, an anthology of contemporary rhyming poetry – as if rhyme itself constituted a distinctive aesthetic platform and was not simply a commonly available resource that any poet might avail himself of should the need arise.

The 1987 Nobel Prize winner Joseph Brodsky is a keen advocate of rhyme, as you might expect from a poet whose original language is inflected and therefore particularly rich in rhyme. About English, however, Brodsky is not to be trusted. In his essay on W. H. Auden's 'September 1st 1939', Brodsky states authoritatively that one should 'never rhyme the same parts of speech. Nouns you can, verbs you shouldn't, and rhyming adjectives is taboo.' Any page of Pope will contradict the law he promulgates against rhyming the same parts of speech. Nearly any page of Brodsky's poetry in his own translations will persuade you that in English this law is suicidal: despite the automatically awarded acclaim and the ceaseless broadcast of remarks designed to demonstrate his sensitivity to language, Brodsky is capable of rhyming 'not the' and 'nostril'. He can write a line as touchingly incompetent as this in order to provide a rhyme for 'city' later on: 'Twice I have drowned, thrice let knives rake my nitty-gritty.' Obscure? I will translate Mr Brodsky's translation. 'Thrice let knives rake my nitty-gritty' means that he has undergone surgery three times for a heart complaint. A new Rhymers' Club has formed itself around Brodsky. I do not think him a reliable guide in questions that affect the English ear – any more than I would be a reliable guide to Russian poetry.

The only resources I am against are those which do not exist, like Eliot's famous theoretical construct, the auditory imagination. At the end of his essay on Arnold, Eliot defines the auditory imagination as follows: 'what I call the "auditory imagination" is the feeling for syllable and rhythm, penetrating far below the conscious levels of thought and feeling, invigorating every word; sinking to the most primitive and forgotten, returning to the origin and bringing something back, seeking the beginning and the end. It works through meanings, certainly, or not without meanings in the ordinary sense, and fuses the old and obliterated and the trite, the current, and the new and surprising, the most ancient and the most civilised mentality.' This auditory imagination has been with us so long – since 1933 – that we feel assured of its existence and shocked to think it might only have the status of a discarded concept like the fancy. Eliot had a wonderful ear, but this auditory imagination is really something improvised to mount an attack on the music of Arnold's poetry. Now, Arnold has some fine sound effects, particularly the end of 'Sohrab and Rustum' and 'Dover Beach' – his description of the 'shorn and parcelled Oxus' as 'a foiled circuitous wanderer', or the sea and 'its melancholy, long, withdrawing roar' with the drag of shingle passed from 'draw' to 'roar'. However, Eliot isn't interested in being fair to Arnold. He owes him too much. Therefore, he invents a faculty which penetrates 'far below the conscious levels of thought and feeling', then implies that he, Eliot, possesses this gift, while Arnold does not. We should hang on to our common sense at this juncture. If the auditory imagination operates 'far below the conscious levels of thought and feeling', it is, of course, irrefutable. Yet if it is 'far below the conscious levels of thought and feeling', how is it that Eliot can provide us with such a detailed account of its mystical operations?

The answer is probably the work of F. Max Müller. Eliot has assimilated the poet to the philologist, as if Max Müller's scholarship eloped with Coleridge's secondary imagination. The auditory imagination is a romantic union, a fantastic pairing, a chimera – which 'dissolves, diffuses, dissipates, in order to re-create' and romantically declares with Max Müller that 'every word, as soon as we hear it, carries us off to near and distant memories. They float about us like thin gossamer filaments in autumn.' When Müller gives an example, though, it serves only to show how comparatively impoverished, how amateurish, how unscholarly Eliot's auditory imagination must be without special-ist knowledge spanning several languages: 'in Sanskrit this root helps us to express cattle, pasu, which is the Latin *pecus*, Gothic *faihu*, German *vieh*, cattle; also *pecunia* and *pecus*, our lawyer's *fee*. It supplies, besides, pasa, fetter, and similar words. Now, when we have a word for animal, such as *pecus*, we have also the material for expressing such concepts as *peculiar*, the transition of meaning being clear enough from *peculium*, one's private property, to *peculiaris*, anything that is one's own – anything that is proper, singular, individual, and, it may be, odd. It is difficult to resist the siren songs of language, and not to follow her into all her flights of imagination.' That last breathless declaration may be the germ of Eliot's new-found mental faculty. To my mind, the history of the language, though useful to a poet, is far less important than an infallible sense of the way language is currently used. As a critic of individual authors, Eliot is *sans pareil*, but his theoretical coinages, as he himself acknowledged, were more dubious: 'one of the two or three phrases of my coinage – like "objective correlative" – which have had a success in the world astonishing to their author.'

Not that anyone should think, because I am sceptical about Eliot's auditory imagination, that I am against musicality in poetry. That, too, is a resource. As are discord and dissonance. Stale cadences – unless they are used ironically, as in Larkin's 'Sad

Steps' – are always to be avoided. Poetry, I believe, teaches the language to sing. When a person talks to you, you hear the meaning and you understand. If someone were to sing the same words to you, each word would be made to vibrate for longer, to have a significance in itself, beyond the meaning. The difference between singing and talking is the difference between kissing and shaking hands. Poetry cannot actually sing of itself, but it uses words with a comparable attention to their individuality and their compatibility with each other. Arnold's 'melancholy, long, withdrawing roar' has a music which it is impossible to divorce from the sense and which is virtually untranslatable. Just these words and no others can produce that particular effect. Cervantes said that translation is the other side of the tapestry. The sound as an echo to the sense may be a primitive trope, but it exercises a profound effect on the human mind. Poetry that *is* translatable – the poems of Miroslav Holub and, in the other direction, say, the poems of Tony Harrison – is a poetry which has deliberately chosen to ignore many of the resources that distinguish poetry from prose. With Harrison, how would a translator preserve the dialect awkwardness, the deliberate anti-music of 'for the bus you took from Beeston into town / for people with no time like you in Leeds'? Easily enough, if it is already the other side of the tapestry, if, like Tony Harrison, you have already artfully opted for the artless.

Coleridge's Notebooks

One of Coleridge's unrealized projects was a selection from his notebooks – a *Memoriae Memorandorum*. Fortunately, he never managed to find the time to prune, polish and censor, so that the notebooks exist in their raw state, untidy and intensely human. They stand, unlike Valéry's *Analects*, without veneer. And taken as a whole, they represent a kind of accidental *Ulysses*, an epic, all-inclusive self-portrait – with Coleridge doubling as the philosophical Stephen Dedalus and the earthily poetic Bloom. Recipes for piles, the itch, for killing the smell of the closed-stool, jokes, remembered anecdotes, puzzles, lists of flower names, and vocabularies co-exist – in the earlier volumes – with philosophical speculation illustrated by homely observation. Take his Cartesian meditation on the unreliability of the senses: 'Feel a pimple, and measure it in *feeling* – and then look at it – how very small it is compared with what you expected it to be.' At his best, Coleridge did not *write* but, as he pointed out, simply *thought* pen in hand.

In this new volume* he is, by comparison, downright dull. He is no longer quietly observing the 'flux and reflux' of his mind, but preparing his thoughts for publication – in *The Friend*, the *Lay Sermons*, the Shakespeare lectures, *Biographia Literaria* and the *Philosophical Lectures*. The intimate tone has gone. Dedalus has vanquished Bloom. The stream of consciousness has become a

The Notebooks of Samuel Taylor Coleridge (Vol. 3) 1808–19: Notes and Text in two volumes edited by Kathleen Coburn, Routledge and Kegan Paul.

238

mere torrent of intellect. Coleridge has gone indoors – to the library – to work. Those who admired the vividness of his earlier natural observation will be struck by its absence in this new volume.

Instead of describing the rising sun 'in a fine Egg of light', instead of displaying his unusual sensitivity to colours ('raspberry and milk colored crags'), instead of wasting his time profitably by observing in the fire 'a conical Volcano of coal, half an inch high, ejaculating its inverted cone of smoke', instead of risking rheumatoid arthritis by going on nature trails to notice a spider's web's 'exquisite Network of Film so instinct with gentle motion which, now the shower only steadies, and now it melts it into such a mistiness as the Breath leaves on a mirror' – instead of this, Coleridge (urged by industrious friends) spent his time swotting up lugubrious aphorisms from Jean Paul and worked at his philosophy. 'I feel the Clouds – yet sure there is something here,' he writes, an old man in a dry month, waiting for rain.

With the resolve to work comes a certain priggishness, a tendency for his prose to slide into prayer, a new Chadband-Coleridge: 'Confidence – faith – faithful confident reliance on Man and on God is the last and hardest virtue! And wherefore? Because we must first have earned a FAITH in ourselves. Let the Conscience pronounce – Trust in thyself! – Let the whole Heart be able to say – I trust in myself – And then whomever we *love*, we shall rely on . . .' Even those who relish the criticism of Wordsworth in the second half of the *Biographia* will find it a high price to pay for the interminable dullness of his reflections on Virtue, Charity, Faith, Grace, Redemption and Punctuation.

Those who had begun to think of the notebooks as Coleridge's real *œuvre* will not reconcile themselves easily to the change – the change from a detailed yet catholic eye to a broad intellectual vision, from an elliptical telegraphese to a style which is a stranger to the full stop. The difference in outlook can be illustrated by a comparison of the late Coleridge eulogizing bird-shit with the early Coleridge praising urine or feminizing a landscape: 'The soil that fell from the Hawk poised at the extreme boundary of the Sight thro' a column of sunshine – a falling star, gem, the fixation,

& chrystal, of substantial Light, again dissolving and elongating like a liquid Drop . . . What a wretched Frenchman would not he be, who could shout out – charming Hawk's *Turd*!' Typically, the word appears only to be censored, whereas, in the early note-books, Coleridge meditates (Bloom-like) on tenderness and cowardice, stimulated by the action of his bowels.

Or, going to Malta, he describes with harrowing detail his enema on the high seas. Again, he writes: 'perfect serenity / that fat round backside of a Hill . . . the road appeared a sort of suture, in many places exactly as the *weiblich tetragrammaton* [i.e., feminine four-letter word] is painted in anatomical Books! I never saw so sweet an Image!!' This Coleridge would never have exclaimed against a harmless word like 'turd', denouncing it as 'the Language, of the swinish Slaves of the Circe', in a paroxysm of inarticulate rectitude.

Perhaps it was this piety which led Wordsworth to contradict Coleridge's distinction between love and lust with a denial of love – except as 'a compound of Lust with Esteem and Friendship, confined to one Object, first by accidents of Association, and permanently, by force of Habit & a sense of Duty'. The quarrel with the Wordsworths, which provides most of the human interest of this volume, had lain dormant since the friction on their Highland Tour in 1803, but in 1810 the real split occurred. It is difficult to apportion blame in what was clearly a clash of temperament between Wordsworth's unemotional egotism and Coleridge's emotional egotism. The relevant entries are ridicu-lous and agonizing by turns: sometimes Coleridge is as absurdly prolix in his trouble as Dostoevsky's Stepan Trofimovitch; sometimes his choked pithiness brings a lump to the throat. 'Sunday Night. No Hope of me! absol. Nuisance! God's mercy is it a Dream!' The (presumably unfounded) sexual jealousy is painfully vivid too: 'But a minute and a half with ME – and all that time evidently *restless & going* – An hour and more with Wordsworth *in bed* – O agony! – & yet even . . .' Here, Coleridge speaks to us directly whereas elsewhere it is like listening to George Steiner on a crystal set – certainly learned, vaguely intimidating, vaguely unintelligible.

There are, of course, scattered moments of light relief. Even as Coleridge struggled to conquer his opium habit, even as he lamented his love for Sara Hutchinson, he was capable of jotting down a piece of fortuitous Joycean wordplay: ' *"Officious for Equivalents"* (I was speaking of the small German Potentates) This my Amanuensis wrote – *"Fishing for Elephants"* – which as I at the time observed was a sort of *Noah's* angling, that could hardly have occurred except at the commencement of the Deluge.'

However, but for Kathleen Coburn's tireless industry and relentless annotation, this new volume would be unreadable, for Coleridge, as he grew older, became more interested in dramatic ideas than in supporting them with evidence. Opinion which shuffles off the responsibilities of proof with a hasty formulaic &c &c is finally dull because unchallengeable. In April of 1819, Keats met Coleridge by the side of Lord Mansfield's park and walked with him and Mr Green ('our Demonstrator') for nearly two miles. 'In those two Miles he broached a thousand things', and Keats appends a list of topics. At least one item is authentic, namely 'a dream accompanied by a sense of touch – single and double touch'. It is a Coleridgean theme with a long history.

Two things are significant in the anecdote: first, Keats shrewdly assesses Coleridge in the single word *broached*. Secondly, though Coleridge invited him to call at Highgate on their parting, there is no evidence that Keats took up the invitation. The restless gourmet of ideas would not have allowed him more than a taste before broaching the next, and the upshot would have been a subtle form of intellectual starvation – with Keats crying, as the door banged behind him, 'O for a Life of Sensations rather than of thoughts!'

The modern reader feels more rebellious than Keats, more like the sceptical Carlyle. Undeterred by the sweep and éclat of Coleridge's mind, one simply notes the revealingly deleted word in this entry: 'That Life can manifest itself only by Poles, under the two forms of Indifference and Identity, we [supposed – crossed out] begin from as already proved.' Or when Coleridge elaborates his teleological theory of Man's divinely guided evolution to Christianity – as a synthesis of the Hebrew patriarchy, Greek idealism and Roman materialism – the reader recites a liturgy of omissions from this world-view. What about the head-hunters of New Guinea, the Aborigines, and the Buddhists, for example?

It is the fate of all great men not to be challenged in their lifetimes. Coleridge is exceptional only in being more Micawber-ish than most. As he became more esteemed, as fewer people interrupted, Coleridge was able to discharge his promissory notes with the characteristic and increasingly frequent &c. Professor Coburn, in her notes, the result of devoted research, has added substance to what Coleridge called his 'far-stretched series of Et Ceteras'. For this we, as well as Coleridge, must be immeasurably grateful.

Coleridge: the I and the World

In the first chapter of this important and provocative book,* Owen Barfield remarks that 'the definitions of *subject* and *object*, and the true nature of the relation between them, are the *pons asinorum*' of the whole endeavour. One can only agree. It seems simple enough. Why, then, do so many commentators begin with their hands on the ropes, and end tied up in knots? It is a paradox of Coleridge studies that biographers are severe and pernickety, while those who study the thought are correspondingly indulgent. (See, for instance, Donald Sultana's meticulous documentation of Coleridge's abuse of Rickman's franking, and Thomas MacFarland's lenient attitude to Coleridge's plagiarisms.) Coleridge's thought needs a sympathetic approach *and* a massive injection of that detachment so conspicuous in biographical studies. Finally, it is the flaw of Mr Barfield's excellent book that there is insufficient distinction between himself and Coleridge.

Literary people tend to react to the subject/object antithesis as they perhaps would to the Jekyll/Hyde antithesis – in a word, uneasily. In fact, it is overdue for demystification; Coleridge studies can only profit from its becoming less occult. It is a late stage in a long argument which began with Descartes. Descartes's starting point was the search for certainty in a predominantly sceptical age, an age typified by Montaigne's 'Apologie de Raimond Sebond' in which Montaigne argues that all reasoning is open to doubt. For him, even doubt is uncertain: 'When they

*What Coleridge Thought by Owen Barfield, Oxford University Press.

say I doubt, you have them fast by the throat to make them avow, that at least you are assured and know that they doubt', and yet, they excuse themselves with a racily physiological analogy: 'When they pronounce, I know not, or I doubt, they say, that this proposition transportes itself together with the rest, even as the Rewbarbe doeth, which scowred ill-humours away, and therwith is carried away himselfe.'

Descartes's method was to adopt the extreme sceptical position, to concede everything to his opponents. He begins by questioning the validity of sense experience. In the First Meditation, for instance, he demonstrates the unreliability of eyesight by pointing out that the Sun is very large, yet we can blot it out by simply holding up a hand which we know to be smaller. Similarly, a tree in the distance will look smaller than a man who is standing beside us. From this piecemeal sniping at the senses, Descartes quickly moves to a more radical demolition of their validity. He asks the question, *How do we know that we are awake?*

The short answer to this, now as then, is that there are no certain criteria for establishing whether we are awake or asleep. Russell, in *Human Knowledge*, summarizes for us: 'I dreamed last night that I was in Germany, in a house which looked on a ruined church; in my dream I supposed at first that the church had been bombed during the recent war, but was subsequently informed that its destruction dated from the wars of religion in the 16th.C. All this, so long as I remained asleep, had all the convincingness of waking life. I did really have the dream, and did really have an experience intrinsically indistinguishable from that of seeing a church when awake. It follows that an experience which I call "seeing a church" is not conclusive evidence that there is a church, since it may occur when there is no such object as I suppose in my dream. It may be said that, though when dreaming I may *think* that I am awake, when I wake up I *know* that I am awake. But I do not see how we are to have any such certainty . . .'

Descartes, having now established his doubt, turns to the problem of certainty in his Second Meditation. First, he postulates a demon, the Arch Deceiver, whose purpose is to deceive man. This hypothesis, as A. J. Ayer says in *The Problem of Knowledge*, 'may be regarded as a picturesque way of expressing the fact that intuitive conviction is not a logical guarantee of truth'. The problem is, then: is anything certain, given the existence of the Arch Deceiver? Descartes writes: 'Let him deceive me as much as he will, he can never cause me to be nothing so long as I am something.' In other words, everything we think may be incorrect, but we cannot doubt that we are thinking. This is the Cartesian certainty.

Given the certainty that the self exists, Descartes asks *what* this self is. The answer to this question creates the whole mind/body problem which is the central subject of the *Biographia Literaria*. Descartes's method of reaching the essence of something is to strip off attributes to see if their absence radically alters that something. In the case of the self, he removes the body attributes and discovers that doubting the existence of his arms and legs does not make him doubt the existence of himself. His conclusion, therefore, is that the essence of self, the *sine qua non*, is thought. This is the Cartesian Cogito – I think, therefore I am. The essence of man is thought, and thought does not occupy space.

In his Third Meditation, Descartes sets about discovering the essence of matter, using the same method. The attributes of a piece of wax are as follows: figure (shape), hardness, magnitude (extension, that which takes up space), colour, smell and other tactile properties. The attributes of the piece of wax alter when Descartes heats it: shape alters, it becomes soft instead of hard, it no longer sounds when tapped, the smell evaporates, the colour changes, it is hot instead of cold, and its size has increased. Descartes then asks: 'Does the same wax still remain after this change? It must be admitted that it does remain; no one doubts it, or judges otherwise. What then was it I knew with so much distinctness in the piece of wax?' His answer is that only one thing remained unchanged – extension. The heated wax took up more space, but the constant factor was that it took up space. Matter, then, becomes that which is extended, that which takes up space.

As such, it is exactly opposite to the mind which does not take up space.

The problem of knowledge is, then, this 'polar opposition between mind and matter' (Gilbert Ryle). How is there communication between the mind and its opposite, matter. How can we know anything of the external world? An analogy would be oil and water; how can the two things mix?

Coleridge states the problem crisply in chapter eight of the *Biographia*: 'The soul was a thinking substance, and the body a space-filling substance. Yet the apparent action of each on the other pressed heavy on the philosopher on the one hand, and no less heavily on the other hand pressed the evident truth that the law of causality holds only between homogeneous things, i.e. things having some common property, and cannot extend from one world into another its opposite.' The problem is really very simple: the only thing which complicates it is terminology. Coleridge, in particular, dons and discards terminology like a model at a fashion show. The root antithesis is between Mind and Matter, but this is expressed indifferently as *Scire/Esse*, Thought/Thing, Man/Nature, Mind/Body, and, of course, Subject/Object. The importance of that last term is, as we shall see, crucial.

Descartes's attempts to solve the problem he had created are failures. His theory of animal spirits explains only how the body works, and, in order to explain how the animal spirits affect the mind, he is forced to violate his own premise that the mind does not exist in space, by locating it in the pineal gland. The Princess Elisabeth, a philosophical amateur, persuaded Descartes, in a series of letters in 1643, to acknowledge the contradiction. His 'solution' is really a restatement of the problem. The philosopher sees that mind and body are mutually exclusive; the philosopher is right. The man in the street, on the other hand, knows that the mind affects the body. He knows this from common sense. The man in the street is right. Our difficulty is that it is not possible to hold both positions at once.

In the *Biographia Literaria*, Coleridge attacks putative solutions to the mind/body gap. His criticism is always the same in essence. It is that in order to establish a *rapprochement* between Mind and Matter, philosophers *falsify* one of the terms. Hartley, for example, discusses the mind as if it were a machine subject to mechanical laws. Priestley falsifies the *other* term: 'He stript matter of all its material properties; substituted spiritual powers; and when we expected to find a body, behold! we had nothing but a ghost! the apparition of a defunct substance!'

Actually, Coleridge illustrates Priestley's error better than Priestley. By 'better', one means 'more enjoyably', for it is in Coleridge's 'Conversation Poems', written under the influence of Priestley, that one finds matter 'stript of all its material properties'. 'This Lime-Tree Bower', for instance, turns on a contrast between two radically different scenes. The first is the 'roaring dell' where Nature is a kind of life-in-death devoid of inner force:

> that branchless ash,
> Unsunned and damp, whose few poor yellow leaves
> Ne'er tremble in the gale, yet tremble still,
> Fann'd by the water-fall!

One might compare Eliot's image of pseudo-Life, of survival rather than genuine existence:

> A broken spring in a factory yard,
> Rust that clings to the form that the strength has left
> Hard and curled and ready to snap.

The prospect changes to a many-steepled tract where:

> all doth seem
> Less gross than bodily . . .

Similarly, in 'Reflections on Having Left a Place of Retirement', a prospect is gradually deprived of its material properties: '*Dim* coasts, and *cloud-like* hills' (my italics).

The myth, started by Coleridge, is that his philosophical interests killed his poetry. The truth is that philosophy fed Coleridge's poetry, but so well that we often do not recognize it:

the icicles, for instance, in 'Frost at Midnight' express symbolically the mystery of the Mind/Matter antithesis. 'The secret
ministry' (my italics) is a *spiritual* force that hangs up icicles
which are matter. The spiritual becomes palpable. It is a brilliant
example of Valéry's dictum that 'stark naked thoughts and
feelings are weak as naked men. So they have to be clothed.' The
best comparison would be Marvell's 'green thought in a green
shade' – a perfect union of Thought and Thing. Other poets have,
on the whole, expressed the terrible chasm between Mind and
Matter: 'Giue me an Ounce of Ciuet; good Apothecary to
sweeten my immagination', and 'Twill hardly buy a cap-case for
one's conscience . . .'

By the time he was writing the *Biographia*, however, Coleridge
had rejected Priestley's solution and was looking about for a
solution of his own. In chapter twelve, he refers to Leibniz's
assertion that the true philosophy would 'at once explain and
collect the fragments of truth scattered through systems apparently the most incongruous'. This was what Coleridge hoped to
do. Thomas MacFarland's painstaking *Coleridge and the Pan-
theist Tradition* has demonstrated conclusively that Coleridge
believed all philosophies could be reduced to two essential
positions – namely, the IT IS, and the I AM. In other words,
Materialism and Idealism, which will eventually arrive, via
different routes, at a solution of the Mind/Matter problem.

Mr Barfield does not distinguish sufficiently between the two
approaches. Rather, he offers a brilliant exegesis of the Materialist route, by amassing Coleridge's sprawling comments scattered
around his works, and by using his *Hints Towards A More
Comprehensive Theory of Life* to effect a striking synthesis. In the
Biographia, Coleridge's account of the Materialist route is
extremely brief and, ultimately, nothing more than conjecture: 'in
nature itself the more the principle of law breaks forth, the more
does the husk drop off, the phaenomena themselves become more
spiritual . . .' Mr Barfield's expansion of this passage can be
summarized as follows: equating *thinking* and *imagining*, he
takes Coleridge's definition of the Primary Imagination – 'a
repetition in the finite mind of the eternal *act* of creation in the

infinite I AM' (my italics) – and describes, using *Hints Towards A More Comprehensive Theory of Life*, what the eternal act of creation was for the poet. Coleridge saw creation not as a fixed, material thing, but rather as a *combination* or polarity of matter (*Natura naturata*) and end-directed *energy* (*Natura naturans*). This energy of Nature combines, relates and communicates with Mind because Mind too, in the *act* of thinking, exhibits a similar combination of Thoughts and energy. Thus, although Mind and Nature initially seem heterogeneous, they do actually have a common factor, which is energy. If Coleridge could have seen Mr Barfield's schematic two-page summation of this, he would probably have disowned it for its clarity.

After this success, Mr Barfield's next move is to consider the Idealist route. It is disappointingly skimped, and, instead of heading into the Ten Theses, Coleridge's Golfo Placido where the SS *Schelling* steams in fog and gloom, Mr Barfield opts to go straight to the periphery of things: 'A detailed exposition of the whole would be out of place, since the intention is that its content should be allowed to transpire from this book taken as a whole.' In other words, the conclusion to the Materialist route should 'rub off' on the rest. But, this is to falsify the way in which the question is set by Coleridge: 'the transcendental or intelligential philosopher is equally anxious to preclude all interpolation of the objective into the subjective principles of his science'.

Mr Barfield's account of the Idealist route is as follows: from the *single* certainty which is I AM, the Idealist must deduce the existence of the real world, which includes sense data. Mr Barfield begins by saying that Coleridge's distinction between Man and Nature is not the conventional one. Presumably he means that the Man and Nature distinction is really the distinction between Mind and Matter, where Matter includes the human body. He then says that the Subject/Object distinction is not the same thing. By this, he appears to mean that there are two kinds of object – mental objects which are Thoughts and natural objects which are Things. And in a sense this is true: Subject means the Percipient, and Object means the Thing perceived. But, this analysis of the Mind tells us nothing about the world. The

Cartesian dualism will not be solved by dividing the Subject into Subject and mental Object. In other words, *pace* Mr Barfield, Subject and Object must be effectually *synonymous* with Man and Nature if the problem is even to be confronted. Coleridge himself is very firm here: 'Now the sum of all that is merely objective we will henceforth call *nature*, confining the term to its passive and material sense, *as comprising all the phaenomena by which its existence is made known to us* [my italics]. On the other hand, the sum of all that is subjective we may comprehend in the name of *self* or *intelligence*. Both conceptions are in necessary antithesis . . . the one as conscious, the other as without consciousness. Now in all acts of positive knowledge there is required a reciprocal concurrence of both, namely of our conscious being and of that which is in itself unconscious. *Our problem is to explain this concurrence, its possibility and its necessity*' (my italics). Only one Object, then, should concern us – the one 'without consciousness'.

Briefly, Coleridge – for all his caution – is, in the Theses, hoist with his own petard. Like Priestley, Hartley, and now Mr Barfield, he constructs a false Object: in the act of self-knowledge, the Subject contemplates itself as Object, and thus Subject and Object come together. It is a hollow solution which can be recognized as such simply by substituting for the term Object a more earthy alternative like World. The wordploy then becomes apparent.

But perhaps the whole Mind/Matter problem is an empty one. Perhaps Ryle is correct and the whole thing is a category mistake. Perhaps the trouble with Coleridge, like his beloved Hamlet, was not that he could not keep his mind on the problem, but that he could not keep it off it, as witness those compulsive metaphysical shopping-lists which are scattered through his works – Reason, Imagination, Understanding are rearranged constantly as Coleridge fidgets with his absurd map of the unmappable mind. Mr Barfield, for one, would contest this hotly, and devotes much sympathetic attention to teasing out the meaning from these lists, in terms of polarity and Coleridge's theory of an evolving consciousness.

A half-success (no mean feat) is his account of the Secondary Imagination as the Primary raised to a higher level of consciousness. At the Primary level, *thinking* and *Natura naturans* have the common property of energy or *Vis*. This common factor enables us to perceive external nature. Mr Barfield puts it this way: 'imagination at its primary stage empowers experience of an outer world', but only at a rudimentary level. At the secondary stage, the interaction becomes more aware: *Natura naturans* is apprehended not simply as a power or source of productive energy. Rather, the mind understands more fully how *Natura naturans* organizes *Natura naturata*, how it creates more and more complicated manifolds where parts and wholes relate, where a more and more complicated multeity is reduced to unity. Having *experienced* the external world as a series of complex manifolds, the Secondary Imagination can *express* similar manifolds: 'at its secondary stage it both expresses and empowers experience of that outer world as the productive "unity in multeity", which results in a whole and parts organically related to one another.'

Two points should be made. First, if we ask ourselves whether this is a true, or even a possible account of our experience of the external world, we must surely answer with a flat denial. That is Coleridge's problem. Mr Barfield's problem is that this account of the Secondary Imagination leaves him with one type of artist only – the Shakespearian type who works, like nature, from within. In fact, Coleridge envisaged two types of artist, the artist *ab intra* (Shakespeare) and the artist *ab extra* (Milton and Wordsworth). This is a difficulty which Mr Barfield can only circumvent by minimizing Coleridge's fundamental distinction between the two types. He is forced to say that Coleridge 'detected' a 'fine contrast' between Shakespeare and Milton. This will not pass muster as a description.

Mr Barfield's exposition of the Fancy is a good deal more cloudy than this, yet, even if it often seems difficult to take Coleridge's account of the higher regions of consciousness seriously, this is a book to be grateful for.

Coleridge: the Critical Heritage

The praise quite as much as the blame apportioned by contemporary reviewers is notoriously misguided and this collection is no exception.* Necessarily it is of greater interest to the student of nineteenth-century reviewing than to the Coleridge specialist. Apart from a handful of well-informed, *engagé* theological reviews, the pieces suffer from the usual faults – abuse of space, horrendous stylistic flourishes, inattention to the text in question, incestuous and interminable disquisitions on reviewing standards, gossip, grotesque philistinism whenever metaphysics is mentioned and, worst of all, a cornucopia of empty critical concepts ('transparency of genius', 'purity of conception', 'If there be such a thing as poetry of the senses *strung* to imagination, such is his'). Coleridge emerges from this volume as his own best critic: these reviewers lean heavily on his marginal gloss to 'The Ancient Mariner', his dictum that great poets are also great philosophers, his own explication of his motives in treating supernatural subjects, and so on. *In propria persona* the average critic makes for extremely dull reading.

Moreover, the editor has done little to alleviate this by his misguidedly rigid interpretation of his brief. This book is unimaginatively conceived and shoddily executed. There are far too many representatively bad reviews. The space would have been more properly allocated to better reviews written after Coleridge's

Coleridge: The Critical Heritage edited by J. R. de J. Jackson, Routledge and Kegan Paul.

death and now not easily available to the general reader. De Quincey's article in *Tait's Edinburgh Magazine* (September 1834), J. T. Ferrier's 'The Plagiarism of S. T. Coleridge' (*Blackwood's Edinburgh Magazine*, 1840), the relevant section of Sir William Hamilton's 'Supplementary Dissertations' to his edition of the *Works of Thomas Reid* (1846), J. H. Stirling's two attacks on Coleridge, and C. M. Ingleby's adverse comments at least have the virtue of containing factual information, regardless of the slant put upon it. And why did not Mr Jackson include any parodies, like the entertaining 'Rime of the Auncient Waggonere' (*Blackwood's Edinburgh Magazine*, February 1819), or 'Christobell' (*European Magazine*, April 1815), or 'Christabel, Part the Third' (*Blackwood's Edinburgh Magazine*, June 1819), or Hogg's two parodies in *The Poetic Mirror*, 'Isabelle' and 'The Cherub'? In their way they show much more graphically than any bona fide review the helplessness of Coleridge's contemporaries confronted by his irreducible originality. Hogg's parodies, for instance, unlike his excellent parodies of Wordsworth, are failures of a particularly informative kind. They do not parody Coleridge so much as the Lake School. The hits are against Wordsworth rather than Coleridge. The Coleridgean critical heritage has been made over to Wordsworth and, to a lesser extent, Southey.

This misdirection of critical energies begins with the joint publication of *Lyrical Ballads*. It is, therefore, an error of judgement by Mr Jackson to truncate the reviews of those volumes, restricting them to comments on poems by Coleridge. This mutilation can only mislead the uninformed reader. But it is difficult to see what kind of a reader Mr Jackson has in mind: there are footnotes explaining that the poet of Rydal Mount is Wordsworth, and that six exclamation marks after the couplet

> She was most beautiful to see
> Like a lady of a far countree.!!!!!!

are the reviewer's, but elsewhere the general reader will find Mr Jackson stingy with his knowledge. Admittedly, in the absence of a standard edition of the prose works, page references are difficult to give. But this does not apply to the poetry. On p. 519, for instance, a reviewer misquotes 'Lewti' but the reader is told neither in which poem the quotation appears, nor that the last line should read 'And *startle* from their reedy bed', and not 'started'. Often, too, it is not clear whether the reviewer is quoting unfamiliar Coleridge or another author. The reader gets no help from Mr Jackson: readers of Hazlitt's reviews will do better to consult P. P. Howe's Centenary Edition where all quotations are traced. One can only wonder that Mr Jackson did not. But this is typical of the scholarship: on p. 226 the general reader will find an unexplained allusion to Byron. A reference to Marchand, Vol. II, chapter xv, pp. 595ff. would have been in order. Similarly, H. N. Coleridge's claim (p. 636) that Schiller 'in more instances than one, afterwards adopted the hints and translated in turn the interpolations of his own translator', requires some comment from a responsible editor. One is surprised, too, to find that Mr Jackson makes no correlation between repeated images in the reviews which show that reviewers perhaps read each other with more care than the work in hand. An instance of this is the comparison of Coleridge with Joanna Southcote (*sic*) by Hazlitt (p. 264) and Wilson (p. 329). On p. 12 there is an incorrect reference. It should read *C.L.*, IV, 785–6. And on pages 106 and 595 there are misleading misprints. The job has not been well done and this list does not exhaust one's complaints.

Kipling and God

'Young man, how's your soul?' asked General Booth, when he and Kipling received honorary degrees at Oxford. Kipling's answer is not extant. However, the question had been asked before, by Caroline Taylor, whose clergyman father thought he detected Romanist tendencies in his daughter's suitor. Kipling replied with a simple statement of faith: 'I believe in the existence of a personal God to Whom we are personally responsible for wrongdoing – that it is our duty to follow and our peril to disobey the ten ethical laws laid down for us.' A catalogue of negatives succeeds this affirmation. Kipling disbelieved in heaven and hell, in the doctrines of the Trinity and Redemption, and though he reverenced Christ, he could not endorse the belief that the Crucifixion, however sincere the gesture, actually promoted man's spiritual welfare.

This sharp distinction between ethical imperatives and metaphysical speculation recurs throughout Kipling's work. Like Wittgenstein, he believed that 'whereof one cannot speak, thereof one must be silent', an attitude which probably derived from his contact with Buddhism, with its emphasis on the Law (*dhamma*) and its reluctance to speculate – for Kipling was more catholic than Caroline Taylor's father could have conceived. But even the Law, as it appears in the *Jungle Book*, 'Recessional' and elsewhere, is not a fixed set of rules. It stands for rules in the abstract and the need for obedience.

Upbringing as much as temperament accounts for this religious posture. Christianity never had a firm or exclusive hold on

Kipling. His parents were free thinkers of Methodist stock, and even as a tot in Bombay, he had a foot in both camps, like some multi-limbed Indian godling – with his bearer, he attended Hindu rites, while his ayah took him to the Goanese Catholic church. At his English school, Westward Ho!, there was no chapel and the Christian notion of suffering for others was tailored to the needs of Empire, transmuted into the secular idea of service. This Conradian ideal finds expression in 'The Sons of Martha'. Moreover, the vast subcontinent of India diminished the exclusive claims of Christian doctrine.

Like E. M. Forster's Mrs Moore, Kipling could see the nationalistic basis of 'poor little talkative Christianity' – a limitation which led him cordially to detest missionaries, and to pillory religious arrogance in the person of Chaplain Bennett in *Kim*. In life, Freemasonry was a way of overcoming racial, religious and caste barriers. Kipling's tolerance escapes only those who have not read him – in the preface to *Life's Handicap*, he wrote: 'when man has come to the turnstiles of Night all the creeds in the world seem to him wonderfully alike and colourless'. In *Kim*, the Lama and Mahbub Ali repeat the idea – the Lama dismissing his youth as the search for doctrine rather than truth, Mahbub comparing creeds to horses, 'there is a profit to be made from them all'. Even the Babu's Spencerian rationalism respects supernatural phenomena.

Indifferent to doctrine, Kipling was none the less acutely susceptible to extra-phenomenal experience. His father reports that after the death of Josephine, his daughter, Kipling saw her 'when a door opened, when a space was vacant at table, coming out of every green dark corner of the garden, radiant – and heartbreaking'. But like Wordsworth's Matthew in 'Two April Mornings', Kipling tenderly put aside the vision: ' "They" ' and 'Endor' (written after his son was killed) recount the temptation and rejection of occult experience.

The supernatural certainly existed for Kipling – he was a man who could still feel the air shaking to the 'red-hot' belief of dead worshippers in a deserted mosque; a man who, in a proleptic dream, had once seen 'an unreleased roll of my life-film' – but he shared Eliot's conviction that 'human kind cannot bear very much reality'. To Rider Haggard he explained that God intentionally made mystical experience difficult to retain, so that man could work for his fellow-men without distraction. 'The Ship That Found Herself' is his comment on the querulous individual voice and the need to suppress it in service.

Divinity, he felt, was for the unknowable God, not for human beings. 'The Children of the Zodiac' is Kipling's allegorical expression of man's atrophying assumptions of divinity and immortality. Leo and Virgo, when they *are* Gods, fail in human understanding and, in their indifference, undervalue human life. Then the prospect of their eventual end gives life its preciousness – as Wallace Stevens wrote, 'Death is the mother of beauty' – so that their loss of divine status is a valuable weaning. Kipling's version of the Fall (*Enemies Unto Each Other*) restates the point which Wordsworth sums up – 'a deep distress hath humanized my soul'. Adam and Eve ignore the only thing they really possess (each other) in a hubristic search for exclusive divinity, and their redemption is simply an acceptance of their own humanity.

The resurgence of Christian mythology in late Kipling is easily misinterpreted as a quasi-conversion. In fact, nothing had changed since 'The Bridge Builders' (1898) where Kipling shows that the gods are merely man's imaginative projections on to the Unknown – comforting fictions, some versions of the Infinite. Krishna informs the Hindu animal pantheon that the gods change – 'all save one that makes love in the hearts of men'. The survivor, then, will always correspond closely to the needs of the human mind. The story begins with Findlayson contemplating his bridge – he 'saw that his work was good'. This echo of Genesis includes Christianity among the fictions, since it implies that the biblical account of Creation is merely a human emotion writ large. The mind, as Stevens knew, is 'a child that sings itself to sleep' – with comforters.

So, in 'On the Gate', Kipling imagines heaven as a paramilitary bureaucracy, overworked by the increased influx of dead from the First World War; while in 'Uncovenanted Mercies' hell is a replica of King's Cross Station. In each case, the science fiction is a *tour de force* of transparent fantasy – man-created to comfort man. Beyond the glitter of technique here, and in the sustained irony of 'The Gardener' with its visionary ending, is an essentially human message: forgiveness is all. Kipling is no Swedenborg asking us to assent to the literal detail. For who, he implicitly asks, can speak of the unknowable with certainty? Faith, he knew, could only be subjective.

Kipling as a Children's Writer

*O Beloved Kids** gathers the extant letters of Kipling to his son John and his daughter Elsie during the years 1906 to 1915, when John was killed in action at Loos. Kipling had wangled him into the Irish Guards, although the boy had already been rejected by both army and navy because of his eyesight. From Bath, Kipling permits himself a 'gloat', writing of a twenty-year-old acquaintance, anxious to drive cars at the front, but with a certificate of medical unfitness: 'I expect his Mamma was at the back of that certificate.' Carrie, Kipling's wife, was more sturdy and when his old French governess asked why John was in the army, since there was no conscription, Carrie proudly replied, 'Precisely *because* there is no compulsion.' The sentiment is no longer fashionable, yet it is comprehensible and still has the power to move us, as Lowell realized in 'For the Union Dead'. The cause was better, but the principle the same:

> He is out of bounds now. He rejoices in man's lovely,
> peculiar power to choose life and die –
> when he leads his black soldiers to death,
> he cannot bend his back.

Where Colonel Shaw's father, though, 'wanted no monument / except the ditch, / where his son's body was thrown / and lost with his "niggers" ', Kipling gave himself the penitential task of

O Beloved Kids: Rudyard Kipling's Letters to his Children edited by Elliot L. Gilbert, Weidenfeld and Nicolson.

259

working for the War Graves Commission. John Kipling's body, however, was not found and there is a moment of sickening poignancy in his penultimate letter, which includes a request: 'By the way, the next time you are in town would you get me an Identification Disc as I have gone and lost mine. I think you could get one at the Stores. Just an aluminium Disc with a string through it like this . . .' A drawing follows.

Before we judge John Kipling's mother, we should remember that when Kipling was critically ill in New York with inflammation of the lung, Carrie's steely quality saved his life. As he lay in a fever, his first-born, Josephine, died. One can do no better than quote the simple account in Charles Carrington's unsurpassed biography: 'The doctors forbade that Rudyard in his weakness should be told of this calamity . . . When Carrie went from the funeral straight to his bedside, remembering in time that she was dressed in black, she snatched up a scarlet shawl as she entered the room and threw it round her shoulders so that he would ask no question.' Josephine was seven years old when she died. Very, very few people would have had the strength to keep the secret of such a grief. Kipling believed in sacrifice, but not coldly. No one has written more tenderly of children or of what parents feel for them. ' "They" ' is Kipling's classic tribute to Josephine, a story by which he includes himself in the hideous democracy of grief that all parents feel. 'The Gardener' is the tribute exacted by the death of his son and again Kipling's imagination is flexible and delicate enough to include even the ghastly Mrs Scarsworth. In the matter of bereavement, Kipling was a communist who recognized no hierarchies of suffering.

As for John's enlistment, Kipling already knew what loss of a child could mean and, as a war correspondent, he could judge the risks. It was not the glib decision of an uncaring chauvinist. And though these letters contain mainly expressions of pride, we can assess from 'Dymchurch Flit' what went into Kipling's decision. It is one of his greatest stories, largely told in Sussex dialect, which bears comparison with Frost's 'The Witch of Coös' and probably surpasses it. Both Frost and Kipling renew the ballad tradition where the kind of supernatural subject matter they treat would naturally have found expression. The alterations are simple but profound. Both abandon rhyme and literary dialect-equivalent, Frost choosing real American and a flexible blank verse, Kipling going to prose and authentic Sussex speech. When Wordsworth wanted to renew the ballad, he chose to eliminate the sensational event that had been its staple. Kipling and Frost retain the macabre event, but naturalize the form.

In 'Dymchurch Flit', Widow Whitgift is a psychic and, there-fore, a possible channel of communication for the fairies or Pharisees who have been driven into the Romney Marsh as Henry VIII's Reformation gets under way, tearing down 'the Images'. The Pharisees wish to escape to France where the atmosphere is more congenial, where they will be less 'stenched up an' frighted'. After a typically oblique and powerfully elusive exposition of the groundwork, much like Frost's sidling and sidelong approach to his narrative subjects, the tale suddenly accelerates and simplifies: 'Now there was a poor widow at Dymchurch under the Wall, which, lacking man or property, she had more time for feeling; and she come to feel there was a Trouble outside her doorstep bigger an' heavier than aught she'd ever carried over it. She had two sons – one born blind, and t'other struck dumb through fallin' off the Wall when he was liddle. They was men grown, but not wage-earnin', an' she worked for 'em, keepin' bees and answerin' Questions.' Has any writer ever used capital letters with more authority or to greater effect? And there is a marvel-lous and necessary conviction in the way Kipling not only reproduces the dialect so exactly, but also, as it were, an authentic dialect of thought – which barely distinguishes between the relative importance of 'man or property' or between 'keepin' bees and answerin' Questions'. To the speaker, Tom Shoesmith, himself a covert Pharisee, bees and Questions are equally natural and the reader is persuaded by his matter-of-factness.

The Pharisees ask for a boat to take them to France 'an' come back no more'. There is a boat, but no one to sail it, and so they ask the widow to lend them her sons: 'Give 'em Leave an' Good-will to sail it for us, Mother – O Mother!' The conflict is then between her own delimited maternal feelings – 'One's dumb, an' t'other's blind . . . but all the dearer me for that' – and her mother's heart which goes out to the invisible Pharisees and *their* children: 'the voices justabout pierced through her; an' there was childern's voices too. She stood out all she could, but she couldn't rightly stand against *that*.' Finally, she consents, shaking 'like a aps-tree makin' up her mind'. She is rewarded for her charity by the return of her sons and by the promise that psychic gifts will run in her family, but Tom Shoesmith makes it clear that her sacrifice was not made for gain: 'No. She loaned her sons for a pure love-loan, bein' as she sensed the Trouble on the Marshes, an' was simple good-willing to ease it.' Written before 1906, this story throws abundant light on Carrie and Kipling's decision in 1914.

John Kipling emerges from these letters as strikingly ordinary, but perhaps 'all the dearer for that'. Kipling warns him against 'beastliness', 'side' and 'pi-jaw', tells him to keep his head 'shut' and work hard. The boy cannot spell, is academically undistinguished and not particularly good at games. Yet Kipling's stories return ceaselessly to the nature of parental love, its ability to expend inexhaustible passion on apparently worthless objects. There is Wyn Fowler in 'Mary Postgate', 'an unlovely orphan of eleven', who repays Mary's devotion 'by calling her "Gatepost", "Postey", or "Packthread", by thumping her between her narrow shoulders, or by chasing her bleating, round the garden, her large mouth open, her large nose high in air, at a stiff-necked shamble very like a camel's'. There is the Copley family in 'Friendly Brook' who have a 'Bernarder cripple-babe', but not for the money they receive for fostering: 'It's handy,' says Jabez. 'But the child's more. "Dada" he says, an "Mumma" he says, with his great rollin' head-piece all hurdled up in that iron collar. *He* won't live long – his backbone's rotten, like. But they Copleys do just about set store by him – five bob or no five bob.' For Kipling, this isn't an extreme case. It is a human constant he can effortlessly empathize with.

It is this knowledge of parental love, too, which produces some of Kipling's most savage stories. He knows it can be murderous if threatened – as it is, most obviously, in 'Mary Postgate', where the wizened old spinster stands over a German airman with a revolver, luxuriating first in his death (from injuries sustained in a fall from his aircraft) and then in a hot bath. This act of barbarism, Mary knows, would not gain Wyn's approval were he alive. Nor does it, I think, elicit Kipling's approval – only his understanding. The same theme is examined in 'A Sahibs' War', where Kipling's attitude is less ambiguous. The narrator, Umr Singh, is a Sikh who is a kind of adoptive father to a Sahib called Kurban: 'Young – of a reddish face – with blue eyes, and he lilted a little on his feet when he was pleased, and cracked his finger-joints.' How carefully Kipling implies, in the first three phrases, this young man's virtual anonymity, and how carefully he conveys the immense emotional investment of the narrator in the last two descriptive touches, singling out characteristics invisible except to the eye of love. In this story, the narrator attempts to revenge himself on a treacherous Boer family who have killed his 'son', Kurban Sahib. They are not prepossessing: 'an old man with a white beard and a wart upon the left side of his neck; and a fat woman with the eyes of a swine and the jowl of a swine; and a tall young man deprived of understanding. His head was hairless, no larger than an orange, and the pits of his nostrils were eaten away by a disease. He laughed and slavered . . .' When the Sikh narrator plans his revenge, he intends to be exact, a child for a child: 'and the idiot lay on the floor with his head against her knee, and he counted his fingers and laughed, and she laughed again. So I knew they were mother and son . . .' He means to hang the son in front of the mother and Kipling accurately records her anguish: 'the woman hindered me not a little with her screechings and plungings.' Umr Singh, who has taken opium to sustain him, is deflected from his purpose by a vision of the dead Kurban Sahib who orders him to refrain, telling him that this is a Sahibs' war. Mary Postgate has no such assistance back to civilized values and the rule of law – only her tortured instinct, in its full atavism. Nevertheless, though the Boer family survive, Kipling makes us know the force of parental grief. If it is the eye of love that isolates and cherishes that habit of cracking the fingers, it is the same eye, hideously inflamed, that registers the wart on the left side of the Boer's neck.

In his stories, Kipling often measures love by its opposite, and these letters also show how deep this habit of thought and expression went. Though they are entitled O *Beloved Kids*, Kipling's expressions of affection are rarely straightforward. Except for two occasions ('You see, I love you'), Kipling prefers the ironical mode: 'Mummy is better I think every day than she was (perhaps because two yellingly pestiferous brats are away)'; 'she says as long as she hasn't you two horrid little brats to look after she can stand most things'; 'I regret I have not kicked you enough'; 'I think he wants being kicked with love and forethought'; 'if it had been you I should have chastised you with a cricket stump'. Examples of this knock-about stuff would be easy to multiply. Clearly, they conceal an almost embarrassing concern and tenderness, a passion more single-minded and obsessive than the sexual. Despite the tough front, Kipling is completely infatuated and showers gifts on his son while the letters keep up a saving pretence of sternness. Squash courts are built, there are treats at Brown's Hotel followed by music halls, motor bikes are bought, gramophones, and finally a Singer car. There can be no question: Kipling was a sugar daddy.

All the same, it has to be said that these letters are comparatively dull reading. Elliot L. Gilbert, an able Kipling scholar, has contributed an introduction which does its level best to inject interest, but it is largely spurious in its claims. The letters do not amount to an unofficial biography of Kipling's son: we learn a little more but, truly, there isn't a lot to learn. Nor will it do to pretend that this correspondence is of a piece with the stories written for children: 'in one sense, the world has long enjoyed "letters" from Kipling to his children. The *Just So Stories*, we know, were addressed directly to them.' This is a false connection, though one can see the commercial advantage of pretending these letters are like a new volume of stories. They are not. They lack, except very sporadically, Kipling's descriptive gifts: there is nothing here to set against the crocodile's 'musky, tusky mouth', or 'the great grey-green, greasy Limpopo River', or the 'Yellow Man' 'yellow – not from sickness, but by nature – yellow as honey, and his eyes stood endwise in his head'. There is a mildly absorbed description of whaling, but little to match the bravura account of how the Pharisees entered the fishing smack to sail to France: 'Then I saw – then, they say, she had to brace back same as if she was wadin' in tide-water; for the Pharisees just about flowed past her – down the beach to the boat, *I* dunnamany of 'em – with their wives an' children an' valooables, all escapin' out of cruel Old England. Silver you could hear clinkin', an' liddle bundles hove down dunt on the bottom boards, an' passels o' liddle swords an' shields raklin', an' liddle fingers an' toes scratchin' on the boatside to board her when the two sons pushed her off. That boat she sunk lower an' lower, but all the Widow could see in it was her boys movin' hampered-like to get at the tackle . . .'

O Beloved Kids demonstrates that, though Kipling was a master at writing for children, he was noticeably less good at writing *to* children. It seems a paradox, perhaps to be explained by Kipling's theory of inspiration:

This is the doom of the Makers – their Daemon lives in their pen. If he be absent or sleeping, they are even as other men.

As an explanation of the difference between Kipling the artist and Kipling the correspondent, it has at least the virtue of familiarity. Henry James's story 'The Private Life' advances much the same thesis, with the bluff social animal at the dining table while his industrious and inspired doppelganger is covering reams upstairs. James's story is usually thought to be based on Browning, but a conversation between Blanche Adney and James's narrator, after Blanche has seen the doppelganger, may point also to Kipling. 'We understood each other,' she says. 'By flashes of lightning?' the narrator inquires. There is a real thunderstorm, of course, but it is just possible that James, always baffled by Kipling's crude enthusiasm for the motor car, is alluding delicately to Oscar Wilde's famous pronouncement: 'as one turns over the pages of his Plain Tales one feels as if one were seated under a palm tree reading life by superb flashes of vulgarity.'

A nearer explanation of Kipling's failure as a letter writer to his children involves a proper understanding of his children's stories. Professor Gilbert's theory is a trifle sentimental in my view: for him, Kipling is a great children's writer because he preserved inside him the undamaged soul of a child. He supports this view with a quotation from a letter to Amelia Clifford in 1890: 'Why can't you frivol and be a baby now and again as I am always.' Two additional pieces of 'evidence' are pressed into service. Professor Gilbert feigns to be unable at first to distinguish the moustached Kipling from the children he is sitting crosslegged among in a photograph. And he claims that a comic sketch of John in a huge overcoat amounts to another sighting of his theory – the enduring child in grown-up togs. It is clever, novel and daft. After all, this overcoat could be reversible and one could argue from it that Kipling's work for children is essentially adult, despite its childish starting point – that the overcoat has the greater bulk. At least this would not contradict Kipling's own view of his children's stories, as he expresses it in *Something of Myself*: 'yet, since the tales had to be read by children, before people realized that they were meant for grown-ups; and since they had to be a sort of balance to, as well as a seal upon, some aspects of my "Imperialistic" output in the past, I worked the material in three or four overlaid tints and textures, which might or might not reveal themselves according to the shifting light of sex, youth and experience . . . So I loaded the book up with allegories and allusions, and verified references until my old chief would have been almost pleased with me.' There seems no good reason to dispute this account. Kipling, though he believed in his daemon, as any writer must if he is not to force his talent, also makes it clear in 'The Wrong Thing' that his art had no place for guess-work. It was conscious and critical after the Inner Voice had played its part: 'iron's sweet stuff,' says Hal, 'if you don't torture her, and hammered work is all pure, truthful line, with a reason and a support for every curve and bar of it.'

It is difficult to imagine any child grasping this piece of aesthetic theorizing from *Rewards and Fairies*. It is a warning to adults that nothing can be skipped, that every detail is relevant. Obviously, though the stories in *Puck of Pook's Hill* and *Rewards and Fairies* are finally aimed at a sophisticated readership, the ostensible readership demands some compromise, but surprisingly little. In fact, Dan and Una are frequently deployed by Kipling to pre-empt and disarm uneasiness. They act as surrogates within the story: 'I think this tale is getting like the woods,' says Dan, 'darker and twistier every minute'; 'I don't understand a bit,' says Una; 'I don't understand all of it, but I like hearing about the little Picts,' says Una, extending her bafflement in a companiable way to the youthful reader. Sometimes these declarations provoke explanation; sometimes they do not. Occasionally, too, Kipling inverts the procedure by conceding wider knowledge to Dan and Una (and, of course, the reader) than the actual narrators possess. They are, for instance, more than a match for Sir Richard Dalyngridge in 'The Knights of the Joyous Venture': they understand the compass ('the evil Spirit strove day and night to return to his country, and therefore, look you, the iron needle pointed continually to the South') and they realize that Sir Richard's Devils are actually apes. By judicious flattery, by a certain amount of conceded exposition, by displays of ignorant solidarity, Kipling contrives to draw children through to the end of his demanding tales.

Even so, there are clearly moments when a young reader will be utterly lost – Tom Shoesmith's elliptical résumé of the Reformation, for instance, or the unexplained reference to Tom Doughty in 'Simple Simon' which is, in fact, crucial to the unravelling of the Aunt's psychic prediction for Francis Drake. Sometimes, too, it is clear that Kipling has included a joke for adults at the expense of his younger readers: in 'A Doctor of Medicine', Puck teases Culpeper about his astrological gifts and asks him to identify a star which is in actuality the midwife's cycle lamp, as Culpeper realizes. 'Wrong, Nick,' says Puck. ''Tis a singular bright star in Virgo, declining towards the house of Aquarius the water-carrier, who hath lately been afflicted by Gemini.' Una 'contradicts' Puck: 'No. It's the village nurse going down to the Mill about some fresh twins that came there last week.'

In 'Marklake Witches', Kipling's miniature *Wings of the Dove*, the failure of Una to comprehend fully is essential to the pathos of the story. Philadelphia, the peppy heroine, is dying of TB but does not know it. She is merely irritated by a troublesome cough and tells her story with such panache and vim that few young readers will grasp the significance of the experiments with primitive stethoscopes ("'tis wonerful like hearin' a man's soul whisperin' in his innards'). At the story's end, Philadelphia doffs her tomboy persona to play the host at her father's table where the Duke of Wellington is guest. Kipling's description of her clothes is detailed and drenched with the sense of a womanhood that will be wasted: 'But Cissie had laid out my very best evening dress, the white satin one, vandyked at the bottom with spots of morone foil, and the pearl knots, you know, catching up the drapery from the left shoulder. I had poor mother's lace tucker and her cornet comb.' Kipling's finest touch is to make Una envy this poor doomed adolescent: ' "Oh, you lucky!" Una murmured.' And, at the last, after Philadelphia has recounted how she played her harp ('not very difficult fingering, but r-r-ravishing sentiment'), Kipling permits himself to sound the note again: ' "I wish I'd been you," said Una, clasping her hands.' The song Philadelphia sings encompasses Kipling's recurrent dread of children's mortality:

> I have given my heart to a flower,
> Though I know it is fading away,
> Though I know it will live but an hour
> And leave me to mourn its decay!

As he said, these stories were 'meant for grown-ups'. Only a grown-up could place that song correctly and critically, yet feel its full force in the context.

Kipling knew his audience. Even the simplest *Just So Stories* are spiked with jokes for adults who had to read them aloud. Like Mr Sleary in *Hard Times*, Kipling knew that 'people must be amuthed, Thquire, thomehow'. People, in this case, were the paying customer – the adult. In his children's stories, Kipling made the adult laugh, but more often made him cry.

Words and Things in Wallace Stevens

Stevens was reluctant to explain his poetry. In 1928, he wrote to L. W. Payne, Jr: 'It is shocking to have to say this sort of thing. Please destroy these notes. I don't mind your saying what I have said here. But I don't want you to quote me. No more explanations.' And yet, there were more explanations, particularly to Henry Church, Renato Poggioli, his Italian translator, and Hi Simons, to whom he confessed that he was 'a little horrified'.

The reason for this change, despite a persistent theoretical revulsion, was Stevens's concept of the poet's role in society: 'After one has abandoned a belief in God, poetry is that essence which takes its place as life's redemption.' In his essay, "The Noble Rider and the Sound of Words' (1942), Stevens outlined this neo-Arnoldian position by using Freud's *Future of an Illusion* as an example of the tendency against which he was struggling. Freud, he wrote, 'disagrees with the argument than man in general cannot do without the consolation of what he calls the religious illusion and that without it he would not endure the cruelty of reality. His conclusion is that man must venture at last into the hostile world and that this may be called education to reality. There is much more in that essay inimical to poetry and not least the observation in one of the final pages that "The voice of the intellect is a soft one, but it does not rest until it has gained a hearing." This, I fear, is intended to be the voice of the realist.' Here, in brief, is the impulse behind Stevens's work. It examines the relationship of man to an inhuman universe; it portrays the bleakness of that universe, as in the chilling 'No Possum, No Sop,

No Taters' where Stevens sees a winter landscape as a human being in the last stages of deracination. The 'broken stalks / Have arms without hands', 'trunks / Without legs or, for that, without heads', the scene is dumb, and 'Snow sparkles like eyesight falling to earth': the landscape, according to the fantasy, is like a person about to die. At this point, a crow with 'malice in his eye' croaks in macabre emulation of a death rattle, and the human element is dead because the forbidding scene has provided nothing for its sustenance – no meat (possum), no drink (sop), and no vegetables (taters).

But Stevens was not solely interested in seeing 'the object as in itself it really is'. In this Spinozist world where man is not the final cause, poetry, by wedding reason to the imagination (in an orthodox Arnoldian manner), should console us by naturalistic interpretation and moral interpretation. The earth may not be 'the mother that held men as they fell', as 'The Man with the Blue Guitar' tells us, alluding to Arnold's quarrel with Ruskin in 'On Translating Homer'. But it can seem so, as in the exquisite 'In the Carolinas':

> The lilacs wither in the Carolinas.
> Already the butterflies flutter above the cabins.
> Already the new-born children interpret love
> In the voices of mothers.
>
> Timeless mother,
> How is it that your aspic nipples
> For once vent honey?

If, however, poetry is to console us effectively, it must reach a large audience. For Stevens, the poet 'fulfils himself only as he sees his imagination become the light in the minds of others'. In 'Country Words', he lamented his provincial predicament:

> I sang a canto in a canton,
> Cunning-coo, O, Cuckoo cock,
> In a canton of Belshazzar
> To Belshazzar . . .

– to Belshazzar notorious for his inability to interpret or understand. 'Country Words' makes it clear, in its final line, that poetry is impotent unless it has wide circulation: 'It wants words virile with [Belshazzar's] breath.'

This, coupled with Stevens's distress that his poems appeared to give pleasure to no one, accounts for the pages of explanation which fill the letters. Some of these explanations are unsatisfactory: Stevens wrote, 'It is very difficult for me to change things from one category to another', and he made mistakes, or could not remember. But early criticism was sadly in need of them, as the first half of Irvin Ehrenpreis's volume demonstrates.* R. P. Blackmur, after a misty page-long analysis of one word, concludes lamely: 'The whole thing increases in ambiguity the more it is analysed, but if the poem is read over after analysis, it will be seen that *in the poem* the language is perfectly precise. In its own words it is clear, and becomes vague in analysis only because the analysis is not the poem. We use analysis properly in order to discard it and return that much better equipped to the poem.' Would he have written this if he had read Stevens's comment on him? 'As an expositor of ideas Blackmur fails, not for lack of ideas, but for not knowing what his ideas are. Nothing shows this more clearly than ten or twelve pages of his work from which one usually comes away – longing for sex and politics.'

Even now, the letters have not made their fullest impact: criticism has largely relied on the poorly written and generalized essays of *The Necessary Angel* and *Opus Posthumous*, causing an inevitable over-concentration on the general orientation of Stevens's *œuvre* – on the collected poem at the expense of the Collected Poems. There are some successes: Yvor Winters writes definitively about 'Anecdote of the Jar', Michel Benamou about 'The Worms at Heaven's Gate', and David P. Young, in the best of these essays, on Stevens's relationship to Santayana. But on the whole there is little to be said about the ongoing critical debate except that it goes on. And on. Now, as in 1928, Stevens could say: 'I am sure that I never had in mind the many abstractions that

Wallace Stevens: A Critical Anthology edited by Irvin Ehrenpreis, Penguin.

appear in your analysis.' As Professor Ehrenpreis unhappily admits: 'I have planted the greenery of a few poems among the sand dunes of scholarship.'

Wallace Stevens and the Symbolist Imagination represents an extreme example of this trend.* M. Benamou, with his statistical tables showing the distribution of key words, with his extensive reading in the literature of anthropology, is frankly uninterested in Stevens's avowed intentions: 'If there is no meaning in a poem beyond what an author meant it to mean, as soon as its inspiring influence has been exposed all its meaning vanishes.' Long familiarity with the 'Intentional fallacy' urges an easy assent to this proposition. And yet, it is, at second glance, difficult to see how the meaning of a poem *can* vanish. Where, one wonders, does it vanish *to*? But M. Benamou is too infatuated with the structuralist subtext of the collected poem, with the euphemization, the mastery, and the sublimation of death, to stop and ask himself. One is irresistibly reminded of a letter to Hi Simons: 'A long time ago I made up my mind not to explain things, because most people have so little appreciation of poetry that once a poem has been explained it has been destroyed.'

It is surprising that M. Benamou did not seize upon the highly suggestive remark of Hi Simons in 1945 that 'the intellectual lyric framed on the Symbolist principle of implication' is 'his genre'. Simons reduced this technique to what he called the radical or pure *metaphor* – or, as Mallarmé wrote to Cazalis, 'peindre non la chose, mais l'effet qu'elle produit'. Stevens, in his 'Adagia', put it thus: 'Reality is a cliché from which we escape by metaphor. It is only *au pays de la métaphore qu'on est poète.*' The principle is best explained by illustration. 'Earthy Anecdote', which Yvor Winters called 'willful nonsense', describes the way in which a 'firecat' appears to herd and organize some bucks, forcing them to swerve in 'swift, circular lines' to the left and right. Actually, this is a metaphorical description of a prairie or forest fire which causes the bucks to stampede. When everything is burnt to the

---

Wallace Stevens and the Symbolist Imagination by Michel Benamou, Princeton University Press and Oxford University Press.

ground (hence the title), the 'firecat closed his bright eyes / And slept', or, in other words, the fire went out. The reader's pleasure is in the paradox between the actual subject and the way in which Stevens describes it. An agent of panic and chaos is seen as an agent of order. 'Things seen are things as seen', Stevens says in 'Adagia'.

This technique of using metaphor not as embellishment but as the *substance* of poetry, the *raison d'être*, is central to Stevens's work. Take the 'darkened ghosts' who carry lanterns in 'Of Heaven Considered as a Tomb': they are, in fact, clouds and stars. Again, when Stevens writes:

> Violets,
> Great tufts, spring up from buried houses
> Of poor, dishonest people, for whom the steeple,
> Long since, rang out farewell, farewell, farewell

– he is actually describing a graveyard, as we can see from Emily Dickinson's 'Because I could not stop for Death', where Death shows her

> . . . a House that seemed
> A Swelling of the Ground –
> The Roof was scarcely visible –
> The Cornice – in the Ground –

It is, therefore, unfortunate that Randall Jarrell should have written of these lines: 'This is a map with people living on it.' Without an imaginative visual sense, a just appreciation is impossible. Take, for example, this description of a sunset in 'A Weak Mind in the Mountains', Stevens's poem about vertigo:

> There was the butcher's hand.
> He squeezed it and the blood
> Spurted from between the fingers
> And fell to the floor.
> And then the body fell.

274

Initially, the image is simply visual and as bloodily extreme as Eliot's

> When the evening is spread out against the sky
> Like a patient etherised upon a table . . .

— or MacDiarmid's

> His corpse owre a' the city lies
>   In ilka square and ilka street.
> His spilt bluid floods the vera skies
> And nae hoose but is darkened wi't.

Sometimes, of course, there are no visual aids to help the reader with this difficult poetry of implication. 'Asides on the Oboe' is a case in point. Here, Stevens's subject is the poetry of the growth and decline of the Christian myth which, typically, he never mentions by name. On the contrary, his examination of the paradox of a God at once personal and omnipresent gains immensely in freshness from his refusal to use traditional imagery. The whole myth is rethought and recast into a fresh idiom. He thus avoids a language which, as Valéry said, is 'essentiellement provisoire comme est provisoire le billet de banque ou le chèque, dont ce que nous appelons la "valeur" exige l'oubli de leur vraie nature, qui est celle d'un morceau de papier généralement sale'. Stevens begins by rejecting certain clearly obsolete creeds — nature-worship, the pagan gods who have been enfeebled by the classical revival, and the hero worship of great men and their statues — then he considers the 'impossible possible philosophers' man', the Christian God. Instead of listing the traditional monotheistic attributes, Stevens produces metaphorical equivalents. Since He is inconceivable, He is impossibly possible. Since He is invisible, Stevens makes Him completely transparent: He is 'the man of glass'. Because we are made in God's image and we pray/talk to Him, He is 'responsive / As a mirror with a voice'. Because every human being is a unique image, God must 'sum us up' 'in a million diamonds', with the infinite number of reflecting facets which it implies. The second section is a straight-forward quasi-psalm divested of all the usual imagery:

> He is the transparence of the place in which
> He is and in his poems we find peace.

This corresponds to the idea of omnipresence, already touched in by the epithet, 'the human globe'.

> He sets this peddlar's pie and cries in summer,
> The glass man, cold and numbered, dewily cries . . .

That is, He gives us our daily bread; He is numbered because He is Donne's 'three person'd God'; He is cold because He lives in Pascal's 'espaces infinis':

> Clandestine steps upon imagined stairs
> Climb through the night, because his cuckoos call.

That is, creation presupposes a creature. The final section, because Stevens has moved so far from traditional imagery, is more difficult to interpret. There are two verbal clues. One is the word 'jasmine' whose alternative spellings include 'gethsamine' from which it is only a short step to the Garden of Gethsemane. The other occurs in the line: 'We buried the *fallen* without jasmine crowns.' The transition of man from a state of primal innocence to a knowledge of evil is transposed into the metaphor of a war in which people *fell* and lost a Kingdom: 'We buried the fallen *without jasmine crowns*.' In this section, we see Christ the redeemer praying, 'the glass man', 'chanting for those buried in their blood'. He does this in 'the jasmine haunted forests' so that Gethsemane becomes a ghostly type of the Garden of Eden, where jasmine (symbolizing innocence) has been lost. Paradoxi-cally, the appearance of God-as-a-man destroys the mythic potency of the omniscient God, 'the man who has had the time to think enough'. It becomes clear that God was man-created, a fiction of the imagination:

> . . . we knew
> The glass man, without external reference.

Unless criticism takes into account this technique of implication in Stevens's poetry, it will be forced into unproductive procedures, like M. Benamou's belief that this poem alludes to Schopenhauer and alchemy, or like Hi Simons's belief that it alludes to the Second World War. Belshazzar offered a chain of gold to the one who could 'read the writing, and make known to me the interpretation of it'. He would have awarded it to no one in these two volumes.

The Poetry of What There Is: Wallace Stevens

The publication of Wallace Stevens's prose works – *The Necessary Angel, Opus Posthumous*, and *Letters* – has made it impossible for anyone to mistake the general direction of his poetic effort. It is now a commonplace that the central axis of his work is the relationship between defunct religion and its substitute, a 'sufficing belief', a supreme fiction created by poetry which weds imagination to reality. The saving ideal is 'the great poem of the earth', now that 'the great poems of heaven and hell have been written'. Everywhere in his prose, Stevens expounds the broad lines of this ideological skeleton. The central problem is that, while it has obvious general relevance to the poetry, it does not explain the difficult details. Nor was it meant to. It was intended only as a push in the right direction. We must draw the detailed map for ourselves. As Stevens somewhat testily remarked to an inquirer, 'I do not think that a thesis should be based on questions and answers like an interview. On the contrary, I believe in pure explication de texte. This may in fact be my principal form of piety.' It ought to be the principal form of piety in critics of Stevens's poems. Too often it isn't – and Stevens's prose gloss is frequently used as a varnish which covers more than it reveals.

Lucy Beckett's book* is a case in point, excellent on the background and disappointingly weak on the actual poetry. Holding Stevens's prose to the light, she shows clearly the influence of Santayana and I. A. Richards – glowing like a

Wallace Stevens by Lucy Beckett, Cambridge University Press.

watermark on many pages. (And, incidentally, she reveals in Santayana Eliot's unacknowledged source for the objective correlative.) Shrewdly, she discounts the influence of Emerson, whose transcendentalism conflicts with Stevens's commitment to reality. With aptly chosen quotation from Wordsworth and Coleridge, she demonstrates a clear parallel in their ideas of the interrelation of imagination and reality – while, at the same time, rejecting any direct influence. Equally, she makes no mistakes in her assessment of Stevens's overall orientation and its para-Christian end-point – a 'spiritual centre' outside himself. But that is where she stops.

Misguidedly tactful, unwilling to bully the poetry with questions, afraid of 'arid abstractions', Dr Beckett confines herself, on the whole, to long quotation followed by modest disclaimers. The poems remain enigmatic and difficult precisely because she will not step outside Stevens's guiding lines. 'More harm than good is done to the poems by attempts to define what Stevens was so careful to create without definition.' For many of her pages, she is simply running on the spot, leaving things as she finds them. Except, that is, in the case of *Harmonium*, the bulk of whose poems stand to one side of Stevens's later preoccupations. Here she distorts – impatient to reach *Notes Toward a Supreme Fiction*, where Stevens's prose is more helpful.

Take 'Le Monocle de Mon Oncle', for example. Dr Beckett's remarks are so far from an 'explication de texte' that it is frankly difficult to see what she means. It is 'about the waste land, and about the search of a man confronting it for something that will reconcile him to it'. Finally, it appears to be about something 'which in another age . . . would have been called "the love of God" '. On the contrary, Stevens's 'uncle' belongs with those other ageing characters – Joyce's Gabriel Conroy, Mann's Aschenbach, Svevo's Emilio – whose hearts are 'fastened to a dying animal'. Middle-aged aliens in a young world, they are gathered under a banner, designed by Giacomo Joyce, which reads, 'Love me, love my umbrella'. For them, romantic emotion is without the self-justifying, graceful simplicity which the young bring to passion. It is passionately farcical and would avoid mirrors.

'I had in mind a man fairly well along in life', forty-eight-year-old Stevens explained, 'looking back and talking in a more or less personal way about life.' The poem contains his thoughts about the 'origin and course of love' – touching on the inevitable loss of physical beauty and the survival of something which hardly answers to traditional descriptions of love. This emotional residue is made up of libido, romantic feeling and memory. As Stevens examines it, he moves from disillusion to a cagey affirmation.

The radical antithesis between the young and the old (an opposition finally modified) is, for most of the poem, its clearest element. At his most bitter, Stevens (for the uncle is the thinnest of fictions) is prepared to resign to the young: love 'is a theme for Hyacinth alone' – Hyacinth who, killed in his prime, never grew old. Watching Venus, the brightest star, he abdicates:

> In the high west there burns a furious star.
> It is for fiery boys that star was set
> And for sweet-smelling virgins close to them.

Being one who wishes he might be 'a thinking stone', one for whom the 'verve of earth' means little or nothing, he adds:

> For me, the firefly's quick, electric stroke
> Ticks tediously the time of one more day.

What Hardy called 'the recuperative power which pervaded organic nature' is inoperative in him: unlike the red bird, pressing on hopefully to join its joyous choir, he is without a future – 'a man of fortune greeting heirs', for whom the 'choirs of welcome' choir farewell.

More problematic is the identity of the woman addressed in the opening lines, which burlesque the extravagant hyperbole of traditional poetry. Raleigh, for instance, writes:

> She is neither white, nor brown,
> But as the heaven fair;
> There is none hath a form so divine
> In the earth, or the air.

Stevens's mocking version of such claims is:

> Mother of heaven, regina of the clouds,
> O sceptre of the sun, crown of the moon.

Given this transparent irony ('And so I mocked her in magnificent measure'), it is an absurd blunder to identify this woman, as Dr Beckett does, with the One of Fictive Music, 'the poetic concept'. The straightforward opening lines of that poem ('Sister and mother and diviner love') cannot be promiscuously bracketed with Stevens's bitter mockery – a mockery which is continued in his declaration of love: 'There is not nothing, no, no, never nothing.' In other words, there is 'something', an emotional residue, expressed here via a diffident cluster of negatives; so little does it resemble the spontaneous overflow of powerful feeling.

In the absence of biographical information, one could conclude (not that it matters) that Stevens is addressing his wife. More importantly, however, he plays with the idea of divinity – particularly the Goddess of Love, Venus Anadyomene:

> The sea of spuming thought foists up again
> The radiant bubble that she was.

But it is clear from the past tense that she is no longer beautiful. Nor is she immortal: Stevens dismisses her pretensions to kinship with the stars as make-believe, story-telling, nothing to set against his own certain knowledge of imminent death:

> No spring can follow past meridian.
> Yet you persist in anecdotal bliss
> To make believe a starry *connaissance*.

The woman, then, is a Venus stripped of beauty and immortality – in a word, of divinity.

Add to this Stevens's other negatives, and his pessimism seems complete – the knowledge of physical ugliness ('warty squashes', 'bald amorists'); the decay of beauty ('This luscious and impeccable fruit of life / Falls, it appears, of its own weight to earth'); the futility of cosmetics ('not one curl in nature has survived'). And yet the residue remains and the woman keeps some of her disturbing physical presence. She is still able to recreate the beauty of Botticelli's sea-borne paragon:

> Why, without pity on these studious ghosts,
> Do you come *dripping* in your hair from sleep?

(My italics.) In person and in memory, she retains the power to move. 'There is not nothing.'

This residue requires its own special poetry:

> In verses wild with motion, full of din,
> Loudened by cries, by clashes, quick and sure
> As the deadly thought of men accomplishing
> Their curious fates in war, come, celebrate
> The faith of forty, ward of Cupido.

One word, *clashes*, refers the reader back to an earlier puzzling line:

> There is not nothing, no, no, never nothing,
> Like the *clashed* edges of two words that kill.

The explanation is two-fold: first, the ungainliness of love at forty requires a poetry of dissonance, not euphony. (And such language has its own appeal, as Stevens explained: 'In addition to the excitement of suave sounds, there is an excitement, an insistent provocation in the strange cacophony of words.') Secondly, the language of love at forty has edge, an extra seriousness – it can 'kill', it is like the noise of battle in which some men die – because, to translate the hyperboles, in middle age death is closer, and language should express this too.

Having rejected both the eternal in his loved one ('your first imagery / Found inklings of your bond to all that dust'), and the eternal arriving from outside ('a damsel heightened by eternal bloom'), Stevens searches for an appropriate image for what remains – the earthy facts. Again he rejects the dignifying metaphors of religion or glamorizing mythology ('Memorabilia of the mystic spouts'), and chooses a 'yeoman's' image. A gigantic tree represents Love. On its summit all birds perch – but only for a time. Nevertheless, the summit, love's fullest experience, remains – for others to achieve, while the rest remember. It is the Stevensian equivalent of Joyce's Howth Head, to which Molly and Bloom direct their most romantic thoughts.

The pigeon which closes the poem sums up Stevens's attitude to middle-aged love. Such love is the same thing as love in youth, but seen from a different angle. The pigeon in flight is blue, the tired pigeon on the ground is white. It is, just the same, the identical bird. The title repeats this idea wittily – *monocle* and *mon oncle* are different and 'identical'. The penultimate stanza explains the way in which youthful romantic feeling and sexual passion survive in the old. Romance is 'that first, foremost law', but the sexual urge also continues, slightly grotesque in its survival. The moonlit night, complete with lilies and a 'pool of pink', is disturbed by the incongruous boom of a frog – 'from his very belly odious chords'. Love me, love my belly.

No detail of this kind emerges in Dr Beckett's account because she mistrusts 'the clumsy gloves of paraphrase' – criticism's central tool, however crude. Adalaide Kirby Morris is more confident.* Using the Concordance with rare intelligence, she scours Stevens's poetry for his assault on rigidified theology and its creative concomitant, a systematic transvaluation of its forms and symbols. Thus, the sacraments of marriage and communion image the merging of imagination and reality. Heaven, hell, and

---

Wallace Stevens: Imagination and Faith by Adalaide Kirby Morris, Princeton University Press (AUPG).

paradise become interior psychological landscapes – the first two representing respectively imbalances of imagination and reality, while the third stands for their integration. Satan is now the man who denies divinity to the world, Eve the person who commits the sin of pathetic fallacy, Adam he who trusts to reason. The Fall becomes a self-awareness separating man from the world, to be countered by Grace which is the moment of fortuitous delight supervening from nature. Christ is the imagination incarnate in the poet-hero – and so on. A bare summary cannot convey the critical scrupulosity with which Dr Morris tests these ideas against the poetry itself. For, unlike Dr Beckett, she is not afraid to volunteer detailed explanations. And if she is sometimes wrong, she is never silly or obscure. These things make *Imagination and Faith* a book to be sought out.

Even when Stevens's prose is most relevant, with *Notes Toward a Supreme Fiction*, Dr Beckett is inclined to write: 'The figure celebrated in these lines [Section IX of 'It Must be Abstract'] like the supreme fiction itself, cannot be named.' Of this poem, Dr Morris confines herself to a general reference to the Nativity. Actually, a closer analysis supports her theory of transvaluation. In the Museo del Correr in Venice, there is a Pietà, by Cosmé Tura. It depicts a haggard and (but for a loin-cloth) naked Christ on the lap of a young Madonna. The artist's implicit irony is in the contrast between the young girl and the crucified Christ. It is not simply a deposition; we are being asked to remember the Infant Christ on his mother's lap, and to compare the tenderness. In Section IX, Stevens asks of his reader something similar.

We contemplate 'he that reposes / On a breast forever precious for that touch', whom Stevens, as a non-believer, describes as 'This foundling of the infected past'. Since he is 'swaddled', we have at first no difficulty in recognizing who it is that Stevens has in mind. But this particular infant is 'swaddled *in reverie*'. He is, therefore, Christ and not-Christ, just as Cosmé Tura's Pietà is also a Nativity. He is Stevens's brain-child, whose origin is not apotheosis, but reason:

> But apotheosis is not
> The origin of the major man. He comes,
>
> Compact in invincible foils, from reason,
> Lighted at midnight by the studious eye . . .

Not, we notice, lighted by the star of Bethlehem. The Infant whom Stevens invokes is not one who will be crucified at Easter:

> For whom the good of April falls tenderly,
> Falls down, the cock-birds calling at the time.

Not, we again notice, the cocks who crowed for Christ's betrayal. Stevens sings the glory of the abstract Infant, who needs no 'romantic intoning', no 'declaimed clairvoyance' – only '*accurate* songs'. And yet, Stevens is compelled to admit, there *is* something of apotheosis, something of Christ, in the abstract ideal of the Child:

> He is and may be but oh! he is, he is,
> This foundling of the infected past, so bright,
> So moving in the manner of his hand.

This last line's biblical cadence, its language of the previously abjured romantic 'intoning', identifies Stevens's brain-child, the abstract Infant, with the Infant Christ. But having praised, he ends with a warning against the literal application of the traditional echoes he has used:

> Yet look not at his colored eyes. Give him
> No names. Dismiss him from your images.

In other words, grasp the ideal essence of the Infant, traditionally embodied in Christ, but reject any and all particular images, because the supreme fiction must be abstract. In these terms, Christ is the object of

> The hum of thoughts *evaded* in the mind,
> Hidden from other thoughts . . .

Hidden, that is, from thoughts of suffering and betrayal. This Child has no particular embodiment; he is a feeling at the heart:

> The hot of him is purest in the heart.

And, one might add, this Child therefore becomes part of the 'great poem of the earth'.

Wallace Stevens: A Centenary Essay

'The trouble with this figure', Wallace Stevens humorously remarked of Albert Schweitzer, 'is that one does not associate it with anything except an ant-proof organ on the equator and a pair of mustaches like African ferns.' For most of his life, Stevens himself was, of course, clean-shaven, as you might expect from a man who described himself thus: 'Doing a selbsportrat in the space of an inch or two requires that I should say very briefly that I was born in Pennsylvania in 1879, studied at Harvard, am a lawyer, practiced in New York until 1916 and then came to Hartford, where I am in the insurance business.' In fact, Stevens became vice-president of the Hartford Accident and Indemnity Co. and, if he was always friendly with other poets like William Carlos Williams, he generally chose to present himself as the typical business man. It was an unworried idiom that suited Stevens's modesty. 'Don't worry about my gray hair,' he joshes. 'Whenever I ring for a stenographer she comes in with a pistol strapped around her belt.'

All the same, however much he pretended to belong, he was, like Schweitzer, an incongruous figure – the man with the blue guitar and the indestructible *Harmonium* in Hartford, the town he named 'Oxidia, banal suburb, / One-half of all its installments paid'. Under the letter 'C' in the index to his *Letters*, we find (appropriately enough for the author of 'The Comedian as the Letter C') this whimsical juxtaposition: 'Confucius, 171, 508' and 'Congress of Industrial Organizations, 351'. In their mild way, the two entries epitomize Stevens rather better than Mary

McCarthy's hectic description of him as 'John D. Rockefeller drenched in attar of roses'. Judging by his correspondence, Stevens felt little conflict or contradiction between his interests in poetry and business, though he guessed that outsiders saw him differently: 'How difficult it seems for people to take poets and poetry naturally,' he groaned. 'One is either tripe or the Aga Khan of letters . . .'

An assiduous observer of social forms, as that bogus, calculatedly red-blooded remark about the stenographer shows, Stevens could be very impatient with other poets who transgressed social or political proprieties. Asked to speak Dylan Thomas's funeral oration, he refused, explaining confidentially to a friend, 'He was an utterly improvident person. He spent what little money he made without regard to his responsibilities. He remarked that he had done what he wanted to do in this country, that is to say, that he had met so and so and Charlie Chaplin, and had insulted a rich industrialist.' As a rich business man himself, Stevens could scarcely be expected to countenance Thomas's boorishness. He admitted no special licence. Pound, too, brought out the morally fastidious in him: 'While he may have many excuses, I must say that I don't consider the fact that he is a man of genius as an excuse. Surely, such men are subject to the common disciplines.' Only a change in the *Zeitgeist* could trap Stevens into an indiscretion remotely comparable to that of Pound – as when he passes through his birthplace, Reading, and records his disappointment in a town 'about as agreeable as a hardware store on a misty day'. It was, he writes to his wife, 'like returning from the wars and finding one's best beloved remarried to a coon'.

Despite this solecism, and a few others like it, Stevens emerges from his letters as an attractive, drily ironic customer with a firm grasp on reality. The commercial and critical failure of his first book, *Harmonium*, produces this wry sally: 'My royalties for the first half of 1924 amounted to $6.70. I shall have to charter a boat and take my friends around the world.' Though Stevens was undoubtedly hurt by the reception of *Harmonium*, he kept it to himself, virtually ceased writing for five or six years and turned instead to the insurance business and what he later described as the salvation of work: 'Our own days are the days of wind and rain, like today,' he wrote to a friend in France, towards the end of his life. 'Yet it is precisely on such days that we give thanks for the office. Sometimes one realizes what an exceeding help work is in anyone's life. What a profound grace it is to have a destiny no matter what it is, even the destiny of the postman going the rounds and of the bus driver driving the bus. Well, one prizes this destiny most particularly when the wind is blowing from the north-north-east . . .' As it was in the years of neglect immediately following *Harmonium*, though this encomium was written in 1954 when Stevens was at last becoming recognized. By then, of course, he had become aware that poetry, too, had its business side, noting with approval of Carl Sandburg that 'they are going to give him a gold medal shortly in New York and, with a shrewd eye to business, that becomes any poet, he has just issued the first volume of an autobiography which it appears can be added to indefinitely'.

Shy, intensely private, a frigid performer at his rare readings, Stevens was less of a hustler and, when success came, he professed to find publicity 'a thing that degrades one'. Only his letters record a patient willingness to promote his art. He is particularly keen to deny any influences, in a way that might make one suspicious, were it not that he is a conspicuously original, even, some might say, a dangerously private poet.

Critically, too, he was quite independent. To José Rodriguez Féo in 1947, he wrote: 'For my own part I like to live in a classic atmosphere, full of my own gods and to be true to them until I have some better authority than a merely contrary opinion for not being true to them. We have all to learn to hold fast.' In 1908, this meant something different from what it meant later. Early in his career, Stevens visibly set out to be an interesting minor poet: 'don't you agree with me', he wrote to his fiancée, 'that if we could get the Michael Angeloes out of our heads – Shakespeare, Titian, Goethe – all the phenomenal men, we should find a multitude of lesser things (lesser but a *multitude*) to occupy us? It would be like withdrawing the sun and bringing out innumerable stars.' That is recognizably the note of self-interest and the paragraph ends just as it should from the poet who modestly entitled his first volume *Harmonium*: 'Let us leave the great things to the professors – substitute for majestic organs, sylvan reeds . . .' In 1908, Stevens had no idea that his tiny harmonium would have ambitions to be a majestic organ, even in the great blank-verse poems of his first book, as well as later – where the grand style exacts its characteristic penalties, until we empathize with Browning's organist struggling with obscure Master Hugues of Saxe-Gotha:

> *Est fuga, volvitur rota.*
> On we drift: where looms the dim port?
> One, Two, Three, Four, Five, contribute their quota;
> Something is gained, if one caught but the import –
> Show it to us, Hugues of Saxe-Gotha!

The pride in being his own man, critically speaking, persists in Stevens, leading him, for instance, to prefer the work of Jean Cavaillès to that of Vuillard – a bizarre judgement that can probably be explained in terms of Stevens's own eclipse by Eliot and Pound. Certainly, there is some displaced bitterness in his comment that Vuillard 'is what he is, not because he is good, but because he has French taste and knew lots of the right people'. By the time Stevens was beginning to feel and relish his own stature, however, we notice his dismissal of Arp as 'too much a man of taste to be a leader like Picasso'. The minor, simply because it was minor, was no longer guaranteed a sympathetic response. Stevens's sympathy is modified by judiciousness: Arp's 'limitation shows itself in the mere dimensions of his work. The long and short of it is that the human spirit need not fear him. Yet so much having been said by way of sizing him up, how exquisite his things can be. How much I should like to have one of the smoother pebbles.' There is a similar residual affection, long after Stevens had deliberately expanded the dimensions of his art, for the short early poems of *Harmonium*.

Taken together, these judgements of Vuillard and Arp illustrate the strength and weakness of the position in which Stevens found himself. He fished by obstinate isles, a loner by temperament reinforced by neglect. The assessment of Arp as flawless but 'fastidious not forceful' is, accordingly, independent and just. But the dismissal of Vuillard is merely perverse. The reward of standing alone may be originality, but the price is sometimes eccentricity. If the eccentricity was unconsidered or confined to critical asides in the correspondence, Stevens would be no different from many other writers. What are we to make, though, of his explanation of the Arabian in *Notes Toward a Supreme Fiction*?

> We say: At night an Arabian in my room,
> With his damned hoobla-hoobla-hoobla-how,
> Inscribes a primitive astronomy
>
> Across the unscrawled fores the future casts
> And throws his stars around the floor . . .

Here, the poetry is infected and no amount of critical piety could elicit a cry of *Eureka*. 'The fact that the Arabian is the moon is something that the reader could not possibly know,' Stevens admits. 'However, I did not think it was necessary for him to know. Even without knowing – ' And so the explanation limply breaks off, showing us a poet entirely out of touch with the world of mere readers, a man who had been deprived of the necessary audience he woos elsewhere with straightforward, if momentary, lust – in, for example, his description of a bear as 'the ponderous cinnamon', or when he writes in 'An Ordinary Evening in New Haven' of 'the infant A standing on infant legs, / Not twisted, stooping, polymathic Z'. It is impossible to forget, too, the immediately seductive lines in which Stevens evokes 'the ever-hooded, tragic-gestured sea' or catches 'A light on the candle tearing against the wick'.

Like Whitman, he was a self-made poet, almost inevitably uneven, and his verdict on his predecessor has a peculiar aptness to himself: 'It is useless to treat everything in Whitman as of equal merit. A great deal of it exhibits little or none of his specific gifts.

He seems often to have driven himself to write like himself.' Any reader familiar with the range of Stevens's *œuvre* (hardly the easy task it may appear) will acknowledge the involuntary element of self-description in this verdict. Stevens had very few themes – the relationship between reality and imagination, the need for poetry to replace religion as a source of belief –and if he felt he had never quite exhausted them, he can exhaust his readers. Read in bulk, he can be profoundly monotonous. In 1951, he wrote to Bernard Heringman: 'As both you and Mr Wagner must realize, I have no wish to arrive at a conclusion. Sometimes I believe most in the imagination for a long time and then, without reasoning about it, turn to reality and believe in that and that alone.'

The result, in his middle period, was that Stevens wrote 'like himself', mechanically tinkering with the balance of his two abstractions. His great periods are his first and his last, the former full of life, the latter touched by the imminence of Stevens's own death – and in both he felt reasonably sure of an intelligent audience. In between, the poetry, though it is never without redeeming flashes, often declines into a stale commentary on the two spectral abstractions as they square up to shadow-box – here gaining a round, there losing a round, but always entirely devoid of the necessary stuffing to knock out of each other.

Take, for example, Section XXIII of 'The Man with the Blue Guitar'. It begins with an undertaker, smelling of drink and singing as he digs a grave. Stevens postulates an harmonious duet between him and a voice in the clouds, whereas, in a religious poem, one might have expected an argument – the undertaker expounding earth's finality, the ethereal voice advancing the idea of an after-life. Instead,

> the voice
> In the clouds serene and final, next
>
> The grunted breath serene and final,
> The imagined and the real, thought
>
> And the truth, Dichtung und Wahrheit, all
> Confusion solved . . .

In this finale, the abstractions arrive with bonging predictability, driving out the undertaker's whisky breath and his effortful grunts. These touches of reality are replaced by Reality and the potentially Shakespearian gravedigger is revealed as the merest pretext. Like the shadowy Mrs Rance in *The Golden Bowl*, who enters Adam Verver's billiards room solely and speechlessly to threaten his widowhood and set the plot in motion before disappearing forever, the undertaker is invested with no intrinsic interest. Both are bits of machinery, ticking audibly during their brief appearances as authorial helpmates.

Berryman's 'So Long? Stevens' puts the case bluntly against this kind of poetry:

> That metaphysics
> he hefted up until we could not breathe
> the physics.

Of course, Stevens was aware of this weakness ('my real danger is not didacticism, but abstraction') and yet increasingly attracted by its rhetorical possibilities. Tempted by metaphysical pathos, the victim of his own grand manner, he substituted a choir of sounding phrases for the simply sensuous. In his study of evil in a secular world, 'Esthétique du Mal', one turns with relief from the rag-bag of high-sounding pensées towards the (dangerously intermittent) fictional intermediary and the details of his life. The man 'at Naples writing letters home' who ruminates for Stevens (when he can get a thought in edgeways) has at least some concrete existence – though not enough to hold this long poem together in the way that Stevens intends. We carry away from the poem not only the picture of the moon as 'round effendi' but also the memorable detail of the contrast between the protagonist's nurse and his sartorially resplendent but socially distant mother:

> the softest
> Woman with a vague moustache and not the mauve
> *Maman.*

That the nurse should prove to be 'reality, / The gross, the fecund' cannot injure the genuine reality of her moustache.

The last section of 'Esthétique du Mal' is, for those rare readers who actually reach it, a grand celebration of the physical world, the paradise we haven't yet patented:

> And out of what one sees and hears and out
> Of what one feels, who could have thought to make
> So many selves, so many sensuous worlds,
> As if the air, the mid-day air, was swarming
> With the metaphysical changes that occur,
> Merely in living as and where we live.

This is so life-enhancing in argument that we are prone to take it at Stevens's own valuation, as 'the thesis scrivened in delight, / The reverberating psalm, the right chorale'. Yet it scarcely stands against the end of 'Sunday Morning', the early poem it rewrites, where Stevens actually evokes the delights to which 'Esthétique du Mal' merely refers us:

> Deer walk upon our mountains, and the quail
> Whistle about us their spontaneous cries;
> Sweet berries ripen in the wilderness;
> And in the isolation of the sky,
> At evening, casual flocks of pigeons make
> Ambiguous undulations as they sink,
> Downward to darkness, on extended wings.

The pigeons are at once real and tinged with old imaginative associations. Stephen Dedalus experiences a ribald equivalent when he notices the Pigeon House on Sandymount Strand and parenthetically repeats a joke to himself:

> *– Qui vous a mis dans cette fichue position?*
> *– C'est le pigeon, Joseph.*

Stevens, however, is totally serious as he transfers a quasi-religious significance to his wholly secular birds. A single phrase, 'ambiguous undulations', endows them with mystery and permits us to hear the echo of an ancient religious chord. It is the finest possible suggestion – unlike the nudging vocabulary of 'psalm' and 'chorale' in 'Esthétique du Mal', or the enriched diction of ugly superlatives like 'immensest', 'tenderest', 'grossest' and 'savagest' on which Stevens came to rely for facile suggestiveness in his later poetry.

In *Harmonium*, then, the crucial polarity between reality and imagination is already present, as the casual flocks of pigeons demonstrate. It is, though, less relentlessly abstract and hardly ever appears *in propria impersona*. Rather, Reality is a snowman, or a blackbird that defies us in thirteen different ways to say it is other than a blackbird in its transactions with us – even though it constantly flirts with meaning and coquettes with relationship. Finally, external reality retains its enigmatic, alien status. 'To the Roaring Wind', the last poem in *Harmonium*, makes the point less bafflingly:

> What syllable are you seeking,
> Vocalissimus,
> In the distances of sleep?
> Speak it.

Other *Harmonium* poems concentrate on the way imagination transforms a reality that has lost, temporarily, its recalcitrance. It is of these that Stevens is speaking when he writes to Ronald Lane Latimer in 1935 that 'when HARMONIUM was in the making there was a time when I liked the idea of images and images alone, or images and the music of verse together. I then believed in *pure poetry*, as it was called.' In his essay, 'The Irrational Element in Poetry' (tentatively dated 1937 by Samuel French Morse), Stevens defined *pure poetry* as 'poetry in which not the true subject but the poetry of the subject is paramount'. Obviously, this is a neo-symbolist position of the kind outlined by Mallarmé, whose famous dictum ('paint not the thing but the effect it produces') entails poetic cryptography: 'to name an object is to banish the major part of the enjoyment derived from a poem, since this enjoyment consists in a process of gradual revelation'. Clearly, there is an element of riddling in this type of verse, something to be solved. In the case of Stevens, not much solving took place in 1924 when *Harmonium* appeared and not much has taken place since – a critical failure best summed up by Chesterton's 'The Point of a Pin', in which Father Brown sagely remarks, 'It isn't that they can't see the solution. It's that they can't see the problem.'

It is hardly surprising that Stevens began to underrate the importance of being fully understood. In 'The Irrational Element in Poetry', he is frankly contemptuous of a M. Delahaye who had quoted 'Ornières' from *Les Illuminations* and indicated that the true subject was, in fact, an American circus which visited Charleville when Rimbaud was a boy. True, the explanation is ridiculously overdocumented, particularly since Rimbaud clearly has a *fair* in mind, but it is not entirely despicable as an interpretative attempt.

One gets the feeling that Stevens, deprived of the intelligent audience he might have expected, decided that the true subjects of his poems were his own business. As no one appeared with the correct solutions, Stevens's metaphors became more and more arbitrary and less and less frequent. Consider, for instance, Section VI of 'Esthétique du Mal' where the sun is 'in clownish yellow, but not a clown' and is fed upon by a 'big bird'. The latter, primarily, is the moon, which borrows the light of the sun:

> The big bird's bony appetite
> Is as insatiable as the sun's. The bird
> Rose from an imperfection of its own
> To feed on the yellow bloom of the yellow fruit
> Dropped down from turquoise leaves. In the landscape of
> The sun, its grossest appetite becomes less gross . . .

We don't, in other words, see the moon when the sun is out. The maundering lines are a prosy failure, of course, but it is the arbitrariness of Stevens's metaphorical starting point that is most depressing – even though one can find a parallel (equally arbitrary) in 'God is Good. It is a Beautiful Night': 'Look round, brown moon, brown bird, as you rise to fly.' This, like the Arabian as moon, shows something has gone sadly amiss in Stevens's relationship with his readers.

Discussing the notices of *Notes Toward a Supreme Fiction*, he complained that 'people never read poetry well until they have accepted it; they read it timidly or they are on edge about it, afraid that something is going to go wrong with the sentence after next'. But that is exactly what does happen in 'Continual Conversation with a Silent Man'. The silent man, 'a turquoise monster', is not only the sky but the total atmosphere outside us. So much is clear. More, if we live and die between 'the old brown hen and the old blue sky', a process of elimination means that the hen must be the earth on which we live. The central section of the poem, however, is an enormous, opaque sentence that begins with an unresolved comparison and lacks any main verb. Not even the realization that death is 'the broken cartwheel on the hill' can help us to construe the central sentence, which I quote entire:

> As if, in the presence of the sea,
> We dried our nets and mended sail
> And talked of never-ending things,
>
> Of the never-ending storm of will,
> One will and many wills, and the wind,
> Of many meanings in the leaves,
>
> Brought down to one below the eaves,
> Link, of that tempest, to the farm,
> The chain of the turquoise hen and sky
> And the wheel that broke as the cart went by.

Suddenly, fatally, the syntax simply melts, as though Claes Oldenberg had tampered with one of the Hartford Accident and Indemnity Co.'s typewriters.

It may be that Stevens intended the syntactic breakdown to mirror life's sudden cessation *in medias res* as the wheel breaks, but one remains sceptical in spite of the directive from Head Office not to fret about the sentence after next. The earth as 'old brown hen' does at least seem a less arbitrary image than some others in Stevens's middle period – a just metaphor that spans the requisite, surprising gap between tenor and vehicle. The initial difficulty is, of course, the symbolist mode in which the tenor is left unstated. We have to infer that the earth is the true subject, the thing signified. The context is, however, so arranged by Stevens that the necessary inference is inevitable – as it is in the *Harmonium* poems which adopt this poetic strategy.

'Earthy Anecdote', for instance, suppresses its true subject, a fire, and substitutes the imaginative replacement of a 'firecat'. Similarly, the infanta of 'Infanta Marina' is actually the sea. Her plumes in this exquisite fantasy are the sails of ships and she is the untroubled relation of the 'tragic-gestured sea' in 'The Idea of Order at Key West':

> She made of the motions of her wrist
> The grandiose gestures
> Of her thought.

Of course, this poetry is not easy, even after the reader has realized that there are riddling problems to be solved. 'The Paltry Nude Starts On a Spring Voyage', a poem about innocence eventually confronting the final experience of age, has misled many commentators. The nude is, one guesses, a sailing boat – archaic and beautiful in an age of steam and propelled instead by the wind 'Blowing upon her hands / And watery back'. Later, the ship will be weather-beaten, a 'goldener nude', and will eventually sink.

By comparison, 'The Doctor of Geneva' is a much easier poem, taking as its subject the hubris of rationalism in the face of nature's chaos. The Doctor confronts the sea:

> He did not quail. A man so used to plumb
> The multifarious heavens felt no awe
> Before these visible, voluble delugings . . .

The sea responds by setting

> his simmering mind
> Spinning and hissing with oracular
> Notations of the wild, the ruinous waste,
>
> Until the steeples of his city clanked and sprang
> In an unburgherly apocalypse.
> The doctor used his handkerchief and sighed.

That is to say, the rationalist receives a comic come-uppance – the indignity of a racking sneeze. 'The Plot Against the Giant' is another brilliantly simple structure, in which the senses boast about their capacity to escape death, the 'yokel' with his 'hacker'. Stevens only employs three of the senses – smell, sight and hearing – but delicately suggests the absurd confidence of youth in its own invulnerability.

In his last period, Stevens returned to this poetry of implication but, a sadder and a wiser man, accommodated himself to the audience that was at last beginning to gather round him, repaying politeness with politeness. 'The World as Meditation', for instance, treats the relationship between the sun and the earth in terms of Ulysses and Penelope. It is a beautiful and intelligible poem that requires little exegesis. The same is true of 'The Woman in Sunshine', 'The Planet on the Table', 'Vacancy in the Park', 'World Without Peculiarity', 'The Hermitage at the Centre' and 'The Beginning'. A hundred years after Stevens's birth, these poems and many others make an imperious claim on our attention as perfect artifacts. Though he never entirely forsook the symbolist method, his late poetry values lucidity and makes greater use of the simile with its straightforwardly powerful equation of tenor and vehicle. Moreover, in his very last letters, he snorted impatiently and significantly over Valéry's

Eupalinos: 'Taken by itself, while it has many values, as all nice books by civilized thinkers have, yet it seems much less because of the difficulty Valéry shared with other poets of not being explicit as to his real conception, which he likes to suggest or imply, not state.' In 1952, two years previously, he was making the same point against an exclusive and rigid symbolist aesthetic. Of Bryher, he noted that 'she has the typical indirectness of an imaginative poet' but continued in a critical spirit: 'For instance, her big event is the battle of Hastings. But she does not face it directly. It happened over the hill or beyond the woods . . . She is sentimental: not crudely so, but delicately, obscurely: yet all the same sentimental . . . One is not looking at real things but reflections of real things.' Stevens, on the other hand, by now at ease with his audience at last, was free to risk breathtaking directness:

And the wind sways like a great thing tottering . . .

Geoffrey Hill and Ted Hughes

You may recall Arnold's melancholy, long, withdrawing roar as he retreated into classicism, took down the ancients and drew the curtains of his study against the intractable subject matter of his time. The age, he complained to Clough in 1849, was 'not unprofound, not ungrand, not unmoving – but *unpoetical*'. In some sense, the null and worthy *Merope*, more thesis than poetic drama, was already on the index cards. Clough's real reply came in 1858 with *Amours de Voyage*. He solved Arnold's problem by accepting it. While Arnold toiled studiously up Mount Parnassus, short of oxygen, somewhere beyond the vegetation line, where imagery peters out and only great undressed boulders of philosophy survive, Clough pottered around in the flatlands, far from these touchstones, twisting the hexameter into comic, unpoetical shapes: 'Am I prepared to lay down my life for the British female?' his anti-hero ponders. The effect is much the same as a Betjeman iambic pentameter apostrophizing Virol or Sanatogen. *Amours de Voyage* is a great poem of its kind, with its own ironical pity and terror, yet it is Arnold who is read, even if *Merope* is never taken up twice. Why?

The reputation of Geoffrey Hill is relevant here. In some ways, he has inherited not Arnold's mantle but his hair-shirt. His poetry is full of high seriousness. You can't miss the noble application of scruples to life. The purged cadences, the bitter medicine of his syntax appeal to the puritan in us: even when the poetry is difficult, obscure and painful to read, we know it is doing us good. It makes no concessions to our intellectual and moral self-esteem. It administers a wonderful snub. Moreover, history plays much the same role in Hill's poetry as the classics do in Arnold's, acting, in a recherché way, as a transparency through which the glare of immediate experience is filtered. Finally, both are academic poets, though Arnold has everlasting oases of greatness. And Hill?

Mercian Hymns, Hill's last collection, showed just how good this kind of poetry can be. Using the historical, underdocumented figure of King Offa, Hill was enabled to write about his unpoetical childhood self: 'Then, leaving Ceolred, he journeyed for hours, calm and alone, in his private derelict sandlorry named *Albion*.' In context, I find this nearly as moving as the end of Rimbaud's 'Le Bateau Ivre':

> Si je désire une eau d'Europe, c'est la flache
> Noire et froide où vers le crépuscule embaumé
> Un enfant accroupi plein de tristesses, lâche
> Un bateau frêle comme un papillon de mai.

Some of the hymns are marvellously funny, too. The epic mode appropriate to Offa nicely judges and places the seriousness of the only child. A diary full of grudges is comically transposed into this heroic paragraph: 'It was there that he drew upon grievances from the people; attended to signatures and retributions; forgave the death-howls of his rival. And there he exchanged gifts with the Muse of History.' The childish mania for signing one's name becomes 'the seals of gold and base metal into which he had sunk his name'. And this section ends with homework, with the pathos and broad comedy of 'he wept, attempting to master *ancilla* and *servus*'. Why, it might almost be Clough.

But if we take that phrase 'forgave the death-howls of his rival', we can see why it isn't. The historical structure of the sequence means that we are forced to take it seriously, as well as on the level of a child's brutal, self-aggrandizingly magnanimous fantasy. The same thing is true of the 'derelict sandlorry named *Albion*': the name chides us pedantically until we remember that Offa constructed Offa's Dyke, that he was 'overlord of the M5'.

As the hymns progress, the structure becomes the subject and the hymns collapse under its weight: Hill's scrupulosity, his high seriousness gradually drive out the low, personal material.

Though the strict forms might make it seem a new departure after the free verse of *Mercian Hymns*, *Tenebrae** continues the trend. Broadly speaking, the poems are about Hill's passionate yet agnostic relationship to Christ. You might expect, therefore, a personal poetry of raw directness. Hill, however, has chosen to filter his dilemma through imitations of Robert Southwell's frigid religious poetry, anonymous Spanish ballads and Lope de Vega. We are back to Arnold and *Merope*. And the use of Spanish verse also marks a return to 'The Songbook of Sebastian Arrurruz' in *King Log*, described by Hill as 'the work of an apocryphal Spanish poet'. Hill also added, somewhat otiosely in my view, the warning that 'the Arrurruz poems contain no allusion to any actual person, living or dead'. Except for odd moments, no one reading the Songbook would dispute that for a minute. The woman lamented there is more than covered by Eliot's comment on Arnold's Marguerite: 'a shadowy figure, neither very passionately desired nor very closely observed, a mere pretext for lamentation.'

In 'The Pentecost Castle', Christ is equally shady, largely because Hill's method is to hitch a lift from anonymous Spanish profane poetry and one Lope de Vega lyric which he marginally improves. Given his agnosticism, the shadiness may be intentional. However, the epigraph from Yeats promises something more passionate: 'it is terrible to desire and not possess, and terrible to possess and not desire.' Promises, premises. Not even the loaded epithet, 'your lord', can transform 'Olmedo's flower' into Christ. The profane remains profane in its anonymous way.

'Lachrimae' ends with another imitation of Lope de Vega, this time a direct address to God. Even with my pathetic Spanish, it is clear that Hill hasn't equalled his original. This is J. M. Cohen's translation of the final lines: 'How many times did the angel say to me: "Now, soul, look out of your window, and you will see

---

*Tenebrae by Geoffrey Hill, André Deutsch.

how lovingly he persists in knocking!" And how many times, oh
supreme beauty, did I reply: "I will open tomorrow"', only to
make the same reply upon the morrow.' This is Hill's version,
somewhat truncated by the requirements of his sonnet:

> So many nights the angel of my house
> has fed such urgent comfort through a dream,
> whispered 'your lord is coming, he is close'
>
> that I have drowsed half-faithful for a time
> bathed in pure tones of promise and remorse:
> 'tomorrow I shall wake to welcome him.'

Hill's agenbite of inwit, his remorse of conscience, has replaced
Lope de Vega's brilliant 'see how lovingly he *persists* in knocking'. For the concrete, Hill gives us the enfeebled abstract of 'pure
tones of promise and remorse'.

The Jesuit martyr-poet, Robert Southwell, is a more important
influence than Lope de Vega in this sequence. 'Lachrimae' takes
its epigraph from Southwell's prose work *Mary Magdalens
Funerall Teares*, an Ignatian spiritual exercise that finally transcends its somewhat rigid formula. Southwell's subject is the
Bible's economical account of Mary Magdalene's despair at
finding the tomb empty and her subsequent error when she
mistakes Christ for the gardener. Southwell's purpose is to make
the bare text live and, after a wordy beginning, he succeeds
brilliantly. For instance, the Magdalene imagines that Christ's
body has been taken by thieves. Southwell argues passionately
against this hypothesis: 'when thy Maister was stripped at the
crosse, thou knowest that his only garment being congealed to his
goary back, came not off without many partes of his skin, and
doubtless would haue torne off many more, if he had beene
annointed with myrrh . . .' He urges that thieves would have had
to work hastily and in darkness, that any such abduction would
inevitably leave behind hairs and remnants of flesh, whereas the
opposite is the case.

It is a wonderful and profoundly imagined circumstantial

account which culminates in her failure to recognize Christ. Briefly, Southwell is exasperated until he realizes that her eyes are so full of tears she can only see a dim shape. Hill takes none of this exemplary immediacy from Southwell. His interest is fatally limited to the idea of Mary Magdalene as a well-known sinner lamenting for an absent God, a predicament that matches his own case:

> I cannot turn aside from what I do;
> you cannot turn away from what I am.

Moreover, Christ's indwelling presence cannot be guaranteed by prayer or the rejection of sin,

> however much I pander to your name
> or answer to your lords of revenue,
> surrendering the joys that they condemn.

The manner is that of Southwell's poetry, with its oddly stilted English, though the content is Hill's. Those 'lords of revenue' may allude to Luke 20:25 ('Render, therefore, unto Caesar the things which are Caesar's, and unto God the things which are God's') but that hardly saves the line from looking both archaic and periphrastic.

Perhaps it is unfair to set Southwell's vivid prose imaginings against Hill's poetry, since Hill's point is that he cannot empathize with anodyne, standardized images of the crucifixion:

> self-withdrawn even from your own device,
> your trim-plugged body, wreath of rakish thorn.

All the same, the general traditional diction makes for glum reading. You can't wring much blood from an already well-wrung stone. Beside the terrible sonnets of Hopkins, the fastidious angst of *Tenebrae* looks archaeological, willed and impersonal in the wrong sense.

Ted Hughes is the least academic of poets, totally unfazed by the unpoetical nature of the age. In *Gaudete*, whatever its structural obscurities, his confident, unselfconscious talent simply assimilated awkward items like the WI and Jaguar cars – rather as if Hughes was some X-ray visionary who could see the myth throbbing under the bonnet. The common criticism of Hughes is that he is a kind of linguistic Quilp, forcing huge beakers of boiling language down the throats of his readers and wolfing down words with their shells on. Indeed, I once heard him read a poem about a cricket match which verged dangerously close to self-parody: batsmen thumped the ball beyond the furthest stars only to find it returning on elastics. By the end, the beer tent was filled with twenty-two charred cricketers, bent like spent matches, barely able to contemplate cheese and chutney sandwiches after their cosmic ordeal.

Occasionally in *Cave Birds** the rhetoric seems excessive but it is nevertheless a very successful book, the best since the careless brilliance of *Season Songs*. Much simpler than *Gaudete*, it is an 'alchemical drama' devoted to the single subject of death: death as an irrelevance that suddenly and sickeningly becomes relevant; death as something to be dreaded in a variety of ways; death as cosmic salvation. As a subject, it is equal to Hughes's strenuous verbal gifts. One could spend a good deal of time simply quoting: 'Mountains lazed in their smoky camp'; 'Calves' heads all dew-bristled with blood on counters'; 'a seed in its armour'. The achievement, though, isn't in the fine touches; it is in the way Hughes has taken something impossibly abstract (as death and dying must be) and made it convincingly concrete: 'And you flare, fluttering, black-out like a firework.' This is Death addressing the dying, with impeccable line-breaks:

> Just as surely as you are my father
> I shall deliver you
> My firstborn
> Into a changed, unchangeable world
> Of wind and of sun, of rock and water
> To cry.

Cave Birds by Ted Hughes, Faber and Faber.

Cave Birds has faults, idiosyncratic shorthand like 'a filament of incandescence', but it is a stupendous work, far better than *Crow* from which it grew.

Basil Bunting

Overdrafts is Basil Bunting's witty half-title to his imitations of classical authors, Latin and Persian. It could have been used on the spine. Glancing wryly at a lifetime's poverty, ironizing his debt to tradition, the word 'overdraft' lastly adumbrates Bunting's poetic method throughout his work. Readers need to be familiar with the borrowed capital if they are to appreciate the interest – the something over. In the straight imitations, to which Pound's *Homage to Sextus Propertius* stands godfather, this is relatively simple. Bunting's version of Horace's 'Cum tu, Lydia, Telephi' (*Odes* I. XIII) takes the urgently jealous Latin and recasts it into stylized gangsterese, the modern pastoral of Bogart:

> Take my advice, better not count on your
> tough guy's mumbling your pretty mouth
> always.

The tone is now a modernized sidelong mutter. Yet it is not intended to obliterate Horace with irony: his underdraft reappears in the last lines ('Only the thrice blest are in love for life') and the opening's apache dance acknowledges its relationship with the classical *pas de deux*. The ironies are equal and the end result is assimilation.

The same thing is partially true of Bunting's first major poem, 'Villon', which fuses Villon's incarceration with Bunting's two spells in stir – the first as a Quaker conscientious objector in

Wormwood Scrubs (1918); the second in Paris when, after a drunken evening, he entered the wrong apartment, tried to expel the rightful tenant and, it's rumoured, bit a policeman. Bunting acknowledges minor differences but only to assert their essential similarity:

> Whereinall we differ not. But they have swept the floor,
> there are no dancers, no somersaulters now,
> only bricks and bleak black cement and bricks,
> only the military tread and the snap of locks.

Apart from sophistications in police methodology, like Alphonse Bertillon's system of anthropometrics, their suffering is the same. Accordingly, Bunting appropriates Villon's words and, for much of the poem, shares an 'I' with him.

The extent of Bunting's overdraft is, however, the extent of Villon's riches:

> My soundbox lacks sonority. All but inaudible
> I stammer to my ear:
> Naked speech! Naked beggar both blind and cold!
> Wrap it for my sake in Paisley shawls . . .

Circumstances compel Bunting to borrow where Villon created *ex nihilo* 'L'emperieres au poing dorez', the line chosen by Bunting to epitomize Villon's remarkable achievement. Out of the iron came forth sweetness, a matchless miracle that survives its creator – the bare forked animal elegized by Bunting who shared his pain.

In 'Villon', the debits and credits are clear. Bunting borrows the magnificence and recreates the anguish forgotten even by early admirers of Villon like Clément Marot, whose 1533 preface is quoted in all its thoughtlessness:

> 'whose words we gathered as pleasant flowers
> and thought on his wit and how neatly he described things'.

In 'Attis: or, Something Missing', though, the debts are more widespread. Catullus (LXIII) is invoked in the epigraph, while in the course of the poem one finds references to Dante's *Inferno* IX, Book II of Lucretius's *De Rerum Natura* and Milton's 'Methought I saw my late espousèd Saint'. Of these, Catullus seems the major creditor. (There are echoes of *The Waste Land*, too – 'Oh Sis! I've been 'ad' – but they seem merely derivative.) Catullus's Attis sails to Phrygia, emasculates himself in a religious frenzy for the Earth Mother, Cybele, sleeps it off and wakes up regretting the deed. In particular, he realizes that he'll never be able to return to his homeland, especially since Cybele unleashes a lion to shoo him back into the undergrowth.

Broadly, Bunting follows this scenario, though the emasculation is figurative and the young Attis is now sixty, 'out of puff' and running to fat. There is no shortage of solutions to the problem of his 'impotence'; the difficulty is in reconciling them to each other. On the one hand, it's partly the result of boredom and age:

> Long loved and
> too long loved, stale habit, such decay of ardour,
> love never dead, love never hoping, never gay.
> Ageslow venom self-secreted.

On the other hand, there's amorous cowardice after a jilting:

> I dare no longer raise my eyes
> on any lass
> seeing what one of them has done to me.

Most importantly, there's another kind of cutting off, on which poetic sterility follows – self-exile in an alien environment. Catullus's 'abero foro, palaestra, stadio et gymnasiis' is comically reworked as

> I also won the 14 carat halfhunter goldwatch
> at the annual sports and flowershow . . .

This is a theme to which Bunting returns, more personally, in his great tragic masterpiece, 'Briggflatts'. It begins with beautifully evoked memories of a childhood love in Briggflatts, a village south of Sedbergh:

> He has untied the tape
> of her striped flannel drawers
> before the range.

The simplicity of the gesture is matched by the simplicity of diction. This love was 'laid aside' when Bunting's literary ambition took him abroad. In Paris, he was editorial assistant on Ford Madox Ford's *Transatlantic Review*; he stayed with Pound at Rapallo; spent some time in Berlin; visited the States, meeting Zukovsky and Carlos Williams; lived in Tenerife; was for a time the skipper of a millionaire's schooner; and was the *Times* correspondent in Persia. Most of these wanderings are present, obliquely and non-factually, in the poem.

During this long exile, wilfully self-imposed, Bunting felt cut off from true creativity and, Attis-like, describes himself as 'self-maimed', conscious that 'amputated years ache'. Moreover, something was missing from his poetry, the instinctive song of Briggflatts:

> It looks well on the page, but never
> well enough. Something is lost
> when wind, sun, sea upbraid
> justly an unconvinced deserter.

Two historical figures, Alexander and Eric Bloodaxe, are employed as objective correlatives by Bunting, since both were ambitious, self-seeking exiles. Bloodaxe, son of the Norwegian Harold Fairhair, was King of Dublin, Orkney and York before he was mysteriously murdered at Stainmore. Alexander's pursuit of conquest took him to the ends of the earth and an early death at thirty-three. Neither is admirable in Bunting's terms, and in

Part III Alexander's futile ambition ('But we desired Macedonia') is bitterly ironized.

Conflating Dante's *Inferno* VIII and Firdausi's *Shahnama* XX:29, Bunting begins with a scatological portrait of ambition and ends with Alexander's encounter with Israfel or Azrael, the Koran's angel of death. It is a powerfully phantasmagoric indictment, drawing on the *Shahnama*'s account of Sekandar's (Alexander's) failure to find the Water of Life. Instead, the angel confronts him with the futility of his life and his imminent death: 'Oh thou slave of greed! Toil not so much, because some day a call will reach thine ears.' In the poem, the Water of Life is a spring at Briggflatts, Bunting's relinquished Macedonia.

There, true creativity waits with the girl of Part I whose objective correlative is Pasiphae. Pasiphae is conquered rather than conquering: she suffered the bull and 'gloried in unlike creation'. Wise passiveness, the poem argues, achieves the desired song and the girl is always remembered as 'laying the tune frankly on the air'. 'Briggflatts' closes with the realization that she is the guiding star, part of the music of the spheres. 'Ridiculous the waste sad time / Stretching before and after.'

Bunting is a great master and we must educate ourselves to read him. Nevertheless, anyone with an ear or an eye will immediately appreciate his extraordinary lyric gift and his acute visual sense:

> Frost has put rowan down,
> a russet blotch of bracken
> tousled about the trunk.

In 'Briggflatts', the voice is totally achieved – clipped, consonantal, shy of Tennysonian *bel canto*, chary of the definite article, mutedly alliterative. The overdraft is paid off.

John Betjeman

Symbolically enough, when John Betjeman, celebrant of the *thé dansant*, published his *Collected Poems* in 1958, the British left-wing intelligentsia was gathered in a coffee bar. If, that is, we are to believe A. Alvarez's 'Exile's Return' in the *Partisan Review* for Spring 1959. With insufficiently few reservations, Alvarez reported that a new magazine, *Universities and Left Review*, showed 'signs of life and activity that are unusual in the London intellectual world. One of the signs is to have opened up a coffee-bar, *The Partisan*, which, when it has paid for itself, will plough back its profits into the *ULR*. *The Partisan*, officially, is an anti-coffee-bar coffee-bar: no plants climb up your leg if you sit there more than half an hour; no stuffed parrots eye you coldly through bamboo lattice-work; there is no background music to put you off your food; the only gesture towards current Bohemian café fashions is the optional chess-sets. Instead, the place has been designed in the best air-raid shelter style; sparsely painted concrete, skeletal stairs, two levels, and a dug-out within the dug-out below for the boys.' The 'inmates', Alvarez observed without detectable irony, were unusually cheerful 'as though they were all there to sign up for some crusade'.

This, then, was the critical context in which Betjeman's *Collected Poems* appeared – an heroically stateless bunker, chilly and comfortless, filled with rigorous types whose thought processes were the intellectual equivalent of cold baths, khaki shorts, bare knees and the reintroduction of rationing. No wonder that Betjeman and his crowd of 90,000 admirers were stopped at the door by Alvarez – and even less surprising, perhaps, that Betjeman should refer (in a later volume) to 'journalism full of hate' and 'the prods of prigs', as well as to 'One-seven Alvarez Cloister'. Typical, one feels, that the coffee bar would have to be an anti-coffee-bar, a monkish cell with only room for anti-heroes of a particular kind. The Betjeman sort of anti-hero ('bald and old and green' like a threadbare tennis ball, guilty of 'neglect and unkindness', 'I remembered her defencelessness as I made my heart a stone', 'I am thirty summers older, / Richer, wickeder and colder') was bound to be refused admission to *The Partisan*.

Betjeman was insufficiently glum, and likely to ironize that 'sparsely painted concrete' or wonder why Alvarez should think it necessary to say that the chess-sets were optional. Frankly, Alvarez explained, the man just wasn't serious: 'all the creative effort of Eliot, Yeats and Auden, and the painful fight to establish critical standards and a fresh tradition by men like Richards, Leavis and Empson, have apparently done no good at all.' Reviewing *Summoned by Bells* in the *Observer* two years later, John Wain reiterated the charge: 'it does not follow from this that Betjeman's work is foolish. It is merely that the strength and appeal of what he writes lies elsewhere, away from the kind of discriminations that must be used when "real" poetry is in question.' Ah yes, discriminations:

> I'm making some changes next week in the organization
>   And though I admire
> Your work for me, John, yet the need to increase circulation
>   Means you must retire:
> An outlook more global than yours is the qualification
>   I really require.

Betjeman has never had the required global outlook so prized by his detractors. 'Greek Orthodox', virtually his sole poetic excursion abroad, loses itself with absent-minded rapidity in English preoccupations, as Betjeman spots 'The semblance of an English chancel screen'. Unlike his critics, he has never been a globetrotter.

In fact, John Wain's absence in America, his discriminations neatly folded in his battered suitcase, was one of the reasons Alvarez cited for Betjeman's sudden popularity: 'with the young men off the field, the Old Guard moved back in force. The occasion was the publication of *The Collected Poems of John Betjeman* . . . Now, Mr Betjeman is a skilful, harmless minor writer of light verse, who is most successful when hymning *les petits plaisirs des riches*; he writes little panegyrics on bullying tennis girls, the nostalgia of boarding schools and the hidden charms of Victorian monstrosities. His subjects, in short, are the rather delicious trials and tribulations of being upper middle class.' And, Alvarez avuncularly concluded, 'no one, apart from a few mildly eccentric English dons at Oxford, had ever taken it particularly seriously'.

For someone so keen on discrimination and 'the painful fight to establish critical standards', Alvarez's account is strangely inaccurate. A fine little grouping of outers. Neither Edmund Wilson, Auden nor Philip Larkin, all of them staunch supporters of Betjeman's poetry, could be described as 'mildly eccentric English dons'. And one is curious to know where exactly Alvarez locates nostalgia for boarding schools. In the lines ' "You're to be booted. Hold him steady, chaps" '; 'So all the previous night I spewed with fear'; 'The dread of beatings!'; 'And by its fishtail gas-jet nursed my fear'? Well, no. Only the first quotation appears in *Collected Poems* (1958), the others are from *Summoned by Bells*. There are 130 poems in *Collected Poems* (1958) and of them only one refers to school – a day-school, as it happens. What bone-idle, irresponsible mendacity. The 'bullying tennis girls' are another figment of Alvarez's indolence. Betjeman may *wish* to be manhandled by these big girls, but what he mostly allows us to see is their complete indifference to him – by no means the same thing.

Presumably, too, it is the 'fresh tradition' which prompts Alvarez's remark, 'he also writes bad religiose poems about death'. For 'religiose' read 'agnostic'. And I find nothing religiose in Betjeman's deservedly famous 'Death in Leamington'. On the other hand, Patrick Taylor-Martin's plodding analysis of the poem*, written from an avowedly friendly standpoint, reminds one of nothing so much as a vet administering a fatal injection to an old favourite. Betjeman's superbly particular realization – the incongruous flirtation between 'the ev'ning star' and the uncompromisingly modern 'plate glass window', the vivid clutter suggested by 'Breast high 'mid the stands and chairs', the grim symbolism of 'She covered the fire with coal', as opposed to 'And then on the fire *put* coal', the telling finality of 'She moved the table of bottles / Away from the bed to the wall' – all these touches, delicately angled over the net, go for nothing in Mr Taylor-Martin's account. Betjeman might be merely warming up. The final, utterly absurd, misplaced *politesse* of 'tiptoeing *gently* over the stairs' is an ace that Taylor-Martin simply does not see. For him, this lonely, ominous poem retains its 'delectable freshness and sparkle'. One could ransack the *OED* for months and not come up with a word less applicable to 'Death in Leamington' than delectable.

> Do you know that the stucco is peeling?
>> Do you know that the heart will stop?
> From those yellow Italianate arches
>> Do you hear the plaster drop?

Eliot once wrote that Rosamund Vincey, in *Middlemarch*, frightened him far more than Goneril and Regan. In the same way, this startling direct address to the reader chills more than Eliot's 'I will show you fear in a handful of dust'. It is less hieratic, perhaps, but horribly insidious. Of it, Taylor-Martin, unstirred and scarcely shaken, comments: 'place, action and feelings are a unity so that the physical decay of the spa town images the old lady's lingering death.' Correct, of course, but totally inadequate, as his later conclusion makes clear: 'the poet's attitude being at one with the nurse's clinical matter-of-factness.' Never mind that 'tiptoeing gently'. Actually, one might go back to Dunbar's 'Lament for the Makeirs' to find a comparably awesome example of *Timor*

John Betjeman: His Life and Work by Patrick Taylor-Martin, Allen Lane

Mortis Conturbat Me. Those unanswerable questions form a prophecy applicable to everyone, including the poet.

Taylor-Martin, however, is not really in sympathy with Betjeman and his study blunders on, uniquely deaf to tone and eager to recommend inferior poems while demoting better ones, or simply misunderstanding them. 'Exeter' is a case in point, though Betjeman's play with tenses provides Taylor-Martin with the vestige of an excuse. Again, 'what is undeniably tragic is overlaid with farce' because of Betjeman's 'total detachment'. Taylor-Martin's reading of 'Exeter' gives us a doctor's wife whose faith is restored after her husband's death in a car accident. 'The neat inversion of the two stanzas describing the wife's alternate loss and recovery of her faith is too slick, a device which enables the poet to tie up the ends of his poem neatly. It is, in fact, just a skilful piece of versifying and the pleasure it gives is of the shallow sort afforded by light verse.' Despite Taylor-Martin's bluff avowal in his preface that 'literature, let us not forget, exists to be enjoyed, not to be evaluated', this looks strikingly similar to those painful discriminations so dear to Alvarez, and no more accurate.

'Exeter' describes a loss of faith, *tout court*. There is no recovery. Taylor-Martin has been misled by the use of the historic present in the third stanza: 'The doctor jumps in his Morris car.' The next stanza, which reverts to the past tense, makes this clear:

> They brought him in by the big front door
>   And a smiling corpse was he;
> On the dining-room table they laid him out
>   Where the *Bystanders* used to be –
> *The Tatler*, *The Sketch* and *The Bystander*
>   For the canons' wives to see.

In other words, before her husband's death and her subsequent loss of faith, the doctor's wife, with harmless snobbery, used to lay out smart magazines to impress her clerical neighbours. Now she doesn't bother. Trivial social concerns, and aesthetic pleasures ('Wulfric's altar and riddel posts'), are erased for her by mortality, as they were for Betjeman:

> You ask me to believe You and
> I only see decay.

Betjeman has always known the steep price to be paid for atheism – riddel posts, squinches, carven swags, fiddle-back vestments, baldachin pillars, brass-studded baize, incense and box-pews. To renounce these pleasures, as the doctor's wife does, is an index of death's terrible power.

Taylor-Martin is excusably wrong about the scenario of 'Exeter', but inexcusably wrong about its tone. The quality of 'burlesque' that he isolates results from his own imaginative failure: in Betjeman's world, the cancellation of a magazine subscription, even to the *Tatler*, can be the outward sign of a great spiritual upheaval. Betjeman understands petty snobbery from the inside and perceives the depths of its tenacious roots. In this suburban milieu, to cast off such things causes a reverberation like a diminished echo of Lear's 'Off, off, you lendings' – bereft of tragic dimension, quite unpublic, undramatically painful and tellingly serious. But, then, few are gifted with Taylor-Martin's trenchant prose ('a sledge hammer seems to have been used to crack a walnut'; 'the agony is laid on with a trowel'; 'Lord Birkenhead hit the nail on the head'; 'Betjeman struck a rich vein of poetic ore') and his complementary critical insight.

The best thing in *John Betjeman: His Life and Work* is the biographical section. There, all too briefly, we are spared Taylor-Martin's rich critical prose ('it is a spirited and accomplished poem, something of a *tour de force*, with its skilful internal rhymes, its well-managed transitions and subtle variations of mood') and released into Betjeman's hilarious and troubled life. We learn about Betjeman's fits of depression and other personal facts – that his forceful wife and he led separate lives to some extent and that his son (in an act of rebellion?) became a Mormon in the United States. With Auden and MacNeice, he writes the great erotic couplet:

> I often think that I would like
> To be the saddle of a bike.

In Ireland, during the war, he signs his correspondence 'Sean O'betjeman' and dates all minutes according to the liturgical calendar. As a film critic, he persuades Myrna Loy to claim an interest in English Perpendicular architecture. And at the white-tie Savoy dinner to celebrate his marriage, he snaps his specially made elastic bow-tie throughout the meal to irritate his snobbish in-laws. This ability to let rip in life is responsible, of course, for a poem like 'Slough', which Taylor-Martin approaches with all the caution of a tax accountant, chiding the 'intemperate and quite uncharacteristic savagery' and noting, in mitigation, that Betjeman very properly exculpates the 'bald young clerks'. On the whole, Taylor-Martin is uneasy with satire: on sober reflection, it sometimes seems unfair.

It is odd, then, to note that he almost puts his finger on Betjeman's most important technique: 'Part of the pleasure – though it is a very secondary one – must derive from the reader's awareness of the strangeness of the enterprise', he writes of *Summoned by Bells*. 'It gives one something of a *frisson* to have the febrile world of Oxford in the twenties described in a form which the Victorians reserved for ponderous and moralising epics . . . This presentation of the modern world in the forms of a traditional poetic technique is, of course, the hallmark of all Betjeman's writing.' It is indeed. All the same, Taylor-Martin finds it 'secondary' and *Summoned by Bells*, Betjeman's serio-comic masterpiece, is given the thumbs down. Taylor-Martin is all thumbs. For him, Betjeman's long poem 'falls short of his august models'. As, it is necessary to add, Betjeman intended.

Betjeman uses the blank verse of his illustrious predecessors for his own, utterly modern, mock-epic purpose in *Summoned by Bells*.* So it is absurdly beside the point to complain that the poem displays triteness or lapses into banality. When Frank Kermode considers 'Deeply I loved thee, 31 West Hill!' and concludes that this 'would not be a tolerable line in a local

*See p. 301.

newspaper poet', Taylor-Martin finds a simple negative judgement. But Kermode fully appreciates what he happily calls Betjeman's 'comic astigmatism' – the play of tone and the role of parody in Betjeman's work. When Betjeman writes:

> Come, Hygiene, goddess of the growing boy,
> I here salute thee in Sanatogen!

Professor Kermode can presumably hear the subversive reminiscence of, say, Wordsworth's 'Ode to Duty'?

> Stern Daughter of the Voice of God!
> O Duty! if that name thou love . . .

Betjeman is plainly disowning the oracular mode and guying it: he knows he isn't the type and that life, to be honest, just isn't like that. His verse autobiography is nearer Joyce's Bloom than Homer's Ulysses:

> I see the asphalt slope and smell again
> The sluggish, sour, inadequate latrines.

The joy of *Summoned by Bells* is that, for all its camp poetese, it escapes Poetry altogether:

> Tons, if you added them, of buttered toast
> Had she and I consumed through all the days.

Once jettisoned, the blank-verse line and its expectations create the rich literary comedy of 'House slippers, sponge-bags, pyjams, Common Prayer' – not to mention the Proustian vividness of 'Salt and hot sun on rubber water-wings . . .' It is useless to approach poetry like this in the Arnoldian spirit of high seriousness. Betjeman is not interested in the noble application of ideas to life. He is interested in the thing itself – life – and he succeeds marvellously, without recourse to the Grand Style. 'And now if you will find my spectacles' – what a blank-verse line. What flat-footed brio. No use furrowing the brow; get out the handkerchief and dab your eyes.

You can scarcely understand Betjeman's poetry until you have grasped that he writes 'badly' in order to write well. It is a brilliant device and one which has disorientated his critics. In essence, Betjeman employs a faintly dated, antique style – Timeless Classical by Golden Treasury – and spikes it with ephemeral detail, knowing that nothing ages quicker than the eternal and that nothing lasts like dross. By and large, Betjeman's lines break every modernist rule. They might have been written, in the spirit of contradiction, with Ezra Pound's 'A Few Don'ts By An Imagiste' propped open at his elbow. It is futile, however, to set up a conflict between Betjeman and modernism, as Alvarez and Wain do, and as Betjeman's greatest admirer, Larkin, seems to do. It is possible to admire Eliot and Betjeman – but only if you can see that Pound's eminently sound rules have been broken by an exceptional poet.

If one reads Betjeman solemnly, the ironic play between, for instance, 'runneth' and the rest of the line in 'May-Day Song for North Oxford' will be baffling: 'And a constant sound of flushing runneth from windows where / The toothbrush too is airing in this new North Oxford air'. This is funny, as much of Betjeman is, in a way that does not preclude authenticity. The 'poetic' is emphasized to accommodate and throw into relief the unpoetic. Or consider 'Old Friends', which begins with Betjeman taking down a bolt of Laura Ashley and measuring off a foot or two:

> And over the west is glowing a mackerel sky
> Whose opal fleece has faded to purple pink.

Soon this standard stuff, a kind of poetic comforter, is replaced:

> Where is Anne Chancel who loved this place the best,
> With her tense blue eyes and her shopping bag falling apart,

And her racy gossip and nineteen-twenty zest,
  And that warmth of heart?

The technique is precisely that used by Dr Johnson in his 'On the Death of Dr Robert Levet', where he modulates from average elegiac ('Well tried through many a varying year, / See LEVET to the grave descend') to accurate observation:

Yet still he fills affection's eye,
Obscurely wise, and coarsely kind . . .

Coarsely kind. Tense blue eyes. We have before us not the recipient of an elegy but a real person. The method is unorthodox, but it works. Modernist poetic decorum is flouted and replaced, then the replacement is flouted in its turn. Betjeman is a great poetic southpaw.

When Ian Hamilton reviewed *The Best of Betjeman* in 1978, he noted, comparing Larkin with Betjeman, that: 'The principal difference between the two poets is that where Larkin uses metre and rhyme as a means of strengthening and elevating ordinary speech, Betjeman more often than not appears to be the creature of his metrical correctness.' Accordingly, Hamilton offered to rewrite a few bits of Betjeman to eliminate inversions: 'the proposition is merely that many rich, heartfelt, beautifully observed moments in his poetry get unnecessarily jauntified by his uneasiness with the tight forms he's committed to.' Though Hamilton is clearly sympathetic and finally rejects his own editorializing, one can detect in his reservations a commitment to poetic decorum – the sense that 'lightness' and 'jauntification' have no place in 'real' poetry. We are, in short, back with John Wain. Or, to give him a rest, with Thom Gunn, who reviewed the *Collected Poems* in the *Yale Review* for June 1959 – an essay he has chosen not to reprint in *The Occasions of Poetry*.

Gunn was (rightly) puzzled by Lord Birkenhead's prefatory assertion that Betjeman is not 'a "funny" poet'. Gunn patiently noted the humour in the poetry, adding: 'but Mr Betjeman wants something more; he wants to be beautiful as well as humorous, as, for example, in the following stanza:

> When shall I see the Thames again?
> The prow-promoted gems again,
>   As beefy ATS
>   Without their hats
> Come shooting through the bridge?
>   And "cheerioh" and "cheeri-bye"
>   Across the waste of waters die,
>   And low the mists of evening lie
> And lightly skims the midge.

'The reference to the ATS', Gunn continues, 'is *quite* amusing, though far from original, but it is at complete variance to the previous two stanzas, to the "poetic" reference to gems of light in the water, and to the equally serious lines that follow. The mixture makes me uneasy. I know that funny-looking people are to be seen in beautiful scenes, but Mr Betjeman has merely noted the discrepancy (with a shudder of repugnance) and the fact itself is not particularly interesting.' Where Ian Hamilton might find jauntiness in the 'beefy ATS', Gunn discovers a 'shudder of repugnance'. Surely both are mistaken? Betjeman has a more elastic sense of beauty and joy than either – one which includes the low mists of evening *and* the ATS, evocatively free of their regulation headgear. Decorum must learn to bed down with the truth of Betjeman's emotional response.

The problem is both modernist and perennial: Wordsworth faced it when he wished to write about an idiot boy, Eliot when he wrote of 'cigarettes in corridors / And cocktail smells in bars'. The anonymous *TLS* reviewer commented drily: 'the fact that these things occurred to the mind of Mr Eliot is surely of the very smallest importance to any one – even to himself. They certainly have no relation to "poetry", and we only give an example because some of the pieces, he states, have appeared in a periodical which claims that word as its title.' Of 'The Idiot Boy', Coleridge complained: 'the author has not, in the poem itself, taken sufficient care to preclude from the reader's fancy the disgusting images of *ordinary morbid idiocy*, which yet it was by no means his intention to represent.' Baudelaire, in his review of the Salon of 1845, encapsulated the problem – the need to 'snatch its epic quality from the life of today'. The epic, on the whole, is not Betjeman's aim. A more modest truth will do, but modern life is what he sets out to capture:

> Miles of pram in the wind and Pam in the gorse track,
>   Coco-nut smell of the broom, and a packet of Weights
> Press'd in the sand . . .

That packet of Player's Weights stands for much that is conventionally unpoetic in Betjeman's work: 'The Lynams' cess-pool like a body blow'; 'Lock'd is the Elsan in its brick abutment'; 'Last year's tea-stained *Vogues*'; 'Do six balls make an over? Help me, God!'; 'Striving on to prunes and suet'; 'Fleas round the tamarisk, an early cigarette'; 'Home and Colonial, Star, International'; 'Oh, Fuller's angel-cake, Robertson's marmalade'; 'And Heinz's ketchup on the tablecloth'. So much that is personal, universal and true finds its way into Betjeman's poetry – which is At Home to everything.

And how is it done? Take 'Parliament Hill Fields':

> Up the hill where stucco houses in Virginia Creeper drown –
> And my childish wave of pity, seeing children carrying down
> Sheaves of drooping dandelions to the courts of Kentish Town.

Everyone has seen something similar, just as we've seen the 'ginger-beery surf', or 'one child [who] still zig-zags homewards up the lane' – but Betjeman makes poetry of it by evaluating his pity as 'childish', by specifying the flowers and by playing on the romantic Golden Treasury associations of 'courts', while insisting on the ironic urban reality.

Auden and Larkin recognize in Betjeman's poetry a vision of England which they share. In 'Margate, 1940', Betjeman ponders

what 'we are fighting for'. His answer is one that the Larkin of
'Show Saturday' might have provided:

> Oh! then what a pleasure to see the ground floor
> With tables for two laid as tables for four,
> And bottles of sauce and Kia-Ora and squash
> Awaiting their owners who'd gone up to wash.

Betjeman may not like this world of Wilfred Pickles's *Have-a-Go*,
any more than Larkin likes the 'cut-price crowd', but both *love* it.
As Auden did, even in America, where he wrote in *The Age of
Anxiety* of 'country curates in cold bedrooms'. In 1947, introducing *Slick but not Streamlined*, a selection from Betjeman, Auden
professed to believe that Betjeman had been taken over by the
spirit of his favourite Aunt Daisy: 'how else could he have entered
so intimately into my childhood? How else could he be so at
home with the provincial gaslit towns, the seaside lodgings, the
bicycles, the harmonium, above all, the atmosphere of ritualistic
controversy?' And, one might add, so at home with Auden's sense
of quotidian evil, as we find it in Betjeman's

> The milkman on the road stood staring in,
> The playground nettles nodded 'Now begin' –
> And Evil waited, quivering, for sin.

As for the seaside lodgings, of *course*: 'ten minutes from the
shore. / Still unprepared to make a picnic lunch / Except by notice
on the previous day.' A quotation from boarding house regu-
lations and a quotation from every English life. We all have an
Aunt Daisy and a childhood littered with brand-names and guilt.

Larkin has also written an introduction to Betjeman for
American readers. It would be interesting to know whether this
extraordinarily English poet travels well, or if, as I suspect, that
wonderfully clear stuff arrives in New York looking muddy and
tasting strange. After all, what are Americans to make of a writer
who, in his essay 'Topographical Verse', had this to say about
Hardy's poem 'At the Draper's'? 'We all know that sad little

Satire of Circumstance about the wife ordering mourning before her husband was dead. But it is the atmosphere created by Hardy which makes the poem memorable for me. "At the Draper's". What a title! I can see the shop he stood at the back of – called Cavendish House, smell of calico, wires going to a cash desk with carriers whizzing among the incandescent lights and the Congregational minister's wife being served at the next counter.' Brilliant, but not for export.

As a thirteen-year-old attending an obscure Northern public school, my first encounter with poetry was 'A Subaltern's Love Song'. It meant less than nothing to me. The Home Counties might have been another continent. So *this* was poetry, I thought – being beaten at tennis by a girl. I turned up the collar of my gabardine and headed for the nearest coffee bar. However, I never forgot Miss Joan Hunter Dunn. It takes time to grow up to Betjeman. America may manage it yet. But there's probably no hope for Alvarez. Was there ever?

Elizabeth Bishop's Prose

In Elizabeth Bishop's work, poetry and prose, there is a hidden rule. It is this. Everything is an exception to the rule. All explanation is a cup which overflows rather than contains. Ultimately, there are no rules.

> When we came to Hustler Hill,
> he said that the mare was tired,
> so we all got down and walked,
> as our good manners required.

Elizabeth Bishop was refined. Manners interested her, as *The Collected Prose* makes clear.* She can remember learning 'how to behave in school' with more recall than most people: 'this meant to sit up straight, not to scrape your feet on the floor, never to whisper, to raise your hand when you had to go out, and to stand up when you were asked a question.' Fifty-odd years later in Brazil, she teaches manners to two little girls who are following a crazy woman and giggling at her: 'I give them a look.' At the same time, she could see the limitations of manners, could see beyond their immediate and important utility as guides to behaviour. She realizes that manners are provisional. They change. Which is why her poem, 'Manners', carries the ironical epigraph, *For a Child of 1918*. Elizabeth Bishop knows that this rigid six-inch ruler, serviceable in its way, cannot measure the

*The Collected Prose of Elizabeth Bishop edited and introduced by Robert Giroux, Chatto and Windus.

larger reaches of human behaviour. 'Manners', then, isn't quite the charmingly simple, didactically home-spun affair it pretends to be. It is an elegy for a lost, straightforward world. Present, too, squally and intractable, is the unmentioned problematic present.

'A Trip to Vigia' is a comedy of manners masquerading as a travel essay, in which the manners of a 'shy poet, so soiled, so poor, so polite' are anthropologically scrutinized by another shy poet, Elizabeth Bishop, whose financial advantages are mysteriously rendered impotent: 'the car was on its last legs; it had broken down twice just getting us around Belem the day before. But what could we do? I couldn't very well flaunt my dollars in his face and hire a better one.' Everyone means well but the occasion comes to resemble a curious courtship in which neither party can advance the issue and make the trip a relaxed affair. The formality of manners somehow outflanks both parties, as if they were speaking different languages – which, in a way, they are. A fine packed lunch proves to be an embarrassment because it reflects on their host's poverty: 'finally M. and I miserably gobbled up some lunch by ourselves.' When the trip is over, Dona Elizabeth offers their guide a drink. He will accept only coffee and somehow contrives to pay for the lot behind their backs. The high spot of the trip is not the church which is their destination, but a passage of behaviour, a little epiphany of etiquette that appeals to the connoisseur of manners: 'we had met Ruy just two days before. That morning I asked M. to let me know when the mystic moment arrived and she'd shift gears from addressing him as "Dr Ruy" to "you". This use of the *você* or second person is always a delicate problem and I wanted to see how M. who has the nicest Brazilian manners would solve it.' The metaphor, 'shift gears', nicely places the transaction by reminding us of the actual vehicle. They are travelling over difficult social terrain in a ramshackle, makeshift affair which keeps breaking down. For once, the Americans are not in the driving seat dictating the direction.

In the stunning memoir of Marianne Moore, this preoccupation is, if anything, more pronounced. Again, there is the same mixture of tactful respect, forbearance, even admiration, and a wry agnosticism. The absolutes promulgated by Miss Moore ('we called each other "Miss" for over two years') and her mother are enormously attractive – yet shown to be provisional and, on occasion, battily arbitrary. On the one hand, their manners are charming, other-worldly, a refreshing change from 'the crass atmosphere of the twentieth century': 'what I remember most is that at the proper floor, as the passengers stared, Marianne and her mother both bowed to the elevator boy pleasantly and thanked him, Mrs Moore the more profusely, for the ride. He was unaccustomed to such civility, but he was very pleased and tried hard not to push his handle or close the doors as quickly as on other floors. Elevator men, subway changemakers, ticket takers, taxi drivers – all were treated to these formalities, and, as a rule, they were pleasantly surprised and seemed to respond in kind.' On the other hand, the system can be inelastic: 'a very well known and polished writer, who had known Marianne since he was a young man and felt great admiration for her, was never invited to Cumberland Street [the Moore residence] although his friends were. Once, I asked innocently why I never saw him there and Marianne gave me her serious, severe look and said, "He *contradicted* Mother".'

The failure here is, perhaps, on both sides – a kind of double fault. But at other moments, Elizabeth Bishop is amused, gentle but firm in her disagreement with the code: 'Besides exercising on the trapeze, Marianne was very fond of tennis. I never saw her play, but from the way she talked about it, it seemed as if she enjoyed the rules and conventions of the game as much as the sport. She engaged a young black boy to play with her, sometimes in Prospect Park and sometimes on the roof of the apartment house. He was finally dismissed because of his lack of tennis manners; his worst offense seemed to be that instead of "Serve!" he *would* say "Okay!" '

Her own finesse and tractability didn't always prevent Elizabeth Bishop from coming into conflict with the rules: she is criticized for using the word 'spit' in a short story and later for the impropriety of using 'water closet' in a poem. 'But by then I had turned obstinate.' In any case, this deliberately shaped memoir shows that these rules were necessarily strained, often by simple emotions of the baser kind, like human curiosity: 'several times over the years Marianne asked me abruptly, "Elizabeth, what do you have on under your dress? How much underwear do *you* wear?" '

And it is this maverick behaviour, these exceptions to the rules, which appeal to Elizabeth Bishop because they reveal the irrepressible individual – the non-conformist who took tango lessons; the baseball enthusiast; the eccentric who, however much she flattened her headgear, nevertheless possessed and wore 'the Holbein/Erasmus-type hat, and later the famous tricorne'; the zany who learned to drive at a dangerously advanced age and preferred the front seat of the roller-coaster at Coney Island.

In the essay on the primitive painter, Gregorio Valdes, Elizabeth Bishop concludes: 'there are some people whom we envy not because they are rich or handsome or successful, although they may be any or all of these, but because everything they are and do seems to be all of a piece, so that even if they wanted to they could not be or do otherwise.' Marianne Moore is a case in point: her poetry is packed with moral nostrums and eccentric detail; it is of a piece with what Elizabeth Bishop calls her '*chinoiserie* of manners'. As a person and as a poet, she adored rules, but was a natural non-conformist: she would telephone her young friend for a rhyme or to check on the metre of a poem. 'These were strange requests, coming from someone who had made contemporary poets self-conscious about their crudities, afraid to rhyme "bone" with "stone", or to go *umpty-umpty-um*. Marianne was doing her best, one saw, to go *umpty-umpty-um* when she sensed that La Fontaine had gone that way, but it seemed to be almost – I use the word again – physically impossible for her to do so.' The endeavour to conform takes her at last to a poetry workshop run by Louise Bogan, where her innocently Socratic questions about the art consistently embarrass the instructor. It is charming yet ridiculous – but never held up for ridicule by Elizabeth Bishop who rather concludes sombrely, meditating on 'the rarity of true originality and also the sort of alienation it might involve'.

Clearly, Elizabeth Bishop's poetry owes a great deal to Marianne Moore. Yet she, too, is a true original and the difference between them as poets is the difference in their manners: the mandarin social manners of Marianne Moore find their poetic counterpart in what she herself called 'all this fiddle'. Elizabeth Bishop is just as sensitive, but straighter, less fiddly. And this, too, is part of her total personality: she is more sceptical, even of herself, and can refer boldly to her own 'neurotically "kind" ' personality. Her general verbal attack is less mannered, less finicky than her mentor's.

A further difference, also related to manners, shows up in Elizabeth Bishop's themes. For Marianne Moore and her mother, manners are a set of rigid rules, instructions for living, tested ways of making life work smoothly. Essentially, they are an extension of religion, whereas Elizabeth Bishop has no faith and this colours her poetry, giving it a distinctive shade. The area where the two part company is here: 'Marianne was intensely interested in the techniques of things – how camellias are grown; how the quartz prisms work in crystal clocks; how the pangolin can close up his ear, nose, and eye apertures and walk on the outside edges of his hands "and save the claws / for digging"; how to drive a car; how the best pitchers throw a baseball; how to make a figurehead for her nephew's sailboat. The exact way in which anything was done, or made, or functioned, was poetry to her.' It isn't that Elizabeth Bishop isn't interested, too. Clearly, she relishes this delicious catalogue. But her underlying attitude is different from this transposed Deism, which is founded on a general confidence that she does not share – a belief in rules and explanations, in finality. Her own world is less confidently certain. Explanations, knowledge, are less forthcoming. Her poetic manner is provisional:

It is like what we imagine knowledge to be:
dark, salt, clear, moving, utterly free,
drawn from the cold hard mouth
of the world, derived from the rocky breasts
forever, flowing and drawn, and since
our knowledge is historical, flowing, and flown.

This coda from 'At the Fishhouses' is more explicitly eloquent than anything else in her poetry, surprisingly akin to the finale of Arnold's 'Sohrab and Rustum'. Usually, Elizabeth Bishop is less dramatically inconclusive about the provisional nature of human knowledge. One thinks, for instance, of 'The Bight', a poem which resolutely refuses to reach for significance. Baudelaire, the idea of correspondences, a metaphysical metonomy in which the small can signify a larger whole, are raised and regretfully dropped. 'The bight', we are told, 'is littered with old correspondences.' And the poem ends with stoical low-key accuracy, fading quietly to its anti-climax:

> Click. Click. Goes the dredge,
> and brings up a dripping jawful of marl.
> All the untidy activity continues,
> awful but cheerful.

Unlike her talentless students, corresponding out of their loneliness to the USA School of Writing, Elizabeth Bishop knows how to deploy her detail and how to desist from the neat moral: 'there was also the same tendency in both primitive painting and writing to make it all right, or of real value to the world, by tacking on a grand, if ill-fitting, "moral", or allegorical interpretation.' She, on the contrary, insists on the pattern of having no pattern – something frequently seen in her prose too.

'To the Botequim & Back' is typically inconsequential. Nature is brilliant; the people, today at least, are fairly awful; and the piece ends with a characteristic aposiopesis: 'and this is where the stream disappears, like the sacred river Alph in Coleridge's dream. It fans out over the red stone, narrows and rises in cold gray ridges, disappears underground, and then shows up again farther off, dashing downwards now through more beautiful rocks. It then takes off downwards for the Underworld. You can hang over the rocks and see it far below. It keeps descending, disappears into a cavern, and is never seen again. It talks as it goes, but the words are lost . . .'

'Primer Class', the first, deceptively guileless reminiscence of her childhood in Nova Scotia, is true to the merely contingent nature of experience and yet has its own subtle significant form. The detail is lavish: 'we ate porridge from bowls, with a cup of cream at the side. You took a spoonful of porridge, dipped it into the cream, then ate it; this was to keep the porridge hot'; 'my grandmother had a glass eye, blue, almost like her other one, and this made her especially vulnerable and precious to me'; 'there was a poor boy, named Roustain, the dirtiest and raggediest of us all, who was really too big for Primer Class and had to walk a long way to school, when he came at all'. (How much more raggy 'raggediest' is than the alternative 'most raggy'!) On the other hand, there is the artist's conscience, the duty to make sense of it all, the pressure of form as Henry James apprehended it: 'really, universally, relations stop nowhere, and the exquisite problem of the artist is eternally but to draw, by a geometry of his own, the circle within which they shall happily *appear* to do so.' In 'Primer Class', Elizabeth Bishop's solution to these two conflicting artistic demands of unfettered inclusiveness and the desire for form is arrived at without illusion or falsification. There is no geometry, only arithmetic. The memoir's thrillingly rich detail exists within formal brackets: it begins and ends with arithmetic, the memory of 'mysterious numbers, the columns, that impressed me so much – a mystery I never solved when I went to Primer Class in Nova Scotia!' For Elizabeth Bishop, experience will never add up – and she concludes, stubbornly, beautifully, emblematically, as she began: 'it was utterly incomprehensible. Those mysterious numbers.'

After her father's death, her disturbed mother was committed to an institution and Elizabeth, after a delay, transplanted brusquely to Boston where her paternal grandparents lived. There the manners were different – formal, unquestionable, without true tenderness. Though she is unwilling to criticize explicitly, her grandfather is an immediately recognizable egotist: 'now he descended, god-like and swearing, swept Grandma out of the way, and wedged himself in the lower berth'. This behaviour on the Pullman is her introduction to Boston manners and things do not change significantly: the servants are in a state of permanent revolution; when the cook leaves, Grandma cooks (appallingly) and her grandfather goes off to an hotel. At first, the young orphan is intimidated and submissive to her new role, her only reaction a series of psychosomatic illnesses. Gradually, though, she realizes the absurdity and inadequacy of this new social code. The moment of truth occurs one day when Beppo, the Boston bull terrier, punishes himself for an offence against propriety: 'when he was "bad", he was punished by being put in a large closet off the sewing room and left there, out of things, for half an hour. Once when I was playing with him, he disappeared and would not answer my calls. Finally he was found, seated gloomily by himself in the closet facing the wall. He was punishing *himself*. We later found a smallish puddle of vomit in the conservatory. No one had ever before punished him for his attacks of gastritis, naturally; it was all his own idea, his peculiar Bostonian sense of guilt.' And what was Elizabeth Bishop punishing herself for? What was her own idea of herself that created the long series of illnesses?

I don't think that she ever knew, which is why this memoir was not included in her projected list of contents for a collected prose. The answer, however, isn't far to seek. As ever, it is to do with manners. On that Pullman, her grandma introduced her to the certainties that were to be imposed on her: 'Yes, I was beginning to enjoy myself a little, if only Grandma hadn't such a confusing way of talking. It was almost as if we were playing house. She would speak of "grandma" and "little girls" and "fathers" and "being good" – things I had never before considered in the abstract, or rarely in the third person. In particular, there seemed to be much, much more to being a "little girl" than I had realised.' Her failure to be this 'little girl' was what she was punishing herself for. And the memoir ends with a prose version of her extraordinary poem, 'In the Waiting Room', where she encounters, not the social fiction, but her true self as she felt herself to be, and it disgusts her: ' "You are not Beppo, or the chestnut tree, or Emma, you are *you* and you are going to be *you* forever." It was like coasting downhill, this thought, only much worse, and it quickly smashed into a tree. *Why* was I a human being?' Like Marianne Moore, she could not be 'in the third person'. She was rather the first person singular and horrified by her singularity. At seven years of age, Elizabeth Bishop could match Hopkins's 'selfyeast of spirit a dull dough sours'.

In 'The USA School of Writing', she continues to examine her own queer individuality, stimulated by her bogus identity as Mr Margolies, a previous instructor whose role she has inherited. Again, the conflict is between her own free-floating uncertainty about life and a colleague's Marxist panacea – another rigid code she cannot accept, preferring instead a bogus association with anarchism, though temperamentally she belongs nowhere. And 'The Baptism', an early story, examines the penalties exacted by certainty. Quietly, firmly, she insists on the absurdity of belief. Lucy, unlike her sisters, wishes to join the Baptist Church. They are Presbyterians, unfanatical, but not untouched by theological pedantry and its attendant callousness: 'her news was that her sister's baby had died the day before, although they had done everything. She and Emma, Flora, and Lucy discussed infant damnation at some length.' Finally, Lucy dies of her religious literalness: 'but a problem came up that she had not considered. She now believed ardently in the use of total immersion as practised by the Baptists, according to their conception of the methods of John the Baptist. She could not join without that, and the river, of course, was frozen over. She would have to wait until the ice went out.' She does, but the immersion kills her.

'The Baptism' is an uncharacteristically bitter story, a settling of scores with these score-keepers who can coolly tot up a baby's chance of damnation. Eventually Elizabeth Bishop repudiated it: 'I published a very bad short story a year or two after I first knew the Moores and I was reprimanded by both of them for having used the word "spit".' In his introduction, Robert Giroux incorrectly identifies the offending story as 'The Farmer's Children' – an implacable masterpiece which he stigmatizes as 'more conventional and sentimental than anything else she wrote'. 'The Farmer's Children' is devoid of sentimentality, full of controlled sentiment, even better than the more famous 'In the Village' and deserves to take its place, alongside Kipling's ' "They" ' and

Joyce's 'The Dead', as one of the greatest short stories of the twentieth century. Mr Giroux has been misled by the reference to spitting (which occurs in both stories). 'The Farmer's Children' was published in 1948, long after Elizabeth Bishop met the Moores in 1934, whereas 'The Baptism' was published in 1937, with this brilliant aside as the immersion takes place: 'one boy or young man, of course, always dared to spit over the railing.'

Like 'The Baptism', 'In Prison' and 'The Sea & the Shore' are apprentice work, but they disclose the same concerns – the randomness of experience and the desire for certainty. 'The Sea & the Shore' is an account of Edwin Boomer's life as a litter collector. He clears the beach of its daily detritus of newsprint and is insanely absorbed in its classification. Three categories present themselves in his effort to make sense of what he finds: 'everything that seemed to be about himself'; 'stories about other people that caught his fancy, whose careers he followed from day to day in newspapers and fragments of books and letters; and whose further adventures he was always watching out for'; and, finally, 'the items he could not understand at all, that bewildered him completely but at the same time interested him so much that he saved them to read. These he tried, almost frantically, to fit into first one, then the other, of the two categories.' Elizabeth Bishop's 'The Bight' is her mature treatment of this theme, a theme which also generates 'In Prison' – a story related in a bizarrely frigid nineteenth-century patois, whose narrator is eager to embrace the certainties, the rigid rules of penal confinement.

Elizabeth Bishop's attitude towards her experience is best summed up, not in her own words, but in a telling quotation from a letter from Hopkins to Robert Bridges which crops up in her preface to 'The Diary of "Helena Morley" '. Hopkins is exercised by the bristling technicality of *Two Years Before the Mast*, 'which I most carefully go over and even enjoy but cannot understand'. For Hopkins, 'the charm and the main point', even of terrible things like flogging, are this: '*it happened.*' Elizabeth Bishop's poetry and prose are filled with things that have happened, things which she enjoys but cannot understand – things she will not pretend to understand. No writer is further from glibness. 'The Farmer's Children' demonstrates her quiet pessimism and its terrible clarity.

This story concerns two step-children, Emerson and Cato, who have to guard the equipment in distant barn by sleeping there overnight, while their father and Judd, the hired man, are on an expedition to the town. The boys have done this several times before, with Cato always fantasizing the two of them as Hansel and Gretel, though the step-mother isn't wicked, merely off-hand, a little short-tempered and preoccupied with her own smaller children. An early sentence whispers horribly to the reader: 'most of these facts later appeared in the newspapers.' It is like a brief glimpse of a razor. There follows a miraculous, methodical inventory, an inspired double-counting of the small-change of childish existence. Nothing is skimped. We are plunged into the intricacies of a game of shipwreck so graphic that it ends in tears. Every item on the supper table is described from a child's point of view. As Cato steals bread to lay a trail of crumbs, 'his thoughts sounded loud and ominous to him'. The boys dress warmly for the barn. A sister has maliciously hidden a pair of gloves. He knows by her sly look. On the way to the barn, the two boys discuss a bicycle seen in a hardware store window. They invent and reject various implausible routes to ownership. They climb a telegraph pole and, listening to the wires, discuss the fate of bees in winter-time. The cold weather forces itself on them as a topic of conversation – whether it is too cold to snow. Finally, crumbs dropped in a trail, they reach the barn where, failing to find the blankets, they snuggle under the hay. As Cato is falling asleep he thinks 'the disks of the harrow looked like the side – those shields hung over the side – of a Viking ship'. Then Elizabeth Bishop simply and swiftly wipes out all this accumulated detail which, as it piles up, makes that early sentence fade to a mote in the middle distance.

He turned to Emerson and called his name, but Emerson only moaned in his sleep. So he fitted his knees into the hollows at the back of his brother's and hugged him tightly round the waist.

At noon the next day their father found them in this position.

The story was in all the newspapers, on the front page of local ones, dwindling as it traveled over the countryside to short paragraphs on middle pages when it got as far as each coast. The farmer grieved wildly for a year; for some reason, one expression he gave to his feelings was to fire Judd.

Reading this unflinching, stoical envoi, I was reminded of Elizabeth Bishop's account of learning to write in 'Primer Class': 'what I liked best about the slate was washing it off at the kitchen sink, or in the watering trough, and then watching it dry. It dried like clouds, and then the very last wet streak would grow tinier and tinier, and thinner and thinner; then suddenly it was gone and the slate was pale gray again and dry, dry, dry.' 'The Farmer's Children' shares the same lovingly observed minor events and the same remorselessly blank conclusion. By comparison, Beckett looks a little mannered, a little over-insistent, a touch melodramatic.

Miss Bishop's artistic manners are impeccable. Her art is the art of refinement, or precision. Somehow it is typical that she should write not about the famous Lady of Shalott, but about her more obscure relation, the Gentleman of Shalott. On that Pullman to Boston, she is sick: 'I threw up, yellow, into something I referred to . . . as a "hopper".' That 'yellow' is priceless, funny, and an example of good manners – even vomit has its individuality and deserves its share of attention. As a writer, she sometimes waited for years for exactly the right word, having resolved 'never to try to publish anything until I thought I'd done my best with it, no matter how many years it took – or never to publish at all'. At a time when, in English poetry, we are often asked to admire the agonized perfectionism of a Geoffrey Hill or a Donald Davie, with its inbuilt grunts of effort, it is worth considering the perfection, *tout simple*, of Elizabeth Bishop. 'Why had no one ever written about things in this clear and dazzling way before?' she asked herself on first reading Marianne Moore. It applies equally to her own work. The critic, weighing words, testing them, is banished from the final draft. She does not agonize in her work about her work: she simply gets it breathtakingly right. Nor does she bore us, profound though she is, by insisting on her profundity. The whole operation is made to seem as natural as reaching for the right fork.

It seems entirely right that, at their first meeting, Robert Giroux should have noticed 'her excellent manners'. Now may we have the collected letters, please.

A Note on Elizabeth Bishop's Poetry

There is pain but no turmoil in Elizabeth Bishop's measured work. As she wryly acknowledged, 'one almost envies those Russian poets a bit – who feel they are so important, and perhaps are . . .' Yet she was a great poet, too, of a different kind. It is not to Akhmatova that one turns for suitable comparisons but to Chekhov, who was a qualified physician. In her poetry, Elizabeth Bishop examines life, even in extremity, with the calm and precision of a gifted family doctor. Of a fish she has caught, she writes:

> I thought of the coarse white flesh
> packed in like feathers,
> the big bones and the little bones,
> the dramatic reds and blacks
> of his shiny entrails,
> and the pink swim-bladder
> like a big peony.

Unhurried, methodical, humane, she pronounces a true but merciful verdict on our precarious existence. In this case: 'And I let the fish go.' Few poets are more alert to the humble accessories that surround tragedy. For a poet, her bedside manners are impeccable. Uniquely among poets, she seems to listen rather than talk, however brilliantly. She is patient with her patients and attentive to her subjects in an exemplary way. She misses nothing:

> The crooked
> towel-covered table
> bears a can of talcum
> and five pasteboard boxes
>   of little pills,
> most half-crystallized.

In its unemphatic way, this makes over to us the poverty of illness and its circumscribed concerns.

All poets have a distinct poetic personality if they are any good. It is an unlooked-for bonus that Elizabeth Bishop's should be so attractive, though one could forgive any poet a lot who was able to write so memorably. Of a map: 'the names of seashore towns run out to sea.' Of fireflies: 'exactly like the bubbles in champagne.' Of a yacht: 'the social being, / that danced on the endless polished floor, / stepped and side-stepped like Fred Astaire.' There is so much that one simply wants to quote: 'the lint / of the waterfalls cling', 'light and nervous water hold / their interview', 'the still explosions on the rocks, / the lichens . . .'

These are brilliant images that any poet would give his left anapaest for and I had always thought of Elizabeth Bishop as a writer for whom images were common currency. Reading *The Complete Poems*, however, makes it clear that she has a plain style in which the images appear like sovereigns. Her great gifts lie elsewhere. She takes her time in a way that no other poet (except Frost) would dare and her best effects come from a fidelity to experience that requires patient exposition:

> I went down to the river
> and the moon was burning bright
> as the gasoline-lamp mantle
> with the flame turned up too high,
> just before it begins to scorch.
> I went down to the river.

'I went down to the river'. Few poets would have the courage to repeat themselves so straightforwardly, but it is a trick Elizabeth

Bishop brings off again and again: 'At four o'clock / in the gun-metal blue dark / we hear the first crow of the first cock / just below / the gun-metal blue window / and immediately there is an echo . . .' The diction here mirrors the identical cries of the roosters, but it also insists in a general way that if a word ('gun-metal') was true once, it can be true twice.

Plain truth is something we find more frequently in Elizabeth Bishop than in most poets. When her friend Robert Lowell was cluttering his poetry with Calvinist theology and Catholic impedimenta, she was altogether less grandiose, less obscure and more frightening. For her, the world is worthy of celebration, yet has a dark side we can all understand, which she looks at unflinchingly. In 'Sleeping on the Ceiling', we accept her fantasy:

> It is so peaceful on the ceiling!
> It is the Place de la Concorde.
> The little crystal chandelier
> is off, the fountain is in the dark.

Yet the horrors are quickly imagined:

> We must go under the wallpaper
> to meet the insect gladiator,
> to battle with a net and trident,
> and leave the fountain and the square.

Elizabeth Bishop is not afraid of simple fear. Her famous poem, 'The Man-Moth', is more than a beautiful fantasy based on a newspaper misprint for 'mammoth'. It describes brilliantly the timorous side we all possess, isolated from all the social mechanisms by which we normally survive. 'But what the Man-Moth fears most he must do': in our little way, we all know this to be so. Elizabeth Bishop, whose world is ravishing but without a metaphysical system, reminds us how brave we often are. She is a doctor who can tell us we have to die — without anyone weeping. Her wonderful poetry is full of prescriptions for facing things with our eyes open. There is something 'tonic and fortifying', to use Arnold's words, and there is something extraordinarily gay and unexpected on every page. One last quotation, about what it would be like not to have travelled:

> And never to have had to listen to rain
> so much like politicians' speeches . . .

The Life of Auden

'To speak phrenologically,' remarked De Quincey of his relationship with Wordsworth, 'the organ of veneration must have received an inordinate development in my case.' Not that its growth impeded his candour – 'the Wordsworthian legs were certainly not ornamental, and it was really a pity, as I agreed with a lady in thinking, that he had not another pair for evening dress parties'. Stephen Spender's absorbing collection of reminiscences* shows a similar mixture of *estime de succès*, tender reverence and frank observation. If De Quincey can present his hero cutting the pages of Burke with a buttery knife, if Crabb Robinson can venture that Wordsworth is 'sloven & his manners are not prepossing [*sic*], his features are large & course [*sic*]', Robert Craft can match them.

His Auden inattentively bolts Stravinsky's carefully selected Château Margaux, is 'shabby, dandruff-speckled, and slightly peculiar-smelling', and turns up to rehearsals in Venice wearing 'a white linen suit, polka-dotted in front with Chianti stains'. And, in Orlan Fox's memoir, Auden emerges naked from his ritual bubble-bath to sniff disapprovingly at his guests for prolonging dinner beyond the sacred hour of 9.30. Observations like these do not, of course, illuminate the poetry, the penetralia of the mystery, but neither do they damage Auden in the way he evidently feared. His friends have calculated finely in their disclosures which, if they are often trivial, never trivialize. They

*W. H. Auden: A Tribute edited by Stephen Spender, Weidenfeld and Nicolson.

commemorate those 'little, nameless, unremembered acts' that (to adapt Wordsworth) form a portion of any man's life. There is something endearing in bizarre, intimate facts like Auden's anagram for T. S. Eliot ('litotes'), or Pound's version of Robert Bridges ('Rabbit Britches'). Their frailness needs no apology.

Together, Professor Spender's contributors create a fully human portrait, moles and all – though one of them is mislocated by Cyril Connolly, as the excellent photographs testify. It is a *moving* picture, in every sense: there is the physical progression from the brilliant youth with 'egg-white skin and straight yellow hair', via a middle period when he resembled 'a big, mad, white rabbit', to the final 'wedding cake left out in the rain'. There is also the psychological change, from the extrovert spell-binder, 'Uncle Wiz', to the grumpy, touching, withdrawn and boring old man.

'Auden . . . Auden . . . Auden', writes Nicholas Nabokov, 'getting older, crankier, lonelier, cracking the same jokes . . . Repeating himself'. Nothing could be less hostile, or more baffled, than Nabokov's concluding paragraph lamenting the change. The high-flyer of his generation is, as it were, a wrecked jumbo jet – overtaken by mental fatigue, fuelled by vodka-martinis, with the radio still crackling on amid the debris. As Eliot's lady remarks, 'our beginnings never know our ends'. Auden's beginnings were prodigiously ordinary. A scholarship in Natural Sciences brought him to Christ Church, Oxford, and from this point a genuine uniqueness and a certain bogus eccentricity begin to show.

He was oblivious to Betjeman's snob friends. He contradicted Betjeman's poetic preferences and lent him an unreturned book on sanitation, soil-pipes and domestic privies. Nature as such did not interest him, unless it was hallowed by a patina of decrepitude, or had some faint human significance: Michael Yates remembers Auden comparing stretches of Icelandic lava to 'the uninteresting and useless debris of an orgy'. Later, this quirkiness showed itself as a frank boredom with the natural world – 'A *walk?* What on earth *for?*' One thinks of Dr Johnson drawing down the blinds of his carriage.

The shabby dress, the period when Auden was (in his own words) 'stripped of self-control and self-respect', the bossiness, the monologues, the use of nature only to carry moral ideas – these things, too, remind one of Johnson. But, most of all, Johnson comes to mind in Auden's semi-humorous rudeness and his friends' unflagging delight in it. As a guest, he was liable to get up during the night to scoff a leg of lamb and all the cold potatoes. He liked weight on him while he slept and calmly took down curtains and pictures to pile on his bed. Once, he even took up a stair-carpet. Arriving late down to breakfast at Gabriel Carrit's, he announced 'in his flattest voice, "Mrs Carrit, my tea tastes like tepid piss" '. She loved him for it, as all his friends did. Much later, we hear of him informing a crowd of dons that 'everyone pees in his bath' – another example of deadpan buffoonery designed to call forth the love he so much needed. 'They loved me!' Stephen Spender reports him exclaiming after a poetry reading in Milwaukee. But by this time, Auden's appetite for affection seems to have increased, while his methods of gaining it declined, rigidified and grew charmless. Increasingly, he became the slave of his eccentricities.

The zest and effervescence – encapsulated in Cyril Connolly's vignette of Auden impulsively ordering Spanish champagne in Valencia – gradually evaporated. After this first meeting in Spain, Connolly was so mesmerized by the poet and his homosexuality that he dreamed of him naked to the waist, indicating two small breasts – 'Well, Cyril, how do you like my lemons?' In its way, this represents a peak in his ability to fascinate.

America seems to mark the turning point, the inauguration of the long change. Some of the clowning remained. Hannah Arendt relates how, sometime in the late fifties, his trousers wore so thin they split from top to bottom. At forty-five, his uppers crashed ('my dear') into a neighbour's teacup when he blew out the flame under a silver kettle. Ursula Niebuhr remembers him stalking her roast beef, asking for 'the smackers' (dollars) before delivering a lecture, and camping up his pleasure in having an article accepted by *Theology*: 'nothing could so delight Mama who has, I hope by now, reached the sixth form in purgatory. I hope, though, she isn't boring her fellow penitents with the news.' As a major in US Intelligence, he shambled round in carpet slippers, failed to wear his regulation helmet liner, and drove like a maniac.

To an outsider, it is strange that so few of his friends question the motive behind the eccentricities they catalogue so evocatively. They present oddities as involuntary and inevitable *données*. But surely, at some deep level, even Auden's notorious rudeness and his despotic directives – go easy with the lavatory paper; bring your own cigarettes – were efforts to be *interesting*. Lurking somewhere was the demand for love, and the fear of being boring. Somehow, though, in later life, he was less and less able to work the trick to his own satisfaction. His many friends went on loving him in spite of his cantankerous behaviour: Auden evidently wished to be loved because of it. At the touch of pity he withdrew inside the famous carapace.

The most telling anecdote in this book is by Cyril Connolly. He had a difficult relationship with his father, and Auden advised him to take a tough line with the old boy. 'The people just batten on one, real emotional harpies, they've got to be taught a lesson. Stand up to him, make him see you don't need him any more.' Connolly took the advice and, after lunch, did not invite his father home for brandy and further conversation: 'I bade him an abrupt farewell and gave the driver his address. Clutching his two thick cherrywood sticks with the rubber ferrules, his legs crossed, his feet in pumps, for owing to arthritis he could not stoop to do up laces, he fingered his grey moustache while a tear trickled down his cheek. I don't know which of us felt more unhappy.' We might condemn the young Auden ('charming but ruthless') more roundly if the later Auden had not applied the prescription so ruthlessly in his own case. He never permitted the tear. He gave the address to the driver himself, and went home to the 'House' to die – a burden on no one. Like his own Prospero, he may have thought that:

> Over there, maybe, it won't seem quite so dreadful
> Not to be interesting any more, but an old man
> Just like other old men, with eyes that water

Easily in the wind, and a head that nods in the sunshine,
Forgetful, maladroit, a little grubby,
And to like it. When the servants settle me into a chair
In some well-sheltered corner of the garden,
And arrange my muffler and rugs, shall I ever be able
To stop myself from telling them what I am doing –
Sailing alone, out over seventy thousand fathoms – ?

In the event, he seems not to have told even his friends. They had
to guess.

Auden and Religion

'At thirteen I was confirmed. To say that shortly afterwards I lost my faith would be melodramatic and false. I simply lost interest.' Auden's reversion to Christianity was not sudden or spectacular. Over a decade, random experiences, tentative in themselves, accumulated until they took on a single meaning. He was led to Christianity as gradually as Darwin uncovered the trail that ended in the theory of evolution: hints and clues created a problem; the problem resolved itself into a pattern of solution. Finally, Auden was able to say, 'I believe again' – with all that statement's implied advance on the unreflective acceptance of a traditional Christianity which says, 'We believe still.'

In 1933, he experienced a vision of Agape. Sitting with four colleagues, male and female, at the prep school where he taught, Auden felt himself invaded by a power. 'For the first time in my life I knew exactly – because, thanks to the power, I was doing it – what it means to love one's neighbour as oneself . . . I knew that, so long as I was possessed by this spirit, it would be literally impossible for me deliberately to injure another human being.' Unlike the mystic vision of Eros described by Auden in his introduction to *The Protestant Mystics*, this vision was completely asexual. It was also temporary and lasted for two days before it finally faded.

Then, in Spain, during the Civil War, he was surprised to find himself seriously disturbed by the compulsory closure of the churches, realizing that they were more important to him than he had previously supposed. Shortly afterwards, in 1937, he met

349

Charles Williams in a publisher's office, 'and for the first time in my life felt myself in the presence of personal sanctity'. Williams, without discussing religious matters at all, not only impressed Auden by his aura of goodness, but also probably dissipated the poet's early prejudice that 'people only love God when no one else will love them'. As a result, Auden began experimental visits to church, and started to read Kierkegaard, whose Christianity seemed appealingly bohemian and non-institutional.

More, Kierkegaard's writings were to Auden what spectacles are to the short-sighted. Auden's problems took on shape, outline and sharpness. In particular, the three Kierkegaardian categories (aesthetic, ethical and religious) organized within a system Auden's jumble of apparently heterogeneous worries about the nature of evil. According to Kierkegaard, if a man lives aesthetically, he exists without any moral system – good and evil, happiness and unhappiness, are irreversible *données* of chance or fate. 'There is no one to blame', to quote from Auden's 'Memorial for the City': man is either fortunate or unfortunate.

On the other hand, if he lives ethically, man adopts a rationalist attitude to life which bears no true relationship to empirical fact. Evil is the product of ignorance, the ethical attitude argues, and once the Good is known, man must obey the categorical imperative. Each of these prima-facie dry abstractions, and their ultimate inadequacy, was fleshed out from Auden's personal experience. 'It is probably true', he wrote, 'that nobody was ever genuinely converted to Christianity who had not lost his nerve, either because he was aesthetically unfortunate or because he was ethically powerless, i.e., unable to do what he knew to be his duty. A great deal of Kierkegaard's work is addressed to the man who has already become uneasy about himself.'

Auden had lost his nerve. In his personal life, at this time, he was 'aesthetically unfortunate', 'forced to know in person what it is like to feel oneself the prey of demonic powers, in both the Greek and the Christian sense, stripped of self-control and self-respect, behaving like a ham actor in a Strindberg play'. For this inner evil, there was no explanation – as an unbeliever, Auden had to accept it as a condition of life.

Moreover, he was 'ethically powerless': in the public sphere, the advent of the Nazis had destroyed his faith in the ethical imperative. Hitler and the German people were neither ignorant nor barbaric, and yet they could openly deny the Good – the self-evident tenets of liberal humanism. The Nazis made it clear beyond doubt that the moral imperative was by no means categorical. Kierkegaard offered an explanation of evil, and an alternative way of living, which resolved Auden's dilemma. Man could live religiously – the third Kierkegaardian category.

In the first two categories, the aesthetic and the ethical, man is effectively deprived of freedom. He cannot be genuinely evil, that is, *choose* not to be good. The former tells man he is what he is. The latter tells man that if he is evil, he is merely ignorant of the Good, and that, if he is not ignorant, he must obey the categorical imperative. But the religious view allows mankind free will, and, from this assumption, it follows that man may know what is good and choose the evil. Why? Kierkegaard answers that man's pride desires to assert his autonomy by an act of rebellion against his relationship with God. In this way, Auden explains the Fall as an act of pride, 'a wish to become like God, to derive his existence from himself, and not through sensuality or any of the desires of his "nature" '.

In retrospect, Auden saw that earlier influences on his thought were all Christian heresies. Marx's classless society after revolution was a version of the Apocalypse, where the last should be first, in a community of total harmony. D. H. Lawrence sought salvation through the flesh. Freudian psychoanalysis saw evil as repressed desires in the limbo of the unconscious, which the analyst would release as Christ harrowed hell. All, to the Christian Auden, were rough prototypes. Poetically, however, the transitions were less easy.

Audenland was already a going concern before Auden was converted to Christianity. The poet's 'secondary world' was a mosaic, constructed from an idiosyncratic selection of features from the 'primary world, the given world outside ourselves in which we are born, live, love, hate and die'. Glaciers menaced its domestic warmth. Defunct lead mines with arcane, rusting machinery kept their secrets. Dogs pricked their ears uneasily. Secret agents brooded over inevitable fates. Leaders went to their doom. Fairy tales and nursery rhymes acquired a queer menacing note. The detective story and the thriller took on an obscure mythic significance. All in all, it was as if something had gone badly wrong with the *Boy's Own Paper* – expeditions were bound to fail; crucial boats were inexplicably missed. Audenland was, in fact, primarily a place of unhappy endings: the world of innocent adventure seen under dream conditions. To the insular, essentially English, coherent ethos, Auden added the disruptive quality of nightmare. The cosy, private myth is wrecked by the private horror, the intimate angst.

Consider, for example, Auden's ballad, 'O What is that Sound?' It begins as a celebration of the redcoats: 'O what is that sound which so thrills the ear?' But, by the finale, we are far from such innocence, beyond even the pat ironies that the general debt to Housman might suggest. The lover deserts. The soldiers break down the door:

> Their boots are heavy on the floor
> And their eyes are burning.

The imaginative point is not that the traditional soldier has, in the twentieth century, become a species of secret police. The suggestion is there, but ultimately, the soldiers remain a blank space which Auden (like Henry James in *The Turn of the Screw*) compels one to fill in with a private horror. It is a ballad viewed under dream conditions: ordinary ballads carry a complete narrative, but Auden's has only a vestigial beginning and a truncated end. Like 'The Ancient Mariner', it exploits a bizarre poetry of the inexplicit and private, in a genre which is normally explicit. It is a proto-dream expressing angst and, at the moment of crisis, we cannot wake up.

After his conversion, Auden, like his Melville, 'sailed into an extraordinary mildness': 'Goodness existed: that was the new knowledge.' However, it was commonplace knowledge, far removed from the private knowledge on which his poetic temperament had previously thrived. Christianity offered public symbols. Further, it tempered proximate suffering with a final happy ending. In other words, it ran completely counter to Auden's natural gifts. At his worst, therefore, he can manage only the feeblest echoes of Eliot ('For the garden is the only place there is, but you will not find it / Until you have looked for it everywhere and found nowhere that is not a desert') and Yeats ('Self-educated William Blake / Who threw his spectre in the lake, / Broke off relations in a curse / With the Newtonian Universe'). The matter was further complicated by his theological scruples. Auden was made uneasy by poetry like Donne's and Hopkins's which expressed 'a poet's personal feelings of religious devotion or penitence'. Thus he eliminated a possible poetry of private doubt and faith.

On the other hand, one might expect Auden, as a Kierkegaardian, to revel in the angst caused by man's realization of his metaphysical freedom. Actually, he has only mixed success, since Kierkegaard provides him with an explanation. Angst is no longer an inexplicable fact, a disturbing centre without a circumference. The compasses are there to hand, as is the compass – expeditions are only temporarily lost, and the poetry is curiously sapped:

> Tonight a scrambling decade ends
> And strangers, enemies and friends
> Stand once more puzzled underneath
> The signpost on the barren heath
> Where the mountain track divides
> To silent valleys on all sides,
> Endeavouring to decipher what
> Is written on it but cannot,
> Nor guess in what direction lies
> The overhanging precipice.

What inert stuff it is, this imitation Auden, rambling on until it finally bumps against the real thing:

> And intense in the mountain frost
> The heavy breathing of the lost.

Other once-potent properties reappear in the later poetry, sagging visibly. Satan, for instance, in Auden's early demonology was an unspecified personification – the Supreme Antagonist, the Adversary, the death-wish and defeatist in us all. After 1940, the Devil is still interior, but tricked out with traditional props, verging on a comfortably baroque caricature. In 'New Year Letter', Auden patronizes him affably, with the detached urbanity of Browning's Blougram. He becomes 'poor cheated MEPHISTOPHELES', working against his own interest, pushing us 'into grace'.

Lead mines return, too. In the early 'Watershed', they were 'an industry already comatose', whereas in 'The Prophets' they foreshadow a love of God: 'all their lack of answer whispered "Wait" '. Contrast this with the earlier unsettling repetition of

> Go home, now, stranger, proud of your young stock,
> Stranger, turn back again, frustrate and vexed:
> This land, cut off, will not communicate . . .

This hostile landscape eventually became (in 'Horae Canonicae') a snug, antiquarian paradise of 'beam-engines' and 'overshot waterwheels', and antithesis of the technocrat's chill, modern New Jerusalem. Bereft of danger, its comfy qualities lend themselves to the guided tour. The later poetry has its charm, but it is markedly inferior. In 'Memorial for the City', the effective passages are not those which summarize church history with febrile internal rhyming. They occur in the opening where Auden sketches in an extra-Christian view of history: 'The soldiers fire, the mayor bursts into tears.' This is authentic – the vivid, unexplained fragment of the young Auden, at once particular and private.

Whatever compensations and comfort Christianity brought to Auden as a human being, it eventually became something inimical to his poetic gifts. It may well be that the greatest Christian writers have been those who were most disturbed about their faith.

Isaac Bashevis Singer

In his novel, *Enemies*, Isaac Bashevis Singer has the character Masha interrupt one of her typically headlong speeches with the words, ' "Why am I bringing this up? Oh, yes!" ' And she is away again.

That fractional hesitation is so true, one can almost see her lost thread, the wispy end of it moistened between her lips, before she continues to stitch up her case against a God who can countenance suffering – a theme which is central to this gathering of three previously published autobiographical reminiscences, with a new preface, under the general title, *Love and Exile*.* The pause is a wonderful touch – as life-like as the moment in Chekhov's 'My Life', when the provincial hero first kisses Masha and scratches his cheek on her hat-pin; as accurately set down as the faintly ridiculous turmoil of Katya in Chekhov's 'A Dreary Story', to the misery of which is added the ironical observation that 'her hat falls off and hangs bobbing on its elastic'. In each case, as Singer states in *Love and Exile*, the power of the writing is located not in language but in life itself: 'I had made up my mind a long time ago that the creative powers of literature lie not in the forced originality produced by variations of style and word machinations but in the countless situations life keeps creating, especially in the queer complications between man and woman. For a writer, they are potential treasures that could never be

*Love and Exile by Isaac Bashevis Singer, Jonathan Cape.

356

exhausted, while all innovations in language soon become clichés.'

Every writer will recognize the force and justice of this fiat. Literature is the great enemy of literature. This is a sub-theme of *Love and Exile* which has been largely ignored. From his earliest days, Singer could see the shortcomings of Yiddish literature. The young apprentice could see that the spirit-level had been tampered with, so that the higgledy-piggledy raw material of Jewish life, with its whores, pimps, thieves, devils, demons, dybbuks, became artificially straightened and straitened: 'Yiddish literature with its sentimentality and slow pace wasn't ready for such a transformation. The same writers who told astounding stories at the Writers' Club trembled the moment they took pen in hand lest, God forbid, they slip into melodrama.' Throughout these memoirs, Singer is aware of the tyranny exerted by literature on life, of the censorship that imposes itself in the act of writing. When Singer believes he has missed a crucial meeting in Toronto, a meeting which should ensure that he will not be deported to Poland, the phone in his hotel room suddenly rings, telling him his vital contact is now in the lobby. He hurries from his room, but the lift has simply vanished. He cannot see it for panic: 'the writer within me observed, Literature hasn't even touched on the fantastic tricks that sick nerves play on people.' Well, it has now. On board ship to America, the young and disoriented Singer hesitantly leaves the sanctuary of his cabin in search of food – and immediately forgets its number in his state of stress, remembers it, and forgets it again. In Singer, the mind is not so much a servant as an absent-minded despot full of arbitrary imperatives, not all of them comic. Singer is wry about the cabin number but conveys the sick resignation that he may have to spend the entire voyage walking the corridors because none of the staff speaks Yiddish.

Sex is another facet of life which Singer introduced into Yiddish literature, to the dismay of his Yiddish readers – dismay because sex, as Singer reports it, is far too like the real thing to produce anything in the reader other than a certain uneasy recognition. We don't like being caught with our trousers down and Singer is an expert at showing the power of matter over mind. In his story, 'The Destruction of Kreshev', the section called 'Secrets of the Chamber' is a disturbing examination of the role that pornographic fantasy plays in extended sexual relationships. There, the Evil One is blamed, but it is clear from these memoirs that Singer was writing out of his own experience, driven by the facts of his own life. In America he meets Nesha, whose husband Boris has committed suicide. Her loss is paralleled in Singer's life by the death of Gina, an older woman with unruly sexual gifts. Gina is, in Bellow's phrase, a 'sack-artist'. But, then, so is Nesha: 'while Nesha was with me I lost all my worries, all the fears. I called her Gina and she called me Boris. We played with the idea that by some cabbalistic combinations of letters we were able to resurrect Boris and Gina for the time of our love game and all four of us indulged together in a mystic orgy where bodies and souls copulated and where sex play and heavenly knowledge became identical.' After reading this and altering the scenario a little, you wonder if everyone isn't a sack-artist in fact – for this is, I submit, an accurate picture of the vivid commerce between sexual partners.

Only Ian McEwan and Joyce (in *Exiles*, as well as *Ulysses*) have so faithfully mapped the trickling subways and foisty culs-de-sac which supply us with sexual imagery and excitement. Joyce, writing to his brother Stanislaus, was confident that he could generalize from a sample of one. Singer is diffident but equally firm: 'somewhere I had the suspicion that what was going on in my head went on in many other heads as well.'

And, of course, literature is the enemy of this candour: 'in the novels I had read in my young days, the lovers were one hundred percent monogamous, certain of their love,' Singer observes; 'it occurred to me more than once to write about myself as I really was, but I was convinced that the readers, the publishers, and the critics (especially the Yiddish ones) would consider me a pornographer, a contriver, mad.' At the divorce court of his rabbi father, Singer had already learned that 'anything is possible between a man and a woman' and he is quick to relate this to literature's inadequacy: 'powerful affection sometimes went hand in hand with shameless betrayal. I often heard critics employ such words as "implausible" and "unrealistic", but I learned that many things that some consider impossible occur daily.'

Sex is the most striking example of literature's blurred representation of life, but Singer finds literature wanting in other respects. Having heard Nesha's life story and divulged the intimate details of his own life, Singer looks at his wrist-watch: 'a half hour had not yet passed since we were introduced. The writer in me has often pondered about how quickly things happen in stories and how slowly in life. But it isn't always so, I said to myself. Sometimes life is quicker than the quickest description.' The problematic congress of fact with fiction affects all literature, since literature at once enables us to see and at the same time interposes its threadbare archetypes: 'from reading the world literature I had realised that the Gentile writers too lacked the perception to describe the epoch in which they lived. They were also rooted in a literary tradition which discouraged them from writing what their eyes saw.' Or felt. One of the strengths of Singer's sexual writing is that he is true not only to the wilder reaches of the imagination, but also to the subsequent mental detumescence – the world of underpants, retraction, pragmatism, hat-pins and bobbing hats.

Singer is a great writer, but *Love and Exile*, despite its occasional power, is not a great book. It relies too much on the axiom I quoted earlier that not style but situation is 'inexhaustible'. Without style, 'the queer complications between man and woman' are not enough. They can be exhausted. Take the brilliant pause with which I began this essay. Why did I bring that up? On page 67 of *Love and Exile*, Gina is telling Singer about her astral experiences: ' "Why am I telling you all this? Yes, to prove that I don't lose consciousness so easily." ' On page 124, another woman, Stefa, is describing her love-life to Singer: ' "Why am I telling you all this?" ' Ship-board for America, Singer meets Zosia, who runs through her curriculum vitae, only to pause with ' "Why am I telling you all this?" ' The truth of

Singer's observation is true only once. Situations, like stylistic innovations, can become clichés, if the writer's accountancy is slipshod. Life is allowed to repeat itself, but literature is not, and Singer, his translator, or his editor should have picked this up. Why am I telling you this? Because in all his work, even the best, Singer is overindulgent towards repetition and in *Love and Exile* more than usually. One chapter begins: 'The new Polish Republic was barely four years old, but in that brief time it had already gone through a war with the Bolsheviks, party struggles that led to the assassination of a President, attacks upon Jews . . .' Fifty pages later, a chapter begins: 'The revived Polish nation was barely seven years old, but within that short time it had already gone through a war with the Bolsheviks, an assassination of a president . . .' On page 41, a worm is described as a divine masterpiece and commended in the same words on page 229.

These are details. More importantly, *Love and Exile* is obsessed with Singer's endless attempt to reconcile human and animal suffering with the idea of God. There are countless repetitions of the possible choice between the impersonality of Spinozism and the Cabbala. Singer says in his foreword that 'the full tale of any life would be both utterly boring and utterly unbelievable'. This may not be the full tale, but there are moments of utter boredom, which can be summed up by Sylvia Plath's poem, 'The Courage of Shutting-Up', in which the mind is pictured as a gramophone playing the same record: 'tattooing over and over the same blue grievances'. You believe Singer's sincerity, but sometimes even sincerity should be edited. The furniture of his mind is large-scale, but uncomfortable to sit in for protracted periods, since one's legs rarely touch ground. When they do – in the finely recalled memory of his father wiping his pen-nib on his skull-cap, or the young Singer finding red hairs from his father's beard or fringes of his robe in books – they serve to remind one of how dangerous ideas are to a writer with their vulgar banality, with their *poshlost* and, ultimately, of how thin *Love and Exile* is beside Nabokov's autobiographical masterpiece, *Speak, Memory*. To which these reminiscences cannot hold a candle, particularly a Nabokovian candle whose 'groggy flame squirms and ducks'. But, then, Nabokov believed in style.

Autobiography

In *Speak, Memory*, the five-year-old Nabokov is led down from the nursery in 1904 to meet a friend of the family, General Kuropatkin. 'To amuse me, he spread out a handful of matches on the divan where he was sitting, placed ten of them end to end to make a horizontal line and said, "This is the sea in calm weather." Then he tipped up each pair so as to turn the straight line into a zigzag – and that was "a stormy sea". He scrambled the matches and was about to do, I hoped, a better trick when we were interrupted. His aide-de-camp was shown in and said something to him. With a Russian, flustered grunt, Kuropatkin immediately rose from his seat, the loose matches jumping up on the divan as his weight left it. That day, he had been ordered to assume supreme command of the Russian army in the Far East.' And there the incident might satisfactorily end, with the ten matches in immortal disarray – a slow freeze of sudden technicolour from the sepia past which is impossible to forget.

But it doesn't. There is a sequel, an historical rhyme. Fifteen years later, Nabokov's father, in flight from the Bolsheviks, is accosted on a bridge 'by an old man who looked like a peasant in his sheepskin coat'. The old man, Kuropatkin, asks for a light, and the artist comments: 'Whether or not old Kuropatkin, in his rustic disguise, managed to evade Soviet imprisonment, is immaterial. What pleases me is the evolution of the match theme . . . The following of such thematic designs through one's life should be, I think, the true purpose of autobiography.'

Dan Jacobson would agree.* In his foreword to these thirteen austerely beautiful recollections, he commits himself not only to the truth but also to shapeliness, to design, to form, to narratives 'which would appear to begin naturally, develop in a surprising and persuasive manner, and come to an end no sooner or later than they should'. It looks like an impossible prescription – the writer as servant of two mistresses, the homely familiar, and the shapely piece on the side. Indeed, brilliant though *Speak, Memory* is, Nabokov never again achieves a moment comparable to the Kuropatkin incident where *Dichtung* and *Wahrheit* embrace so closely and satisfyingly. His chapters have their rough unities – a chapter arranged around his mother; a chapter touching on English themes from Pears soap to imported tutors; a lepidoptery chapter; another about journeys abroad, and so on – but the Kuropatkin interlude serves only to show how difficult it is to achieve such perfect symmetry. And perhaps also how undesirable this might be on a large scale since, in the end, Nabokov's subject is memory itself – a genre in which details carry with them their own validity. Those aerobatic matches, a bathroom thermometer 'with a bit of damp string in the eye of the handle', a senile grandfather who, when shown a pretty pebble by the infant author, examines it and slowly puts it into his mouth, 'a silvery rustle spelling "Suchard" ' – these details, gold-plated by the act of remembrance, are the treasures one takes away from *Speak, Memory*.

For when memory speaks, it is in a voice burdened with emotion, as Maupassant realized when he had Jeanne return to the lost house of her childhood in *Une Vie*: 'In Mamma's room she found, stuck behind a door in a dark corner by the bed, a slim gold-headed pin she had put there long ago (she remembered it now) and for which she had searched for years. No one had been able to find it. She took it as a priceless relic and kissed it.' Dan Jacobson's tone is cooler but just as intent: 'nothing is more mysterious to us than the processes which suddenly present to our awareness a long-forgotten face or phrase from childhood.' And

Time and Time Again by Dan Jacobson, André Deutsch.

there are moments of piercing recollection throughout *Time and Time Again*: just as Nabokov can picture his son's 'bare back crisscrossed by the shoulder-straps of his knitted navy-blue shorts', so Dan Jacobson rediscovers his son 'wearing a green knitted jersey with a stand-up collar and buttons at its neck, and a pair of orange pants of a coarsely woven material that seemed to come no more than about two inches down his thighs'. In an earlier piece, clothes also appear, powerful, mysterious, almost crackling with static electricity: 'why should the movement of his body in his shirt, even the buttons on one particular blue, coarse-woven shirt, still be vivid in my memory after so many years?' Again, he is able to reconstitute his English master's wardrobe: 'he had three suits woven in hopsack, in improbable colours – one in green, one in purple, and one in a kind of mauve. Each of these suits had a matching pair of suede shoes. They would have made him an extravagant figure almost anywhere, let alone in a drab, dusty mining town like Kimberley.' One of his childhood neighbours, Jamie Dalhousie, a victim of Down's syndrome, 'invariably wore on his close-cropped head the cap of the local high school – which he would never be able to attend.'

Though there is no shortage of detail in *Time and Time Again*, there is no profusion either. Dan Jacobson is not a helpless genius of memory like Nabokov or Saul Bellow. His details strike deeply home, but Bellow and Nabokov are St Sebastians, martyrs to detail. Bellow, characterizing Herzog, also delineates himself: 'Almost certainly, Nachman ran away from the power of his old friend's memory. Herzog persecuted everyone with it. It was like a terrible engine.' Jacobson has no such headlong retrieval system. But he is therefore able to fulfil the promise of his foreword. His essays are more shapely than Nabokov or Bellow because he is not at the mercy of his memory to the same extent. Patterns present themselves: one could add to the clothing above the odd vivid accessory, like school cricket pads with string instead of buckles, or a colleague's umbrella which is always firmly clutched 'half-way down its length, in his right hand'. These are not the author's shapes and designs, yet one makes them because one is not overwhelmed – Jacobson isn't drunk on detail, so his reader stays sober.

If that sounds drab, it isn't meant to. The pleasure offered by *Time and Time Again* is different from that offered by *Speak, Memory*. Though these memoirs have been widely praised, their autobiographical slant prevents a just appreciation of their art. With fiction, the reader constantly asks *why*? Autobiography apparently answers this question before it can be asked: incidents, details, are included *because they happened*. Yet take the essay 'Fate, Art, Love, and George', which is an account of how Dan Jacobson came to marry his wife. It was, you could say, an accident. In bald summary, George, a virtual stranger to the author, by making an inquiry about economics in the smoking room of Kimberley library, effectively introduced Dan Jacobson to another person – who became a friend and subsequently introduced him to his future wife. The story is a story of fate – and of how, but for this intervention, Jacobson's life might have been utterly different. Though everything in 'Fate, Art, Love, and George' is true, it is only by reading it as fiction that the artistry of the telling becomes visible: alternative lives – a theme with variations.

Consider the sentence 'Not only was I never to speak to him again, I was never to see him thereafter, never to hear anything about him in any context whatever.' Surely the slight tinge of contractual legalese here is deliberate? Jacobson's pact with fate is already signed, sealed, delivered and signalled in the prose. Throughout *Time and Time Again*, one encounters subtle, calculated linguistic effects. The title itself, one gradually realizes, marvellously encapsulates the Jacobson journey through time – which begins tenderly with a small boy being handed through a train window from mother to father, and ends with the author in hospital, seeing not himself in the mirror but his father. Time, and time again has passed. And yet more time. Elsewhere, Jacobson gently shows himself as a callow, would-be writer, merely by referring to 'John Keats and Alfred Tennyson' – two real writers sporting their Christian names like new ties. A similar give-away is planted on the young teacher, fresh from the colonies, who says of himself, 'I was always putting a foot wrong.' The idiom is wonky to just the right degree – neither 'I was always putting my foot in it', nor the usual 'I couldn't put a foot wrong.'

The landlady in 'Fate, Art, Love, and George' is named from Oscar Wilde. She is Miss Bunbury – another glance at alternative lives – and she keeps old personal columns with certain advertisements encircled in red. For some reason, too, Miss Bunbury refers to Dan Jacobson as 'David' – an odd, striking detail, which in addition to being true, contributes to the theme of alternative existences. By contrast, Jacobson's wife is not named in the memoir: she is 'the young woman', another gesture, it seems to me, towards what Stephen Dedalus calls 'the room of the infinite possibilities' that events have ousted. Near the end of the narrative, Jacobson and his future wife watch Miss Bunbury from their rented window: 'she puts down her bags. Exhausted already? No, she has something else in mind. She proceeds to rummage in her bags, first in the one, then in the other. Evidently she believes herself to be unobserved. It turns out that what she has been looking for is a bottle of milk. She puts the bottle to her lips, tilts her head back, and drinks ravenously from it.' Why is this included? Simply because it happened? Again, Jacobson touches his theme: this old spinster, the owner of property in Highgate and in Swiss Cottage, is seen for a moment in a convincing, hypothetical role – that of a bag-lady.

Sometimes Dan Jacobson's attempts to shape his raw material are less successful than this quiet masterpiece. The opening essay, 'Kimberley', sketches the town brilliantly – its dust, its racial divisions, 'the stinging shriek of cicadas' – but ends like this: 'One hears little English in the streets. The trenches dug by the English defenders of the city during the siege, which my brothers and I once combed through for souvenirs, have been covered over and are now the site of a drive-in cinema. At night, from miles away across the veld, one can see the imbecile blinkings and starings of its enormous screen. But no sound comes from it. Instead a multitude of dogs suddenly raise their voices on the outskirts of town. One has only to listen to them for a moment to realise that their language, at least, is unchanged, and that they have nothing new to say for themselves.' I find this last sentence little more than a rhetorical flourish – as if the final paragraph had become a para, face blacked, somehow camouflaged, and dropping into suggestive darkness.

'The Calling', on the other hand, is faultless – an account of a writer realizing his vocation, thanks to a single word in, of all things, A. W. Kinglake's *Eothen*. The word *chemise* crops up in class and even the precocious Jacobson can come no nearer its meaning than 'obviously it was something that women wore'. The master, a homosexual nicknamed 'Dainty' by the boys, writes the word on the blackboard: 'then he returned to his chair, which, as always, he had moved away from his desk and put down directly in front of us and on a level with us. He settled himself comfortably in it, legs apart and stretched out before him. His eyes found mine again. He took a fold of the fine cloth of his shirt between thumb and forefinger, at the level of his nipple, and pulled it away from his body, towards us. For a moment he rubbed the cloth backwards and forwards between his fingers. The room was so quiet we could all hear the sound: furtive, dry, tiny, no sooner picked up than lost.'

Dan Jacobson's direct comment on this erotic pantomime is: 'if you knew a word like that you could use it; if you used it, its power became yours. Words were not signs or posters pointing to meanings outside themselves; they *were* their meanings.' Exaltation and vocation follow – but 'The Calling' of the title isn't limited only to art. 'His eyes found mine again': in this one sentence, Jacobson conveys to us the forbidden, public yet private appeal of the master to the young boy, which is never repeated. Except in a minor key: going home, Jacobson encounters a gang of convicts, blacks, one of whom meets his eyes. But 'their gaze told me nothing but that I had passed across it, as close to them and as remote from them as a figure in a dream'. They are being punished. Mr Dainty is more careful of the law: 'he did not invite me to join his court or his clique' but instead leaves presents in the young Jacobson's desk, nothing too compromising. 'The Calling' is a wonderfully restrained, understated narrative, in which the adult forgoes the temptation to spell out what was unclear to his young self. Everything in the story seems merely contingent and circumstantial until the black convicts are introduced – when, like magnets, they gather every detail of the tale and point up its implicit shape.

Like the best fiction, everything in *Time and Time Again* is carefully and casually arranged – yet there are moments when patterns arise which, you feel, the author has not prepared. The memoir of F. R. Leavis is a case in point. The man is created unforgettably in a rare adjectival burst: 'it was the most complicated scalp I had ever seen: flecked, freckled, blotched, mottled, pitted, bumpy, bordered at the back and sides by a fringe of long, fine, unkempt, colourless hair.' The metaphysical man is also captured: Jacobson feels protective because Leavis 'was as little capable as a child of distancing himself from what he felt about anything or restraining himself from uttering whatever happened to be in his mind'. In the event, however, it is Leavis who protects Jacobson – from Mrs Leavis, who is as little capable as a child of restraining herself. The memoir ends, brilliantly, tenderly: 'in the years that followed I dreamed about him, improbably and affectionately, several times.' Reading this piece, I was immediately struck by the theme of protection and reminded of Dan Jacobson's father, as portrayed in the second essay: 'once his temper was lost he was quite incapable of controlling himself.' In fact, Jacobson senior, we learn, was twice formally charged for assault. Could it be that, all these years, he has actually been dreaming about his father, 'improbably and affectionately', disguised as Dr Leavis? Perhaps not: I mention the possibility only to illustrate what a rich mine this exile from Kimberley has opened for at least one grateful re-reader.

Elias Canetti

Just before his death, the speechless Kafka scrawled this wry joke on a conversation slip: 'Tremendous amount of sputum, easily, and still pain in the morning. In my daze it went through my head that for such quantities and the ease somehow the Nobel Prize . . .' Why was Elias Canetti awarded the Nobel Prize in 1981? For the English reader, any answer must be provisional, because the American translations of the autobiographical volumes, *The Tongue Set Free* and *The Torch in My Ear*, are not yet available in this country. We have only the following: the novel *Auto-Da-Fé*, *Crowds and Power*, best described as synthetic anthropology, a few plays, and now *The Human Province*, a collection of notebook jottings from 1942 to 1972.* Judging from all this, one answer to the question might be that the Nobel Prize was given to Canetti because he asked for it so persistently.

Not literally, in so many words. Rather, in so few words, over such a long period – the twenty years it took to write *Crowds and Power*. Recent Nobel laureates have something in common which explains why Canetti is now one of their number. Take two worthy winners, Beckett and Bellow – the one notoriously costive, the other famously wordy. What they share is seriousness, long years of obscure postings out at the frontiers of consciousness. Beckett may seem playful and funny to some readers, myself among them, but he is generally regarded as

The Human Province by Elias Canetti (translated by Joachim Neugroschel), André Deutsch.

369

unflinchingly serious – a writer capable of taking to his flinty heart Canetti's rebuke of 1969 that 'not even Pascal was serious enough'. Bellow, too, has a serious side, heavily ironized in *Herzog*, but persistent nevertheless. John Updike shrewdly isolates it thus: 'there is in Bellow a kind of little professor, a professor-self, who keeps fluttering round the characters . . . It's this professor, this earnest sociological man who somehow wants us to be better than we are.' The Nobel Prize comes only to those who have realized the importance of being earnest. Elias Canetti is very earnest.

An example from *The Human Province*. In 1943, Canetti notes: 'For many years now, nothing has so deeply moved and filled me as the thought of death. The highly concrete and serious, the admitted goal of my life is to achieve immortality for men.' I promise you I am not making this up. Oh, is *that* all, you think, faced with this incredibly torpid ambition. Why doesn't he try for something a little less ostentatiously miniaturist than mere immortality?

In fact, Canetti isn't stupid. He can foresee, as well as any reader, that there are a few teething troubles in the offing – a snag here, a wrinkle there, people 'dying by the millions'. Accordingly and unsurprisingly, he at first turns to fiction as the most hospitable medium. Yet even gullible, grasping fiction gags on 'the admitted goal' of Canetti's life, *Immortality – for Men!* Even in fiction the hero cannot succeed: 'an honourable death was planned for him; he was to be slain by a meteor.' Would it have been a dishonourable death, then, if he had been 'slain' by something less exalted and kitsch than a meteor – like a heart condition, say, or kidney failure? Fruitless to ask, since in the end Canetti rejects fiction: 'the cowardly use of a character as a front is to no avail. I have to perish on this field of honour, even if they bury me like a nameless cur, decry me as a lunatic, avoid me as a bitter, an obstinate, an incurable torment.' Or give me the Nobel Prize, one is tempted to add, for services to grandeur on the 'field of honour' – no matter how silly the ideas actually are. As a thinker, Canetti hardly bears thinking about sometimes.

But he isn't always as stupid and posturing as this. Now and then he is merely opaque: 'dwarf helicopters that land on bald heads'. This gnomic utterance from 1966 may be an ironic comment on the thinker as revered intellectual monument. Or it may not. At any rate, now it conveniently raises the question of Canetti's status as culture-hero. How did that come about? Sometimes, it has to be said, he delivers the goods, as in this 1947 entry about Kafka: 'The commandments become qualms for him. Of all writers, he is the only one never to be infected by power; he never exercises any kind of power whatsoever. He has stripped God of the final vestige of fatherliness. What remains is a dense and indestructible net of qualms concerning life rather than the demands of his begetter. The other poets imitate God and act like Creators. Kafka, who never wants to be a god, is never a child either. What some people see as terrifying in him and what disturbs me too is his constant adulthood. He thinks without commanding, but also without playing.' As a description of Kafka's queasy *gravitas*, this is brilliant – for once – and it enables us to define Canetti by contrast.

Canetti's thoughts are always commanding yet fickle: his distaste for the Romans, he notes narcissistically, stems from his dislike of the toga. Always the aphorist, he lays down the law, asserting confidently and fearlessly, with the aphorist's licence not to explain or argue the toss. In this sense, he resembles the pithy, dogmatic friend we all of us value and respect – the man with the weeded garden, whose trains run always on time, who never has to nip across to a neighbour to ask for a cupful of answers. Even so, Canetti is the least convincing of aphorists: Auden, who left him out of the *Faber Book of Aphorisms*, was sounder in his judgement than John Gross, who allowed Canetti several entries in the *Oxford Book of Aphorisms*. Nevertheless, like all aphorists, Canetti starts with the implicit authority the form inevitably supplies: 'If you have seen a person sleeping, you can never hate him again.' We all like authority. Until it makes us suspicious. How many divorced wives would underwrite that last maxim? This scepticism is all too frequent with *The Human Province*. In 1955, Canetti is fearful: 'I fear the analysis and explanation of names, I fear them more than murder', he writes.

To which one replies, irritably, for one has by now reached page 157: 'No – you don't.' And for emphasis, one picks up a meat cleaver. Intellectual authority is volatile and easily squandered.

It may be that notebook jottings are not what one should judge Canetti by. Clearly, there is much here which, unlike Kafka, is playful and provisional – like the postulated man 'who wouldn't have to eat and yet thrives, who behaves like a human being, intellectually and emotionally, although he never eats'. As a fictional hypothesis, an imaginative construct, this is acceptable. But with Canetti, the whimsical has a way of turning serious. As it does here: 'that would be the highest moral experiment conceivable', he continues. It would also be quite impossible, one is compelled to add, and therefore the most worthless moral experiment conceivable.

All the same, admirers would argue that these jottings have not the finished quality of the heroic *Crowds and Power*, with its patina of twenty years. Consider this statement, however: 'All demands for justice and all theories of equality ultimately derive their energy from the actual experience of equality familiar to anyone who has been part of a crowd.' Does Canetti expect us to believe this as a literal truth, or only as a poetic truth? Either way, it is open to two objections. The first part of the statement relies on its unverifiability. No one can check. The second half, however, can be checked by anyone who has been in a crowd. If you are small, as I am, crowds tend to make you acutely aware of your inequality as some lanky galoot blocks your view.

And what about this gem which might have been culled from any eighteenth-century treatise on the origin of poetry? 'Rhythm is originally the rhythm of the feet.' Well, yes, unless it is originally the rhythm of the heart or the lungs, both of which we hear *in utero*, long before we take our first intoxicated, arthythmical steps. Canetti prefers feet as the prime rhythmic source because feet imply crowds – and he can see a crowd where the rest of us see only the concept of the Resurrection, a shared religious belief, or handful of sperm. Truth to tell, Canetti has a bit of a swarm in his bonnet about crowds. The dead are a stagnating crowd, according to Canetti, unable to disperse until the Last

Judgement. Believers are a 'slow crowd', whose members are characterized by anonymity 'for they live dispersed in many cities and countries'. If the dead constitute a crowd, and if believers who are geographically separate also constitute a crowd, then why aren't the living, everyone on earth, a crowd too? Surely if spermatozoa qualify as an 'invisible crowd' because 'they are equal among themselves and in a state of very great density', then it's hardly just to exclude anyone or anything. On the other hand, spermatozoa *aren't* equal: the high density is necessary in part because a percentage is actually deformed or damaged.

Crowds and Power is a wonderfully dubious book – ingenious, untrue, witty, and vulnerable to common sense. Take Canetti on public executions: 'Disgust at collective killing is of very recent date and should not be over-estimated. Today everyone takes part in public executions through the newspapers. Like everything else, it is more comfortable than it was. We sit peacefully at home and, out of a hundred details, can choose those to linger over which offer a special thrill . . .' Like much of what Canetti writes, this is plausible – for about five seconds. Which newspapers can he have been reading that contain these detailed inventories of public executions? Or does he mean only descriptions of grisly murders? Actually, he means executions – though it is hard to be certain, since occasionally you feel that Canetti lives in a different world from the rest of us: meditating on war, for example, he is frankly puzzled. 'But how does a belligerent crowd *form*? What, from one moment to another, creates that uncanny coherence? What is it that suddenly moves men to risk their all? The phenomenon is so mysterious that it must be approached with a measure of caution.' At the risk of appearing incautious, one might suggest the following efficient causes – patriotism, conscription, courts-martial, firing squads, press-gangs. There doesn't seem to be *that* much mystery, unless you happen to have a particularly cloudy mind.

Canetti, however, is passionate and easily carried away. Discussing the sea as a crowd symbol, he writes: 'But the sea has, in addition, the constancy which the crowd lacks. It is always there; it does not ooze away from time to time and disappear.'

Picture Canetti in a deck-chair at Brighton, tetchily twitching through *The Times* in search of a juicy execution, while the sea relentlessly oozes away on the ebb-tide. Still, I prefer this other-worldly innocence to the solemn banalities that Canetti sometimes visits on his readers: 'Rain falls in drops. There are many of them, they can be seen, and the direction of their movement is particularly noticeable.' I bet you can hardly keep up. The pace is a *bit* testing and there's more to come: 'the density of rain is variable. Rain can be heavy or light and the number of drops is subject to large fluctuation.' All right, everybody? Good – because I want you to tell me what is wrong with the next statement: 'the width of a river is limited; it cannot grow indefinitely or unexpectedly, and hence its use as a crowd symbol is always in some degree provisional only. It stands for processions . . .' As we know, the width of a river is not limited. It can grow unexpectedly. We call this a flood.

The novel, however, remains – the inexplicably over-valued *Auto-Da-Fé*. 'I am not interested in grasping precisely a man I know,' Canetti avers in *The Human Province* with a slight German accent, 'I am interested only in exaggerating him precisely.' Peter Kien, the loathsome protagonist of *Auto-Da-Fé* and the world's leading sinologist, is probably an exaggerated self-portrait of Canetti. Thoroughly unworldly and bookish, this stilted caricature marries his improbably simplified housekeeper because he suddenly believes that she cares for books more than he does. The evidence? She rests a borrowed book on a cushion, turns over the pages with gloved hands, and claims to read every page a dozen times. Later in the book, Fischerle, the hunchbacked dwarf, persuades Kien that the state pawnbroker actually *eats* books – 'raw with oil and vinegar like salad, or baked in a batter like schnitzel, with salt and pepper, or with sugar and cinnamon'. Kien's response to this likely story is typically temperate and scholarly: 'he smote the pavement with his fleshless fists as though to prove that the hard crust of the earth itself was softer than the heart of man. Sharp anguish rent his bosom . . .' Relishing the prose, you should note that the translation took place 'under the personal supervision of the author' – which is why, presumably, it is so consistently execrable. The real trial of *Auto-Da-Fé*, however, is not the style but Canetti's insistence on completely closed psychology: no character can communicate with another, everyone is the slave of a drastically truncated ego, so that the action is, for the most part, about as elevated as a Punch and Judy show. In the end, like Kafka, one is left speechless: 'Tremendous amount of drivel, easily, and still pain in the morning. In my daze it went through my head that for such quantities and the ease somehow the Nobel Prize . . .'

Hans Walter Gabler's *Ulysses*

This three-volume edition of *Ulysses** gives us the evolving text of Joyce's masterpiece on the left-hand page and the final text on the right. Already acclaimed by Anthony Burgess and Hugh Kenner, it has its starting point in James Joyce's comment on the first edition of 1922: 'I am extremely irritated by all those printer's errors . . . Are these to be perpetuated in future editions?'

Apparently, a great many were, as Hans Gabler tells us in his foreword: 'any given text of *Ulysses* is erroneous at least seven times per page.' Dear, dear. Learning this, who can suppress the picture of a great masterpiece fallen on hard times? Diaphanously thin in the seat of its pants, zip like a dentist's nightmare, out at the elbows, down at the heels, frayed at the cuffs, seams agape, *Ulysses* mumbles incoherently to itself, while we strain to catch the drift of its genius. In a trice, our wallets are open and the necessary £163 note gladly bestowed. Anything to accomplish the feat of restoration.

But, on inspection, is this impulse quite correct? Those holes in the socks, for instance, which juggle like eggs above the broken shoes – might they not be a figment of a bibliographer's overzealous imagination? Is it the basest ingratitude to cite the example of Stephen's talkative ashplant as it trails noisily along in the first episode? In my Bodley Head edition and in the Penguin text, the stick addresses its owner thus: 'Steeeeeeeeeephen.'

**Ulysses: A Critical and Synoptic Edition* prepared by Hans Walter Gabler (with Wolfhard Steppe and Claus Melchior), Garland Publishing Inc.

Professor Gabler, quick to pounce on such an obvious solecism, informs us that Joyce intended a more sycophantic characterization of the stick: it now whines, 'Steeeeeeeeeeeephen'. Ah yes. Just so. And when, at the end of 'Sirens', Bloom breaks wind, the Bodley Head render the fart incorrectly as 'Pprrpffrrppfff'. Now, at last, we know it should be 'Pprrpffrrppfffff'. There are, too, a great many unruly commas who don't know their place. One or two colons have played hookey. Professor Gabler ticks them off and gets them into line.

The suit, in other words, was in excellent shape – give or take the odd loose thread and a few bits of clinging fluff. Edmund Wilson, in his fine essay 'The Fruits of the M L A', was once faced with a similar problem. 'It seems', he wrote, 'that eighteen of these Mark Twain workers are reading *Tom Sawyer*, word by word, backward, in order to ascertain, without being diverted from this drudgery by attention to the story or to the style, how many times "Aunt Polly" is printed as "aunt Polly", and how many times "sst!" is printed as "ssst!" ' The robust Wilson decided that the whole enterprise was a 'boondoggle' – or trivial and unnecessary task. Whether you judge this edition a classic boondoggle, or not, depends on your attitude to misprints. Personally, I believe they are irritating but inevitable in any text and, on the whole, I couldn't give a fuppenny tuck.

Professor Gabler, of course, has adopted a less pragmatic, more idealistic view of what is possible. Praiseworthy, perhaps; essential in a bibliographer even; but wrong – as an epic misprint in his own edition demonstrates, despite the aid of two assistants, computers and collation machines. At a certain point, the correction of mistakes merely leads to new mistakes. God seems to have written this into our contracts, lest we suffer the sin of hubris. So, on page 403 of volume one, Professor Gabler has corrected a 'howler': some *incredibly* careless person (possibly the author himself, but unspecified in either the historical collation chart, or the synoptic apparatus) has added a dash to signify new dialogue when all that is required is paragraph indentation because the same person is speaking. The dash is, therefore, eliminated. However, the indentation continues mistakenly for the next six lines. And the error is mirrored in the synoptic text on the opposite page. I hope Professor Gabler doesn't have too many sleepless nights over it. It isn't *that* important, like so many of his own corrections.

A few emendations, though, are worth recording. When Stephen, in the third section, reminisces about his return from Paris, he quotes the telegram that brought him back: 'Mother dying come home father.' It is typical of Joyce's meticulous imagination that the text of the telegram was intended to incorporate a misprint, a misprint that was 'corrected' by someone on the fifth set of proofs. We now have the true text: 'Nother dying come home father.'

Professor Gabler's great find of this sort occurs in the library episode – five lost lines which solve a famous interpretative crux. In the later brothel chapter, the drunken Stephen asks his dead mother's vision, 'Tell me the word, mother, if you know now. The word known to all men.' Scholars have expended many hours trying to identify the word known to all men. Professor Richard Ellmann now proves to have been correct in his *Ulysses on the Liffey*. The word is 'love', as we know from five lines which Professor Gabler has retrieved and put in the library episode, including 'Love, yes. Word known to all men.'

It is nice to know for certain, but I doubt whether this extra fact radically alters our reading of *Ulysses*. And I doubt, too, whether the five lines should be admitted to the final text. In doing so, Professor Gabler has preferred the reading of an early fair copy to a later corrected typescript. He argues that, in copying, the typist omitted the crucial lines because his/her eyes skipped from one set of dots to another set lower down the page. This is plausible, but no more than that. Joyce may have omitted the lines deliberately, or he may have condoned the typist's error. Either decision would make aesthetic sense.

But I am no bibliographer. Indeed, I emerged into the real world from these three volumes richly confused, rather like one of those wizened Japanese soldiers tottering out of the jungle into the dazzling sunlight of 1958. Professor Gabler's *apparatus criticus* would tax a code-breaker at GCHQ. My counter-argument, then, is necessarily tentative. In the library episode, Stephen is bullshitting about Shakespeare ('I think you're getting on very nicely,' he says to himself, 'Just mix up a mixture of theolologicophilolological. *Mingo, minxi, mictum, mingere*'). His interlocutors are trying to show off and trip him up. Mr Best gracefully alludes to Victor Hugo's *L'art d'être grandpère*. Stephen interrupts him, either at *L'art d'être grandp* . . ., or at *L'art d'être grand* . . . The latter is a typeset reading which Professor Gabler rejects in order to restore the five lines which continue the argument about parentage. In my view, the latter (that is, the art of being great) is what Stephen hears – and, in his argumentative anxiety, goes off at a tangent to the idea of great men: 'His own image to a man with that queer thing genius is the standard of all experience.' Professor Gabler's addition makes the argument more coherent, but that isn't Joyce's point about Stephen's theory of Shakespeare. It shouldn't make sense and by omitting the five lines Joyce is serving the idea of verisimilitude. Accordingly, I retain my scepticism and I advise other readers to do the same.

The real reason for buying this edition is not to acquire a final, perfect text of the greatest book of the century, but to follow the moves of a brilliant writer at work, however partially since not all the documents survive. The final text will always be argued about: Professor Gabler is too often willing to accept readings from the fair copy of the Rosenbach manuscript in preference to later typescript readings for his edition to be beyond question. However, the left-hand page of this edition shows us the work in progress – the way Joyce added, deleted, rewrote extensively in proof – and for those with the patience this is worth £163.

The Man Who Broke the Bank

It is a whimsical coincidence that two of the century's greatest literary assets – Joyce and Eliot – should have found temporary refuge in the banking business. Eliot, though, was a credit to the profession, and stuck at it from 1917 to 1924, remarking to John Quinn in April 1923: 'I don't know whether I have ever explained this to you, but the Bank is a secure job for life, with a pension at 60.' Joyce was a decided debit. Working from July 1906 to February 1907 in the Nast-Kolb Schumaker Bank in Rome, he squandered his salary, wore holes in the seat of his trousers, covered them with his tail-coat even in the hottest months, and was reprimanded for slovenly posture. Where Eliot displayed his life-long tact and adaptability, Joyce displayed his royal Irish arse and, like Stephen Dedalus, would not serve – behind desk or counter. Eliot tailored himself to the job, po-faced, pinstriped, with a gold chain carefully mountaineering across a granite-black waistcoat; Joyce in 'new secondhand clothes', tennis shoes and carrying an ashplant, cried (Larkin-like) *Stuff your pension* and tried the most difficult route to the top of Parnassus.

Essentially a loner (he once told Beckett, 'I don't love anyone except my family'), Joyce cleared his route of friends and literary helpers. In Paris for the first time, he was the recipient of shrewd paternal advice, retailed in his mother's thriftily punctuated letters: 'you cannot get on in your line without friends', his father insisted with bourgeois caution. Joyce, meanwhile, ignored this memo and, like an uncommercial traveller, used her daughter

380

Iseult's temporary quarantine as an excuse to keep his ill-shod foot out of Maud Gonne's influential door. Other potentially useful doorsteps were crossed by Joyce but (shades of *Portrait of the Artist as a Young Dog*) were methodically dunged on as he left. Lady Gregory got him reviewing for the Dublin *Daily Express*, only to be subsequently panned by her protégé; George Russell and Yeats both helped him out, only to find themselves belittled in *The Holy Office*. It was years before Joyce was confident enough and desperate enough to accept the help of Ezra Pound, and even then he managed, while receiving a pair of secondhand boots, to daunt Eliot and Wyndham Lewis with his muted arrogance. Money debts never bothered Joyce, but literary debts were another matter – in the latter respect, he could have answered Mr Deasy's question in *Ulysses* ('Can you feel that? *I owe nothing*. Can you?') with an honest yes. Instinct made him offend before any literary loans of importance could be transacted, and if he was not a borrower in this sense, neither was he a lender: when Gogarty lifted one of the titles Joyce used to collect for future use (a creative trait common to him and Wallace Stevens), Joyce read Gogarty's essay and tore off what belonged to him.

He guarded his literary capital avariciously, as his dealings with Synge show. Sensing a rival, though one who could give him first-hand advice about starvation, Joyce carried off the dramat-ist's *Riders to the Sea* from the Hôtel Corneille in Paris. To Stanislaus in Dublin he reported gleefully: 'I am glad to say that ever since I read it, I have been riddling it mentally till it has not a sound spot.' But it is the conclusion to this letter which discloses his real worry – 'thanks be to God, Synge isn't an Aristotelian'. Joyce, the recent re-interpreter of 'pity and terror', *was*. In fact, Synge had not trespassed on Joyce's territory but, unable to forgive the moment of fearful apprehension, Joyce prosecuted just the same – returning the blunt verdict of 'dwarf-drama' when he gave back the manuscript.

This determination to be original is reflected in his comment on *Dubliners*: 'The stories in *Dubliners* seem to be indisputably well done but, after all, perhaps many people could do them as well. I

am not rewarded by any feeling of having overcome difficulties.'
They were, for all their gauntness, too conventional. The Bank, so
to speak, failed to give him job satisfaction. Moreover, the great
experiments which followed – *A Portrait*, *Ulysses* and *Finnegans
Wake* – are mirrored in Joyce's life by equally extraordinary
business ventures. Safety did not interest him. Like Blougram, his
interest was on 'the dangerous edge of things'. A natural
innovator, an inventor in the round, Joyce vindicates Carlyle's
notion that the great man contains the potential for many roles.
The King of prose, with a retinue of professors, might easily have
been the Emperor of Ice Cream, for as Stanislaus remarked, 'In
my brother, business lost to poetry a "go-getter" on the American
model.'

His schemes, all of which came to nothing, were as radically
visionary as his fiction – Joyce was ever the prospector, never the
young man with good prospects. Being first, being original, was
more important to him than security. His bright ideas included an
early attempt to establish himself as a joint stock company and
sell off shares, a plan to develop Galway as a major transatlantic
port, another to set up the first Irish weekly on the continental
model, another to export fireworks and Irish tweeds to Trieste,
yet another to found the first cinema in Ireland. In retrospect,
curiously enough, it is the wildest scheme which now looks most
attractive – the joint stock company. The rest are shrewd and,
typically, ahead of their time. They failed, however, partly
because Joyce's personal magnetism was a less powerful attraction to capital than the ubiquitous Bank (or timid backers cut
their losses at the first difficulty), and partly because his versatility
was fatally fertile. A man with only one idea is inevitably single-
minded in his perseverance, but Joyce moved on restlessly to the
next and the next. In any case, that fugitive feeling of 'having
overcome difficulties', which he missed in the composition of
Dubliners, was not something that mere business could give him
– finding the necessary capital was simply his day-to-day sponging writ large, as dull and irritating as finding a printer for *Ulysses*
once it was written.

In literature, on the other hand, the idea itself is nothing until the execution is complete. Content is form and the pathetically thin plot of *Ulysses* (a day in the life of a Jewish cuckold) is drab beside the obvious glamour of Dublin's first cinema. It needed all of Joyce's 'descriptive lust', as a Triestine pupil perceptively called it, to make the idea live. Nevertheless, despite this difference, these commercial ventures are siblings of the great experimental works and demonstrate the essential wholeness of Joyce's life. It was all of a piece – Joyce's elopement with Nora Barnacle becomes the sexual frankness of *Ulysses*; the spatio-temporal puns Joyce arranged in his life (eating wild duck when meeting Ibsen's translator) find their counterparts in the linguistic coincidences of *Finnegans Wake*; singing in the quintet from *Die Meistersinger* produced the form of the Sirens episode; Joyce's nifty projects suffer ironic alchemy in the Barmecidal business wheezes of Bloom.

The weakness of Stan Gébler Davies's new biography* is that, unlike Richard Ellmann's elegant and detailed work, it does not explore the crucial symbiosis of life and art. Mr Gébler Davies chooses to ignore the work and concentrate on the life, with the glib disclaimer, 'my book is short on critical waffle'. And though he points out the most obvious correspondences, he cannot match Professor Ellmann's wide-ranging awareness of how the tiniest incidents, the most obscure acquaintances fed the work. This new biography is a gay scamper of disenchanted prose, but it cannot begin to challenge Professor Ellmann's biography, which does for Joyce what Livingstone Lowes did for Coleridge in *The Road to Xanadu*. Thus, Mr Gébler Davies tells us that Joyce read D'Annunzio: Professor Ellmann tells us that Joyce admired *Il Fuoco* for turning an iconoclastic life to fiction, eliminating action, and using lyrical prose. *James Joyce: A Portrait of the Artist* is the thin end of the Ellmann wedge, omitting much and adding only the speculation that Joyce and his father may have contracted syphilis, and the more certain probability that Joyce

James Joyce: A Portrait of the Artist by Stan Gébler Davies, Davis-Poynter.

slept with Marthe Fleischmann in Zurich. It is not a dull book –
Joyce's life was not a dull one – but there are more debits than
credits.

Pygmy Scribblers

Family conversation is a habit, a continuous performance whose *déjà vu* is a powerful narcotic. And even when the blood-dimmed tide is loosed and quarrels come, *mauvais mots* are overrehearsed – yes, even the best lack all conviction. No wonder they are so hard to forget. Ordinary conversation, on the other hand, happens quickly, like a road accident: we are involved, hurt or hurting, without quite remembering what took place. To make an accurate statement, one needs to be a witness, not a participant. Detachment is all. Boswell, for example, after Johnson had initially bloodied his nose, confined himself to tactfully drawing the Doctor out, retreating at the first signs of displeasure and taking copious notes. Johnson had his catalyst, Goethe his mirror. Eckermann once dared to question his excellency's theory of colours only to be told: 'With your idea of coloured light you belong to the fourteenth century, and with the rest you are in the very abyss of dialectics.' Later on, Goethe came round somewhat, but remembering the 'half-laugh and half-sneer', Eckermann resumed his habit of admiring assent.

The scribbling pygmies Boswell and Eckermann, having accepted their roles, were admitted into the family. There, Eckermann could hear Goethe rehearsing his conviction that a flourishing national culture was essential to great literature, and other frequently broached topics. Boswell, too, faithfully records Johnsonian repetitions and, as a member of the family, consistently denigrates his rivals in Johnson's home circle (Mrs Thrale,

Levet and Mrs Williams) while accurately reproducing the very tones of the paterfamilias.

Both men were so much part of the furniture that even quirky behaviour was in the open: Goethe tells Eckermann how much he hates people who wear spectacles; Boswell hears from Maxwell how Johnson fondled a female Methodist from Staffordshire. Arthur Power was robust enough to resist an intellectually passive role, but it limits the value of his memories.* He spent his time disagreeing with Joyce, and with praiseworthy candour portrays his young self as an Ajax to Joyce's Ulysses: 'I had not been greatly impressed by his books.'

As Irishmen they had common ground, and both were fascinated by the details of the Bywaters and Thompson murder case: powdered electric light bulbs and a six-shilling knife. But in literary matters they were poles apart. Joyce admired Eliot, Tolstoy, Dostoevsky, Ibsen, Gide, Proust, Stendhal and Hemingway's *A Clean, Well Lighted Place*; Mr Power, with the exception of the last, did not. He preferred Turgenev, Pushkin, Synge, Hardy, Lamartine's *Graziella*, Browning, Braque and the Ballet Russe; Joyce was alternately scathing or indifferent about each item on this list. At least they agreed about the merit of Chekhov.

On wider issues like religion, Joyce wore his heart, not on his sleeve, but firmly buttoned under his waistcoat. 'Indeed, one of his marked characteristics was his avoidance of giving a direct opinion about anyone or anything,' writes Mr Power, though he is honest enough to report Joyce's hardly indirect opinion of himself – 'You are talking like a philistine.' But more often, Joyce remained 'impassive, polite but impassive, answering a query when he was asked one, but no more'. Clearly, this aggressively argumentative young man was scarcely a Frank Budgen (Joyce's sympathetic helpmate), let alone a Boswell or an Eckermann. This in itself would disqualify him as a chronicler, even if it was not supported by internal evidence. Mr Power claims to have worked from notes – so, by and large, there is no reason to

---

Conversations with James Joyce by Arthur Power, edited by Clive Hart, Millington.

dispute his general impressions – but can Joyce *really* have said, 'a book, in my opinion, should not be planned out beforehand'? Where does that leave *Ulysses* – a book organized with more care than the average moon-shot?

It is noticeable, too, that in their literary conversations both men's speech is interchangeable. 'Indeed,' remarks Joyce, 'some people think that the decline of the patron has caused a decline in art . . . You must admit that patrons have played an important part in the arts. Indeed in many cases they would not have been created but for their help. Indeed what was the constant tragedy of the *Quartier* but lack of money?' 'Indeed,' volunteers Power, 'I have been told that the nearest man to compare with Proust is Saint-Simon.' In his introduction Clive Hart shrewdly suggests that Joyce was primarily interested in Power's Irish speech rhythms, with an ear to *Finnegans Wake*. But, indeed, little or nothing of them, or those of Joyce, survives in these pages. Processed by time, Mr Power's reminiscences are oddly flavour-less.

The great memoirists knew that art must help the truth, that listening carefully was only part of the secret. The crux is contained in Browning's rhetorical question from *The Ring and the Book*: 'Is fiction which makes fact alive, fact too?' The answer is evidently 'Yes' if one looks at Eckermann, Boswell or Ford Madox Ford. Did Eckermann actually see a charred fragment of *Tasso* among the ruins of the Weimar theatre? Was it truly 9 July 1827 that 'we rose to go, but Goethe was so full of life that the conversation was continued awhile standing'? Isn't it the novelist in Boswell, rather than the reporter, who spices his accounts with stage directions – 'blowing with high derision', 'puffing hard with passion', 'rising into warmth'? There is art also in Boswell's description of Johnson's walk, like 'the struggling gait of one in fetters'. When Ford Madox Ford depicts James rolling his eyes and his periods, what does it matter that the details are exaggerated or even untrue? James is *there*, as Johnson is there, as Goethe is there: in Mr Power's version, Joyce is not.

Joyce: New Secondhand Clothes

I

When Leopold Bloom goes to the kitchen sink of 7 Eccles Street to fill the kettle for two cups of Epps's soluble cocoa, information about the source flows endlessly from the innocent tap. Behind the simple drumming of water into a kettle, Joyce shows us an orchestrated water system, a massed band of silent facts awaiting a sign from the conductor's baton. They have their music too. Richard Ellmann's new book, *The Consciousness of Joyce*, examines Joyce's treatment of his literary sources and, with Joycean diligence, appends an indispensable list of the books in his Trieste library, carefully supplemented by other well authenticated titles. Unlikely works, such as the Revd J. C. Woods's *Common Objects of the Sea Shore* and Maurice Clare's *A Day with Shakespeare*, can now be heard striking their triangles in the music that is *Ulysses*.

Primarily, however, Professor Ellmann concerns himself with Joyce's use of *Hamlet* and Homer. Though Joyce was dismissive of Homer in conversation with Nabokov, and though he told his Aunt Josephine to 'buy at once the *Adventures of Ulysses*' (Lamb's unscholarly abbreviation), Professor Ellmann approaches Homer on the lines initiated by Stuart Gilbert under Joyce's supervision. His Joyce is a cunning impresario, bent on subduing to his purpose a trio of scholarly prima donnas. Under his hands, the soloists are persuaded to sing a chorus of sorts. The talktapes are selectively spliced. The opening of Gilbert's pioneering work has always struck me as largely irrelevant and a little specious in its use of Homeric scholarship and pseudo-scholarship. Joyce was not a Greek scholar himself. Yet he condoned Gilbert's excess of zeal because he saw it would confer respectability on what was widely regarded as a pornographic work. He knew the value of the expert witness.

The main experts were Samuel Butler (who thought Homer was a woman), Victor Bérard (who thought Homer was a Greek, but Ulysses a Phoenician), and Francis Bacon (who believed the *Odyssey* should be read allegorically). Professor Ellmann calls them 'an unlikely trio' and yet believes that Joyce read them out of respect for Homer, rather than to amuse himself. But the truth is that Joyce's attitude to Homer is there in the text. Homer makes a personal appearance, in disguise of course, but as recognizable as Hitchcock taking a furtively fat bow. The blind poet is transformed and ironized as a blind piano tuner who passes unobtrusively through the narrative just as references to Homer's work run through the book. Joyce is careful to nudge the attentive reader. For example, ostensibly pointless questions are asked: when Bloom helps the tuner across the street, he wonders 'if he has a name'. How many people, we ought to wonder in our turn, don't have names? Homer is the sole candidate since, as Professor Ellmann remarks in another context, he was known to antiquity simply as 'the poet'. Later, in 'Sirens', Miss Douce comments: 'The tuner was in today . . . tuning it for the smoking concert and I never heard such an exquisite player . . . *The real classical* you know. And blind too, poor fellow' (my italics).

In other words, Homer is reduced to the status of piano tuner. He sees to the harmonics and mechanics of *Ulysses*. He improves the tone by his presence in the book. But it is Joyce who will, as it were, dominate the stage in evening dress, acknowledge the applause, and spread his tails before seating himself at the piano where he will accompany himself in a song cycle of his own composition. Homer is a 'blind stripling' (the regularly applied Homeric epithet) who sneaks back wordlessly for his forgotten tuning fork. Professor Ellmann is right to say that Joyce suffered from none of Harold Bloom's anxiety of influence. But he is incorrect in his supposition that Joyce, though scarcely abased, deferred to Homer. He stole, cavalierly, what was useful and ignored the rest. The tap, tap, tap of the tuner's chipped white stick (Bloom is probably a Freemason) is also the tap of a trowel laying the foundation stone on which Joyce built the towering work. Joyce's methods involved not only parallels (which, as Professor Peake, in *James Joyce – the Citizen and the Artist*, scrupulously points out, are sometimes elaborate, sometimes intermittent) but also *parallax* – the same story seen from an entirely different point of view. It is no accident that the word parallax sounds through *Ulysses*.

Professor Ellmann can hear hooves too. One of the sharpest questions in his absorbing book concerns the whereabouts of Homer's Trojan horse in *Ulysses*. He finds it thudding surreptitiously on a great many pages and provides an almost exhaustive list of equine images – but the homework has been done too well and, as elsewhere, Professor Ellmann's wide knowledge works against him. The correct answer is there in the list – lost in the stampede of candidates. The Trojan horse is, in fact, the unfancied outsider who wins the Gold Cup – it is Throwaway. Like the Trojan horse, it is a free gift: unknowingly, Bloom gives the tip to Bantam Lyons for nothing. Joyce later underlines the point when Bloom is given a throwaway – i.e. a *free* leaflet. The element of deception in the free gift is forcibly emphasized when Bloom chucks the leaflet into the Liffey and notes that the gulls are not gulled into thinking it bread. Moreover, every time the Gold Cup race is mentioned, a covert, transformed Throwaway appears, *in disguise* to underline the idea that it is a secret weapon: a newsboy is *thrown out* of the office; M'Coy pushes aside some dangerous banana peel that someone has *thrown away*; Boylan pitches 'a broad coin down'; and, when Nosey Flynn asks Davy Byrne for a tip, Bloom meditates 'Nice piece of wood in that counter', thus bringing together the ideas of wood and horse. Only a few pages on in 'Lestrygonians', still in Davy Byrne's bar, Paddy Leonard mentions 'some bloody horse up his sleeve for the Gold Cup' and Throwaway is obliquely alluded to in two different ways. First, the dyspeptic Tom Rochford '*spilt* [my italics] powder from a twisted paper into the water set before him'. Secondly, Bloom muses on the idea of Röntgen rays which make it possible to have 'insides entrails on show' – an invention that might have saved Troy. In the 'Cyclops' episode, one throwaway dominates the entire passage – the biscuit tin the Citizen hurls after Bloom – an epic object to cover a multitude of references to the Gold Cup: 'Gob, if he got that lottery ticket on the side of his poll he'd remember the gold cup, he would so.' In 'Oxen of the Sun' we learn that Madden has lost money on Sceptre, the horse ridden by his namesake, O. Madden. We are quickly reminded that, earlier in the day, Madden and his girlfriend have encountered Father Conmee – an event recorded in 'Wandering Rocks': 'the young woman abruptly bent and with slow care detached from her light skirt a clinging twig', which, of course, she throws away. Finally, Throwaway is an outsider, like the horse left by the Greeks outside the walls of Troy.

Politically, Joyce was a dark horse. In his biography, Professor Ellmann found that he 'cultivated disengagement'. Here, he modifies his opinion and offers Joyce as a political writer. Professor Peake agrees and I dissent. First, Professor Ellmann presents a definition of politics from Roland Barthes which is unacceptably elastic: 'the whole of human relations in their real, social structure, in their power of making the world.' Thanks for everything/nothing. Secondly, he argues that Joyce had a 'message' which, however obliquely expressed, was against the tyranny of Church and State and for individual freedom and the truth of the self. To me, this message amounts to little more than a mistrust of the messages and generalities that in practice make up politics. *Non serviam*, the theme that structures *A Portrait*, is not a political creed. Thirdly, Professor Ellmann, in spite of admitted ironies, assumes an identity between Joyce and his two protagonists when they themselves agree. This is possible. Political opinions, however, are required by verisimilitude. They are an aspect of life and, therefore, occur in *Ulysses*. It does not follow from this that Joyce is a political writer in the usual sense. Orwell, an extremely political writer, believed rightly that Joyce's strength lay in his anti-intellectual indifference to politics.

Although Bloom has connections with moderate Sinn Fein, they are only a small part of his general intellectual curiosity. As for Joyce, Stanislaus, his brother (who was interned for *his* politics), was cynical about James's socialism with its hand-outs for impecunious artists. Joyce's attitude to Ireland always fluctuated, and if he saw a vague hope in Griffith and Sinn Fein, he never gave up his right to criticize. In the First World War, he praised the German offensive and changed his paper from the pro-allied *Neue Zürcher Zeitung* to the pro-German *Zürcher Post* – largely, it seems, because he quarrelled with the British Consulate on a personal matter. 'As an artist', he remarked in 1918, 'I attach no importance to political conformity . . . The state is concentric, man is eccentric.' Most of these facts and quotations come from Professor Ellmann's brilliant biography where he got most of the answers right the first time.

C. H. Peake's study of Joyce is orderly and, in the best sense, elementary. All those who have been injured in collisions with sophisticated Joyce criticism will find a first aid kit here. Professor Peake's thesis, that Joyce's *œuvre* exemplifies the reconciliation of the idealist and the realist, is not new, but some subtle and sound new emphases are touched in. He is particularly good on *Dubliners* and I liked the idea that Stephen's artistic theory is peripatetic in presentation as well as scholastic in exposition. Sometimes his ideas are a little near-fetched: many of Joyce's intricate patterns, like the preponderance of flowers in 'Lotus Eaters', would not, in his opinion, strike the reader without Joyce's advance publicity. They work only as distant music, suggestive but unclear. How was it, then, that Walter Whiter noticed Shakespeare's image patterns in the eighteenth century? Metempsychosis? Nevertheless, Professor Peake's work, in conjunction with Professor Ellmann's biography, would be an excellent place for anyone to start with Joyce. Clear information pours from them both like a tap.

II

More recently, the case for a politically committed Joyce, a writer with a 'republican and proudly anti-colonial imagination', has been forcefully argued – or arguably forced – by Tom Paulin. In his essay, 'The British Presence in *Ulysses*', Paulin marshals a great many political references from *Ulysses*. The resultant eight-page concentrate inevitably creates the impression that *Ulysses* is saturated in politics – which it isn't. Neither are all the references germane to the British presence that Paulin would have us believe was resented by Joyce. The status of others is rather less 'anti-colonial' than Paulin, as an Irishman and therefore as an authority, tends to believe.

The Martello tower, for example, installed by Pitt against a possible French invasion, is an historical fact, hardly to be gainsaid, yet less galling than one might reasonably assume. The tower prompts Stephen to ruminate on Ireland's subservient position: 'I am the servant of two masters,' he remarks. This seems promising for Paulin's argument – except that Goldoni's play, *The Servant of Two Masters*, is a light comedy, in which, moreover, the servant is strategically more adept than his nominal masters. This ironic tinge is ignored by Paulin and Stephen's tone is misrepresented as factual rather than playful. And then Paulin makes the Roman Catholic Church, the second of Stephen's two masters, subordinate to the British Empire, because he wants Joyce particularly to resent the British presence: 'the Roman Catholic Church is here presented as a servant of Britain,' Paulin confidently, mystically and incorrectly asserts, without a wisp of justification.

Less mystically, Paulin identifies Blazes Boylan with the British presence in Ireland. For Ireland, the British occupation is 'the stranger in her house', as Boylan is the stranger in Bloom's home. The identification is confirmed for Paulin by Boylan's appearance at the end of 'Lestrygonians', 'immediately' after Bloom has seen a placard on which the Lord Lieutenant is mentioned. Snap. The argument here is vulnerable to several objections. First, when Bloom initially sees Boylan from the carriage in the 'Hades' section, the association made, if any, is between Boylan and 'Sir Philip Crampton's memorial fountain bust'. There is no reason why the technique of contagion, as identified later by Paulin, should be conveniently suspended in this instance. Crampton was a Dublin surgeon, a man significantly insignificant. 'Who was he?' Bloom asks himself. Secondly, the proximity between the Lord Lieutenant and Boylan's appearance in 'Lestrygonians' isn't conclusive. Two paragraphs, one longish, the other a sentence and two phrases, separate the two men: as zeugma, it isn't the perfect example one might present to undergraduates as an obvious illustration of the literary mechanism. Thirdly, grant that Paulin is right to identify the British occupation of Ireland with Boylan's adultery and problems are created elsewhere in the book.

I am thinking particularly of the passage in 'Eumaeus', where Bloom sees in the Parnell, O'Shea, Kitty O'Shea triangle a reflection of his own predicament with Boylan and Molly. 'Whereas the simple fact of the case was it was simply a case of the husband not being up to scratch with nothing in common between them beyond the name and then a real man arriving on the scene.' This passage is an indisputable parallel with Boylan's sexual proficiency and Bloom's failure to have full sexual intercourse with Molly since November 1893. The difficulty lies in the implications of this parallel if we pursue Paulin's earlier parallel. If the adulterous Boylan equals the British invader, then the adulterous Parnell equals the British invader, too, since Bloom unmistakably identifies with O'Shea in the 'Eumaeus' episode. Given that Parnell's entire political career was dedicated to ridding Ireland of the British presence, the equation is manifestly absurd. Finally, if Boylan is a symbol of the British presence in Ireland, then surely Bloom should resent him keenly? In fact, the question is put in the 'Ithaca' section. 'With what antagonistic sentiments were his subsequent reflections affected?' The answer is: 'Envy, jealousy, abnegation, equanimity.' That last emotion is fatal to the political view Paulin wishes to impart to Joyce.

And then there is Haines. He is, of course, British and unquestionably a presence in the Martello tower, a presence whom Stephen would like to be rid of. Haines looks like hard evidence. However, Stephen seems to be nervous of Haines's gun and his tendency to talk in his sleep – rather than resentful of Haines's Britishness. Inconveniently for the anti-British views which Tom Paulin is anxious to attribute to Stephen (and, therefore, to Joyce), Haines happens to be a particularly supine British specimen who regrets the colonial past and who is passionately interested in the Irish language. Haines speaks Irish better than the old milkwoman who is associated with Ireland – 'silk of the kine and poor old woman, names given her in old times.' The milkwoman admits, 'I'm ashamed I don't speak the language myself.' The irony, it seems to me, is directed fairly and squarely at Irish sentimentality about their extinct native tongue. At any rate, Haines emerges with credit – unless, of course, you choose to see his care and conservation of a language abandoned by its own people as a further example of usurpation. This difficulty for his argument is solved by Tom Paulin briskly enough. He leaves it out.

'We feel in England,' Haines awkwardly concedes, 'that we have treated you rather unfairly. It seems history is to blame.' Lest we should find this surprisingly un-British in its mildness, Paulin 'corrects' the impression with his weighted commentary: 'Here, Haines sounds lofty and patronising, and Stephen later transforms him into a symbol of naval supremacy.' A quotation from the 'Nestor' episode is adduced by Paulin in support: 'The seas' ruler. His seacold eyes looked on the empty bay.' Yet, just as one begins to think that, by Jingo, Haines does seem an imperious British presence in *Ulysses* after all, the full quotation comes to mind. In its entirety, the quotation makes it clear that Stephen finds it difficult to sustain reflex prejudice: 'The seas' ruler. His seacold eyes looked on the empty bay: history is to blame: on me and on my words, unhating.' That last word 'unhating' subverts the drift of Paulin's argument and it was shrewd (or slipshod) of him to edit it out. There is no hatred in Haines's 'seacold eyes'.

Because he is a political animal, Paulin's political conclusions are, to him, inescapable and obvious. Yet, for me, most of his argument has the impacted quality of small print in a contract. It isn't concerned to explain itself to the uninitiated reader and there is a strong temptation to give difficulties the go by – and sign on the dotted line rather than fidget and haggle. Even so, the case of Robert Emmet is unwontedly clear and it takes all Paulin's argumentative skills – which are formidable – to stand the evidence on its head. Leaving the Ormond hotel in the 'Sirens' episode, Bloom sees 'a gallant pictured hero in Lionel Marks's window' and immediately recalls 'Robert Emmet's last words'. They are as patriotic as could be desired by a 'republican and proudly anti-colonial imagination'. Tom Paulin's strategy is to quote them complete – for a change – but inaccurately, because the moving speech is fragmented in Joyce's text and ironically punctuated by a series of farts. In historical fact, Emmet said: 'I have but one request to make at my departure from this world. It is the charity of silence. Let no man write my epitaph. When my country shall have taken her place among the nations of the earth, then, and not till then, let my epitaph be written.' In this form, the speech is moving perhaps. As transcribed in *Ulysses*, it cannot be: '*When my country takes her place among.* Prrprr.' And so on. Repeatedly, as Bloom/Ulysses resists the siren voice of political eloquence. It is a ticklish moment for Paulin, but if you listen carefully you can hear the argument raising its voice and talking more quickly, lest it be interrupted. Paulin explains about it and about it: Bloom's 'reaction to the portrait of Robert Emmet', we learn, is 'a rejection, *less of Emmet's example* [my italics] than of sentimental nationalism and martyrology.' The real target of Joyce's irony, Paulin concludes on our behalf, is not Robert Emmet. Not at all. Contrary to appearances, apparently, Joyce has in his sights Pearse, for whom he had 'an intense dislike' – so the mockery is aimed exclusively at '*Pearse's echo* of Emmet's last words' (my italics). Which, of course, as you probably noticed, rescues Paulin's profoundly endangered argument very conveniently, and allows him to proceed to his confident, almost predestined, conclusion – that *Ulysses* is Robert Emmet's real epitaph, because Joyce's novel has given Ireland a 'national and international identity'. Reluctantly, I have to say that this connection is more rhetorical than real. It may have been Joyce's achievement to vindicate Emmet's last words, but Paulin has no justification for confusing achievement with intention. It is naive to pretend, even for a sentence, that Joyce would have welcomed the subordination of his great egotistical epic to Emmet's political aims. And if this wasn't Joyce's intention for *Ulysses*, I can't see that Paulin's determination to see the novel in this light is either here or there.

Nor is Bloom's scepticism sufficiently appreciated by Paulin in other areas. He omits to mention Bloom's comment on 'The Croppy Boy': 'he must have been a bit of a natural,' Bloom observes with detachment, 'not to see it was a yeoman cap[tain].' Another patriotic icon offhandedly ironized. Paulin prefers to notice that Joyce 'credits Bloom with giving Griffith the idea for Sinn Fein'. This is not strictly accurate. John Wyse credits Bloom, as the narrator of 'Cyclops' reports: 'they were at it dingdong, John Wyse saying it was Bloom gave the idea for Sinn Fein to Griffith to put in his paper all kinds of jerrymandering, packed juries and swindling the taxes off the Government and appointing consuls all over the world to walk about selling Irish industries.' When Wyse asks Martin Cunningham for confirmation, he replies, 'That's so. Or so they allege.' Not exactly positive confirmation.

What is certain is that Bloom is opposed to the extreme, bigoted nationalism of the Citizen. When the latter aggressively proposes a toast to 'the memory of the dead' – following their argument about 'the brothers Sheares and Wolf Tone beyond on Arbour Hill and Robert Emmet and die for your country, the Tommy Moore touch about Sara Curran', Bloom courageously opposes this patriotic slither and bluster with the brave words, 'You don't grasp my point.' Bloom profoundly mistrusts politics and, in 'Eumaeus', recalls the trammelled incautiousness of his own views of twenty years previously – 'it goes without saying, not contributing a copper or pinning his faith absolutely to its dictums, some of which wouldn't exactly hold water, he at the outset in principle, at all events, was in thorough sympathy with peasant possession'. From the particular example, Bloom turns to the general: 'so far as politics themselves were concerned, he was only too conscious of the casualties invariably resulting from propaganda and displays of mutual animosity and the misery and suffering it entailed as a foregone conclusion on fine young fellows, chiefly, destruction of the fittest, in a word.'

Given this general orientation, how likely is it that Bloom was instrumental in the inception of Sinn Fein? Of course, Sinn Fein in the initial stages – whatever it became later in the hands of people like the Citizen – did not advocate violence, but passive resistance to all things English, and was extra-parliamentary. Bloom might have been attracted, but even Molly's soliloquy proves only an acquaintance, if an admiring acquaintance, with Griffith: 'and he was going about with some of them Sinner Fein lately or whatever they call themselves talking his usual trash and nonsense he says that little man he showed me without the neck is very intelligent the coming man Griffith is he well he doesnt look it thats all I can say still it must have been him he knew there was a boycott.' *Ulysses* is rife with rumours about Bloom. His role in Sinn Fein must remain one of those which are unconfirmed. Were it relevant to speculate outside the novel – which it isn't, because the process is endless – one might venture to say that Bloom might have found Griffith's anti-Semitism a problem.

Stephen Dedalus is, on the face of it, a more likely candidate for political election. If Tom Paulin is stretching a point by describing such a heavily ironized protagonist as 'heroic' – because he possesses 'the epic imagination' – it is certainly true that *A Portrait of the Artist as a Young Man* concludes with an apparently nationalistic prophecy. 'Welcome. O life! I go to encounter for the millionth time the reality of experience and to forge in the smithy of my soul the uncreated conscience of my race.' Even allowing for a little covert irony in the apostrophe to life and the excess of 'millionth', the ambition ostensibly expressed consorts oddly with Stephen's previously established pattern of refusals – the rebellious Lucifer's formula of *Non Serviam* has been consistently applied by Stephen to the Roman Catholic church, to McCann's petition for universal peace, temperance and votes for women, to Irish nationalism as represented by Davin. To Cranly, Stephen summarizes his position: 'I will not serve that in which I no longer believe, whether it call itself my home, my fatherland, or my church.' This anti-credo is contradicted, it seems, by the final, positive declaration already quoted. Or is it?

Automatically, one translates that last diary entry, so that it reads: 'forge in the smithy of my soul the uncreated consciousness of my race.' *Conscience* is emended to *consciousness*, even though *A Portrait* can supply, at a rough count, six examples of 'conscience' in the usual sense ('the threefold sting of conscience') and many more of 'consciousness' also employed in the conventional way.

Perhaps one should assume that Joyce meant what he wrote? We know that Stephen shares with Lucifer 'rebellious pride of the intellect'. Is this not another example of supreme egotism, rather than a statement of altruism? An affirmation not of national pride, but of personal pride? Isn't it a resolve to forge his own conscience by which he will judge the more conventional moralities of his countrymen? This conscience, as opposed to conventional ideas of conscience, has yet to be created. On 4 October 1906, Joyce wrote to Stannie, infuriated by Gogarty's hypocritical public fulminations against 'venereal excess': 'Am I the only honest person that has come out of Ireland in our time?' On 13 November 1906, Joyce returned to the subject and, in doing so, provides us with an expanded version of what it might be to be the conscience of one's race, Joycean style: 'Anyway my opinion is that if I put down a bucket into my own soul's well, sexual department, I draw up Griffith's and Ibsen's and Skeffington's and Bernard Vaughan's and St Aloysius' and Shelley's and Renan's water along with my own. And I am going to do that in my novel (inter alia) and plank the bucket down before the shades and substances mentioned above to see how they like it: and if they don't like it I can't help them. I am nauseated by their lying drivel about pure men and pure women and spiritual love and love forever: blatant lying in the face of the truth.' Against the truth, hypocrisies would be judged.

The ambition expressed here isn't narrowly political. It isn't even broadly political. The ambition expressed here is moral and literary. Joyce is interested in politics less in terms of issues and pressing questions than, it seems to me, in terms of their human consequences. The quarrel in *A Portrait* between Dante and Mr Casey and Simon Dedalus is a perfect illustration of Joyce's perception of politics. The issues are important for the way they issue in human behaviour; the political details interest Joyce less than the details of the quarrel, its triggers, its eddies, its angers, disguised and eventually open. Joyce shows us how people quarrel. What they are quarrelling about is merely the pretext for his art – which produces a scene matched only by Shakespeare (the quarrel between Brutus and Cassius) and D. H. Lawrence (the tiff between Ursula and Birkin). 'Those big words' which make Stephen so unhappy (a phrase used in 'Nestor', but recycled by Joyce from a review of the Sinn Fein poet Rooney) are less original than Joyce's observation of human behaviour: 'Then he asked uncle Charles was it tender. Uncle Charles could not speak because his mouth was full, but he nodded that it was.' We have all seen this – but without noticing it. It is so unnoticed that it is remarkable; so familiar, yet no writer has ever recorded it before. Opinions for and against Parnell have often been rehearsed. I think Joyce was amazed that they could still generate such passion – as amazed in his way as Balzac is when, in *La Cousine Bette*, he sends the ruined and decrepit Baron prowling priapically in search of the new maid. Politics are important but they are also commonplace – manifestly so, as is evident from reading any of our important political analysts as they work their changes, like master chefs, on the two or three issues in season on any particular week. There isn't much you can do in the way of originality with either swede or politics.

III

Except cook the books, as I believe Tom Paulin, inventively, nimbly, tenaciously and mistakenly, does with *Ulysses*. The question which interests me is why critics wish to politicize texts they admire. Behind, for instance, Dominic Manganiello's fascinating study, *Joyce's Politics*, itself Paulin's starting point, is a little tumour of guilt. Early on, Manganiello nobly states that one of his aims, perhaps his major aim, is to 'exculpate' Joyce from the charge of irresponsibility to the history of his own time. In order to achieve this, Manganiello deploys Robert Dahl's definition of 'political' as 'any pattern of human relationship that involves to a significant extent, power, rule, or authority'. Manganiello is sure that Joyce would accept such a definition. On what basis he never discloses. As a definition of politics it seems to me as unacceptably broad and question-begging as that of Barthes offered by Ellmann. But I suppose, adopting the Manganiello scenario, if you were an author who stood accused of irresponsibility in the face of contemporary history, you might very well be glad of a definition broad enough to secure an acquittal. Vague enough to have the charges thrown out of court.

For a great many people, I realize, politics – rather than being a guarantee of the commonplace, of consensus rather than individuality – are a guarantee of the importance of human behaviour, a guarantee of seriousness. This is why it is commonly maintained that all literature is political – a dogma which, I confess, baffles me, though I encounter it in European seminars frequently enough. Obviously, all literature can be viewed from a political perspective – just as it can be viewed from a vegetarian or animal rights perspective. It may not be the most appropriate way to read, say, a song like Burns's 'Red, Red Rose', but it can be done: Burns's invented Lallans might be discussed in the context of class and literary decorum. One could subordinate, as we have seen, Bloom's 'minor' preoccupation with his wife's adultery to the more 'important' issue of the British presence in Ireland. Jane Austen might be interpreted in class terms, as Auden did, brilliantly, surprisingly, in 'A Letter to Lord Byron':

> You could not shock her more than she shocks me;
>   Beside her Joyce seems innocent as grass.
> It makes me most uncomfortable to see
>   An English spinster of the middle class
> Describe the amorous effects of 'brass',

> Reveal so frankly and with such sobriety
> The economic basis of society.

That last line is a poignant reminder of a time when literary criticism of the Marxist persuasion was employed in disclosing the economic basis of literature, because *Kapital* had demonstrated the central role of economics in all aspects of human society. Quite soon, this approach began to seem crude and was replaced by a variety of related techniques for locating ideologies, historical contradictions, and structures of power – all designed to ensure that literature remained political and, therefore, important.

How else can one explain, in the case of Joyce, the refusal to accept several unambiguous statements? When Nancy Cunard sent Joyce a questionnaire about the Spanish Civil War, he retorted, 'I won't answer it because it is politics. Now politics are getting into everything.' In 1932, Joyce refused to be guest of honour at a St Patrick's Day party. He thought that an acceptance, in the presence of the Irish ambassador, would imply an endorsement of the Irish Free State: 'I care nothing about politics,' he wrote back unequivocally. In 1918, Joyce told Georges Borach that 'as an artist, I attach no importance to political conformity'. No one would deny that the young Joyce had his flirtations with politics, specifically socialism and moderate Sinn Fein, but the arc of his career and writing is away from politics. Frank Budgen remembered that 'on one subject he was more uncommunicative than any man I know: the subject of politics. He often spoke with admiration of Parnell, but it was the mystical realist navigating the bark of his reputation through the whirlpool of the *Times* commission that interested him and not his political principles.' Joyce's fascination, in other words, is with behaviour not beliefs. Budgen continues: 'An occasional vague reference to the pacific American anarchist, Tucker, was the only indication I ever heard of a political outlook. His view seemed to be that government is work for the specialist; and the artist, another specialist, had better leave it alone.'

Against this weight of evidence for the apolitical Joyce, a writer more interested in political behaviour than political beliefs, is a prejudice in favour of politics – a prejudice not unrelated to the prejudice towards unhappiness in poetry, what Larkin, even as he extricated Stevie Smith from the implications of her dangerous whimsicality, called the 'authority of sadness'. This prejudice in favour of politics is exemplified by the critic Arnold Kettle. In his 'Introductory' to *An Introduction to the English Novel*, this acute and relatively sophisticated Marxist ('the novel, like every other literary form, is a product of history') dismisses *David Copperfield*. It is a failure because it lacks analysis: 'it is a novel almost completely lacking what I mean by pattern.' In fact, *David Copperfield* is replete with pattern, like all Dickens's mature novels. The specific figure in the carpet, the key design, is responsibility and its opposite: there is the institutionalized business arrangement of Jorkins and Spenlow, two lawyers who regularly shift the responsibility for their decisions on to their absent partner; there is Micawber with his professions of responsibility and his actual financial fecklessness; there is the abuse of parental responsibility by Murdstone and Creakle; Steerforth's irresponsible behaviour with Emily and Peggotty's assumption of responsibility for her; there is Tommy Traddles who provides not only for Sophie, but the tribe of his in-laws, and so on. Had Kettle noticed this pattern, I imagine he would have revised his bizarre verdict: 'though *David Copperfield* conveys something of life it tells us very little about life. It is hard to say what it is about, except that it is about David Copperfield, and there again David's life is not presented to us in a way that can reasonably be called significant . . . it is all (or most of it) quite interesting and frequently very amusing; but that is all. There is no pattern.'

What a rich declaration of poverty. What an apt illustration of the critic's preference for belief rather than behaviour: '*David Copperfield* conveys something of life [but] tells us very little about life.' Less behaviour, Dickens, more belief. 'It is all (or most of it) quite interesting and frequently very amusing; but that is all.' *But that is all.* As if interest and amusement were a little low, something of which a *serious* person might be slightly ashamed. Later in his 'Introductory', Kettle warms to his chilly, moralistic theme, rather in the stonily intemperate manner of F. R. Leavis. 'Interest' and its crony 'amusement' are transformed by Kettle into something decidedly disreputable – 'human interest'. The latter, we are sternly informed, 'implies today a concern with life which is not a generalised moral interest'. The whole passage displays a set of attitudes, a set of superiorities, which belong in a museum, but have survived and evolved: 'the atom bomb is dropped on Hiroshima and the event of it is front-page news, "dramatic", "sensational", "of far-reaching consequences" according to taste. The political and moral implications are examined, with whatever inadequacy, in the leading articles. And then, gradually, there creep in the "human interest stories": what it felt like to be in Hiroshima when the bomb fell, what it felt like to pull the lever that dropped the bomb, the kind of life the pilot led when he wasn't dropping atom bombs, how long the trams stopped running, how Mr Mitsuoto made his miraculous escape. It is precisely the fact that the "human interest story" in our newspapers is nearly always presented from a morally neutral standpoint, without significance, that makes it so often rather disgusting.' *Rather disgusting* – how Mr Mitsuoto made his miraculous escape. *Without significance* – what it felt like to be in Hiroshima when the bomb fell. It is difficult to believe that Arnold Kettle isn't intent on some dramatic Swiftian irony, bent on a scathing satire of moralists – moralists interested in human behaviour only as it illustrates general beliefs.

The piece, then, isn't the relic it seems. Its underlying attitude is shared by all those critics who find human interest somehow unworthy of Art, by all those critics intent on ushering the detailed life of the novel into retirement and presenting the reader with a solid moral precept or two to be placed at either end of the mental mantelpiece. These critics mistrust humour, light verse, and eccentricity. They feel safe and serious by definition when they find politics. Otherwise, there may be human interest, but where is the content? This is Tom Paulin on Ian McGilchrist's *Against Criticism*: 'this harmless Sitwellian waffle makes me wonder whether English studies will go the way of phrenology.' Not criticism, you notice – English studies. The threat of marginality is vividly present to Paulin, who, in an essay on translation, attributes his own worry to Peter Porter: 'the basis of his complaint is that in England the poet can be neither dissident nor dignified laureate, and is therefore condemned to be a harmless and neglected figure.' *Condemned* is a remarkably strange word to use in this context. One thinks of a 'harmless and neglected' poet like Cavafy, or Hardy, or Elizabeth Bishop – and wonders in what sense any of the three can be thought of as 'condemned'?

The oppositions are wrongly framed as they usually are in these discussions – either 'dissident' or 'dignified laureate' or the alternative, 'a harmless and neglected figure'. Although, knowing them to be questionable, Seamus Heaney therefore questions a related set of oppositions, these oppositions nevertheless generate the substance of *The Government of the Tongue*. 'Why should the joyful affirmation of music and poetry ever constitute an affront to life?' Heaney asks, rhetorically and unanswerably. All the same, Heaney has inherited and accepted the artistic guilt felt by Eastern European poets – who see the lyric impulse as an affront to suffering and the need for social responsibility. Even as he repudiates this position, he experiences a pang of doubt: 'I do not in fact see how poetry can survive as a category of human consciousness if it does not put poetic considerations first – expressive considerations, that is, based upon its own genetic laws which spring into operation at the moment of lyric conception. Yet it is possible to feel all this and still concede the justice of Czeslaw Milosz's rebuke to the autocracy of such romantic presumption.' Heaney is partly motivated by a becoming modesty in the face of European political experience and partly victimized by the mind's nostalgia and appetite for simple binary oppositions, which have been with us since the invention of good and evil – two absolutes hardly ever sighted in their pure form after their first appearance in the human brain.

No wonder, then, that we overvalue those who claim to have seen pure specimens. Anita Brookner, whom I have already mocked in my title essay, is susceptible like Heaney to a pleasurably puritan abnegation: 'these writers are more dangerous than their English counterparts: bitterness, regret, wildness, fascination with God and the devil mark them out as heavyweights, not to be trifled with. When Milosz lectured to American students he "openly acknowledged the existence of good and evil, a stance they dismissed as irredeemably reactionary". No doubt they preferred to watch television.' Despite that tart final sentence – with its implication that the alternative to Milosz is a life sentence of game shows on television – I am inclined to agree with the students who are sceptical about the existence of those moral dinosaurs, good and evil. And on our side of the argument, I would be joined by Jane Austen, George Eliot, Graham Greene and Milan Kundera. These writers know that evil, alas, hardly ever comes in reassuringly melodramatic guise, for which the pantomime hiss is an adequate and appropriate response.

And we should be wary of those who, however impeccable their credentials, simplify the world of truth. In this, I include writers I admire like Rozewicz and Milosz. Both, after the Second World War, despaired of the value of literature. 'Famine and death are more powerfully expressive', wrote Milosz, 'than the most inspired stanza or the most beautifully painted picture.' Similarly disturbed, Rozewicz turned to literature 'for practical help' and 'became angry and disillusioned with the greatest works'. I find these pronouncements self-indulgent, hyperbolic, inaccurate, illogical, ridiculous and self-important. Is the relative power of poetry and death a matter for such pained and eloquent surprise? Of course death can alter your life more radically than a sonnet on your mistress's eyebrow. Of course you cannot eat a poem if you are starving. Who ever thought differently? The opposition between famine and poetry is an hilarious category mistake. There is no logical opposition, no conflict, no pressing choice that has to be made. Art is relatively unimportant most of the time to most people. If you are starving, art is absolutely unimportant all of the time to everyone.

Art is about pleasure – complicated pleasure, but pleasure nevertheless. Many people value the purer pleasure produced by chocolate, beer, cigarettes and sex. Some people are lucky enough to enjoy all of those things and art. Art's greatest virtue, apart from the pleasure it gives to a limited number of people, is that it is, with rare exceptions, harmless. Harmless: the word much bandied by Tom Paulin, as he excoriates 'this harmless Sitwellian waffle', or notes the possibility of being 'a harmless and neglected figure'. It is not that Tom Paulin wants poetry to be the opposite of 'harmless'. He does not want it to be 'harmful'. But he would like it to be as important as politics. It can only be as important as politics if it is as banal and commonplace as politics.

Art, as Zbigniew Herbert has said, is opposed to politics: 'the languages of politics and literature are entirely different and so are the mentalities. Politicians are concerned with "far-reaching" goals, personal games, gangster-style tricks. What interests me is human fate. What does me good is bad for politicians: what suits them I find indigestible. We use two separate styles. I have tried to use the conditional. I hesitate, I appeal to conscience. I dislike the imperative, exclamation mark, black and white divisions.' This credo, this declaration of interest in human fate, can be set against those who, like Arnold Kettle, find mere human interest insufficiently lofty. I would also cite Chekhov: 'great writers and artists must take part in politics only in so far as it is necessary to put up a defence against politics.'

But perhaps the crucial figure in this debate is Orwell – a political writer increasingly drawn to the neutralizing of politics by the weighty trivia of ordinary human interests. Twice in his essays, Orwell commends and endorses E. M. Forster's comment on the wartime publication of 'The Love Song of J. Alfred Prufrock': 'I should have felt, like E. M. Forster, that simply by standing aloof and keeping touch with pre-war emotions, Eliot was carrying on the human heritage.' *Nineteen Eighty-Four* is not simply a pessimistic book in which Winston is defeated and forced to conform. There is a muted positive in the presence of the proles. They will not overthrow the Party, but they exist outside it. And, as Orwell said, 'in all societies the common people must live to some extent *against* the existing order'. Even in the cells of the Ministry of Love they retain their subversive vitality – in contrast to the Party prisoners.

The common people have private lives. They are unaffected by political events: pigeon-fancying, darts, walking the dog and so on induce what Orwell calls a 'semi-anaesthesia'. And it is a recognition of this impulse in himself which led him to note in his wartime diary: 'Not much news – i.e. only news of world-wide importance; nothing that has affected me personally.' The process of life is unaffected by politics: 'I never read the proclamations of generals before battle, the speeches of fuehrers and prime ministers . . . without seeming to hear in the background a chorus of raspberries from all the millions of common men to whom these high sentiments have no appeal.' Similarly, Orwell's essay on the postcards of Donald McGill is a tribute to the durability of ordinary life: he believes in the indestructibility of the dirty joke. In the same way, Orwell interprets the Fool in *King Lear* as a McGill figure: 'his jokes, riddles and scraps of rhymes, and his endless digs at Lear's high-minded folly . . . are like a trickle of sanity running through the play, a reminder that somewhere or other, in spite of injustices, cruelties, intrigues, deceptions and misunderstandings . . . life is going on much as usual.'

The Second World War demonstrated to Orwell that the common people 'preserved the ordinary pattern of their lives to a surprising extent even amid the disorganisation caused by the bombing. As William Empson puts it, "Three fathoms down the sea is always calm".' Orwell believed passionately in the continuity of popular culture ('it is continuous . . . there is something that persists, as in a living creature') and this belief finds expression in *Nineteen Eighty-Four*. The prole woman, whose beam-end is a metre wide, has stepped straight out of a McGill postcard: the thread stretches unbroken from the early 1900s to 1984, and beyond. Winston's fate is Orwell's prediction for the intelligentsia who need an orthodoxy to replace religion. The Quixotic element in Orwell was afraid but the Sancho Panza element, the 'average sensual man', was in the pub – having a drink with Henry Miller and the prole woman with the 'rasping red skin', inside the whale.

Saul Bellow

According to Oscar Wilde, before Dickens, there were no fogs, and before Turner no sunsets. Wilde is merely exaggerating a truth, practising the art of aphorism, drawing our attention to this precept: we need art so that we can see what we are seeing. On his way to the Hebrides, Dr Johnson pulled down the blind on what a future generation of writers would take for their subject matter – wild, 'romantic' nature. Johnson, had he lived, would not have seen the point of Wordsworth's 'single sheep, and the one blasted tree, / And the bleak music of that old stone wall'. But if art enables and liberates its audience, it can also disable and enslave the subsequent generation of writers. In *To Jerusalem and Back*, Saul Bellow notes that 'in every generation we recognise a leader race of masterminds whose ideas ("class-struggle", "Oedipus complex", "identity crisis") come down over us like butterfly nets.' This insight applies to artists as well as thinkers.

After Dickens, as it were, the weather took a turn for the worse, as Virginia Woolf recorded in *Orlando*: 'The great cloud which hung, not only over London, but over the whole of the British Isles on the first day of the nineteenth century stayed, or rather, did not stay, for it was buffeted about constantly by blustering gales, long enough to have extraordinary consequences upon those who lived beneath its shadow. A change seemed to have come over the climate of England.' In the twentieth century, similar restrictions obtain. Rex Warner recalls how, as Oxford undergraduates, he and Auden used to walk by canals and gasworks because they were 'already sanctified by a phrase in *The*

Waste Land'. Eliot had altered the landscape and it was to be some time before, so to speak, Auden could write in praise of limestone. Meanwhile, Auden's coevals were blindly exploring his idiosyncratic geography of deserted leadmines and overshot waterwheels – and wondering why their own environments felt so drab and unpromising as possible subject matter. Hopkins had the answer to this predicament – admire and do otherwise – a recipe, however, which is more easily assented to than followed.

The classic account of imprisonment by admiration is Ted Solotaroff's essay, 'Silence, Exile and Cunning' (1970), which antedates Harold Bloom's *The Anxiety of Influence* by three years. There, Solotaroff shows how the aspiring writer's mind, locked in the cell of its preconceptions, receives visits from real life, but for the most part gets down to serving the sentence. Flaubert was the model, for Solotaroff and Bellow ('In writing *The Victim* I accepted a Flaubertian standard'). In the years of virtual silence, Solotaroff, 'trying to give the words that quiet, impassive gleam through the ordinary of Flaubert's *Un Cœur Simple* . . . would spend months revising a ten-page story so that it might come out like the poem Yeats dreamed of, "as cold and beautiful as the dawn". These values of "art" persisted, and in the five years after I left Ann Arbor, I wrote exactly seven stories. In terms of experience, they were probably the richest years of my life: I was engrossed in a young, deep, complex, and stormy marriage; we lived mostly in the Village but also in Berkeley and in Maine; I worked in innumerable restaurants and a few gambling houses and racetracks as a waiter or bartender; I was also a psychiatric attendant, a temporary office worker, an eradicator of gooseberry bushes in the Sierras, and an assistant to a Japanese gardener; I twice started graduate school, read a great deal, and even taught myself Latin and German. Virtually none of this went into my writing.'

'Instead,' Solotaroff ruefully recalls, 'I laboured on my few ironic tales of empty lives.' Most writers, when they begin to write, are actually taking dictation from their immediate great predecessors. Someone fully formed like Kipling, with a new subject – India – and a new style to go with it, is a rare event. For the rest, while the pantheon casts a long, blighting shadow, some writer nearer in time, or less weighty, may provide the liberation from Literature. Eliot, in 'To Criticise the Critic', explains that 'just as the modern poet who influenced me was not Baudelaire but Jules Laforgue, so the dramatic poets were Marlowe and Webster and Tourneur and Middleton and Ford, not Shakespeare. A poet of the supreme greatness of Shakespeare can hardly influence, he can only be imitated: and the difference between influence and imitation is that influence can fecundate, whereas imitation – especially unconscious imitation – can only sterilise.' Seamus Heaney has recorded the importance of Ted Hughes to him as an example: 'suddenly, the matter of contemporary poetry was the material of my own life.' Athol Fugard has acknowledged a similar debt to Camus. After apprentice work which struggled to accommodate South African material in the dramatic forms supplied by Tennessee Williams, Clifford Odets, Eugene O'Neill and Arthur Miller, Fugard found what he needed in Camus's treatment of Algeria: 'when I first encountered the articulation of that almost pagan, sensual life lived out in the sun, next to a sea, with warm rocks being, in a sense, the ultimate reality, it struck a resonance in me that persists to this day.' The key word here is surely 'articulation', when it is linked to something fundamentally inarticulate – a landscape and an associated way of life.

For Bellow, as for Nabokov, even more than Nabokov, articulation was caught up in one categorical imperative – Speak, Memory. In *The Victim* and *Dangling Man*, Bellow is paying his dues to modernism, existentialism, Camus – serving his time. 'Ironic tales of empty lives', they are crafted, careful and slightly comatose – except for one page of *Dangling Man* in which Bellow stumbles on what is to be his subject. That is, autobiography, the long clear packed morning of life, evoked in streetwise, high-minded, headlong prose. The hero is cleaning his wife's shoes: 'it was doing something I had done as a child. In Montreal, on such afternoons as this, I often asked permission to spread a paper on the sitting room floor and shine all the shoes in the house, including Aunt Dina's with their long tongues and scores of eyelets. When I thrust my arm into one of her shoes it reached well above the elbow and I could feel the brush against my arm through the soft leather.' When Bellow reaches 'their long tongues', the prose suddenly stirs and Joseph is taken back to St Dominique Street and a series of memories whose vividness is their only justification, ending with: 'two quarrelling drunkards, one of whom walked away bleeding, drops falling from his head like the first slow drops of a heavy rain in summer, a crooked line of drops left on the pavement as he walked.' Cleaning shoes: for any admirer of Bellow, this moment links directly with the end of *Herzog*, where the style is less constrained, more ejaculatory and excitable: 'Moses could remember a time when Willie, too, had been demonstrative, passionate, explosive, given to bursts of rage, flinging objects to the ground. Just a moment – what was it, now, that he had thrown down? A brush! That was it! The broad old Russian shoe brush. Will slammed it to the floor so hard the veneer backing fell off, and beneath were the stitches, ancient waxed thread, maybe even sinew.' This little miracle of particularity, and many others like it, is what we read Bellow for. As Herzog puts it, 'he sometimes imagined he was an industry that manufactured personal history'. This personal history is the placenta which has nourished so many of Bellow's novels, keeping up an endless supply of rich details. Nothing is too small for him to notice. In *Humboldt's Gift*, it might be a clothesline, 'old and dark grey': 'It had burst open and was giving up its white pith.' Or it might be a locker room, where 'hair pieces like Skye terriers waited for their masters'; or a court room, where a lawyer called Cannibal Pinsker has 'a large yellow cravat that lay on his shirt like a cheese omelette'; or an old man's trouser fly, three feet long. As a writer, Bellow sees. He sees the bare toes of Pierre Thaxter 'pressed together like Smyrna figs'. But what he *has* seen, in the past, is, if anything, more vivid: at the Division Street turkish baths, everything remains as it was, and Franush 'crawls up like a red salamander with a stick to tip the latch of the furnace, which is too hot to touch, and then on all fours, with testicles swinging on a long sinew and the clean anus staring out, he backs away groping for the bucket. He pitches in the water and the boulders flash and sizzle.'

Bellow is not one of those purely imaginative writers like Golding or Ian McEwan who invent copiously and logically from first premises. You cannot imagine him wondering what it is like to be an ape married to a young woman writer who is having trouble with her second novel after the success of the first. Or wondering what might transpire if a group of boys was placed on an island without adult supervision. Bellow uses experience, his own life. And so has gone a stage beyond Solotaroff. No surprise, then, to see *The Adventures of Augie March* cited as a key text in 'Silence, Exile and Cunning' – cited because it embraced American experience instead of taking up an alienated posture. Something in Solotaroff's analysis makes this seem like a tactic, almost a lucky break, a trend that he, Solotaroff, didn't spot early enough. Certainly, unlike Solotaroff, virtually everything of Bellow's life in its formative years suddenly gets into his writing with *The Adventures of Augie March*. There and in the best subsequent fiction, Bellow's writing is earthed in the American city. St Dominique Street, Napoleon Street, Jefferson Street – Bellow gives his imaginative source several different names, but it is always the street where he lives: 'here was a wider range of feelings than he had ever again been able to find . . . What was wrong with Napoleon Street? thought Herzog. All he ever wanted was there.'

With this subject comes a distinctively American voice, capable of using a slang word like 'slugger' as well as 'fancy' words like 'tergiversate'. But the Ivy League intonation was always there in Bellow. The slang arrives with *Augie March*, and although the full title acknowledges Twain's *The Adventures of Huckleberry Finn*, it is a reasonable supposition that Salinger's *The Catcher in the Rye* gave Bellow the example he needed of a fluent and formidable vernacular. Certainly, it is difficult to read a sentence like 'But I enjoyed Caroline's company, I have to admit' without being reminded of Salinger even now. And to say that this is merely American is to miss the point. Before Salinger, it was American, but it was not American literature.

In *Herzog*, there is a heart-stopping description of Valentine Gersbach losing his leg in a childhood accident: ' "Seven years old, in Saratoga Springs, running after the balloon man; he blew his little *fifel*. When I took that short cut through the freight yards, crawling under the cars. Lucky the brakeman found me as soon as the wheel took off my leg. Wrapped me in his coat and rushed me to the hospital. When I came to, my nose was bleeding. Alone in the room . . . I leaned over," Gersbach went on, as if relating a miracle. "A drop of blood fell on the floor, and as it splashed I saw a little mouse under the bed who seemed to be staring at the splash. It backed away, it moved its tail and whiskers. And the room was just full of bright sunlight . . . It was a little world underneath the bed. Then I realised that my leg was gone".'

This brilliantly haphazard, grammatically spontaneous narrative, by the man who has stolen Herzog's wife, receives this accolade from Herzog: 'each man has his own batch of poems.' And these poems of experience are repeated, recited by everyone, again and again: 'there were stories about himself, too, that Moses had told a hundred times, so he couldn't complain of Gersbach's repetitiveness.' This weakness is a trait which Madeleine, his wife, satirizes: 'Yes, I know, your darling mother wore flour sacks.' And his mistress, Ramona, is familiar with Gersbach's leg-action: 'As you told me. Like a gondolier.' As Herzog, so Bellow. The novels have their share of repetition. Augie and Herzog both remember having their hair washed with a bar of Castile soap – by a mother who made sheets out of Ceresota sacks. In *Dangling Man*, 'I warmed myself at a salamander flaming in an oil drum near a newsstand.' In *Augie March*, 'down the cold alleys flames tore from the salamander cans of people selling chestnuts'. In *Augie March*, his girlfriend's father wears 'a white drill suit and a helmet with a nipple'. In *Henderson the Rain King*, Henderson has a 'helmet with its nipple at the top'. In *Seize the Day*, Mr Rappaport's ear cartilage is 'twisted like a cabbage heart', while in *Humboldt's Gift* a Pole called Casey has ears that are 'amazingly crinkled, like Chinese cabbage'. Corde, in *The Dean's December*, feels betrayed by some cyclamens which have bloomed in a crematorium, but, since he likes these flowers, he may have to effect a reconciliation with them: 'the irrationality of this did not disturb him. If this was how he was, this was how he was.' Herzog opens his narrative similarly phlegmatic: 'If I am out of my mind, it's all right with me, thought Moses Herzog.'

In fact, though they are quite numerous, these repetitions can usually be discounted because Bellow's memory-hoard is so fecund. There is always plenty that is new, like 'the long hard rays of tendons' on the backs of Mrs Renling's hands, or Gorman the gangster putting away his gun: 'he was reaching inside his sleeve with a lifted shoulder, almost like a woman pulling up an inside strap.' Likewise the drawbacks of Bellow's fast-talking prose, which, though generally effective, can sometimes produce redundancies worthy of a freak show: 'Wilhelm let out a long, hard breath and raised the brows of his round and somewhat circular eyes.' Yet, set beside Bellow's wonderful dialogue, glittering with redundancy and anacoluthon, does the odd failure matter? Isn't it a necessary risk which can produce this: 'I know about suffering – we're on the same identical network'; or 'she was a no-good lay. A broad eighteen don't know even how to shit'; or 'Daisy didn't married yet?' Yes, we say, yes.

And then again, we say no. The new novel, *More Die of Heartbreak*,* is ruined by repetitions and echoes of earlier work, since there is scarcely any redeeming specificity to compensate, nor any form to speak of. It is a dismally thin performance. The characters are the merest tokens: Benn Crader is an Arnoldian representative of pure culture, a natural contemplative, whose botanical interests are pure rather than applied science; his fate is to be mangled in the machinery of modern sexual desire. In physical terms, he has a humped back like a wingcase and eyes that look like the mathematical symbol for infinity. Well, they would, wouldn't they? The central ideas are laughable and garnished with reading which, in other Bellow novels, might generate strenuous discussion, but here amounts to little more than perfunctory citations from a Russian literature binge. Kenneth Trachtenberg, the narrator, teaches Russian literature –

More Die of Heartbreak by Saul Bellow, The Alison Press / Secker and Warburg.

hence the garland of dusty immortelles he hangs on his cousin, Fishl: 'he was flavoured with essences belonging to that period of Rosanov, Meyerhold, the late Chekhov, Mandelstam and Bely.' With as little potential meaning, you might say that someone now was flavoured with the essences belonging to, say, Peter Ackroyd, Anita Brookner, William Boyd, Anthony Burgess and Peter Hall. This is typical, alas.

First repetition: Kenneth has left Paris, even though his father has promised to introduce him to the 'agent who had forced Tsvetayeva's husband to work for the GPU'. Kenneth prefers the mid-West because 'that's where the action is now – the real modern action'. In *The Dean's December*, Albert Corde had written 'a few pieces on the poetess Tsvetayeva as she was remembered by the Russian colony in Paris. How her husband, whom she loved deeply, became a member of the GPU and was forced to take part in killings.' Corde, too, left Paris for the mid-West because 'America is where the real action is.' Kenneth, however, has an additional motive: he wants to remain in close contact with his uncle, Benn Crader, the world-class botanist, who wishes to re-marry – or, in the Swedenborgian lingo of the novel, desires an exchange of souls in love. This, of course, involves sexual needs and, in that sphere, Crader has to compete in a world where women have a composite ideal of the male: 'candid women will tell you, I'd like some of this and some of that – a little Muhammad Ali for straight sex, some Kissinger for savvy, Cary Grant for looks, Jack Nicholson for entertainment, plus André Malraux or some Jew for brains. Commonest fantasy there is.' So common, in fact, that it has already been given an outing in *Mr Sammler's Planet*: 'he fetched back, for example, a statement by Angela Gruner, blurted out after several drinks when she was laughing, gay, and evidently feeling free (to the point of brutality) with old Uncle Sammler. "A Jew brain, a black cock, a Nordic beauty," she had said, "is what a woman wants." Putting together the ideal man.'

Of course, in these trying times, there are external consider-ations, too. AIDS, for instance, though that is 'an elaborate terrifying organic figure' (apparently) for some inner spiritual malaise. In the same way, lead poisoning in *The Dean's December* 'stands for something else that we all sense'. As for sex, it is, for most people, a cure for all problems: 'they turn to sex as the analgesic.' In *The Dean's December*, Corde's sister makes 'an aspirin marriage'. All the same, at first it seems possible that Crader will make it work with his much younger, beautiful bride, Matilda Layamon. After all, perhaps Crader's insight into plants can be transferred to human beings: 'he was wrapped in nature. The whole vegetable kingdom was his garment – his robe, his coat – and that to me meant fundamental liberty from low-grade human meanness, it meant universality. Still, Uncle's garment was incomplete. It didn't quite button.'

Neither did the garment of Von Humboldt Fleisher in *Humboldt's Gift* and look what happened to him – heart failure in a flophouse. 'Humboldt wanted to drape the world in radiance, but he didn't have enough material. His attempt ended at the belly. Below hung the shaggy nudity we know so well.' Shaggy nudity is a feature of *More Die of Heartbreak*, where we learn that 'this literalness, from a sexual standpoint, is lethal. When it becomes a matter of limbs, members and organs, Eros faces annihilation.' Not a lot has changed, in that case, from *The Dean's December*: there 'the horror is in the literalness – the genital literalness of the delusion. That's what gives the curse its finality. The literalness of bodies and their members – outside without insides.' *Insides*, in both novels, means the soul, rather than viscera. Maybe Crader can escape literalness, since he is 'an outstanding "noticer" (there is such a type)'. The parenthesis can be confirmed by anyone who has read *The Dean's December* because there Corde is just such a type: 'He looked out, noticing. What a man he was for noticing! Continually attentive to his surroundings.' Either character, given this faculty, might have noticed that Bellow's use of Baron Hulot, from *La Cousine Bette*, had already been used as an instance of indestructible desire in *The Dean's December* and *Humboldt's Gift*. Or that Forster's aphorism, 'How do I know what I think till I see what I say?', had already appeared (uncredited) in *Humboldt's Gift*, admittedly in a different form: viz. 'Still, I don't seem to know what I think till I see what I say.'

An outstanding noticer might have noticed, too, that Dita Schwartz's 'hive of bandages', following her facial surgery, is a repeat from *Augie March*, where a brawler appears in court wearing 'a bloody beehive of bandages, totter-headed'.

Dita Schwartz, incidentally, shows how inattentive and incompetent Bellow has become in this novel: she is twice mentioned by name before she is properly introduced. On page 113, Kenneth's mother refers enigmatically to 'a young woman named Dita Schwartz', who is 'evidently glad to listen' to Kenneth for the sake of her education. On page 121, Crader refers to 'your friend Dita Schwartz'. But it isn't until page 173 that the reader is given any data to go with Dita. Her role in the novel is to be the ideal woman, with the drawback of a poor complexion. In every way except the physical, she is perfect for Kenneth. She admires his Russian name-dropping and, as only a course student can, she audits him. He, however, is still infatuated with Treckie, the mother of his daughter, but not his wife. Kenneth is considerate and she prefers to be brutalized in bed and, as a result, has shins which are bruised like the markings on peacock feathers. As Herzog remarks, 'nothing can be done about the sexual preferences of women. That's ancient wisdom. Nor of men.' Kenneth is fixated by Treckie's body which is that of a child-woman.

Crader, on the other hand, has married a woman, who, though beautiful, doesn't suit him. Matilda's shoulders are too wide and her breasts are too far apart. Lest these seem trivial considerations, little imperfections that a mature personality might come to love, Bellow is forced to draft in the Swedenborgian system of correspondences. If everything is a sign, these imperfections presumably show that Matilda, for all her beauty, is too like her father – is, in point of fact, a bloke. How else can one explain her father's revelation that, when she was born, it was difficult to tell what sex she was? Crader is in no doubt: physically, she's a woman. But, we are meant to infer, only venture beyond the literal – and she's a bloke for Crader, much like Norman Bates masquerading as his mother in *Psycho*, a film which he finds worryingly pertinent.

By now you may have some notion of how wacky *More Die of*

Heartbreak is. Common sense seems to have deserted Bellow utterly. A strip show in Kyoto provokes Kenneth to reflect, as the women dilate themselves manually: 'Miss Osaka and Miss Nara put it in front of you, as literal as it was possible to be, and the more literal it was, the more mystery there seemed to be in it . . . All these botanists, engineers, inventors of miraculous visual instruments from electron microscopes to equipment that sent back pictures of the moons of Saturn, cared for nothing but these slow openings.' Bellow's conclusion seems to be that the precious life of the mind is ultimately in thrall to an orifice. Which is another version of Kenneth's belief that 'the quality people are always knee-deep in the garbage of "personal life" '. Now this nexus of assertions is comic. I don't myself find it surprising that engineers, botanists, inventors of electron microscopes, or (for that matter) winners of the Nobel Prize for Literature should take a look if a woman chooses to open her vagina for them. Bellow appears to have an exaggerated idea of the dignity of his own mind.

The central theme of the novel is equally nutty in its presentation. It is that more die of heartbreak than are killed by radiation. In the East, there are camps, prison sentences, mental and physical abuse; in Africa, there is famine; in the West, there is heartbreak. Bellow allows his characters to ironize this dichotomy, but it is clear that the purpose of the novel is ultimately to endorse it. Thus, Kenneth's mother, working with refugees in Somalia, herself a refugee from her husband's philandering, parodies the position by setting against the work-camp at Kolyma her husband: 'suddenly Dad was paraded in front of us with all his chicks in various stages of undress. *That* was an ordeal!' The truth is that suffering is manifold and it is very stupid to make meaningless comparisons. Why say more die of heartbreak than of radiation when there are no statistics for either? Unless, of course, you want to trail your coat, or take off into the unprovable – the latter being an area of which Bellow has always been overfond. Sometimes the famous resonance just sounds hollow, and it can be irritating when he pretends to be the last believer in the soul.

One of the worst features of *More Die of Heartbreak* is its depressing gabbiness, which is not unrelated to the rhetorical sauce he ladles out so generously. There is built into the novel a kind of negative commentary of asides and reminders which supply reasons why no one should bother to read it: 'I will remember that I am not here to lecture on history but to relate the strange turns in the life of my uncle Benn'; 'so it's one moment of flashing insight and then a quarter of an hour of pedantry and tiresome elaboration'; 'but let me not be sidetracked again'; 'excuse the language; I'm in a hurry and I can't stop to pick and choose among the available terms'. This digressive garrulity, this formlessness, one might argue, is of no importance in Bellow because his work has always repudiated form. In a *Paris Review* interview, he said: 'I could not, with such an instrument as I developed in the first two books, express a variety of things I knew intimately. Those books, though useful, did not give me a form in which I felt comfortable. A writer should be able to express himself easily, naturally, copiously in a form which frees his mind, his energies. Why should he hobble himself with formalities? With a borrowed sensibility? With the desire to be "correct"?'

In *Augie March*, Bellow's greatest novel, form is accordingly dismissed on the first page. The narrator declares for spontaneity: he will 'go at things as I have taught myself, free-style, and will make the record in my own way: first to knock, first admitted'. And yet, in the midst of Dickensian detail ('loud-breathing and wind-breaking, [Winnie the dog] lay near the old lady's stool on a cushion embroidered with a Berber aiming a rifle at a lion'), in the midst of this, there is a formal polarity to which everything refers. On the one hand, there is the wised-up pragmatic-realist stance of Grandma Lausch, which is responsible for the disposing of the retarded Georgie into a home: 'And now he realised that we would leave him and he began to do with his soul, that is, to let out his moan, worse for us than tears, though many grades below the pitch of weeping. Then Mama slumped down and gave in utterly. It was when she had the bristles of his special head between her hands and was kissing him that she began to cry.' On the other hand, there are the impracticalities of pure feeling, of idealism, which at first are embodied by brother Simon, on whom '*Tom Brown's Schooldays* for many years had an influence we were not in a position to afford'. Even the eagle in Mexico conforms to the pattern – by turning out, after all, to be less than one hundred per cent ruthless; 'well, it was hard to take from wild nature, that there should be humanity mixed with it'. Augie himself is poised between the two poles, though there is no doubt that his final destination will be in the camp of those with feelings.

In *Humboldt's Gift*, the polarity around which the novel is organized is 'rot or burn'. Humboldt, Cantabile, are the obvious exemplars of frenetic activity to which Citrine is attracted, but Citrine's brother, Ulick, an ostensible digression, is also part of the pattern: 'You know what I found the other day? The deed to the family burial plots in Waldheim. There are two graves left. You wouldn't want to buy mine, would you? I'm not going to lie around. I'm having myself cremated. I need action. I'd rather go into the atmosphere. Look for me in the weather reports.' Here, Bellow has literalized Humboldt's philosophy of life: 'if life is not intoxicating, it's nothing. Here it's burn or rot. The USA is a romantic country. If you want to be sober, Charlie, it's only because you're a maverick and you'll try anything.' At the centre of *Humboldt's Gift* is a long exposition of, in effect, Lambert Strether's advice to Little Bilham in *The Ambassadors* ('Live as much as you can, young man. It's a mistake not to'): 'Or as William James put it, human beings really lived when they lived at the top of their energies. Something like the *Wille zur Macht*. Suppose then you began with the proposition that boredom was a kind of pain caused by unused powers, the pain of wasted possibilities or talents, and was accompanied by expectations of the optimum utilization of capacities.'

As you might by now expect, in *More Die of Heartbreak*, this last idea is brought out of retirement. The sexually hyperactive Rudi Trachtenberg, we are told, 'is responding to a talent, and a talent will cause your death if you try to hide it'. Notice how the idea is now overstated, how a possibly flashing insight has become a merely flashy insight.

This is a haunted novel. The dim ghosts of better books are everywhere. For Picasso, the ultimate failure was not to copy others, but to copy himself. *More Die of Heartbreak* is pure Parnassian. At its end, Crader, his marriage in ruins, flees to the frozen wastes of the symbolic Arctic, and it is *The Dean's December* which can supply the most lucid gloss on his behaviour: 'these badgering perplexities, intricacies of equilibrium, sick hopes, riddling evils, sadistic calculations – you might do worse than to return to that strict zero-blue and simple ice.' Like, more or less, Arnold's scholar gipsy taking a rain-check on 'this strange disease of modern life'.

In one important particular, Bellow hasn't copied himself. His real territory – Napoleon Street, for short – has been pushed out of the picture. When Benn Crader, like any Bellow protagonist, wants to reminisce about his youth on Jefferson Street (now replaced by the Ecliptic Circle Electronic Tower) he is discouraged by his bride: 'she doesn't care for that far-away-and-long-ago stuff'; 'she doesn't care for your imaginative background music'. There is a great deal of intuition of souls in this book, which perhaps provides one with an excuse for looking at *More Die of Heartbreak* in the same way oneself. Superficially, the novel exactly fits Citrine's description of 'the insignificant Picasso sculpture with its struts and its sheet metal, no wings, no victory, only a token, a reminder, only the *idea* of a work of art'. This latest effort is without a soul, mainly because it is all about the soul, the soul and ideas. Real life is somewhere else – as it must be for Bellow after the elevation of the Nobel Prize. Unconsciously, he has dramatized his predicament in Uncle Benn Crader, who stands in his rich duplex, feeling uncomfortable, miles above Jefferson Street, listening to the moans of the sycamores far below. Only Uncle Harold Vilitzer comes alive – not smoking, but mashing up twenty cigars a day, still tough in temperament, but physically as hollow as a wicker basket. 'Only the pacemaker unit under his shirt had any weight.' Not that Vilitzer compares with Lollie Fewter, a minor character in *Augie March* on whom the young Bellow lavished his brimming gifts: 'young Lollie Fewter who was fresh up from the coal fields, that girl with her green eyes from which she didn't try to keep the hotness, and her freckled bust presented to the gathering of men she came among with her waxing rags and the soft shake of her gait.' The whole of *More Die of Heartbreak* isn't worth that one hectic, ungrammatical, accurate sentence, utterly unforced in its plenitude.

John Updike

'A cold coming we had of it.' T. S. Eliot's famous line takes on new meaning after one has read *The Witches of Eastwick*,* John Updike's deceptively playful, intricate and absorbing look at feminism, evil and the cosmic set-up. Darryl Van Horne, a first dan of the adultery belt, shows 'supernatural control, and when he did come his semen, all agreed later, was marvellously cold'. After his arrival in Eastwick, a small town in Rhode Island, the familiar desolate couplings are replaced by triplings, lesbian orgies and even a session with a dog – a recreation best described, perhaps, as canilingus. Van Horne, it soon becomes clear, is a devil. Hence the traditionally chilled ejaculate, authoritatively reported as long ago as 1622 in Pierre de Lancre's *L'Incrédulité et mécréance du sortilège* by one Jeanette d'Abadie, who also volunteers the information that the devil's member is scaly and painful. Van Horne's is merely uncircumcised and 'empurpled' when erect. Just the same, Jane Smart, one of the titular witches, 'still ached, at both ends of her perineum'. Van Horne stretches the women physically and artistically: a reporter is encouraged to become a novelist (though a sample of her prose is hilariously calculated to undermine this ambition); a sculptress is guided from miniatures to monumentalism; a cellist to improve her technique.

Much of the fun of Updike's novel is in establishing the supernatural dimension against the reader's expectation. Or that,

**The Witches of Eastwick* by John Updike, André Deutsch.

at least, is the intention. In practice, though there are some deft transpositions, the enterprise is much less successful than, say, Ian McEwan's 'Reflections of a Kept Ape', a story which is narrated by the ape himself in fine belletrist style. McEwan's *donnée* is so outrageous that the reader's hermeneutical instinct frantically reaches for plausible allegory – only to be confronted by some irrefutably ape-like fact, as when the ape sweeps up spilled papers with his left foot. In Updike, the ambiguity evaporates fairly quickly, though it is fun while it lasts. For instance, we are blandly informed that Alexandra's former husband now 'rests on a high kitchen shelf in a jar, reduced to multi-coloured dust, the cap screwed on tight'. We are invited to assume he has been cremated. The phrase quoted leaves room for this possibility. A page later, however, we learn that 'the other witches had experienced similar transformations in their marriages; Jane Smart's ex, Sam, hung in the cellar of her ranch house among the dried herbs and simples and was occasionally sprinkled, a pinch at a time, into a philtre, for piquancy; and Sukie Rougemont had permanized hers in plastic and used him as a place mat.'

Early in the novel, too, one enjoys the *double entendre* which accompanies words like 'cackling', 'damn', and phrases like 'the devil was getting into her', 'the damnedest thing happened back in there just now', as well as mention of 'devilled eggs' and Van Horne's red-hot cocktail snacks. When Van Horne asks Sukie to kiss his arse 'in the middle' because it gives him 'a helluva boost', scholars of the occult will recognize the *osculum infame* of the traditional sabbat. Ordinary readers should turn back to the epigraph taken from Agnes Sampson, whose testimony was preserved for posterity in Robert Pitcairn's *Criminal Trials in Scotland* (1833): 'the deuell . . . caused all the company to com and kiss his ers.' Traditional features like storm-raising are also planted in the narrative. After a while, it begins to look somewhat researched and pedantic, particularly since, when Updike actually invents, the magic is terribly banal – balls metamorphosing while a tennis match is in progress (twice) and the transformation of a wooden spoon. If you are going to invent, it's a good idea to be inventive.

Van Horne, who is an inventor, is more successfully conceived, partly because he is seen exclusively from the outside, except for one moment when we are vouchsafed his thoughts. Despite the nudging name, Updike presents him well. Some of his diabolic features reveal themselves only on a second reading: his trousers, for instance, bag at the back of his knees, inviting the reader to imagine a satyr; the personalized initials on his possessions change disconcertingly, suggesting an assumed human identity, as does his seamed face, which is not merely lined but a construct. His speech, too, is a torrential yet robotic simulacrum. The sulphurous smell in his hallway seems merely chemical for some time.

But *The Witches of Eastwick* isn't simply a comic soufflé. There's something more substantial here which is best anatomized by looking at the minor characters. Felicia, the smug, nattering, intellectually deaf wife of Clyde Gabriel, a newspaper editor, provides a clue to the governing design – before her husband looks up from the open fire and dispatches her with a little murderous pokerwork. She is against the war in Vietnam, pornography, capitalist exploitation of ecological resources – a veritable supermarket of liberal indignation and democratic gripes, though she doesn't actually *like* people. Compare the leftie parson, Ed Parsley, who eventually blows himself up making bombs. He also wants to buck the system.

So does Van Horne – but on a larger scale. As an inventor, he is looking for a loophole in the second law of thermodynamics. As a devil, he is against the cosmos. Where God said, 'Let there be light', Van Horne prefers black sheets on his bed, black couches in his sauna, and preaches a notably secular sermon against the horrors of God's creation – from predacious anthropods, through the syphilis spirochete, to the lung fluke and the tapeworm. 'So vote for me next time, OK?' he concludes. But, as Updike shows us, the devil is not creative but parasitical – inversion, not invention, is his *métier*. By the end of the novel, Van Horne has invented nothing, gone bankrupt and disappeared with another man – the final inversion. Not that this needs spelling out: Van Horne's attitude to art has already blown his cover. As a musician, he is only capable of variations on a given theme – 'The A Nightingale Sang in Berkeley Square Boogie' and 'The How High the Moon March'. His collection of pop art is, significantly, Jim Dine, Kienholz, Oldenberg – 'travesties of the ordinary'.

Clyde Gabriel, on the other hand, puts his trust in Lucretius and the idea that all things operate according to their own laws, without a supernatural sanction. For him, the cosmos is an 'implausible spatter of stars' and creation has come into being accidentally by a fortuitous swerving of atoms. Like Lucretius, he commits suicide – after murdering his wife for disturbing this cosmic peace with her jabbering discontent. The description of the suicide, incidentally, is one of the best passages Updike has ever written – flawless, detailed, unflinching and horribly pessimistic. Just before he dies, Clyde reverts to his adolescent self, the boy who saw no conflict between science and religion. Working out the logistics of hanging himself, he is suddenly taken by the architecture of the staircase. For a moment, the argument from design convinces him: 'it was all as clear as rectified type'. Updike, however, wipes this illusion away, as the rope tightens around Clyde's neck, with one terrible, poetic sentence: 'then a redness in his overstuffed skull was followed by blackness, giving way, with the change of a single letter, to blankness.'

The witches, Alexandra, Jane and Sukie, are also bucking the system. They hate housework and neglect their kids (a neglect which is oddly unrealized by Updike, since usually he is brilliant with the quiddity of children). Without husbands, they are free to have affairs and to fulfil themselves. Clearly, this is related, in Updike's mind at least, to feminism: 'so many of Alexandra's remarkable powers had flowed from this mere reappropriation of her assigned self, achieved not until midlife. Not until midlife did she truly believe that she had a right to exist, that the forces of nature had created her not as an afterthought and companion – a bent rib, as the infamous *Malleus Maleficarum* had it – but as a mainstay of the continuous Creation . . .' On the next page, we are offered a psychological curriculum vitae in summary: 'Alexandra's fat bare toes, corned and bent by years in shoes shaped by men's desires and cruel notions of beauty . . .'

Instead of marriage, drudgery and compliance, the witches give their loyalty to their triune sisterhood. Their adulteries are fuelled by pity as much as desire: 'healing belonged to their natures, and if the world accused them of coming between men and their wives . . . not merely accused but burned them alive in the tongues of indignant opinion, that was the price they must pay.' Those burning tongues are an example of Updike's fudged equation between the natural and the supernatural: the craftsman hammering a screw into the wall, botching the job.

So much for the programme and the liberationist theory. Gradually Updike withdraws his sympathy. In no time at all, the sisterhood is beset with internal jealousies and insistent egos, despite the best endeavours. The artistic aspirations, set in train by Van Horne, come to nothing. More importantly, Updike shows that the feminist myth of the gentler sex – the idea that women would exercise power more responsibly than men – is simply sentimental. These witches casually kill squirrels and dogs out of irritation, torment other women and conclude by giving a fatal dose of cancer to a woman of whom they are jealous. Not even Alexandra's espousal of Nature as a Nietzschean seethe of continuity, nor her hesitant and ineffectual compassion, can justify this act of cruel pique. So much for the healing art. By the finale, Updike has packed his rebellious women back into the boring monogamous system – it claims them, as of right.

The Witches of Eastwick is, then, toughly argued and provocative – a text for our times, despite the supernatural overlay. For the most part, it is intriguingly organized, and the dialogue is superb throughout, but the narrative prose is well below Updike's standards. The earth in winter is as 'hard as iron'; Sukie's face is 'bright as a new penny'; a girl's bikini isn't tight as a drum but 'taut and simple as a drum', as Updike fusses with the cliché. Similarly, Jane Smart doesn't just bristle in the old well-worn way: because she is a witch, 'her voice bristled like a black cat's fur, iridescent'. Another screw splintering the woodwork. Nor do

I think the supernatural motif saves this numb platitude: 'as if in a crystal ball she saw that she would meet and fall in love with this man . . .' Updike, too, overuses a device patented by Saul Bellow, the unpunctuated string of adjectives: 'the ruthless jubilant lucid minds'; 'melancholy triumphant affectionate feelings'. It is a pity, also, that Updike should borrow Joyce's 'white button under the butt of her tail' in the phrase 'the harmless button of its anus'. He is still a master at evoking domestic detritus – a corroded barbecue, a chair arm shiny with dirt, a store-room full of Wellington boots, rakes and pruning shears. But there are too many sentences in which the subject hangs by its fingernails from a cliff-face, overwhelmed by subordinate clauses, until the main verb at last comes to the rescue: 'Marge Perley, whose horrid canary-yellow For Sale signs leaped up and down on trees and fences as on the tides of economics and fashion (Eastwick had for decades been semi-depressed and semi-fashionable) people moved in and out of the town, was a heavily made-up, go-getting woman who, if one at all, was a witch on a different wavelength from Jane, Alexandra and Sukie.' You begin to see what Eliot meant by the 'intolerable wrestle of words' and the terrible thought strikes you that Updike is one of our best writers.

Golding's *Darkness Visible*

The third chapter of *Darkness Visible** opens with a description of an ironmonger's. Frankley's is an old established firm that has failed to get on terms with the twentieth century. Despite the introduction of new lines in garish plastic and the abolition of an overhead network of wires and cannisters that used to whizz to a central till, the premises refuse rationalization. In fact, though it no longer exists, faithful old retainers still reach up automatically for the system of wires. It is a neat symbol, encapsulating Golding's concerns, and only beckoned from its naturalistic obscurity by the space devoted to it. In other words, the old system of metaphysics which gave morality a supernatural sanction is still a felt presence, here symbolized by a spider's web of wires that originally guaranteed financial probity in the employees. Both systems retain a lingering potency, unimpaired by rationalism, as you might expect in a novel whose title is taken from *Paradise Lost*'s description of hell and whose epigraph is a quotation from the *Aeneid* Book 6 where, before descending into the Underworld, Aeneas invokes the powers of Darkness.

This isn't new territory for Golding, though the bold mixture of comedy and terror is an unfamiliar and successful departure. *Free Fall* (1959) ended with Sammy Mountjoy's realization that there were two worlds – the scientific, rational world of his physics master, and the other world of the spirit, of good and evil, that 'touches only the dark things, held prisoner, incommuni-

Darkness Visible by William Golding, Faber and Faber.

cado, touches, judges, sentences and passes on'. The central emblem of this duality was the darkened cell into which the Gestapo thrust Sammy. By daylight merely an emptied broom cupboard with a damp cloth in the centre of the floor, it is, when Sammy experiences it in total darkness, a veritable hell – or would have been, had not Golding's prose, normally aroused by limitation, collapsed into a limp imitation of Poe. *Free Fall* concluded that 'both worlds are real. There is no bridge.'

Darkness Visible is an attempt to sketch that bridge, even as it exploits the comically incongruous gap between the two worlds. For instance, at a kind of seance, three characters experience religious beatitude, yet one of them, a bookseller, is almost overwhelmed by the desire to scratch his nose. Finally, his hands held by the others, he eases the itch on the table – only to have his agonized facial expressions interpreted later, by one of his companions, as the outward sign of an inward spiritual conflict. All the same, in spite of the farce, even because of it, the religious experience is irrefutable.

However lucid this may sound in summary, the theme emerges only gradually from a crowded narrative, full of startling events rapidly told with an insouciant economy that is almost biblical. Further, as in *The Inheritors*, *Pincher Martin* and *The Spire*, Golding abjures what James, in the preface to *The Golden Bowl*, called 'the muffled majesty of authorship'. For most of the novel, we are compelled to inhabit the perplexed consciousnesses of the characters, so it is to be expected that some episodes are as obscure as the allegory on Mr Tulkinghorn's ceiling in *Bleak House*. However, no one is more skilled than Golding at making obscurity compelling – at forcing his reader, in James's formula, to 'live and breathe and rub shoulders and converse with the persons engaged in the struggle'. In fact, when Golding does eventually step back at the very end, we are in a position to see how inadequate such a perspective on the struggle is.

The struggle in *Darkness Visible* is that of supernatural forces, good and evil, to find expression in a rational century. At first, to characters and readers alike, this merely seems an identity crisis. Take Sophy, the twin who is eventually so overpowered by the evil within her that she engineers an abortive, terrorist-aided kidnap attempt – the quasi-apocalypse that provides the book with a sudden excess of plot at its denouement. To begin with, Sophy is aware only of what she calls a *This* inside her head which differs from her social persona: '*This* lived and watched without any feelings at all and brandished or manipulated the Sophy-creature like a complicated doll, a child with all the arts and wiles and deliberate delightfulness of a quiet unselfconscious, oh a quite innocent, naive, trusting little girl.' At one point, Golding calls her 'little friend of all the world', alluding to Kim who, like Sophy, isn't sure who he is and has difficulty in relating to the normal world. But whereas Kim weeps and feels the wheels of his being 'lock up anew on the world without', Sophy is gradually initiated into evil by the force within and, in some sense, outside her.

Initially, she is an ignorant medium, at once enthralled and innocently terrified by what is taking place. She is, for example, inexplicably horrified by the image of a huge wave and, later, by a Rorschach ink-blot – experiences for which Golding volunteers no explanation, leaving the reader to infer that they are images of her condition. A wave is, of course, an invisible force acting *through* the medium of water, just as the ink-blot is itself passive, awaiting the imposition of meaning from outside. Sophy's equally baffling fascination with transistor radios and her enigmatic comment on a glove puppet ('Sometimes I felt – ') belong to the same collocation of images.

Though she manipulates others, Sophy is herself manipulated like a puppet from the inside. Similarly, she is a kind of radio, receiving messages from 'the voice of darkness between the stars'. Her childish temporary belief that the owners of transistors are trapped inside them is a naive formulation, but one that expresses her sense that the *This*-Sophy, the evil spirit, is compelled to inhabit a body. The conflict between the normal girl and this imperious force is finally resolved when, after sundry failures, she achieves orgasm by wounding her dull boyfriend in the shoulder, and sees that the way to pleasure is through the infliction of pain. 'Then for a timeless time there is no Sophy. No *This*.'

Matty, the hero of *Darkness Visible,* is a curious plodder who develops in parallel to the gifted Sophy. While they brush at moments, their two narratives do not engage until the final third of the novel – with a certain crunching of machinery. As with Lok in *The Inheritors,* Matty's innocent dumbness calls forth Golding's prodigious gifts of empathy: his pedestrian journal is recreated brilliantly in all its comic pathos and, seen from the outside, he is utterly compelling. Matty, too, has experienced a life-long crisis of identity. Who am I? he constantly asks. It's a good question and one that Golding is prepared to answer only with hints.

We first see Matty walking, badly burned down his left side, out of a fire that is melting iron and lead. There are two contradictory clues to his identity: as if he might be a force for good or evil, the fire which produces him is described as a burning bush and as the infernal city. Comforted in hospital by a tender nurse, Matty obscurely conveys his psychic powers by making the nurse aware of her spiritual dimension – a process she understands so imperfectly that she can only employ the inarticulate locution, *Matty believes I bring someone with me.*

As this episode implies, unlike Sophy, Matty is a medium for the force of good, and it is he who thwarts the terrorist plot by becoming a burnt offering – as his ludicrous, yet accurate, visions have predicted. Prepared to sacrifice himself for a child, Matty typically blunders into his destiny. Mending a puncture, he goes into the garage the terrorists intend to dynamite, is knocked out by an unseen assailant and burned alive in the explosion – but not before he has rushed out incandescent and scared the kidnappers, whether intentionally or not, into dropping their prey.

Given this role of saviour, why is Matty so closely associated with Lucifer at the beginning of the novel? His disfigured face recalls Milton's 'damaged arch-angel'; like Hephaestus, Lucifer's classical equivalent, he has a limp and is drawn to the forge at Frankley's; reflecting on his mild sexual susceptibilities, he equates himself with the sons of God, the fallen angels of Genesis who 'came in unto the daughters of men'. At the same time, he feels reserved for a high destiny and like the God of the Jews, who was referred to only by initials (YHWH), Matty's surname is never certain: Windgrove, Windrave, Windgraff, Windrove, Wildwort and Windrop are some of the alternatives used to suggest his special significance – as well as his special insignificance. He is a poor instrument to do a noble deed, with a profound sense of his own sinfulness.

This awareness of his shortcomings and the need to forgive the sins of others are part of Matty's awkward religious consciousness – as his middle name, Septimus, implies. Though used only once, it sends the reader directly to Matthew 7. 'Judge not, that ye be not judged. For with what judgment ye judge, ye shall be judged; and with what measure ye mete, it shall be measured to you again.' This text explains why *Darkness Visible* is such a compassionate novel, extending forgiveness and understanding even to the homosexual Pedigree, or 'Pedders' as his pupils appropriately dub him. Those tempted to take a lofty attitude are shown the beam in their own eye: Sim Goodchild, the bookseller, finally admits to himself that his interest in the young Sophy and her twin was sexual. Edwin, who rejects Pedigree's purely social overtures, has something shady in his own sex life. Both men learn from Matty, almost by osmosis, that there is in all of us what Sim calls the 'diabolical *thing* down there disporting itself'. Imperfection must forgive imperfection – so that, just before his death, Matty forgives his own body, the Lucifer within.

Eight years in the writing, *Darkness Visible* is a gripping metaphysical thriller. By Golding's standards, only the Matty narrative approaches his best work; the familiarity of Sophy's seventies' environment somehow renders his meticulously detailed imagination redundant; it is improbable that the Secret Service would televise and record the seance; finally, the potential for good in the twins is mentioned only sketchily as a religious phase in one of them. That said, I don't expect to read a better novel this year.

Golding's Sources

Three contradictory axioms

1. Schoolboys on an island after an atomic war; Neanderthal man recreated, inside and outside, down to 'the little patch of hair over his big toe'; contemporary man prolonging his existence after death; a *Bildungsroman* whose settings range from a slum to a prisoner-of-war camp; the construction of a spire in the middle ages – despite thematic similarities, it is axiomatic that every Golding novel is different from its predecessors, each with a separate patent, each a new invention, as if Golding had decided to take the form at its word. No one's novels are more deliberately novel.

2. Set against this, though, another axiom – that all literary works have their sources, that all novels have navels, so to speak. Why has criticism hardly looked beyond Golding's own citations, *Coral Island* and Wells's *Outline of History*?

3. Then oppose to both a third axiom mischievously promulgated by Valéry in *Analects*: 'what has been believed by all, always and everywhere, has every likelihood of being untrue.' Which of the three axioms is true? Golding, whose *Lord of the Flies* systematically sets out to refute Ballantyne's sentimentality, would be drawn, I imagine, to Valéry's calculated provocation. But perhaps the third axiom is trailing its coat so flamboyantly only because it doesn't have a leg to stand on.

What are Golding's sources? If he is father to a family of disturbingly different one-offs, who are the mothers? Is it possible to confront the paterfamilias with the odd maternity suit? I should like to propose a few plausible candidates. In *Free Fall*, for instance, there is a well-known passage in which Sammy Mount-joy, after much intellectual circling, formulates a statement of polarities that seems central to Golding's fiction: 'All day long the trains run on rails. Eclipses are predictable. Penicillin cures pneumonia and the atom splits to order. All day long, year in, year out, the daylight explanation drives back the mystery and reveals a reality usable, understandable and detached.' This is the world which is rational and operates according to scientific laws. But there is another world, quasi-mystical and anti-utilitarian: 'All day long action is weighed in the balance and found not opportune nor fortunate or ill-advised, but good or evil. For this mode which we must call the spirit breathes through the universe and does not touch it; touches only the dark things, held prisoner, incommunicado, touches, judges, sentences and passes on.' This dualism, with its Cartesian distinction between the world of extension and the world of the spirit, is one of which Sammy concludes: 'both worlds are real. There is no bridge.'

The crux is so characteristic, so individual, that one can almost run a finger over the hallmarks. It is odd, then, to encounter this twin in Aldous Huxley's *Antic Hay*: 'No, but seriously, Gumbril reminded himself, the problem was very troublesome indeed. God as a sense of warmth about the heart, God as exultation, God as tears in the eyes, God as a rush of power or thought – that was all right. But God as truth, God as $2 + 2 = 4$ – that wasn't so clearly all right. Was there any chance of their being the same? Were there bridges to join the two worlds?' Not an identical twin perhaps – Gumbril is less positive than Sammy, Golding more eloquent than Huxley – but the terms in which the problem is framed are strikingly similar. Yet will the bridge between Huxley and Golding take the weight of the source hunter? After all, in every other respect, *Antic Hay* (with its pneumatic trousers, *femme fatale*, and febrile farce) and *Free Fall* share no family resemblance and the metaphor of the bridge between different systems of thought isn't so rare. Does it help, if only tangentially, to note a similarity between *Pincher Martin*'s lust for Nat's girl and that of Anthony Beavis, in *Eyeless in Gaza*, for the girl of his awkward friend, Brian?

But what about *Crime and Punishment*, whose hero, Raskolnikov, begins as a free thinker determined to live in a world of 'daylight explanation', where a murder is neither good nor evil, simply 'opportune' or 'ill advised'? He ends, however, in the world of the spirit – touched, judged and sentenced by his own gagging conscience. To this one might add that Sammy and Raskolnikov share an interrogator – Halde and Porfiry, both of whom are a mixture of terror and compassionate understanding. Not that these general similarities would mean anything without the figure of Svidrigaylov, the man who commits suicide, unable to bear the knowledge that there are two worlds, both of them trivial. He unburdens himself to Raskolnikov: 'ghosts are, so they say, bits and pieces of other worlds, the beginning of them. There is no reason, of course, why a healthy man should see them, because a healthy man is, above all, a man of this earth, and he must, therefore, only live the life of this earth for the sake of order and completeness. But as soon as he falls ill, as soon as the normal earthly order of his organism is disturbed, the possibility of another world begins to become apparent, and the more ill he is, the more closely does he come into touch with the other world, so that when he dies, he goes straight to the other world.' Again, this is scarcely conclusive. However, Svidrigaylov immediately continues in a way that cannot help reminding the reader of Sammy Mountjoy's black vision in the broom cupboard: 'we're always thinking of eternity as an idea that cannot be understood, something immense. But why must it be? What if, instead of all this, you suddenly find just a little room there, something like a village bath-house, grimy, and spiders in every corner, and that's all eternity is. Sometimes, you know, I can't help feeling that that's probably what it is.' The plausibility of *Crime and Punishment* as a source is also increased by another reminiscence, this time of *Pincher Martin*, whose entire plot is encapsulated by the ruminating Raskolnikov: 'where was it I read about a man sentenced to death who, one hour before his execution, says or thinks that if he had to live on some high rock, on a cliff, and a ledge so narrow that there was only room enough for him to stand there, and if there were bottomless chasms all round, the ocean, eternal darkness, eternal solitude, and eternal gales, and if he had to spend all his life on that square yard of space – a thousand years, an eternity – he'd rather live like that than die at once! Oh, only to live, live, live! Live under any circumstances – only to live!' On the other hand, to return to Sammy and the cupboard, there is the Henry James story, 'The Ghostly Rental', where the following passage occurs: ' "Observe closely enough," she once said, "and it doesn't matter where you are. You may be in a pitch-dark closet. All you want is something to start with, one thing leads to another, and all things are mixed up. Shut me up in a dark closet and I will observe after a while, that some places in it are darker than others. After that (give me time), and I will tell you what the President of the United States is going to have for dinner." ' How far, if at all, does this parallel affect the status of *Crime and Punishment* as a source? On the face of it, Dostoevsky, a writer with more temperamental affinity to Golding, seems a likelier influence than Henry James. All the same, before we come out of the closet, we should emphasize that Svidrigaylov's version of eternity, even if it was Golding's starting point, doesn't go very far towards explaining what actually happens to Sammy. Sammy, in his strenuous efforts to explain the horror at the dark centre, never actually touches on the thing that bothers him about the darkness. What he has to confess is not what Halde wants him to confess, namely details of planned escapes. By ending *Free Fall* with the juxtaposition of the insane Beatrice and his release from the cupboard, Golding strongly implies the guilt in Sammy's heart of darkness, but earlier he has been much more explicit. It is, though, an ironic declaration which, at the time, is merely baffling: going off with Taffy, Sammy thinks to dismiss Beatrice with words that only attain their full meaning almost a hundred pages later: 'her only power now was that of the accuser, the skeleton in the cupboard; and in this bounded universe we can easily put paid to that.' This cliché, the skeleton in the cupboard, and all it might mean, is surely a source too? Perhaps, indeed, the primary source.

When Matty emerges from the fire at the beginning of
Darkness Visible, does Golding intend us to recall Robert
Southwell's poem, 'The Burning Babe'?

As I in hoary winter's night stood shivering in the snow,
Surprised I was with sudden heat which made my heart to glow;
And lifting up a fearful eye to view what fire was near,
A pretty babe all burning bright did in the air appear;
Who, scorched with excessive heat, such floods of tears did shed
As though his floods should quench the flames with which his
 tears were fed.
'Alas,' quoth he, 'but newly born in fiery heats I fry,
Yet none approach to warm their hearts or feel my fire but I!
My faultless breast the furnace is, the fuel wounding thorns,
Love is the fire, and sighs the smoke, and mercy blows the coals,
The metal in this furnace wrought are men's defiled souls,
For which, as now on fire I am to work them to their good,
So I will melt into a bath to wash them in my blood.'
With this he vanished out of sight and swiftly shrunk away,
And straight I called unto mind that it was Christmas day.

Clearly, it would be possible to argue that Matty was a more
realistic, more sceptical and intelligent treatment of the concept
of the incarnation than is usual among theologically minded
writers in the Christian tradition. Matty's struggle with the flesh,
brilliantly and comically realized by Golding, may have been
sparked off by Southwell's vivid and quirky poem.

Similarly, one might cite Kipling's 'The Knights of the Joyous
Venture' as a possible source for *The Inheritors* – particularly
since Kipling appears to anticipate Golding's mode of stylistic
innocence which is one of the great joys of *The Inheritors*: 'he was
yellow – not from sickness, but by nature – yellow as honey, and
his eyes stood endwise in his head,' says Sir Richard Dalyngridge,
describing a Chinaman seen for the first time, and sounding not a
little like Lok. In 'The Knights of the Joyous Venture', Sir Richard
and Hugh journey with Witta, a Norseman, to the coast of Africa,

where, after a long sea voyage, they do battle with Devils 'covered with reddish hair'. The Devils are, of course, apes – though Sir Richard has to wait several hundred years to be enlightened by Dan, who has recently read *'The Gorilla Hunters* – it's a continuation of *Coral Island*, sir'. The native population rewards the knights with vast quantities of gold, with the result that, on the homeward journey, they are afraid of almost everything: 'we were troubled for fear that the Wise Iron should fail us now that its Yellow Man had gone, and when we saw the Spirit still served us we grew afraid of too strong winds . . .' Their fear of jeopardizing the cargo of gold makes the knights and the crew as paranoid as *Homo sapiens* in *The Inheritors*, whom Lok describes as 'frightened of the air'.

It should be obvious already from this summary that Kipling's tale is remarkably like *The Inheritors* – if it was told entirely from the viewpoint, not of Neanderthal man, but of Tuami and Marlan. In each case, the unknown creature is perceived as a red devil. Golding, you could argue, has 'merely' shifted the viewpoint, just as, in his use of Wells's *Outline of History*, he has seized on Wells's supposition that Neanderthal man 'made no clear distinction between animate and inanimate things: if a stick hurt him, he kicked it'. In each case, however, you wonder if it actually matters – when you consider the example given by Wells and compare Golding's imaginative depth and reach, which transforms stagnant water to water which is 'not awake like the river or the fall but asleep'. More, Wells would have been incapable of Golding's astonishing negative capability (in the vulgar sense) which endows Neanderthal man with a fear of water – a fear whose cause Golding requires his reader to work out unassisted, so confident is he of his overall portrait. Given the importance of smell to the Neanderthaler, immersion in water and the subsequent loss of scent amounts to a kind of death, as Golding hints when Lok loses all trace of Fa and assumes she is dead.

Still, there are ideas in Wells which Golding builds on. Wells modifies the expert picture himself: 'for the little tribe Mr Worthington Smith described, there has been substituted, therefore, a family group under the leadership of one Old Man, and the suggestions of Mr Atkinson as to the behaviour of the Old Man have been worked into the sketch. Mr Worthington Smith describes a squatting-place near a stream, because primitive man, having no pots or other vessels, must needs have kept close to a water supply, and with some chalk cliffs adjacent from which flints could be got to work. The air was bleak, and the fire was of great importance, because fires once out were not easily relit in those days. When not required to blaze it was probably banked down with ashes.' Golding rejects Wells's supposition that the Old Man was a tyrant who drove out the young men when they approached maturity, so that 'the fear of the Father passed by imperceptible degrees into the fear of the Tribal God'. On the other hand, he appears to accept Wells's version of Neanderthal woman: 'the woman goddesses were kindlier and more subtle. They helped, they protected, they gratified and consoled. Yet at the same time there was something about them less comprehensible than the direct brutality of the Old Man, a greater mystery. So that the Woman also had her vestiture of fear for primitive man. Goddesses were feared. They had to do with secret things.' From Wells, too, perhaps, comes the idea of chopping off Pinetree's finger: 'a queer development of the later Palaeolithic and Neolithic Ages was self-mutilation. Men began to cut themselves about, to excise noses, ears, fingers, teeth and the like, and to attach all sorts of superstitious ideas to these acts.' In this one case, Golding tells us very little more. Elsewhere, his imagination floods Wells's sketch with colour and life: take, for instance, chapter 12 of Wells's *A Short History of the World*, 'Primitive Thought', which Golding also probably read. 'Primitive man probably thought very much as a child thinks, that is to say, in a series of imaginative pictures.' Who but a genius could transform this idea until it is possible for Fa to rebuke Lok with the crushing remark, 'You have fewer pictures than the new one'?

This consideration of Wells puts the whole idea of sources into proper perspective. They account for very little of any great work of art, however interesting they may be. Suppose, for example, that we knew for a certainty that 'The Knights of the Joyous Venture' lay behind *The Inheritors*: would it make the slightest difference to our appreciation of Golding's novel? H. G. Wells, whom we know Golding read, is only of importance because Golding read him and disagreed.

For myself, I believe that the real sources of Golding's novels are not Dostoevsky, Huxley, Henry James or Kipling. They are the books themselves, despite their manifest heterogeneity. This is Ralph running: 'once more Ralph dreamed, letting his skilful feet deal with the difficulties of the path.' In *The Inheritors* this becomes 'Lok's feet were clever.' But if their feet are clever, their brains are less so: both find consecutive ratiocination difficult. Ralph: 'A strange thing happened in his head. Something flittered there in front of his mind like a bat's wing, obscuring his idea.' Lok: 'there came a confusion in his head, a darkness; and then he was Lok again, wandering aimlessly by the marshes . . .' As Lok is to Mal, so Ralph is to Piggy. Ralph thinks in pictures too: 'By now, Ralph had no self-consciousness in public thinking but would treat the day's decisions as though he were playing chess. The only trouble was that he would never be a very good chess player. He thought of the littluns and Piggy. Vividly he imagined Piggy by himself, huddled in a shelter that was silent except for the sounds of nightmare.' In *Ulysses*, Stephen meditates on Eve: 'she had no navel. Gaze. Belly without blemish, bulging big, a buckler of taut vellum.' In my view, this is a good image of Golding as a novelist. In *Lord of the Flies*, he takes a group of civilized children and shows us that they are savages. In *The Inheritors*, he takes a family of savages and shows us that they are more truly civilized than *Homo sapiens*. In *Pincher Martin*, he again inverts his previous idea: from a being, Lok, who can scarcely think, he presents us with a man who can only think, whose existence is predicated on thought. Pincher is completely self-centred, a living example of Descartes's *cogito* – 'I think therefore I am.' In *Free Fall*, he examines not so much the self-centred and selfish human being as the dark centre of the self. *The Spire* continues this debate from a different standpoint. Jocelin, inspired, loses his self in the larger purpose, which is the diagram of prayer – even if Golding finally insists on the necessary imperfection of such transcendence. This, as an account of how writers work, seems to me to be truer than the indebted modes wished on literature by critical procedures. Perhaps Valéry was right after all.

On Not Knowing Much About Art

On 5 May 1974, the Piero Manzoni–Yves Klein exhibition closed at the Tate Gallery. Manzoni was the 'discoverer' of mono-chrome white and Klein the 'inventor' of monochrome blue, latterly known as International Klein Blue, or IKB for short. The catalogue explained: 'On 2 January [1957] the first exhibition of the work of Yves Klein in Italy opens at the Galleria Apollinaire ... It consists of eleven monochrome paintings in ultramarine blue, all severely [*sic*] similar in colour and format, but selling for varying prices according to the different painterly feelings with which they are impregnated.' This unsmiling prose contrasted vividly with the snorts of mirth escaping from two Italian ladies as they contemplated Manzoni's exhibit 54, entitled 'Merda d'artista'. In a state of collapse, they dabbed their eyes, and I read the explanatory note: these neat tins, each containing thirty grammes of Manzoni's faeces, were offered to the public at a price equivalent to their weight in gold.

Despite the photogenic smirks of Manzoni and Klein, their squibs are deliberately humourless, lest we should forget their polemical purpose. IKB, monochrome white and 'Merda d'ar-tista' are, alas, *serious* jokes. They comment ironically on the assumptions of art: for Klein and Manzoni, value is not intrinsic; it is conferred on objects essentially valueless by the beholder, who is prepared to purchase, for an exorbitant price, a square of inexpensive painted canvas – or, in this case, its *reductio ad absurdum*, artist's shit. As a critique, it is profoundly shallow – resting as it does on the most vulgar conception of art, connived

444

at by the public, as a species of magic. (Hence Manzoni's magic bases – stand on them and you become a work of art, by virtue of your context.)

In fact, the artist is not a genius-magician who can transform the banal and worthless into something 'expensive, rich and strange'. Like all magicians, his procedures can be explained, and once this has happened, the element of mystery disappears. In its place is skill. Unfortunately, the public tends to prefer mystery to explanation – as witness the enduring currency of the word 'genius'. As witness, too, Peter Shaffer's 'exploration' of Mozart's 'genius' in *Amadeus* – less an examination of the surviving scores, with their evidence of hard work, than an exposition of the rumour that God once lodged in the frontal lobe of a foul-mouthed vulgarian. Evidence is boring, rumour is replete with theatrical possibilities. My own art, poetry, is notorious for attracting silly and pretentious theoretical declarations. And even when they are not self-evidently daft, some foolish, romanticized assumption may be close at hand. Towards the end of 1984, the friendly but formidable Irish critic, Edna Longley, told me in a Belfast pub that the long poem was a chimera. I found this unsurprising, because the idea is an old prejudice – a veteran that goes all the way back to Poe, for whom, as he explains in his essay, 'The Poetic Principle', the long poem is a contradiction in terms. Meaning that the essence of poetry is the lyric impulse – and that an impulse is an impulse is an impulse. An impulse, by definition, is not extended – it is the shot of spirits rather than the inexhaustible tea urn.

Seamus Heaney's poem 'Stone from Delphi' is an eloquent statement of this theory of inspiration:

> *govern the tongue, fear hybris, fear the god*
> *until he speaks in my untrammelled mouth.*

This prescription is at once modest (because the poet is merely the conduit for a larger force) and only saved from immodesty by the attribution of these imperatives to the stone itself. For a moment, the activity of poetry is elevated to something godlike – but only as a figure of speech. I am reminded of Stravinsky's description of himself as 'the vessel through which *Le Sacre* passed' – a pretence at odds with his copious manuscript changes, or the late alterations Stravinsky made to the instrumentation in response to criticisms of the first conductor, Pierre Monteux. And I expect that the manuscript drafts of Heaney's poem 'Stone from Delphi' record alternative lines – rejected and, presumably, trammelled versions.

Inspiration isn't the simple process – the flash of light, the clap of thunder, the voice from the clouds – we might like it to be. But neither can it be summarily dismissed. Thus Eliot may be scathing about the Yeatsian version of inspiration – 'something like the exaltation to be obtained, I believe, from hashisch or nitrous oxide' – but he has his own version of it. Which is as follows: 'I know', writes Eliot, 'that some forms of ill-health, debility, or anaemia, may (if other circumstances are favourable) produce an efflux of poetry in a way approaching the condition of automatic writing.' Still, I prefer this version of inspiration – inspiration as a disability, rather than something quasi-divine, '*fear the god / until he speaks in my untrammelled mouth*'.

Of course, this latter version of Delphic afflatus isn't innocent. Heaney is no clumping literalist: he is protected by the mask and requires of his reader a tactful translation. He means that the poet should forgo what Hopkins famously defined as Parnassian in a letter to Alexander Baillie (10 September 1864): 'Great men, poets I mean,' writes Hopkins, 'have each their own dialect as it were of Parnassian, formed generally as they go on writing, and at last, – this is the point to be marked, – they can see things in this Parnassian way and describe them in this Parnassian tongue, without further effort of inspiration.' In other words, the poet isn't writing to the top of his bent, and beyond, but is only writing *like* himself.

Faced with the quasi-divine analogy, the proper response is ridicule. Valéry is wonderfully caustic: 'inspiration is an hypothesis that reduces the author to the role of observer.' Yet, faced with the craftsman analogy of Hopkins, one of our most original literary critics, how do we plead? I think the writer must plead guilty, but with his head held high. There is nothing to be ashamed of in Parnassian. Valéry once more: 'it is essential for an artist to know how to imitate himself. This is the only way of solidly constructing a work of art – an undertaking which is bound to be a war on instability, fluctuations of thought and energy and passing moods.'

I find Valéry's pragmatism immensely appealing. Eliot, too, was pragmatic. And despite his personal view of inspiration – in which poetry is a by-product of physical debility – Eliot readily conceded that he could not think 'of Shakespeare or Dante as having been dependent upon such capricious releases'. They were too prolific for that. Such sustained achievement could hardly have been initiated by even the most virulent flu virus. There are two things wrong with Randall Jarrell's formula for great poetry. 'A good poet', he wrote, 'is someone who manages, in a lifetime of standing out in thunderstorms, to be struck by lightning five or six times; a dozen or two dozen times and he is great.' The first thing wrong with Jarrell's image is the image – getting struck by lightning once doesn't sound like a good idea, let alone a dozen times. Secondly, it places poetry in the context of accident rather than skill – and not just minor accident, but major cataclysm. There is something horribly helpless and depressingly drenched in Jarrell's evocation. Stravinsky composed, at the piano, every day, and wrote in his autobiography: 'Fingers are not to be despised. They are great inspirers.'

Forget about lightning, in other words. Trust to those local inspirations that happen at the desk during work in progress – little lifts, sudden buoyancies, unbidden vistas. With those, every practising artist is familiar. And they will occur in the course of any long poem. In any case, should the long poem be judged by the standards of the lyric? Eliot and Valéry, defenders of the long poem, choose identical ground from which to mount a defence. Valéry first: 'it is impossible to construct a poem containing *only* poetry. If a piece contains nothing else, it is not *constructed*; not a *poem*.' This is from the magazine *Tel Quel* sometime in the early forties, but culled from reviews written in the mid-twenties and thirties. Eliot's defence of the long poem may derive from Valéry but it is also a defence of his own practice in *Four Quartets*. In 1948, Eliot took on Poe directly: 'Poe has a remarkable passage about the impossibility of writing a long poem – for a long poem, he holds, is at best a series of short poems strung together. What we have to bear in mind is that he himself was incapable of writing a long poem. He could conceive only a poem which was a single simple effect: for him, the whole of a poem had to be in one mood. Yet it is only in a poem of some length that a variety of moods can be expressed; for a variety of moods requires a number of different themes or subjects, related either in themselves or in the mind of the poet.' Eliot goes on, like Valéry, to insist on construction and the need perhaps for passages which may show 'no lustre when extracted'.

If art is not magic, what is it? It is an exclusively human phenomenon (like pornography) which distinguishes us from animals because (with the obvious exception of architecture) it is absolutely non-utilitarian. We do it for pleasure, not for reasons of survival – like football, all other games, and cooking. In fact, art is a game too. It is, however, a game only imperfectly understood by Manzoni and Klein, who concentrate exclusively on the end-product. Soccer is equally absurd from this limited perspective: twenty-two men risk physical injury to boot, of all things, a piece of leather into a net. This in turn resolves itself into something staggeringly null – a score-line. But soccer, like art, is essentially a *process* during which skill is displayed. When we contemplate a Rembrandt self-portrait, for example, we should see it as a record of the special skills which went into its making – something a mere score-line cannot tell us – that is, if we understand the nature of the game.

Yet, many are like a friend of mine whose painfully weak eyesight was only discovered after five years of watching cricket with his father at Old Trafford – spectacles at last revealed a crucial fact. These men in white flannels were using a *ball*. Before the oculist did his work, my friend watched an occult ballet – a mysterious ritual punctuated by arbitrary cries, inexplicable noises and sudden departures from the pitch. Curiously, he

enjoyed the powerful attraction of the imperfectly compre-
hended.

This is, of course, an extreme analogy. Nevertheless, the
following paradigm is common enough: the artist is an extremely
sensitive person whose art is the product of his heightened
emotional life. When *your* mother dies, you are sad; when *his*
mother dies, the artist experiences a different order of sadness,
the de luxe version: put like that, the arrogance is obvious. In fact,
artists are generally no more susceptible than other people – and
strong emotion cannot transform the ordinary person into an
artist. Only skill can do that. If art moves us, it is through skill,
not through raw emotion. Too often in our appreciation, we
move from the artist's initial emotion to our own, leaving out the
middle term, the *sine qua non* – art. To appreciate that, we have
to master the rules. True, successful creation involves chance –
what game does not? But only the skilful artist is capable of
exploiting lucky happenings. And, in any case, the spectator can
have no way of ascertaining from the finished work what is
exploited chance (a lucky *calculation*) and what is pure calculation. In this matter, the artist retains his secret and offers us
undifferentiated skill, for the appreciation of which we need to
know the rules.

Indolence is not the sole reason for our failure to do so. In any
living art-form, the rules are constantly changed by the artists.
Innovation brings interest. When Ruskin accused Whistler of
flinging a pot of paint in the face of the public, the artist brought a
libel action. In cross-examination, Whistler revealed that an
afternoon had been sufficient to catch the effect of fireworks over
Battersea bridge at night. Asked whether 500 guineas was a fair
price for an afternoon's work, Whistler retorted that he was not
charging for five hours' painting, but for the knowledge of a
lifetime. The barrister thus immortalized was judging by the rules
of brick-laying. Ruskin's failure to see that Whistler had modified
the rules of painting is more surprising – until, that is, one
considers his defence of Turner's neo-impressionism as the
product of profound geological and meteorological study. In

Modern Painters, Turner's skill is subdued to the Victorian work-ethic in a subtle form.

The great artist is like the great cook. Where the average chef follows the recipe, the great cook invents, and his products are sometimes an acquired taste. The general public makes no distinction: the stomach, as it were, has no powers to appreciate the process of cooking – either the skill which follows, or the greater skill which innovates. We devour and pronounce. Occasionally, artists retaliate and draw attention to our failure to appreciate the existence of rules. Thus, Whistler entitled a portrait of his mother, 'Composition in Grey and Black' – insisting that art, unlike the novel, is primarily a game in which the arrangement of colours is of overriding importance. Comparably, a chef might print a recipe on the menu. In France, the symbolists (according to Valéry) were united only by the desire to be obscure to the uninitiated: the rules drawn up were so complex that their presence could not be ignored – a naive participation was made impossible. Similarly, the cubists insisted on the importance of line over realistic representation. As Hardy prophetically put it, 'Angles were taking the place of curves . . . a change constituting a sudden lapse from the ornate to the primitive on Nature's canvas, and comparable to a retrogressive step from the art of an advanced school of painting to that of the Pacific Islander' (*The Woodlanders* – of autumn trees).

One way of resuscitating an ailing art-form is to borrow from another. James's novels transplant from the drama: on stage (whatever liberties a Shaw might allow himself in prefaces and stage directions) action and dialogue must reveal character. Direct authorial comment is impossible. In his quasi-dramatic works, James often tells us what his characters think, but the overall design, the figure in the carpet, must speak for itself. Our only aid in reaching correct moral judgements is characters who function as hidden, and slightly imperfect, commentators. The game is, therefore, complicated by dramatic reticence. For instance, it is the reader's responsibility to grasp the paradoxical form of *The Ambassadors* – in which Lambert Strether sets out for Paris, entrusted with the task of rescuing Chad from the charms of his possibly gold-digging French mistress; in which Lambert Strether concludes by doing his best to persuade Chad to stand by Madame de Vionnet, the hard-hit mistress he proposes to abandon. The design is there, as conspicuous, once it is pointed out, as the Eiffel Tower. James's skill, his greatness as a novelist, is not to conceal it, but never once to look in its direction so the reader can follow his gaze. Likewise, the playwright cannot speak, he can only show.

Strange, then, that James was so unsympathetic to the Goncourts who borrowed from painting: 'The most general stricture to be made on their work is probably that they have not allowed enough for the difference of the instrument, have persisted in the effort to render impressions that the plastic artist renders better, neglecting too much those he is unable to render.' Here James discloses the privileged stupidity of the great theoretician. His comment is only possible to a man who had studied the strengths and weaknesses of both games. For him, the painter is supremely able to render outsides, while the novelist's strength is psychology. His objection is that the Goncourts are less appreciative of these respective possibilities.

In fact, in borrowing from the pictorial arts, they were extending their art. They surpassed their source, rather than lamely imitating it. If a writer wishes vividly to describe beads of rain-water on a black twig, he may compare them to light bulbs on rubber flex, lit by the sun. Where the writer has depicted two things the realistic painter is restricted to one.

Naturally enough, painting soon realized this limitation and borrowed from literature. In the work of Picasso, for example, metaphor comes to play an increasingly important role: in 'The Three Musicians', the holes in a clarinet also double as the buttons down a clown's smock, and the belt of another is simultaneously the strings of a guitar. More familiar instances include the bull's head made from handlebars and a racing saddle, and the gorilla whose face is a child's model motor car. In some sense, too, cubist painting (in its final stages) borrows from sculpture: the same object is painted from different angles, so that the shifting viewpoint presents irreconcilable visual information and creates a three-dimensionality akin to that of sculpture, as opposed to representational painting's *trompe-l'œil* three-dimensionality. Yet, true to form, in its late stages, cubism advances beyond its sculptural source and presents a multi-dimensionality, where our difficulty in resolving the conflicting pictorial information is created by a whole series of contradictory viewpoints.

Cubism's 'broken bundle of mirrors' (to borrow from Pound) strikes many people as a laudable failure. And one must face the possibility that some changes in the rules of any game are not improvements. Byron's *Don Juan*, for instance, borrows heavily from the picaresque novel. *Letters from Iceland*, Auden's imitation, argues by implication that the innovation was useful, not merely idiosyncratic. But, all the same, one feels that the poetry is thin on the ground. Again, this unjustified leaning arises from a misunderstanding of the game – Byron is writing verse, not poetry, and it is idle to expect anything else. Once make this adjustment and the troubled sensation vanishes – as it were, we discover that the disappointing cup of coffee is, in fact, tea.

Whitman's *Leaves of Grass*, on the other hand, are themselves largely to blame for the misapplication of inappropriate criteria. D. H. Lawrence found them ponderously overpoetic and jeered at Whitman's 'I am he that aches with amorous love' – 'reminds one of a steam-engine . . . CHUFF!' James was more soberly stern: 'it exhibits the effort of an essentially prosaic mind to lift itself, by prolonged muscular strain, into poetry.' Only the shrewd Eliot saw that *Leaves of Grass* was not failed poetry but bullied prose: 'Whitman was a great prose writer. It [his originality] is spurious in so far as Whitman wrote in a way that asserted that his great prose was a new form of verse.' It took a man of Eliot's radical disposition to see that Whitman had not changed the rules, but was playing an entirely different game. Eliot watches as Whitman – togged out in snorkel, flippers and swimming trunks – ambles out to score a superb century.

To call art a game does not diminish it, since it is the highest of all games. As Valéry said, 'in the strange faculty of doing certain things irrelevant to life with as much care, passion and persistence

452

as if one's life depended on them . . . there we find what is called "living" '. To return to the charlatans, Manzoni and Klein, we discover that, 'serious' as they purport to be, they are not serious enough. The rules are more complex than the simplistic conventions they belabour so repetitively. In short, they know what they dislike – but they don't know much about art.

At a Slight Angle to the Universe

Erewhon, Illyria, Lilliput, Llaregub, Yoknapatawpha, Greeneland. To some extent, all art is foreign travel through the given world – at once strange and familiar. Think of Hardy's Wessex or Eliot's Waste Land or Dickens's London. No wonder, then, that E. M. Forster described Cavafy as 'a Greek gentleman at a slight angle to the universe'. Or that Wallace Stevens wrote:

> They said, 'You have a blue guitar,
> You do not play things as they are.'
>
> The man replied, 'Things as they are
> Are changed upon the blue guitar.'

Children, too, are a special case. They are foreigners in our world, until they become naturalized. That is why we patronize them, tailoring our language to their ignorance, addressing them in loud pidgin. Their ignorance is bliss – for us, if not for the children. Consider, for example, Pip's slight angle to the universe in *Great Expectations*: 'I remember Mr Hubble as a tough high-shouldered stooping old man, of a saw-dusty fragrance, with his legs extraordinarily wide apart: so that in my short days I always saw some miles of open country between them when I met him coming up the lane.' This distorted perspective, this 'considerable obliquity of vision' (to borrow De Quincey on Mrs Wordsworth's squint), is even more pronounced in Wordsworth's idiot boy. Johnny, after a night out on his pony, describes his inverted adventures:

> 'The cocks did crow to-whoo, to-whoo,
> And the sun did shine so cold.'

Like Benjy in Faulkner's *The Sound and the Fury*, Wordsworth's Johnny will never grow up. His perceptions will always be day for night. He is a perpetual foreigner at an extreme angle to the universe. As such, his world-view is carefully attributed by Wordsworth. There is no attempt to pass it off as the author's own.

Yet that is precisely what it is. Similarly, when Pip describes the Jaggers five o'clock shadow as 'strong black dots of beard and whisker', or when David Copperfield mentions Mr Murdstone's 'dotted indication of the strong black beard', our doubt is alerted by the repetition. Is this a genuine child, or Dickens in a romper suit?

And if we study real children? Do we then find that the parallel between the child and the artist continues to exist? We discover, I believe, that the parallel is convincing but intermittent – no more than a convenient analogue. This is my own daughter describing a juggler: 'there was a man sharing balls between his hands.' With a few minor embellishments, this periphrastic evocation found its way into one of my poems – duly attributed. This is Pip describing a stranger's wink in the Three Jolly Bargemen: 'His head was all on one side, and one of his eyes was half shut up, as if he were taking aim at something with an invisible gun.' Dickens *may* have stolen the idea from one of his many children. After all, his letters record several occasions when life conspired to imitate the Inimitable: one thinks, for instance, of Dickens's eagerness to see a man with a wooden leg, highly decorated with rosettes, who performed the highland fling in music hall. Even so, I think Dickens himself, and not one of his children, is probably the source for Pip's deliberate mistake. In the nature of things, there can be no conclusive evidence either way, but my own experience records the familial donnée as a rare event.

If the artist is a child in any sense, he is untypical, a superbrat –
like the young Christ in the temple, talking theology with the
elders, dominating his father's business premises and exhorting
the employees. In Rembrandt's etching of this subject (wrongly
identified by Arthur Hind, I believe, as 'Joseph Telling his
Dreams') his young hands are spread emphatically. His body is
tilted slightly forward, tense and expository. His immediate
auditor looks him straight in the eyes. The other elders are
listening attentively, too. Not that Rembrandt offers us open-
mouthed, agog facial clichés: he shows us instead slumped,
almost careless postures and eyes which are fixed on some point
other than the speaker's face. They are trying to follow without
distractions. Evidently, keeping up isn't easy with this precocious
young man.

Nevertheless, there must be *something* childlike about Christ in
Rembrandt's etching, just as an iota of the childlike must survive
somewhere in the most sophisticated artist. What of the child the
elders have momentarily discounted? In fact, he's present by
implication, in the anxious expression on Mary's intruding,
crumpled features. He's present also in a delightful, vulgar
foreground detail – a tiny dog, contorted like Houdini over its
spread haunches, is licking its genitals urgently. In the temporary
'absence' of a childish Christ, displaced by a more scholarly alter
ego, Rembrandt sketches in the childish point of view – knowing
that children exist on the fringes of adult life, at ground-level with
the dogs and the dirt between the floorboards, at a slight angle to
the universe. Only a child or an artist would notice the little dog
at such a time.

Rembrandt, as so often, has taken a familiar religious subject
and introduced a naturalistic, tasteless detail which, in the
context, tinges the subject with foreignness – the foreignness of
the child. In the same way, Joyce's friend, Frank Budgen,
recorded this impression of *Finnegans Wake*, a book in which the
history of the world is subdued and assimilated to the idea of
Dublin: 'And therefore I write as one who has visited a foreign
country not yet on Baedeker's list – not as an authoritative guide
but as a traveller with sufficient sensibility, sufficient power of

observation to record an impression that may encourage the adventurous to risk a more extended visit to the same shores.'

But has the child the last word in Rembrandt's etching? Do we merely register the innocent shock of the little dog? I can't help thinking there is a yet further stage in which the artist leaves the child far behind. Why did Rembrandt include the dog? Of course, it is true to life, but how is it true to the picture? Isn't Rembrandt asserting an implicit parallel between the mental gymnastics and the bodily contortions of the dog? Surely we can tell, just by glancing at the dog niggling away, that the theology is extraordinarily complex – a kind of nit-picking, in fact. Finally, but only finally, the image is not at all childlike. It is earning its living in the picture as a whole.

Olivier Deconstructed

*Confessions of An Actor** is, unsurprisingly, more an impersonation than a real piece of writing. In it, Laurence Olivier *acts* writing – an uneasy mixture of the chatty ('All right, I can hear you, reader dear') and the belletrist flourish ('Fortunately for the restoration of my depleted coffers . . .'). What good bits of writing there are (not many) stem equally from Olivier's *métier*: as when, for instance, he arrives in Hollywood to help the mad Vivien Leigh. 'I said, "Hello, darling", and when she spoke to me it was in the tone of halting dreamlike amazement that people in the theatre use for mad scenes when they can't think of anything better. My instinctive reaction was that she was putting it on.' She wasn't. Soon she had to be sedated: 'To my horror I saw that the nurse was enjoying it; she was waggling the syringe and there was a glint in her eye. But there was no time for anything; Danny Kaye and I threw ourselves on top of Vivien and held her down. Vivien fought us with the utmost ferocity as the needle went in, biting and scratching Danny and me, screaming appalling abuse at both of us, with particular attention to my erotic impulses . . .' There is a professional, unadorned quality of observation here that survives the sentence's limp end: 'it seemed an eternity before she went limp and Danny and I were able to let her go, both shattered and exhausted.' The whole incident shows us not only the distraught husband but also the observant actor. Indeed, in Olivier's life, the professional, for the most part, took priority

Confessions of An Actor by Laurence Olivier, Weidenfeld and Nicolson.

458

over the personal: 'I have always believed that if you aspire to be an artist you must be prepared to make such personal sacrifices as separation readily, if not exactly cheerfully. It's tough but it's right.'

This suppression of self is even invoked to explain Olivier's early sexual failure: 'In the first years of Vivien's theatre-acting there was not the passion, the flare, the flame necessary to set the stage alight. It was therefore hard to make her understand, at those times when she was sadly disappointed in the results of my intimate passionate endeavours, that all *that* had gone into my acting . . .' One is reminded of Balzac complaining to one of the Goncourt brothers that he had 'lost a book this morning' because 'sperm for him was an emission of cerebral matter and as it were a waste of creative power'. This theory, shared with Balzac, that 'you can't be more than one kind of athlete at a time', is surely undermined by Olivier's later sexual prowess – the result of a few sympathetic, extra-marital affairs which cured his tendency to premature ejaculation. This, however, isn't the only contradictory theorizing in the book: Lord Olivier is a nice man but no Socrates.

The real truth, in so far as one can glean it, is that for many years Olivier wasn't simply *suppressing himself*. There was no one there in the first place. For such an acclaimed somebody, these memoirs often read like the Diary of a Nobody. This is partly because Olivier, anxious not to appear boastful, invariably presents himself in an ironical light – anything not to be known, as he was at school, as 'that sidey little shit Olivier'. But it is also because one detects that, without a role to play, Olivier suspected that there wasn't much there. He dislikes surprisingly few people and most of those are dead. His opinions strike one as largely borrowed: on homosexuality, for instance, he is conventionally liberal ('It would be dreadfully wrong if any of this should be taken to imply that I ever found anything in the remotest way unrespectable about homosexuality') and yet it is clear he finds the subject deeply disturbing. 'I felt that the homosexual act would be a step darkly destructive to my soul.' Plainly, the liberal attitude is a later graft. Compare, too, his attitude to the General

Strike: 'I have been told constantly in the last few years that I was on the wrong side and should be ashamed of myself.'

The first chapter sounds an authentically Pooterish note with its description of genteel poverty – a childhood of shared baths, rationed lavatory paper and diaphanous slices of meat. With a background like that, the young Olivier would hardly side with the workers. And, apart from his natural gifts, you can see that the attraction of the acting profession was partly social: 'From my own resources, I had to have full evening dress, full morning dress and a short black coat, plus-fours, sports jacket and blazer with grey and white flannels, dressing gowns and night attire, as well as suitable socks, shirts, shoes, collars and ties.' The world Olivier was aiming for was the aristocracy – or rather the pseudo-aristocracy that the stage might provide. Later, in New York, at a time of financial stringency, 'it was natural for the two of us to stay at the St Regis; it would have been misunderstood if we had sought somewhere more economical.' All his life, Olivier appears to have taken his colour from his surroundings. Fortunately, in the latter half of his life, his surroundings improved – less of Noël Coward's chic, as it were, and more of George Devine's scruff. The glamorous world at which he had originally aimed didn't really suit him anyway. When he has supper with Winston Churchill, the occasion is one of Pooterish maladroitness: 'As we three turned to seat ourselves again, I fancied I caught a glimpse of ancient Harrow days as he declared in youthful enthusiasm his appreciation of Vivien: "By Jove," he said, "by Jove, she's a clinker!" He pushed the whisky decanter towards me and, with a slight flutter of dismay at mixing drinks so much, I obediently helped myself: what the hell, I thought, we're *not* only young once. I pushed it on to Soames and reached for the water. Soames passed the decanter to Winston who helped himself and as he reached for the soda syphon, again impelled to that ghastly self-conscious banter, I said: "Excuse me, sir, but have you ever tried plain water with it? I believe it to be the soda that crawls up the back of our necks the next morning." ' I prefer the Olivier on all fours in Moscow being coaxed into bed by his third wife, Joan Plowright. Or even the Olivier who tends to avoid glittering parties because they make him pass out. Either seems more natural to him.

This relatively recently induced naturalness has some bearing on Olivier the performer. He isn't a great theorist: 'At that time, stage-acting and film-acting were thought of as two entirely different crafts, even professions. We know now that this is not by any means a true assessment; the truth is infinitely subtler. They call for the same ingredients but in different proportions. The precise differences may take some years of puzzling work to appreciate; in each case there are many subtle variations accord-ing to the character of the actor.' Thanks very much. That's a great help. Nevertheless, Olivier manages, despite a dangerous amount of unchronological free association, to tell us a great deal about his acting career and its curious shape. I'd pick out three significant moments: his first audition, a remark made by Tyrone Guthrie and his stage fright which lasted from October 1964 until April 1970. My emphases, though, are different from Olivier's. *Confessions of An Actor* is a quarry where you do your own spade-work.

Olivier's rationalization of his profession is endearing and unpretentious: 'The more intelligent of my young colleagues, in ceaseless talks pathetically seeking some rationalization of our lives, agree that their choice of metier was to satisfy an urgent need to "express themselves". When my turn comes I cannot boast that degree of intellectuality; in honesty I have to confess, rather shamefacedly, that I was not conscious of any other need than to show off.' While it is true that, initially, Olivier had no desire to express himself, it isn't quite enough to say of himself that he wanted to show off. It was more complicated. When he applied for a scholarship and bursary at the Central School of Drama, Elsie Fogerty placed her finger in the deep hollow where Olivier's brow met his nose: 'You have a weakness . . . *here*.' True or not, the young actor believed her and afterwards resorted, whenever possible, to nose putty. But it is Olivier's casual, throwaway conclusion which is significant: nose putty allowed him the 'relief of an alien character' and enabled him 'to avoid anything so embarrassing as self-representation'. Far from

461

wanting to 'show off' in any uncomplicated sense, Olivier wanted to hide himself. In a world of Noël Cowards and Gertrude Lawrences, the carapace was all – glittering, hard and protective. There are a number of photographs in this book which show Olivier purloining the moustache of Ronald Coleman and the tidal quiff of Clark Gable. Handsome, yes. Real, absolutely not. At any rate, a million miles away from 'The Laurels', Brickfield Terrace, Holloway, where the Pooters lived.

The good thing to emerge out of this, from the acting point of view, was Olivier's uncanny gift for physical mimicry. Being a nobody meant he could be a great number of people – potentially, at any rate, though his aim seems to have been the matinée idol, a star. One imagines, however, that, in another way, this ontological insecurity disabled him as an actor. At least, this seems a plausible inference from the Tyrone Guthrie incident of 1945–6. Olivier was playing Sergius in *Arms and the Man*, while Ralph Richardson played Bluntschli, the larger part, and gained better notices. Olivier was feeling frankly miffed. Guthrie asked him if he didn't love Sergius? 'Love that stooge? That inconsiderable . . .' Olivier returned, incredulously. Guthrie then said 'something which changed the course of my actor's thinking for the rest of my life. "Well, of course, if you can't love him you'll never be any good in him, will you?" '

For Olivier, the significance of Guthrie's remark is that characters must be played from the inside. But it had a deeper effect on his psychology than even Olivier realized. It marks, I believe, the moment when Olivier subconsciously grasped that acting was more than playing the star roles – in which he could show off as someone else more glamorous than himself. Somehow, Guthrie had implanted the notion that successful acting involved the nobody within – that stooge, that inconsiderable, that Pooterish . . .

Olivier's theories about the use of self in acting are, as one would expect, contradictory. On the one hand: 'The theatre is replete with emotional legends; it is not surprising that those playing Romeo and Juliet are supposed to present a more stirring partnership if they develop the same passion between themselves as that which they are emulating; some believe that Shakespeare's magic depends on it. After long reflection, I must point out that this is a dangerous notion. It would imply that actual death is necessary to the feigning of it, or at least that physical pain is necessary to give a successful impression of it. Such an idea robs the work of its artfulness as well as its artistry. It is a tempting belief, but a bad principle.' Forty-two pages on, however, Olivier tells us: 'It is, as has been said, next to impossible to produce the effect of great suffering without the actor enduring some degree of it.' Olivier's greatness as an actor is inherent in this contradiction: he is a superb technician, a great mimic, *and* he has learned to put himself into his roles. Particularly, one guesses, those bits of his personality which slightly shame him.

This, I take it, is the real explanation for Olivier's six-year period of stage fright – of terror, as he puts it. The cause was the embarrassment of 'self-representation' and began with *Othello* – reasonably enough, since Vivien Leigh had given him ample experience of jealousy and of the chasm between public acclaim and private failure. Olivier was, in a sense, playing himself and took refuge, therefore, in what later became his most famous disguise. Despite stupendous make-up, a new voice and a new walk, Olivier was so afraid of being left alone with the audience during the soliloquies that Frank Finlay (Iago) stayed in the wings where Olivier could see him. Yet, after the early years of massive putty jobs, he had learned that a tiny change could provide a disguise: 'I hit on the practical notion that . . . by changing one feature one can create a whole new face.' By the time he was playing Shylock for Jonathan Miller, his only protection was a set of specially made teeth (in the still, oddly enough, he looks like a handsome version of Ken Tynan on the facing page). Miller had persuaded him to jettison a more complicated Jewish make-up that was based on George Arliss's Disraeli. In the course of playing *The Merchant*, virtually naked, as it were, Olivier found himself cured – though, initially, his terror was so strong he asked the cast not to look him in the eyes.

The terror was real enough, but like many another phobia somehow vague – and one seizes on the few details, like the eye-contact, for a kind of explanation. Might it not be that Olivier was, contrary to his stated belief, putting so much of himself on view that he felt at once threatened by the audience and his fellow actors? At any rate, it is striking that, after *The Merchant*, Olivier overcame a lifetime's reluctance and played James Tyrone in *Long Day's Journey into Night*: 'It was not that I felt inadequate for this role, it was too clearly within my compass; but I had always felt a strong resistance to playing an actor.' Why? The reason Olivier gives is that the part lent itself to stereotype. But I'd guess that the real reason had always been Olivier's reluctance to play himself, the actor. Now, at last, he was prepared to risk himself.

Certainly, in Olivier's personal life, one sees a parallel endeavour to be increasingly frank. Which is why, despite failures in the prose, one comes to admire this brave book. Disclosure follows disclosure – from amorous inefficiency to a haemorrhoidectomy ('too charming'). His personal vanity comes in for criticism, too: 'I grow a moustache partly to hide the scar which has formed two other creases one on each side, but, more secretly, to draw attention away from the displeasingly thin hard line of my upper labium, inherited from my father.' Coshed by a burglar, he reports: 'In phoning the police I was guilty of some over-dramatics.' His wife, Joan Plowright, is partly responsible for this scrupulosity, if one can judge from a letter reprinted here. She is obviously an actress who knows the value of the truth in her profession: 'I remember you saying about Brenda de B. that she "tries to cry" on stage, whereas in real life one tries to stop crying. I think maybe you are trying to believe Cassio's kisses have been on her lips, instead of trying to stop yourself believing.' What a wonderful wife. How crucial she must have been in saving Olivier from the person he was set on being, we can gauge from this telling aside: 'I had eyes for no one but Joan, whose smile at this first meeting had more than a hint of mockery about it; I divined that I stood for everything that the young generation at the Royal Court would find most objectionable . . . I was titled, necessarily self-satisfied, pompous, patronising, having obviously come to visit in a spirit of condescension – I could see it all. It preyed on my mind . . .' Archie Rice, Osborne's great nobody, followed shortly after and Olivier was reborn as an actor.

Joe Orton

When Joe Orton was in Tangier, he noted down the following exchange: ' "You like to be fucked or fuck?" he said. "I like to fuck, wherever possible," I said. He leaned across and said in a confidential tone, "I take it." "Do you?" I said. "Yes," he said, "up to the last hair." "You speak very good English," I said.' Though Orton is aroused, his attention is undeflected. He records the tiny linguistic shock, too, his pleasure in the unexpectedly supple grasp of idiom. On the evidence of these diaries,* the flight recorder, the black box present in all writers, was particularly efficient in Joe Orton. In his plays, the tapes are doctored and played at impossible speeds to produce situations which are heightened, undifferentiated and much less interesting – a scream, in fact. Orton criticized Oscar Wilde for putting his genius into his life instead of his art, but has copied him in this, as in so much else. The plays are a glittering shambles – no longer absurdist, just absurd. Their aerosol polish no longer dazzles and their subject matter has ceased to shock even Orton's middle-class invention, the permanently outraged Edna Welthorpe. The diaries, however, are still effective, because they are less affected. Here, the gaze is unblinking and truthful.

For example, just before Christmas 1966, Orton met 'an ugly Scotsman who said he liked being fucked. He took me somewhere in his car and I fucked him up against a wall.' An ordinary participant, an ugly Scotsman perhaps, might have stopped there,

*The Orton Diaries edited by John Lahr, Methuen.

or discussed his feelings. Orton concludes: 'the sleeve of my rainmac is covered with white-wash from the wall. It won't come off.' All emotion, all sensation, is edited out. But the scene is there – horribly vivid, carefully written. Because Orton's prose is naturally flat and economical, the pose is perfunctory.

Was Orton heartless? 'We were just too late to miss a man who'd decided to commit suicide by jumping from the window of New Zealand House. They caught him unfortunately.' Does this represent the inhuman in all human beings – what Keats, in another context, called 'the feel of not to feel it'? The consensus is that Orton was a promiscuous and chilly sensualist – so unable to empathize with Kenneth Halliwell, the literary mentor and sexual partner he had decisively outgrown, that Halliwell was driven to hammer the point home. Before taking the twenty-two Nembutals which killed him, Halliwell left a suicide note: 'If you read his diary all will be explained. K.H. P.S. Especially the latter part.' In fact, the diaries only complicate the picture – particularly Orton's reputed lack of feelings. When Halliwell is threatening suicide, Orton suddenly erupts: 'I won't have you monopolising the agony market.' Elsewhere, he cheers up Kenneth Williams, who is 'low and depressed', and criticizes him on another occasion for possible tactlessness – talking too freely in front of his own mother. Williams is a good character witness: 'What is heart? If we're talking about compassion and sympathy, I'd say Joe had it. He showed tremendous loyalty to Halliwell.' And while Peggy Ramsay, Orton's agent, noted that 'he didn't give a damn about anybody else', the exception was Halliwell: 'Joe had only one overwhelming relationship allied to loyalty, and that was to Ken.' Orton's first money earned as a playwright was spent on two wigs for Halliwell's baldness: 'he chose a style with a rather endearing forelock' and Halliwell's difficult personality improved. One person, Peter Willes, then head of drama at Rediffusion, is prepared to say of Orton that 'he did not have a heart' – only to continue, 'but I loved what was there instead, which was infinite kindness and good manners'. And the diaries record several straightforwardly human moments, mainly of pity for the old and unwanted – actresses whose beauty has disappeared, a totally isolated old woman whose body rots undiscovered for days, a desolate busker. 'How awful', Orton shudders, much like the rest of us, 'to be alone in a house knowing that no one cared when you died.'

And yet. The diaries begin with his mother's funeral in 1966. Leonie Orton, Joe's sister, told James Fox of the *Sunday Times*: 'He nearly had mother out of her coffin . . . He was picking her head up. "What's all this brown stuff?"; "try and get her rings off". I said, "I don't want to." He said, "I do." He wanted to see her feet, he was opening her dressing gown. "It's incredible," he said, "doesn't she look bizarre." The kids were screaming and I said, "For Christ's sake leave her alone." ' The day before the funeral, Orton picks up a labourer ('a navy-blue coat with leather across the shoulders') and has sex with him in a derelict house ('I put it between his legs'). After the funeral, he sodomizes an Irishman with some difficulty: 'as I lay on the bed looking upwards, I noticed what an amazing ceiling it was. Heavy moulding, a centrepiece of acorns and birds painted blue. All cracked now. Must've been rather a fine room once.' Back in London, Orton produces his mother's false teeth for the cast of *Loot*: 'I said to Kenneth Cranham, "Here, I thought you'd like the originals." ' In *Loot*, a dead mother's teeth function briefly as castanets — a macabre comic prop to match the glass eye which rolls around disturbingly. Cranham 'looked very sick', as well he might, though Orton was making a literary point — defending his play against the charge that it was a fantasy. Going over the same ground with Peter Willes, Orton reports: 'he suddenly caught a glimpse of the fact that I write the truth'.

In a way, there are no surprises here. This is exactly how we expect the playwright Orton to behave. Outrageously. Heartlessly. However, it is worth noting that his sister's account of his behaviour appears to be a fabrication, if the diaries are to be trusted. Before going to Leicester, Orton writes: 'as the corpse is downstairs in the main living-room it means going out or watching television with death at one's elbow. My father, fumbling out of bed in the middle of the night, bumped into the coffin and almost had the corpse on the floor.' But when this connoisseur of the grotesque arrives, the body 'isn't at home as I'd supposed. It's laid out in a Chapel of Rest'. Once there, Orton merely feels his mother's hand and notices its coldness: 'Mum quite unrecognisable without her glasses. And they'd scraped her hair back from her forehead. She looked fat, old and dead. They'd made up her face. When I asked about this the mortician said, "Would you say it wasn't discreet then, sir?" I said, "No. It seems all right to me." "We try to give a lifelike impression," he said. Which seems a contradiction in terms somehow. I've never seen a corpse before. How cold they are.' As we encounter the admission 'I've never seen a corpse before', we reflect that *Loot* is fantasy and suddenly catch a glimpse of Orton writing more than the truth, or less than the truth. Which is why the play's hectic hyperbole is frankly tedious compared to the bleak notation here: 'We all went to the Chapel of Rest. It's a room, bare, white-washed. Muted organ music from a speaker in the corner. The coffin lid propped up against a wall. It said, "Elsie Mary Orton, aged 62 years". Betty said, "They've got her age wrong, see. Your Mum was 63. You should tell them about that. Put in a complaint." I said, "Why? It doesn't matter now." 'Well," said Betty, "you want it done right, don't you? It's what you pay for." '

This dispassionate account of his mother's funeral, once Leonie Orton's hectic embellishment has been removed, irresistibly calls up the opening of *L'Étranger*: 'Mother died today. Or, maybe, yesterday; I can't be sure.' Like an early McEwan narrator, Meursault approaches every event with democratic and innocent pedantry. At his mother's funeral, Meursault smokes, drinks coffee and falls asleep during the all-night vigil by the coffin. He shows no emotion and, confronted by the tears of Pérez, his mother's last 'boy-friend', sees only that 'because of the wrinkles they couldn't flow down. They spread out, criss-crossed, and formed a sort of glaze over the old, worn face.' The next day, Meursault swims, takes a girl to a Fernandel comedy, and starts an affair with her. When he kills the Arab on the beach, he is conscious 'only of the cymbals of the sun clashing on my skull, and, less distinctly, of the keen blade of light flashing up from the knife'. The Arab scarcely features, just as the ugly Scotsman comes second to the whitewash on Orton's sleeve.

For the public prosecutor, Meursault is 'an inhuman monster wholly without moral sense'. For Camus, writing an introduction to an American University edition, Meursault is unambiguously heroic: 'readers have been tempted to look on him as a piece of social wreckage. A much more accurate idea of the character, or, at least, one much closer to the author's intentions, will emerge if it is asked just how Meursault refuses to conform. The reply is a simple one: he refuses to lie. To lie is not only to say what is not the case. It also, above all, means saying more than is the case, and, as far as the human heart is concerned, more than we feel. It is what we all do, every day, to simplify life.' Because Meursault refuses conventional pretence, Camus endows him with 'a passion for the absolute and for truth', despite the murder he has committed – a murder which is artistically functional because, without it, Meursault can never be tried by society for his other 'crimes'. The murder is a mistake, a bald contrivance, try as Camus does to blame it on the sun. Camus's alibi for Meursault is neat – he wouldn't even possess the murder weapon had he not taken it to avoid trouble in the first place – but the alibi cannot expunge the guilt. At the centre of *L'Étranger*, there is not an ambiguity, but an artistic mess. We are asked to admire a murderer.

Orton, having been murdered, at least escapes this problem. Yet he isn't wholly exonerated as a man of absolute truth, speaking the unspeakable. The plays, for all that Orton demurs, are fantastications of the truth, the truth that there isn't much in this world which can properly be called 'normal'. Writing to Glenn Loney, Orton obliquely shows his trump card: 'I don't know what the average member of the public (if he exists) is going to say' about *The Good and Faithful Servant*. '(*If he exists*).'

The average family is another favourite target. Justly enough, when you consider, say, the 1974 BBC series *The Family* which documented a Reading family, the Wilkins, over a number of weeks – and discovered that their youngest child, Christopher, was the deliberate result of an extra-marital affair; that Karen and Gary married at sixteen because Karen was pregnant; that another daughter, Heather, was going to marry a black boy; that yet another daughter, Marion, had sexual relations with her boyfriend in her parents' house. None of which is in any way reprehensible. Yet, without being surprising, or even out of the ordinary, the Wilkins family could hardly be described as typical or average – any more than any other family, in all probability. Orton grasped this but exaggerated his insight. In *What the Butler Saw*, Dr Prentice attempts to seduce his new secretary, Geraldine. Mrs Prentice has actually succeeded with Nick, the page-boy at the Station Hotel. Not that it matters (since the play is the theatrical equivalent of pure mathematics), Geraldine and Nick are their lost twin children, the result of a rape by Dr Prentice on Mrs Prentice before, so to speak, they were introduced and married. The rape, in case you were wondering, took place in a dark linen cupboard at the Station Hotel.

Entertaining Mr Sloane toys with a similar incestuous sub-text. In the main plot, the forty-year-old nymphomaniac Kath shares the murderous orphan, Mr Sloane, with her homosexual brother, Eddie. However, there are broad hints that Mr Sloane is Kath's adopted child. And there are slighter hints that Eddie may be the father of Kath's adopted child. The other candidate for fatherhood is Eddie's adolescent friend, Tommy. Problems of censorship confuse things here. Eddie's father hasn't spoken to him for twenty years, after finding him 'committing some kind of felony in the bedroom' – with either Tommy or Kath. A twenty-year silence indicates incest rather than homosexuality and, increasingly, the friend looks more and more like a 'friend', a fiction to deflect blame. Essentially, though, these complications belong to what was once called Whitehall farce. Orton's variant, Soho farce, is the same thing with knobs on, and a good deal less clear.

In his diaries, Orton is freer to let material take its own shape. He has fewer designs on the truth, is less concerned to make it fit a dramatic timetable. He can afford to be laconic and meticulous. At the time of his mother's funeral, for instance, Orton also records that he has to shave his father because the old man is too upset. He tries to get him admitted to a hospital where he will be properly cared for. A footnote tells us that Orton kept all his mother's letters ('when the ambnleance came to fetch me they saw the specialist come and the doctor so I caused a little exsiment') – kept them and dated them.

The funniest moment in Orton's entire *œuvre* comes in these diaries. It is a very long account of a disastrous trip to Libya. He and Halliwell came back the next day. They didn't like it there and saw no reason to stay and pretend. Meursault would have done the same thing. On their return, a few hundred pounds poorer, Orton went to the Criterion, regaled the cast with his misadventures, then popped into a pissoir near Holloway Road: 'It was dark because somebody had taken the bulb away. There were three figures pissing. I had a piss and, as my eyes became used to the gloom, I saw that only one of the figures was worth having – a labouring type . . .' Overtures are made, there is some jockeying for position, groping begins: 'at this point a fifth man entered. Nobody moved. It was dark. Just a little light spilled into the place from the street, not enough to see immediately. The man next to me moved back to allow the fifth man to piss. But the fifth man very quickly flashed his cock and the man next to me returned to my side, lifting up my coat and shoving his hand down the back of my trousers. The fifth man kept puffing on a cigarette and, by the glowing end, watching. A sixth man came into the pissoir.' And then a seventh man. And finally an eighth, 'bearded and stocky', who 'pushed the sixth man roughly away from the fair-haired man and quickly sucked the fair-haired man off.' The fair-headed one quickly leaves and 'the bearded man came over and nudged away the seventh man from me and, opening wide my fly, began sucking me like a maniac . . . I came, squirting into the bearded man's mouth, and quickly pulled up my jeans. As I was about to leave, I heard the bearded man hissing quietly, "I suck people off! Who wants his cock sucked?" When I left, the labourer was just shoving his cock into the man's mouth to keep him quiet.' And then Halliwell supplies the punch line: 'I told Kenneth who said, "It sounds as though eightpence and a bus down the Holloway Road was more interesting than £200 and a plane to Tripoli." '

For this kind of sexual farce, Orton has found the ideal medium. And it isn't the stage. There, the kinds of truth that Orton was uniquely equipped to tell couldn't possibly be told – merely gestured at, flamboyantly. *The Orton Diaries* are undeniably impressive, given the risk they take. When Joyce wrote *Ulysses*, Orwell commented that it was 'a matter of *daring* just as much as of technique – to expose the imbecilities of the inner mind'. Orton exposes the imbecilities of the outer body: 'he made a motion to the dwarfish creature, rather as someone would call a taxi. The dwarf sucked me off while the other man smiled benevolently.' Moreover, while Joyce guessed that his mental imbecilities were widely shared, Orton must have known he was in a special category among homosexuals. Halliwell, one guesses, made the point brutally.

All the same, my hypothesis would be that Halliwell disapproved of Orton's promiscuity much less than critics generally suppose. In Tangier, they were promiscuous together. 'We sat talking of how happy we both felt and of how it couldn't, surely, last. We'd have to pay for it.' And pay they did – largely, I think, because Halliwell eventually became disgusted. ' "I sometimes think I'm against all you stand for," Kenneth said. "When I'm not here you won't be able to write in this flip way." ' Finally, though Halliwell claimed to be disgusted by homosexuals – an assertion which, rightly, baffled Orton – it was something else which disgusted him. When two homosexuals, Tom and Clive, stray into their ménage, they treat Halliwell 'like shit' and are only interested in Orton's celebrity. Orton is without illusions: 'their simpering over me was all you can expect from people like that. I saw through it. You saw through it.' Halliwell came to hate the way Orton saw through everything. Orton was what Bellow's Herzog calls a reality-instructor. A man, in other words, whose idea of the truth is restricted to what is nasty. Nothing is noble. There are no finer feelings. The incident confirms Orton in his unremittingly low opinion of life, whereas poor Halliwell yearns for something better – something which will soothe his literary and sexual envy. At this point, Orton isn't neutral like Meursault. He is gleeful like Iago – a role that Halliwell couldn't bear to see adopted by someone he cared for, and who, the diaries make clear, cared for him.

Theatre: Chekhov

Chekhov is a great minimalist. Like Jane Austen, who can create interest and comedy from a pencil stub, he makes do with very little. He, too, prefers the sigh and the shrug to the gothic groan, so it seems right that *The Seagull* should share amateur dramatics with *Mansfield Park*. Moreover, it's easy to imagine Mr Woodhouse's fussy hypochondria finding a place in Chekhov's canon. A schoolmaster pinched for cash, a plain girl who takes snuff and drinks, a landowner to whom nothing has happened, a doctor who is past the unadventurous adventures of his youth – these are the brilliantly drab stuff of his art. 'The main thing, my dears,' Chekhov instructed his players, 'is not to be theatrical. The characters are all ordinary, simple people.' And this goes for the famous writer and actress, Trigorin and Irina, whose charisma is quickly subdued until (as Nina observes ruefully) 'they are crying, fishing, playing cards, laughing and losing their tempers like anyone else'. Chekhov would have agreed with Browning's Andrea del Sarto that 'a common greyness silvers everything, – / All in a twilight'. Thus it is entirely appropriate that, when Kostya lets daylight into his head, the noise of the off-stage shot should be passed off by the doctor as an exploding bottle of ether – minimized as it is by the hubbub from a game of Lotto.

There are no bright lights in *The Seagull*. Everyone is a failure, from the inert to the ambitious. The young, stage-struck Nina is quietly deranged by her break-up with Trigorin and the prospect of third-class travel to obscurity in the provinces she hardly left. Even Trigorin, though superficially successful, knows that he is dwarfed by the huge spectres of Tolstoy and Turgenev. Doubtless there was an element of self-portraiture in Trigorin, but Chekhov was himself more resourceful in his dealings with the great art of the past. *The Seagull*, for example, deliberately invokes and challenges *Hamlet* by a series of quotations, some obvious, others not. 'Or I see a cloud over there like a grand piano,' Trigorin tells Nina. 'So I think it must go in a story.' It is, of course, Hamlet's cloud that is 'very like a whale', but appropriately scaled down.

Chekhov, however, doesn't stop at quotation. Kostya's dislike of Trigorin and the subsequent muffed duel are a muted version of Hamlet's oedipal jealousy of Claudius. Trigorin, like Claudius, knows he is behaving wrongly in tempting Nina but is similarly unable to help himself. The quarrel between Kostya and his mother, with its mixture of bitter indignation and tenderness, evokes the bedroom scene in *Hamlet*. Masha, the steward's daughter, dresses in black like Hamlet because she is in mourning for her life. Her father, a bore with a limited fund of theatrical anecdotes, recalls Polonius at his most 'pastoral-comical' tedious. There is a play within the play. Nina goes mad like Ophelia.

It isn't difficult to see what Chekhov found congenial in Shakespeare's play: after all, as the Prince constantly reminds us, nothing happens in *Hamlet*, and very little happens in a Chekhov play. The sporadic references serve to defend *The Seagull*'s inactivity by claiming kin with Shakespeare. They tell us that even the greatest drama consists not of action so much as words, words, words. But more than that, they ironize the panoply of Shakespeare's setting – once recognize *Hamlet* in *The Seagull* and it is impossible not to see the Danish court in its everyday, domestic aspect. *Hamlet* becomes a family squabble in which worried, wordy people are on their way to failure – crying and losing their tempers like anyone else. At the same time, Chekhov claims Shakespearian grandeur for a jilted girl, so that the minimal no longer seems a limitation.

The Seagull, however, is not easy to play, as the transferred Derby Playhouse production amply confirms. The piece is full of calculated risks: towards the end of Act III, Chekhov leaves an empty stage, replete with ringing silence; earlier, he gives Trigorin a realistically interminable speech, leaving his Nina to grin and bear it. Above all, the pathetic elements risk contagion from the surrounding prosaic comedy. They require intensity. Alas, Alan Bates is a zestless Trigorin, bringing to the role the winded lethargy of a long-distance runner, so closely does the novelist resemble the detached observer he played in *Otherwise Engaged*. Georgina Hale is miscast as Nina: in the mad scene her reedy, South Kensington counter-tenor makes her sound, not tragic, but stoned. 'I am a seagull,' she whinges. 'No, that's not right.' Nor is it. 'I am the walrus' would be nearer the mark. Richard O'Callaghan, who plays Kostya, is almost equally handicapped by his face: its natural expression is the grin of a reined-in Derby winner, quite at odds with the melancholy he must convey.

On the other hand, when he mouths the words of his play, the action is thoughtfully picked up and deflated by his mother as she munches Turkish Delight. And among the minor roles, Robert Flemyng is excellent as old Sorin – all hands, and the hands all knuckles, his head waggling like one of those shell-shocked alsatians that dodder in rear windows on the motorway. Gabrielle Lloyd looks right as Masha, with dingy smoker's teeth, oily skin and a cigarette hole in her dress. Otherwise, there is a tear in the sky that needs mending, and sound effects should be audible *before* characters comment on them.

Volker Schlöndorff's Film of *The Tin Drum*

Considerably slimmer than the original, Volker Schlöndorff's elegant adaptation of Günter Grass's novel still leaves plenty on your plate. *Passim*, the food for thought includes roast potatoes *au naturel*, wine and cheese, geese, turnips, soup with paprika and cloves, eels with dill sauce, bay leaf and a twist of lemon, cooked Kashubian goose, stew, smoked fish, raw herring, sardines, sherbert, Dutch chocolate, Hungarian salami, caviar from Stalingrad and coffee to finish. In short, *The Tin Drum* is a film about greed and possessiveness, an allegory of man's appetite for food, sex and, above all, territory. Hence the huge menu that is consumed as we watch and hence, too, those careful specifications of national provenance in the final items: after all, Germany invaded Poland, Holland, Hungary and Russia. If you consume too much, you die of indigestion, whether you are a nation or an individual, Grass would argue. Greed is fatal – as we infer when Roswitha Raguna, the somnambulist dwarf, is killed, risking an artillery bombardment for a cup of coffee; or when Alfred Matzerath (delicatessen owner and gourmet cook) chokes on his Nazi party pin, horrified that the invading Russian troops might see it. Matzerath, appropriately enough, is buried in a makeshift coffin constructed from old apple boxes – a pleasing consistency.

The action of *The Tin Drum* centres on the Free State of Danzig, from 1899 to the defeat of Germany in 1945, covering the First World War, inflation and the rise of the Nazi party. In 1919, a German says to a Pole, 'We'll live in peace', but he is holding negligently between them a fat, phallic mushroom which is a prediction of their sexual rivalry. And that sexual rivalry is itself an emblem of larger political issues – the struggle between Germans and Poles for Danzig or Gdansk – for Grass and Schlöndorff have chosen to filter the history of the body politic obliquely through its gourmandizing, sexually aroused individuals. Thus, Agnes Matzerath (the *appetitlich* Angela Winkler) is torn between her German husband and her Polish cousin, Jan Bronski. She screws her cousin every Thursday in the red light area of Danzig and after one such assignation Schlöndorff directs our attention to a spilt consignment of smoked fish: they are, as it were, stuffing themselves.

Sigismund Markus, toymaker and Jew, represents a third alternative which Agnes Matzerath rejects. Accordingly, he gives her sensible, pragmatic advice, telling her to choose her German husband and reject Bronski, the Pole. As advice, it is essentially political and shrewdly conscious of the *Zeitgeist*. Agnes, however, is pregnant by Bronski as well as sexually infatuated; but though she loathes Matzerath, she continues to live with him, as far as one can judge for entirely political reasons. Her inner turmoil is mute but vividly dramatized in terms of food, the film's dominant metaphor. On the beach, for instance, the trio watch a fisherman haul in a horse's head: eels slither from its mouth, nostrils, ears and eyes. As Donne memorably wrote: 'There is motion in corruption.' Agnes throws up, comforted by Jan Bronski, as Matzerath helps the fisherman and buys a few eels for supper. We watch Matzerath slice off their heads, see the dark blood, hear the knife like a bad electrical connection, watch the severed heads squirm. They are prepared with a dill sauce, bay leaf and a twist of lemon. Agnes refuses to eat them, or any fish, and retires to the boudoir, where Jan comforts her with his courting finger. This, then, is how she feels viscerally.

Just the same, orgasm achieved, she returns to the table and eats. Thereafter, she eats fish obsessively – sardines, herrings, raw haddock – although it is slowly poisoning her. She has made the 'right' decision, just as Danzig has: '*Wir wollen Heim ins Reich.*' The fish kills her and the child she is carrying. At her funeral,

Sigismund Markus is expelled by Nazi sympathizers, but returns later to say Kiddush, the Hebrew blessing of food, over her grave. The gesture is touching, tender and tinged with appetite. Markus has hungered for her too. Meanwhile, at the wake, the guests are gorging again and Matzerath and Bronski play cards – *skat*, a friendly but competitive game.

Danzig finally goes German after the guns have reduced the Polish Post Office to rubble. Bronski sits in the basement, building a house of cards, the frail symbol of Polish aspirations, and goes to the firing squad with the queen of hearts in his hand – he may have lost, but, in a sense, he holds the only card that counts. Matzerath and the other Germans celebrate this and following victories with a meal – a cooked Kashubian goose. The Germans have cooked the goose, just as they will go on to consume chocolate from Holland, salami from Hungary and caviar from Stalingrad. France, unaccountably, is the only occupied country omitted from the list of comestibles.

The Kashubian question perhaps needs a footnote. One deduces finally that Danzig and its environs have a population neither Polish nor German – the indigenous locals, Kashubians whose loyalty is to their fields alone, who are quite impervious to nationalism and ideology. Not that their political quietism can prevent annexation, as the opening scene demonstrates. Richly comic, a delicate pastiche of early silent movies with their jerky continuity, this scene also establishes the pattern of events to follow – the equation of sexual, territorial and ordinary appetites.

Agnes's mother, Anna Bronski, a Kashubian, is sitting in the middle of a field by a smouldering fire of potato-tops. It is 1899 and she is roasting potatoes when she notices a chase on the horizon. The fugitive, a fire-raiser called Joseph Koljaiczek, is soon prostrate before her, with the military not far behind. She extends to him the hospitality of her voluminous skirts and placidly eats a hot potato as the military, a bit puffed, question her and prod her baskets of potatoes with their bayonets. In parallel, Koljaiczek is prodding her with *his* weapon. She has been 'taken', like her district, without her consent but also without protest. It is a rape of sorts and a metonomy in which sexual conquest stands for the larger idea of conquest. Koljaiczek also adumbrates the idea that profit ensues from destruction: when the authorities finally catch up with him, he disappears beneath a flotilla of rafts, never to re-surface. Rumour has it, though, that he is a lonely millionaire in America – selling matches and fire insurance.

Anna Bronski's indifference and quietism is explicit at the end of the film: Kashubia, she states, will be there long after the Poles and the Germans have gone. In the final frame, we see her once more sitting by a fire in a field, a good deal older and more or less clearly presented as Mother Earth – the survivor of all territorial struggle, all ideological claims. But it's hardly surprising that Oskar Matzerath, the titular drummer, should refer to her skirts as he stands below the Eiffel Tower in German-occupied Paris. The parallel isn't merely visual, an analogy between the tower's widespread legs, over-arching shelter and those of Anna Bronski. It continues the equation of sexual and military conquest.

Beautifully played with unblinking gravity by David Bennent, Oskar is the most puzzling feature of *The Tin Drum*. He is a moral enigma. Either the child of Bronski or Matzerath or both, he throws himself down the cellar stairs at three and successfully arrests his growth – partly because he is repelled by the adult world's sexuality after seeing Bronski's stockinged foot probe his mother's thighs under a card-table; partly because he is evidently disgusted by the brown-shirt, Greff's, promise that 'you'll be as big as me'. Greff, a grocer, eulogizes the potato for its protean qualities: it is, he drools, 'forever conceiving new shapes'. Just what you'd expect from a sympathizer with the idea of *Lebensraum*. Are we then to read Oskar's arrested growth as a rejection of the idea of sexual conquest and its counterpart, territorial expansion? Some things point to this: when he is born, for instance, the frames are mimetically inverted to show the contrariness of his values. He doesn't even want to be born, but the umbilicus is cut and he has been promised a tin drum on his third birthday. So far so good. He is, too, a loyal friend of the Jew,

Sigismund Markus, and he disrupts a Nazi meeting by playing waltz time on his drum, until everyone is dancing.

By and large, then, Oskar seems to align himself with the little people – those who, as the dwarf Bebra explains, 'must perform' otherwise 'they will take over the meadows where we pitch our tents. They will organize torchlight parades. They will build rostrums and fill them, and down from the rostrums they will preach our destruction.' However, though Oskar denounces Hitler as 'the Gasman', most of the time he exudes a certain amoral coolness. He blames himself for his mother's death (a complete mystery this), for Jan Bronski's death (he drags him into the Polish Post Office just as the hostilities begin) and we can see that he is directly responsible for his father's death (he deliberately presents him with the carefully hidden Nazi party pin). The last responsibility, of course, partly redounds to Oskar's credit: the old glutton, so to speak, is merely eating his words.

Certain apparently moral ambiguities are easily enough resolved. If Oskar spends some of the war entertaining the German troops, so does Bebra, the spokesman for the little people. In uniform together, they are essentially parodic. They *belittle* German military might. On the other hand, there is Oskar's gift – a voice that can shatter glass, a weapon he uses whenever anyone tries to take away his tin drum, discovered first when the irritated Matzerath tugs at the instrument ('Alfred, why must you always use force?' his wife complains). The tin drum itself appears to stand for the military 'might' of the ineffectual: we see a drum in the Polish Post Office when it is being flattened by German artillery; Sigismund Markus, the Jew, makes the drums; and (only in the novel) we are told that its red and white colours are Polish. In the film, this identification of the drum with the Polish cause is subtly implicit in a brief, beautiful shot of the Polish Post Office, where letters are stamped – rapidly, rhythmically, with a drumming stick.

In any case, whenever anyone tries to part Oskar and his drum, he screams in a spasm of possessiveness – shattering his teacher's spectacles and every bottled sample in a doctor's surgery. He also defenestrates the Stadt-Theater when he discovers his mother's adultery with Bronski – presumably out of jealousy. The gift, then, is primarily destructive (though he can tame it to engrave a heart on glass). The last time we see him use the power is in Paris, where he shatters a glass of champagne in an officer's hand. Seconds later, the sirens start, as if to say the celebratory bubbly was premature. Germany is losing the war. You might conclude that, finally, the gift is intelligently destructive.

Yet, if Oskar's smallness is a virtue, the antithesis of *Lebensraum*, and if his drum is a symbol of how *little* power he has, and if his sexuality is delicate (a play with fizzing sherbert rather than a gross appetite) – why does the film end with his resolution to grow up at last, after he has thrown his drum into Matzerath's grave? Perhaps we are meant to infer that, now his Nazi father is dead, natural growth, healthy growth is possible. It's difficult to say, and David Bennent's performance gives nothing away, either by words or expression.

Radio

David Lane, head of the Commission for Racial Equality, was the first guest on Radio 4's new phone-in, *One Man, One Voice*. As I listened to the yelps and barks of bigotry, it struck me that the receiver resembles a kind of Bakelite bone for most of the callers. It gradually struck me, too, that the tragedy of racial prejudice isn't devoid of farcical elements. For instance, I'd never realized before that Hitler was a negro, yet, according to many callers, we fought the Second World War to keep Britain white. Then there's the hitherto unrecognized importance of the crash helmet to the English way of life: when Mr Lane asked his callers why they thought immigrants wanted to *change* our culture, they replied that the Sikh motorcyclist is allowed to wear a turban instead of a crash helmet. Mr Lane argued that the Sikhs were merely retaining one aspect of their own culture – a pathetically weak argument, I think you'll agree, in view of the crash helmet's crucial, even defining, role in our society.

No, tamper with *that* and the abject surrender of the white community inevitably follows. The Queen will wear Norman Hartnell saris; the Duke of Edinburgh will be kitted out with a fly-whisk and clasp his hands firmly behind his *lungi*. After all, they're into *polo* already. On radio (I say this to bring home the full horror) programmes will be rearranged to reflect the new cultural balance: *The Archers* will go out on Sunday mornings at 7.15 a.m. while *am Apna Hi Ghar Samajhiye* will be broadcast twice daily.

And think of our great national sport – cricket. Since the

Indians, the Pakistanis and the West Indians are the main agents for cultural change, cricket, in no time at all, will be displaced by cricket. Finally, there'll be mass repatriation of the white community to Jutland and Normandy.

Well, Odin forbid that it should ever come to that, but *Return to the Iron Age* (R4) and a preview on *Start the Week* (R4) gave us a pretty good idea of what it might be like to return to our ancestry. Fifteen people were chosen from a thousand volunteers to re-create authentically primitive conditions in a secret rural location. For a year, amazingly, they survived without Gordon's, Grant's or Gauloises – a fate worse than meths. In fact, they seem to have thrived. Rapidly, they ceased to suffer the agony of dental bills. Things called muscles appeared all over their bodies – worrying at first, I'd speculate, but apparently not so bad when you get used to them. Their diet included, so they claimed, large quantities of an Iron Age vegetable – 'roughage' – obviously analogous to the modern cabbage.

Despite the absence of toothpaste and privacy, love-making flourished in the communal roundhouse, even though 'you might have to stop in the middle and say you're bouncing too much'. Another convincing detail, deftly elicited by Malcolm Billings, and one that leads me to Dennis Potter's sermon for Lent, *All in the Waiting* (R4). 'Whenever . . . we make love,' he intoned, 'we are outside normal time; we're in the cauldron of the actual minute and we've suspended or evaded the claims of any other moment except this one.' The delivery was muted yet intense, like John Arlott describing a ball hopping over the boundary rope, but it was pure rhetoric, of course – as those creaking, constrained Iron-Agers could have told him.

Or Mrs Shandy, whose bland inquiry about the unwound clock is timed to Mr Shandy's orgasm in the opening chapter of Sterne's novel. Even intense moments have an admixture of roughage – and so has that phrase, 'the cauldron of the actual minute'. It's got Good Prose written all over it, but it's 90 per cent roughage. Any vicar could be proud of it – the orotund tautology of 'actual'; the inappropriateness of 'minute' as a unit of time to describe either intercourse or orgasm; and, finally, the glibly archaic 'cauldron'. Potter's style is vaguely powerful – ideally suited, in fact, to God who is powerfully vague, but less good for things like love-making that we all know about.

Television

A week of awards. Liam Brady, the players' Player of the Year, had some difficulty in holding back his tears at the Hilton Hotel presentation ceremony (ATV).

It was hardly surprising, though, when you considered the hideous trophy his footballing feats had landed him with. Dizzy with vertigo, a chromium dwarf in his underpants threatened suicide from a plinth the size of the Empire State Building. When will they learn a sense of proportion? The polite Brady said that he would 'treasure' it – a euphemism, I suppose, for burying it in the garden, where it will doubtless be defused in fifty years' time by a fearless disposal expert from the Design Centre.

In the end, weary with watching the BAFTA awards, Miss ATV and the usual presentations of EPNS dog-eared cheque books to the failures on *Blankety Blank* (BBC1), I gave out a few unofficial awards of my own. The overflowing ashtray award for anti-charisma goes to Michael Billington (*Tonight in Town*, BBC1's ineffectual answer to Radio 4's *Kaleidoscope*). As we watched a group of musicians stumble, hard-hatted and clutching their instrument cases, over the concrete debris that one day will be the Barbican Arts Centre, Billington's disembodied voice-over assured us that they were just like racehorses 'feeling the springy turf'.

Worse was to come – an appearance in the flesh of the drama critics' drama critic, a super-clone with chubby roll-neck, manic delivery, perspiring upper lip and those Zorro spectacles that used to betoken crusading intelligence twenty-odd years ago.

487

Fortunately, his image was quickly displaced by the exotic Tina Turner, who confessed to the demure and sensible-ankled Valerie Singleton that her sexy act was just a sexy act. Nine-tenths nude, Ms Turner writhed sexily behind a thin drizzle of sequins, strategically placed to stop you seeing her pancreas.

Unprejudiced image of the week award went to London Weekend's *Weekend World*, which summed up modern French farming methods with footage of a carthorse, complete with lavatory seat and Moshe Dayan blinkers, toiling across a dust bowl on its way to the knacker's yard. Euphemism of the week award went to Bill Maclaren for his commentary on the Wales–England gouge-in. While ears were being tattered and boots spat out like quids of baccy, he mildly observed that there seemed to be a certain amount of 'niggling' in the line-outs and loose mauls.

But on to more serious things. *The Book Programme* (BBC2) devoted half an hour to the manifold genius of Barbara Cartland – novelist, record star, health food oracle, prayer anthologist and trenchant pundit ('people respect purity and innocence'). Turning a typically graceful compliment to this Renaissance versatility, Robert Robinson described her as 'gift-wrapped', a remark only a cynic would take to be an allusion to Miss Cartland's sartorial style.

In fact, it was immediately evident that Robinson was fully prepared for an intellectual encounter of the most testing kind: aware, like Hopkins, that the 'mind has mountains; cliffs of fall', his hair was carefully bandaged to look like the time-honoured prophylactic of vinegar and brown paper; moreover, though deeply versed in Miss Cartland's books, he took the further precaution of establishing his intellectual bona fides with a pair of depressed clericals, over which he peered warily at the great lady.

Actually, she was so much in the pink, nay, the cerise of health, that he could have been forgiven specs a little less studious. A welder's mask, for instance, if more cumbersome, would have given him greater protection from the fiery cosmetic glow and the dazzle of her diamonds. By contrast, the normally rubicund and interesting Robinson looked almost pale and interesting for a change. Equally, his intriguing hair style looked carelessly disarranged, even dull, beside Miss Cartland's stiffly beaten peaks of egg-white. Does her resident chef concoct it anew every morning?

After an amiable glance at the covers of her books, Robinson steeled himself to look straight into Miss Cartland's flamboyantly false eyelashes and risk the philistine question that had been occupying the mind of many a doubting Thomas: did her books have much appeal for intellectuals? In some ways, it seemed a fair enough question, given her own earlier, paradoxical, appraisal ('the reason my books are good, is that they're journalese'), but for a moment the eyelashes threatened to take off like a pair of condors and peck poor Robinson to death. Yet the answer was brisk and unruffled. Miss Cartland's fans apparently include President Sadat and Mrs Gandhi, 'and I suppose you'd call them intellectuals?'

Not any more, you could almost hear Robinson thinking. However, he didn't press the lady – and who can blame him for that? Only Betjeman with his delighted and ambiguous chortle could have wallowed shamelessly in the omnipresent kitsch. *Arena* (BBC2) a few nights later gave us Australia's answer to Barbara Cartland and it was an illuminating juxtaposition. Dame Edna Everage, *la dame aux gladiolas*, reclined in her Dorchester penthouse suite, scoffed Nivea Creme Assortment and reminisced unstoppably *à la* Cartland.

There are, of course, radical differences between these two ladies that no one would deny: Miss Cartland has a pop-eyed peke, Dame Edna two stuffed corgies; Dame Edna has a lepidopterist's collection of spectacle frames, whereas Miss Cartland's eyelashes would be badly crushed by anything other than a lorgnette held at arm's length. All the same, they share star quality, abundant confidence, bold dress sense and soprano voices of uncertain pitch. What they share most of all, though, is an aggressive emphasis on femininity, as if at some deep subconscious level they are desperately afraid of being mistaken for men.

The odd thing about the three unmistakable plays by Samuel Beckett (*Shades*, BBC2) was that the two most minimalist, 'Ghost Trio' and '. . . but the clouds . . .', pared down though they were, dragged so intolerably that one would cheerfully have cut them even further.

Only 'Not I' was an unqualified success: a mouth speaks the circling monologue of a dead woman who, after a life of unmitigated deracination and dumbness punctuated periodically by unintelligible torrents of speech, finds that there is life after death. Horrified by the idea of continuation, she regularly disowns herself ('who? no! she! SHE!') – hence the title.

I gave Billie Whitelaw's gymnastic mouth the maximum score of 9 dead. By comparison, Tina Turner's mobile kisser seemed ailing and arthritic. In fact, only Barbara Cartland could have managed the part with ease – which leaves Robert Robinson the non-speaking role of the Auditor, a part for which he's now well rehearsed.

Gossip

Terry Eagleton, the democratically rumpled folk-singer and charismatic don, concluded a recent article (*New Statesman*, 6 June 1980) with these stirring words: 'Oxbridge would be ill-advised to be complacent. The real root of these recent stirrings is nothing less than a muted, pervasive crisis in the whole meaning and function of "literature" and "criticism" in the West, one not unconnected with wider ideological turmoil.' Apocalyptic stuff, by Engels. Pause a moment, classless reader, until your heart has ceased to behave like a Harlem Globetrotter dribbling desperately for a crucial basket.

Feeling better? Just in case Eagleton's final flourish has conjured up dramatic *événements* – the burning of Dame Helen Gardner in effigy, the public recantation of a blubbing John Bayley – I'd better tell you that Eagleton's starting point was a conference held in Oxford on 8 March, already described by Horner in *Quarto* 5 as a 'banquet of egg-shells', but officially designated 'The Necessity of Theory'. It was, at least the bit I attended with ossified nostrils, a non-*événement*. Eagleton, I have to report to those who have switched from the *New Statesman* to *Quarto*, saw it rather differently. In particular the pre-conference debate on the inadequacies of the Oxford English course, which 'attracted, astonishingly, three or four hundred largely critical students out of a total undergraduate body of some nine hundred – an intriguing comment on the official Faculty line that no serious discontent exists'.

How, I wonder, does Eagleton *know* that the audience was

'largely critical'? By their mere presence? By ESP? Always diffident, I decided to do some checking. According to Carl Schmidt, an English don at Balliol and a participant in the debate, 'perhaps twelve people spoke, some of them several times'. There was, at the stipulation of the organizers, no vote. A sensible procedure under the circumstances. What about that reference to the 'official Faculty line'? It turns out that the Oxford English Faculty's attitude to the syllabus is based on a detailed question-naire sent out to all undergraduates reading English in the university – not just to Eagleton's three or four hundred students most of whom were silent anyway.

In my unrigorous, untheoretical, empiricist way, I'm left pondering Eagleton's motives for these and other omissions. For instance, he made no attempt to outline, let alone refute, the arguments of his opponents, who argue that a structured course would actually circumscribe the freedom of students. At present, there is a wide range of choice from 1100 to 1960 – a liberal spectrum dismissed by Eagleton as a 'blandly innocuous survey'. The 'entrenched ideology' he identifies so certainly isn't, in fact, an ideology at all, but fundamentally pluralistic, catering for personal preference and disagreement. There is no ban on theory, Freudian approaches or feminism. By contrast, it's only Eagleton who wants a compulsory theoretical paper for first-year students – at a time when they are likely to be ignorant of the primary material against which all theoretical positions must be tested. There isn't much point in reading, say, Lucien Goldmann's *The Hidden God* (described by Eagleton as 'a Marxist study of Pascal and Racine, with an important preliminary account of his "genetic structuralist" method') if you haven't first read Pascal or Racine. And there's hardly time for that if you're busy reading Goldmann *on* Pascal and Racine, or practising difficult jargon with a tape-recorder until you're sufficiently fluent to attend an Eagleton seminar without disgracing yourself.

As I say, not much of this is mentioned in Eagleton's piece, which takes it as self-evident that theory is all-important. Perhaps, however, he assumed that his readers would have already digested the full report of the pre-conference debate in the

Times Higher Education Supplement – where his speech, Schmidt's reply and a lively ensuing correspondence were printed. On the whole, I doubt it. He was preaching to the converted, an increasingly common *New Statesman* mode, and he preferred to create the impression of an inert establishment assailed by valiant theoreticians. That way you can borrow a bit of revolutionary glamour and kid yourself that you're 'not unconnected with wider ideological turmoil'.

Why the attraction to theory anyway? In an idle moment, Horner once read Eagleton's untaxing, amiable, idiot's guide to Marxist literary theory: it transpires that Marxist critics are doing much the same thing as any other critic who's any good. Only they spell out their assumptions. Despite Eagleton's lucid exposition, I found myself listening between the lines to the sound of panting – the heavy breathing of a critic solemnly plodding in the wake of an ever-receding vanguard. Theories date so quickly. As Eagleton pointed out in a review of two studies of Lukács, no sooner have you mastered the mysteries than the Marxist structuralists of the left bank expose their theoretical poverty. 'Having sweated over the concept of reification, you had to forget it all straight away; hours of reading went down the drain overnight', he complained. But you'd be stupid to take the complaint at face value. It's really a boast.

Clearly, the main attraction of theory for Eagleton and his *confrères* is that, though it may be finally useless and discredited, it is bloody *hard*. Only *real* intellectual toughies need apply. Theory is a kind of assault course, aggressively unreadable, for those who are prepared to go beyond the pleasure principle, beyond the tree-line into the thin air of abstraction. As currently practised, it is elitist in the worst sense. Anyone who managed to finish David Caute's four-part tribute to Sartre will have noticed the same set of symptoms: '*L'Idiot de la Famille* is hard going. Its vast paragraphs, repetitious and incantatory, fall off the page. Sartre had rarely travelled light but the weight of the spelaeological equipment was now such as could be sustained only by a man capable of generating his own oxygen at any altitude.' There it goes again. Bloody hard, practically unreadable, difficult to

493

follow without breathing apparatus, rarefied – and heroic. Do I detect a note of self-congratulation?

A last quotation from Eagleton: 'there are English dons who regularly return hot-foot from Paris with sample cases of the latest theoretical goods . . .' Doesn't this self-glamorizing image belong to the same constellation? Can't you picture all those dons with their hot *pieds*, rushing back, loaded up with duty-free Gauloises – and more stamina-sapping ideas that will sort out the *hommes* from the *garçons*?

Horner is reminded of an acquaintance who now writes for the *Oxford Literary Review* – a daunting publication that aims for maximum unreadability. Years ago, he told me a dream he'd had. He was on a new campus and vaguely bothered because he wasn't sure what he was doing there. Suddenly he saw a concrete and glass tower: the legend over the entrance read, The Department of Existentialist Criminology. This is for me, he thought, and entered the egg-beater.

Profile: Ted Hughes

1980? About then. We are driving to see Sexton Hyades the 33rd, the most written-about bull in the world. He belongs to Ted Hughes and visiting poets are always taken to pay their respects and instructed to write a poem about him. On the half-hour car journey, Hughes tells me and my wife about river pollution and its effect on the fish. The subject is taken up, investigated and exhausted – a detailed inventory of the different pollutants in the river Taw from source to mouth. It isn't small talk; it's a talk, and after it, I feel I could pass an O level. Hughes is a natural teacher. Every time you meet him, you learn something new – about Rudolph Steiner and homoeopathy; the benefits of Vitamin C ('three grams a day, but you have to keep taking it'); chiropractors; pheromones; scansion; footboards on beds; the ability of human beings to recover, under hypnosis, a sense of smell greater than that of baboons ('you should read Eugène Marais, "The Soul of the Apes" '); dowsing. It's a bit like talking to the *Encyclopaedia Britannica* – but an unauthorized version, an alternative route to knowledge, well off the main trunk roads.

He stops the car at Moortown, the farm he used to work with Jack Orchard, his late father-in-law. He wants to show my five-year-old daughter a snake, 'or maybe a weasel'. In the event, after poking about, he finds neither, but we come on the beehives. 'Now, this is interesting,' he says and points to the mouth of the hive. Two bees are having a tussle with a third. He explains to my daughter that there are robber bees and that two guard bees are ejecting the intruder from the hive. After they have flown ten feet, the two bees drop their burden. Hughes immediately examines it. 'No, it's a dead bee. They must have been undertaker bees.' My daughter is wide-eyed at all this lore. So am I.

Later the same day, he produces a dowsing twig, shows me how to hold it and sends me in the rough direction of where he knows there is underground water. 'You're a poet, you'll be able to do it.' I come back a little crestfallen. Nothing has happened. 'So much for my poetry,' I say. 'I can't do it either,' he replies and we roar with laughter. A short time later, though, my wife is dowsing very successfully, using a wine bottle filled with water: each time she passes the underground source, the balanced bottle on the palm of her hand tips dramatically. We are all delighted – persistence has paid off and persistence is a quality of Hughes, both as a man and as a poet, so much so that you feel there is no distinction to be made. He doesn't just look at things, he looks *into* things with the relaxed raptness of a hypnotist.

Take his poem 'Second Glance at a Jaguar', which was written after he'd spent a few months working as a washer-up at Regent's Park Zoo when he was a young man. He could see the jaguar from the kitchens and, just after he'd left the job, stood in front of the cage and drew it in words, jotting down his thoughts just as they occurred. The poem, this untampered-with direct transcript, isn't a *glance* at all, but an act of possession. The thing is captured alive, after months of persistent, semi-conscious stalking:

> Skinfull of bowls, he bowls them,
> The hip going in and out of joint, dropping the spine
> With the urgency of his hurry
> Like a cat going along under thrown stones, under cover,
> Glancing sideways, running
> Under his spine . . .

Hughes himself is more difficult to capture. On the day of the dowsing, my wife took a number of photographs with her new Pentax, rather warily since we knew he doesn't like photo-calls. Curiously, typically even, none of the snaps came out. 'A shilling life', wrote Auden, ironically, 'will give you all the facts.' Ted

Hughes was born in West Yorkshire in 1930, educated at Pembroke College, Cambridge, married the American poet, Sylvia Plath, who committed suicide in 1963 ('You knocked the world off, like a flower-vase. / It was the third time. And it smashed.'), took up farming, received the Queen's Gold Medal in 1974 and the OBE in 1977. These facts tell you as little about Ted Hughes as Bill Brandt's gloomy, thunder-lit portrait photograph – which looks more like Ted Dexter. The trouble with 'facts' is that they never tell you about robber bees, or any of the things which make Hughes such a phenomenon. Only the poetry can do that.

And the poetry explains why the man is so difficult to epitomize. Keats distinguished between two kinds of poet – the egotistical sublime (like Wordsworth, whose subject is himself) and the Shakespearian or dramatic poet, who gets as much pleasure from creating an Iago as an Imogen. Hughes is firmly of the second category, an invisible poet who enters his subjects and loses himself there. Like his famous otter which 're-enters the water by melting', Hughes vanishes into whatever he is writing about. Prim moralists have sometimes objected that the nature he presents in his work is violent and unpleasant – as if the poet is personally responsible for what he is simply and truthfully recording. But anyone who has worked on a farm, or even thought for a minute or two, will recognize the justice of the poems in *Moortown*, his farming journal, brilliantly dashed off at the end of a hard day's work:

Now over here, where the raven was,
Is what interests you next. Born dead,
Twisted like a scarf, a lamb of an hour or two,
Its insides, the various jellies and crimsons and transparencies
And threads and tissues pulled out
In straight lines, like tent ropes
From its upward belly opened like a lamb-wool slipper,
The fine anatomy of silvery ribs on display and the cavity,
The head also emptied through the eye-sockets,
The woolly limbs swathed in birth-yolk and impossible

497

To tell now which in all this field of quietly nibbling sheep
Was its mother. I explain . . .

Hughes is explaining, as ever, but this time to his young nephew, who is moved (' "And did it cry?" you cry') but also simply interested – as the reader is, if he is honest with himself.

Matthew Arnold said that the aim of literature is 'to see the object as in itself it really is'. Anna Akhmatova, introducing her great poem of the Terror, 'Requiem', describes how, standing in a prison queue, she was recognized by the woman behind her: ' "Can you describe this?" I said. "I can!" Then something resembling a smile slipped over what had once been her face.' Arnold and Akhmatova agree – the purpose of poetry is to witness and not to look away. By their standards, Ted Hughes must be judged a poet of the first rank, a writer justly honoured by the laureateship and one who will do honour to the office. Everything he has looked at has been seen as it actually is. That dead lamb will live as long as there are readers.

To return to Sexton Hyades the 33rd, I couldn't manage a whole poem. I tried, but it's hard to write an animal poem that doesn't somehow sound like Ted Hughes. Eventually, Sexton dwindled to four lines in a poem about something else:

> and this is her bull
> drooling over his dummy,
> his angular buttocks
> crusted with cradle cap.

Two days after I sent my book to Ted, he was on the phone: 'Great, but I hope that isn't *our* bull. His buttocks aren't angular at all.' I knew I hadn't looked hard enough.